Dialectic and Narrative

Contemporary Studies in Philosophy and Literature 3
Hugh J. Silverman, Editor

Dialectic and Narrative

Edited by
Thomas R. Flynn and Dalia Judovitz

State University of New York Press

Production by Ruth Fisher
Marketing by Fran Keneston

Published by
State University of New York Press, Albany

Printed in the United States of America

For information, address the State University of New York Press,
State University Plaza, Albany, NY 12246

Library of Congress Cataloging-in-Publication Data

Dialectic and narrative / [edited by] Thomas R. Flynn and Dalia Judovitz.
p. cm.—(Contemporary studies in philosophy and literature ; 3)
Includes bibliographical references and index.
ISBN 0-7914-1455-8 (cloth : acid-free paper).—ISBN 0-7914-1456-6 (pbk. : acid-free paper)
1. Dialectic. 2. Literature—Philosophy. 3. Heidegger, Martin, 1889–1976. 4. Postmodernism. 5. Philosophy, Modern—20th century. I. Flynn, Thomas R. II. Judovitz, Dalia. III. Series.
B809.7.D48 1993
101—dc20

92-25668
CIP

10 9 8 7 6 5 4 3 2 1

Contents

Acknowledgments

We would like to thank Emory University for its sponsorship of the International Association for Philosophy and Literature Conference at Emory University, April 1989, and for its continued support for the publication of this volume. We also want to thank Lance Peterson and Ralph Schoolcraft for their editorial assistance. Additional thanks go to Heather Dubnick and to Keith Anthony.

Introduction

I.

As a pair, dialectic and narrative seem to reflect the respective inclinations of philosophy and literature as disciplines that fix one another in a Sartrean gaze, admixing envy with suspicion. Ever since Plato and Aristotle distinguished scientific knowledge (*episteme*) from opinion (*doxa*) and valuated demonstration through formal and final causes over emplotment (*mythos*), the palm has been awarded to dialectic as the proper instrument of rational discourse, the arbiter of coherence, consistency, and ultimately of truth.

But the matter becomes more complicated when we recognize the various uses of the term *dialectic* in the tradition. In addition to being synonymous with logic in general, it was held by the ancients to be a specific form of reasoning, one that (1) began from received opinion and/or argued to simultaneously contradictory conclusions, a form that (2) constituted a logic of questioning or of testing hypotheses, or a kind of reasoning that (3) established the conditions for inductive discovery of the first principles of a science. With Hegel and the Marxists, "dialectic" becomes the logic of process, where contradiction is not a sign of defeat but the prod for advancing toward higher viewpoints—a temporalizing and totalizing form of reasoning that subsumes the Aristotelian-Kantian logic of understanding as a dynamic whole sublates its static parts. In the following essays, "dialectic" is employed in both its ancient and its modern, Hegelian usages. At one level of the discussion, the very traditions that inform its meanings and its legacies to modernism and postmodernism will be at issue.

Philosophy has traditionally claimed a critical autonomy denied to other disciplines. Its search for "ultimate principles, causes, and reasons," as one voice of the tradition would put it, or its "second-level" position, to quote another voice, affords it the superiority that comes from distinguishing truth from opinion, *episteme* from *doxa* (always "as such"), along with the self-questioning and detachment that accompany this stance. But the form/content distinction, on which this autonomy relies and that warrants the discipline of "formal" logic, is itself questioned and subsumed in modern dialectic and, with it, the adequacy of the contrast drawn between philosophy and what has come to known as "literature."

Moreover, *pace* Aristotle, the philosophical rage for abstract coherence has itself repressed a drive to construct a philosophy of the concrete, one revived in the existential phenomenological movement of the twentieth century. One has only to recall the emotion Sartre expressed at being informed by Raymond Aron of a method (Husserl's) that would enable him to philosophize about the cocktail sitting before them.[1] This urge testifies to a sense felt by certain philosophers of the inadequacy of their own discipline as traditionally conceived. In our day, for example, this malaise may appear as the experienced limit of formalization before the paradox of revisionist denials of the Holocaust. Recent interest in the philosophical use of narrative discourse may be seen as another variation on this theme of the appetite for a philosophy of the concrete. But with this interest, exhibited by the essays in the present volume, the adequacy of the dialectic/narrative dichotomy tends to be undermined and with it, perhaps, the distinction between philosophy and literature as disciplines.

Narrative, after all, is usually processful, temporalizing, and totalizing, as is Hegelian dialectic. In fact, Hegel's *Phenomenology of Spirit,* the paradigm of dialectical thought in modern times, not without reason has been characterized as a *Bildungsroman.* Given that narrative is often multilevel and, when required, can be self-critical as well, the similarity of its argument to that of dialectic may be very strong. This is especially plausible when what Charles Taylor calls the "richer" concept of 'rationality' supplants the notion of rationality as logical consistency propounded by formal logicians.[2] Indeed, the concomitant questioning of the distinction between philosophy and literature has become a characteristic of postmodern thought.

Two philosophers in this collection address this comparative issue directly. Though scarcely wishing to collapse philosophy into literature or vice versa, each points out the rationalistic presupposition operative in traditional attempts to link philosophy exclusively with dialectic and literature (art) with narrative (nonliteral truth). They correctly underscore the decisive role that philosophy has played in setting the norm for what counts as "knowledge" or "truth," thereby guaranteeing its own legitimacy. The obvious circularity of this move has often been noted by philosophers but politely set aside as one of the unavoidable hazards of epistemology. After all, it is argued, to what else can one appeal in defense of knowledge except knowledge itself?[3] Implicit in what follows is the charge that this ostensible "bad faith" blinds philosophy to its own rich heritage of myth and narrative while impoverishing its dealings with itself and the world.

Thus far we have drawn the contrast between philosophy and literature along the axes of the abstract/concrete. One could also state it in terms of the true/fictive, as some in this volume do. But others, including the poststructuralists and those who are students of the movement, address the contrast in the language of representation/nonrepresentation. This last gives the discussion a totally new focus, while viewing the issue of philosophy and literature from yet another perspective. It circumvents the traditional issue of sense and reference that has captured the attention of analytic and phenomenological philosophers throughout this century. If the representational adequacy of language is in question, then so too is the ability of prosaic philosophy to capture or mirror the real. The Sartrean distinction between "poetry" and "prose" (*What is Literature?*) is likewise in jeopardy and with it the distinction between the imaginary and the real, the fictive and the true. This struggle between representation and language can also be seen as the contemporary heir to the ancient quarrel between philosophy and poetry, mentioned at the outset.

Placed in the context of Foucault's *The Order of Things,* the representational limits of language do not seem to be shared by praxis or by art. Or even by ethics, as the following discussion of the ethically ambiguous role of metaphor in narrative will propose. In fact, we shall see it suggested that Brecht's theater would sublate the very distinction between praxis and art. Does this snatch the palm from philosophy and confer it on literature in our day? Foucault would scarcely agree. To the extent that awards are expected for ultimacy, primacy, or irrefragability (Descartes), Foucault would simply avoid the contest. But "the so-called crisis of representation," as Fredric Jameson terms it, has become another hallmark of postmodernist thought.

Heidegger's implicit critique of representationalism and its attendant questioning of the normative primacy of philosophy-metaphysics, emerges from his meditations on truth as uncoveredness (*aletheia*). We shall see that he mounts this criticism explicitly in his essay, "The Age of the World Picture," while formulating a related critique in his highly influential "The Origin of the Work of Art." If the distinction between philosophy and literature is being questioned in these texts by Heidegger as well, it is in terms of a "poetic" way of dwelling in the world that avoids or, better, precedes the distinction rather than denying or covering it over. And this occurs in the midst of a linguistic turn, albeit one, as we have noted, that does not revolve around the sense/reference dichotomy. Rather, his famous *Kehre* calls the very notion of referential adequacy into question. In fact, we shall see it argued that Heidegger's "turn" continues from language to music, the least representational of the arts.

The often gray but sometimes stark presence of Heidegger throughout this collection is apparent from the outset. It is the explicit object of consideration in several essays, most of which set the discussion in a political framework. Indeed, since the appearance of the controversial documentation of Heidegger's continued association with the National Socialist German Workers' Party, one has scarcely been able to separate the philosophical from the political and the moral in his abstract thought. This very concrete difficulty articulates the postmodern challenge to the ideal of a "pure" philosophy. Such a generalization of the "Heidegger problem" exhibits a thesis dear to existentialist thinkers for decades, but one not readily accepted by many parties to either side of this controversy, namely, the claim that abstract, disinterested, uncommitted consciousness (*la conscience de survol*) is in bad faith. In the very least, this "problematizes" the philosophical "as such."[4]

Only a quartet of the following essays deals with the ethico-political dimension of Heidegger's work. But the larger issue of the adequacy of representational thinking, where Heidegger's influence has been pervasive and profound, as well as the concomitant matter of the distinction between philosophical and literary discourse, is not far removed from any of the articles in this volume.

Shifting to yet another perspective, if one reads the dispute between ancients and moderns, between philosophy and poetry, in terms of reason and will, respectively, as Leo Strauss and Stanley Rosen do, then the ascendancy of psychoanalytic discourse can be read as a properly modernist phenomenon and its Lacanian heresy, a postmodernist deviation. Of course, neither Strauss nor Rosen would have much use for either the modern or its deviant offspring. Presumably, both would cite in support of their diagnosis the nominalist and correspondingly voluntarist strains in postmodern thought, an affliction that has always plagued philosophy in the West inasmuch as it has aspired to be a series of footnotes to Plato.

And this reminds us of a second brooding presence in this volume, namely, the so-called French Freud. Psychoanalysis, as a paradigmatically modernist phenomenon, takes the relationship between dialectic and narrative to be in some respects complementary. Some contributors to this volume acknowledge, at least by implication, their close, if problematic, interrelation. This is expressed, for instance, by relying on a Lacanian account of the origin of the subject, where the contrast is fixed in terms of the imaginary and the symbolic. Whether one claims a Heideggerian "equiprimordiality" for the imaginary and the symbolic or sees a "transmodal" dialectic at work between them, an uneasy, even agonistic, relationship of Lacanian inspiration seems to be acknowledged between the imaginary and the symbolic in diverse cases. Without succumbing to anachronism, one might even extend this Lacanian reading into Adorno's confrontation between literal and artistic truth.

Yet some contributors will underscore the "non-dialectical thinking and non-narrative writing characteristic of postmodernity." To the extent that dialectic and narrative are paradigms of philosophy and "literature" respectively, this claim resonates with the questioning of the end of philosophy that postmodern thinkers have revived, linking it with the corresponding question of the end of literature. What remains? Presumably writing (*l'écriture*) and discourse. Yet even these are chastened by the postmodernist warning to resist "colonization" by various ideologies afoot.

An important issue resting in the wings of these discussions but, unfortunately, not brought to center stage, is that of the contrast between the modern and the postmodern in terms of the valorization of *time* and *space* respectively. To the extent that dialectic and narrative are inextricably bound to temporal sequence, as Sartre, for example, seems to think, their fate appears to rest with that of modernism. On the contrary, inasmuch as one can successfully translate their "arguments" into agonistic relations, diacritical reasoning, and atemporal "plots" (Paul Veyne's *intrigues,* for example),[5] the relative future of dialectic and narrative may be assured, but perhaps at the price of their sharp mutual distinction, if not their very identities. And the consequence of this move for the contrast between philosophy and "literature" is again problematic.

If Heidegger's and Lacan's presences pervade this collection, one glimpses the shadow of Max Weber as well. It hovers over these essays and, indeed, across the entire debate about modernity. His concept of objective possibility, typically intellectualized, seems to lie at the base of Blumenberg's method of reoccupation, for example, and his famous theses about a disenchanted and rationalized society anticipate discussions of instrumental truths, mythic values, and poetic verities that occur in the articles that follow. The secularization thesis, which Blumenberg questions, serves to help characterize modernity.

The tripartite division of value spheres, which Habermas adopts as being characteristically modern, is, of course, explicitly Weberian. And the ultimate inconclusiveness and ambiguity of Weber's own position regarding modernity seems to be shared by several authors in this volume. Of course, the willingness to live with ambiguity is emerging as yet another criterion of the postmodern, one notably anticipated by Merleau-Ponty.[6]

Weber, Heidegger, Foucault, and other harbingers of postmodernity read the by now obviously multifaceted problem of modernity as an issue of *truth and rationality*. The famous debate between Habermas, representing the values of modernity, and Gadamer, upholding a contextualism often associated with the postmodern—though Gadamer would find the link uncongenial—this confrontation is symptomatic of the underlying contrast between a universalizing philosophy and a relativizing literature that has haunted us since the ancient Greeks. Whether one defends a Habermasian position, opts for hermeneutics or finds Blumenberg charting an attractive "middle way" between the two, though scarcely a *via media* between the modern and the postmodern, defenders of each alternative are represented here. There are some, moreover, who, while exhibiting a cautious sympathy for Habermas, would finally side with the (non)position of postmodernism. We place the negative in parentheses to be used *ad libitum,* according as one's negations are "determinate" or free-floating, that is, "Hegelian," if you will, or Freudian.

The uneasy mutual relationship that dialectic and narrative exhibit both in the essays that follow and in the discourse that has come to be known as "postmodern" is symptomatic of that discourse itself. What is being generated is not so much an identity crisis as a *crisis of identity,* Parmenides awash yet again in the Heraclitian stream. More disconcerting still (or is *exhilarating* the word?), is the fact that we seem to be experiencing a *crisis of criteria*. Perhaps the attraction of postmodern "dialectic" (if that is not a *contradictio in adjecto*) is its unwillingness to come to closure or, better, its recognition of closure only in the willing it. The corresponding appeal of narrative might well lie not so much in its retrospective necessities as in its (uncritical?) tolerance. In any case, reflection on dialectic and narrative affords us both a promising perspective from which to view the problem of postmodernity and an especially fruitful instrument for probing the boundaries between philosophy and literature while engaging in both.

II.

It has become almost a truism by now to note the demise of the novel and, by extension, the decline of traditional forms of narration. At issue is less the disappearance of literature than the fact that the literary forms of the past are being supplanted by experimental genres that challenge the definition and bounds of fictional narrative. Although high modernism (embodied in such figures as Proust, Joyce, and Woolf) may involve the breakdown of traditional narrative modes as well as the identity of consciousness, it still presents us with a familiar image of literature because of its experiential character. Contemporary culture displays an assortment of literary forms, a veritable menu within which one must note the predominance of historical, biographical, and nonfictional works, to the detriment of fictional narrative. This is less a symptom of the decline of fiction than, as this volume will show, a sign that its persistence is translated into narrative modes that are no longer readily classifiable and culturally assimilable.

Before addressing in more detail the status of narrative in a postmodern culture, its apparent illegibility and marginality, it is useful to recall Walter Benjamin's comments on the decline of the art of storytelling in the modern age.[7] At issue is less the nostalgia for an art that appears to have reached its end than the fact that this phenomenon corresponds to a shift in sensibility engendered by the emergence of mechanical modes of reproduction. The decay of the art of storytelling is connected by Benjamin to the demise of an epic conception of truth. Rather than viewing this phenomenon as a symptom of the modern age, Benjamin understands it as an effect of the secularizing forces of history that predate the emergence of modernity. The removal of narrative from the realm of living speech corresponds to the rise of the novel and its dissemination through print. The emergence of mechanical forms of reproduction replaces traditional means of communicating and exchanging experiences. Rather than functioning merely as a "symptom of decay," or specifically, as a symptom of the "modern," the disappearance of the art of storytelling signals shifts in cultural sensibility engendered by the continued intervention of technical modes of production. The debates that fuel the effort to distinguish modernity and postmodernity may, in light of Benjamin's observations, be understood as the effort to come to terms with the radical redefinition of artistic modes of production as artistic modes of reproduction.

According to Benjamin, what differentiates the novel from other forms of prose literature is that "it neither comes from oral tradition nor goes into it." However, the autonomy of the novel as a medium of representation is menaced today by the proliferation of information in both print and visual media. Information embodies new forms of communication whose mass accessibility and consumption is made possible by means of mechanical reproduction. It seems that the fate of both oral and written narrative is sealed by the preponderance of information, whose seeming immediacy, verifiability, and plausibility undermine the authority of narrative experience as a subjective and communicative event. The demise of communicable experience is underlined by Benjamin when he cites the experience of the veterans coming home from the First World War: "Was it not noticeable at the end of the war that men returned from the battlefield grown silent—not richer, but poorer in communicable experiences? . . . For never has experience been contradicted more thoroughly than strategic experience by tactical warfare, economic experience by inflation, bodily experience by mechanical warfare, moral experience by those in power."[8]

This poverty of communicable experience marks the decline of experience, its value and efficacity as narrative account. It seems that experience can no longer function as an adequate reflection of human life, since it is upstaged by events whose massive, disruptive, and overwhelming character contradict it and ultimately undermine its legitimacy. Experienced through the immediacy of newspaper accounts and photographs, the authority of information supplants by its verifiability the legitimacy of personal experience. The spatial and temporal space of narration, which relies on a mediating distance, is upstaged by the illusory objectivity of information, which seems to be, to quote Benjamin "understandable in itself." We now begin to understand how personal experience gives way to information, just as narrative forms may cease to function as an adequate representation of events. Thus the poverty of communicable experience in the modern age reflects not the dearth of information but rather its unremitting immediacy and uncontainable excess.

If the novel no longer provides an adequate or even plausible account of experience, does this limitation extend to narrative as a whole? Given Benjamin's contention that information upstages narration, since it "lays claim to prompt verifiability," how are we to conceptualize its impact on and transformation of narrative modes? The answers to these questions will prove to be indispensable to our discussion of narrative, its paradoxical decline, and also its renewed potential in contemporary culture. The essays in this volume provide us with road marks, which enable us to see that the question of narrative is no less strategic to an understanding of antiquity or the Renaissance than is to an understanding of our own age. As this volume suggests, narrative as a genre has been in dispute since its definitions in antiquity. Its adequacy and persuasive capabilities, as a mode of representation as well as its organization as a structured sequence of events, have been at issue from its very origins in myth.

Starting with Aristotle's critique of myth in *Metaphysics,* the utility of mythic narrative as a cognitive mode has been challenged by the emergence of dialectical modes of thought. Narrative appears to have been supplanted by other discursive forms of expression, such as the Platonic dialogues. However, the Platonic dialogue, as the platform of "dialectical philosophy," is also considered, since Nietzsche, to be the model for a surprising new offspring, the novel. Thus dialectic and narrative are intertwined, even as we attempt to define them exclusive of each other. It is unclear whether the critique of myth in antiquity signals the actual demise of narrative or merely a transformation in the way it is conceived. This latter contention is addressed in this volume by exploring the sophist Gorgias's understanding of mythic narratives as ideological formations. For Gorgias, myth no longer serves as the locus of epic knowledge; rather, its significance lies in its rhetorical function as a series of embedded narratives of persuasion.

Does the fact that mythic narrative appears to lose its hold as a privileged mode of representation imply that narrative structure is threatened as well? A quick glance at Aristotle's *Poetics* reveals that myth returns, albeit under a different guise. For *mythos* now designates the essence of dramatic genre as the representation of action or plot. However, the identification of narrative organization with the structure of *mythos* (a properly dramatic function), conflates narrative and dramatic forms. The critical discussions that surround the emergence of the novel as a genre in the seventeenth century announce the redefinition of narrative concerns according to dramatic principles. In the French context, the formal definition of drama in terms of the *three unities* (of plot, place, and time), impacts on the definition of narrative, its criteria of verisimilitude and plausibility. Novelistic narrative becomes subject to conventions that seek to organize it according to a coherent system that subsumes character, plot, place, and time. Like an axis of coordinates, the coincidence of these terms generates prototypes for modern subjectivity, understood as a network where agency, experience, and identity are inextricably melded together. Staging the confluence of being and existence, novelistic narrative conjures through its dramatic structure the haunting specters of reality, subjectivity, and communicable experience, that is, the constitutive elements of identity and consciousness that define the cultural mythologies of modernism.

But, as M. M. Bakhtin's history of the novel suggests, the capacity of narrative to integrate other discursive modes and genres opens up the possibility of conceiving narrative as a "dialogical" space.[9] Defined by its permeability to modal frontiers, narrative emerges as a process of decoding and recoding, which explains its fundamental instability as a genre. This is why narrative may also be identified with those moments where it seems to depart most from its own character. For instance, narrative may be most ethical when it is most suspect, since moral referents rely upon narrative and generic conventions that may shift or even be totally undermined in the course of a work. The generic and narrative instability of the modern novel reflects its double origins. For the birth of the novel, in the modern sense, corresponds to the emergence of the anti-novel, that is, with the emergence of parody as an autonomous literary genre.[10] Parody represents an alternative and parallel tradition to the development of the novel as a proper form. Parody is not simply imitation or mimicry of a style or linguistic mannerisms, nor is it merely a satirical copy of another work. Rather, it embodies a dialogic conception of the novelistic genre, based on the transmodalizing features of narrative.

This brief discussion of parody enables us to reassess Fredric Jameson's claim that postmodernity is best defined in terms of pastiche, as opposed to parody.[11] Pastiche is "blank parody," a type of mimicry that has lost its satirical impulse, that appeals to different artistic conventions without recognizing their normative character. While pastiche, like parody, deliberately manipulates artistic conventions, it differs from it insofar as it scrambles these codes without any regard to their historical specificity. By assembling in one work the signatory trademarks of various artistic conventions, pastiche fakes history by reassembling it without regard to its specificity. Its facticity relies on the actual dismissal of history. Pastiche treats convention as information and thereby liquidates the historical content of tradition, whereas parody resists such reduction, since it posits an active dialogue between convention and information. Since parody takes as its subject matter the formal conventions that define narrative, it redefines the narrative process as a function of its dialogical and transmodalizing features. Thus parody provides us with a conceptual insight into the strategies that characterize postmodernism as a medium for information. The conscious manipulation of novelistic codes, which defines the transcriptive and transcoding function of parody, reveals the mechanisms that underline both the production and the reproduction of systems of information. In so doing, parody challenges the order of representation by deliberately staging its "ready-made" character.

This rapid consideration of the issues by a dialogic conception of narrative reveals and by no means exhausts the problematic status of narrative for both philosophy and literature. In the current philosophical debates regarding modernity and postmodernity, narrative has been under siege because of its perceived complicity with philosophical discourse in the guise of "master narratives of legitimation" (Lyotard). The critique of the hegemony of dialectical reason corresponds to a crisis of logic in philosophy, which poststructuralism, in particular, explores in terms of the limits of formalization. Such an exploration both reveals the difficulty of dissociating dialectic and narrative (Fredric Jameson and Hayden White), and attests to the effort to rethink narrative itself as a strategic site of contestation, of competing forms of discourse and, thus, of logical and rhetorical positions. Hence the style of the essays in this volume attempts to combine philosophical and literary concerns. Whether identified as a critique "internal" to modernity or as a position that exceeds the constraints of modernity, the discussions of postmodernity in this volume suggest a fundamental revaluation of the notion of philosophical critique in the wake of dialectics. Emerging within a field of contesting modernities, could it be that the philosophical articulation of postmodernity might share the transmodalizing features of narrative? If that is the case, the strategic and positional nature of philosophical discourse comes into evidence as a dialogical contestation of its own generic and cognitive limits.

The illegibility of postmodern narrative thus reflects the transformation of the novel as a vehicle for the communication of experience into a medium whose communicative structure is challenged by the advent of information and its consumption as mass-media culture. The effort to classify postmodern narrative must take into account how information as a medium challenges narrative forms and conventions. Works by such authors as William Burroughs, J. G. Ballard, and Don Delillo represent the disruptive and explosive impact of information upon communicable experience. Information, in the guise of systems or networks that substitute their "ready-made" logic for the reality of consciousness, replaces experience. In this context, narrative no longer represents a capacity for fictionalization, a representation of the self in the exterior world, since information implodes this fictional space. Information thus erodes the representational potential of narrative by challenging the ability of fiction to contain and frame it. The space of postmodern narrative is no longer the alternative space of fiction but the space of information where fiction is the only alternative. By exploring the limits of fiction, postmodern narrative restages the facticity of information. In the wake of dialectics, philosophy must face the challenge that narrative assumes as it explores the limits of communicability in the age of information.

Part 1

Philosophy and Literature: Crossing Borders

A fundamental problem haunts the origins and the foundation of philosophical discourse, that of the opposition of philosophy and literature. The initial attempts to distinguish philosophy from literature are concomitant with the birth of philosophy as an autonomous discourse of knowledge. Plato's and Aristotle's efforts to establish philosophy as the voice of truth and philosophical argumentation as its most adequate and appropriate expression rely upon the efforts to distinguish form and content. According to Louis Mackey, Aristotle's critique of myth affirms that truth in poetry and narrative is expressed in an improper form. Improper, because the narrative adornments of myth preserve the tradition in the form of relics whose anthropomorphic or animal character only highlights the alienating aspects of the narrative. The problem may be, as Aristotle had noted, the communication of tradition requires narrativization: the effort to represent and preserve it as a story whose powers of persuasion are founded in the legal and utilitarian expediency of narration.

But as Mackey points out, the utility of narrative as a cognitive mode is challenged in its inception by other modes competing for the communication of knowledge. Thus from Xenophanes's critique of poetry (based on epistemological errors and moral excesses) to the Milesian physicists (Thales, Anaximenes, and Anaximander), rational explanations of the constitution of nature replace mythic accounts of the origins of the world. These rational accounts of the constitution of nature are underlied by a dynamic element: by structures of dialectical transformation whose exposition challenges notions of change and narrative development (e.g., Heraclitus and Parmenides). According to Mackey, we are witnessing the substitution of dialectical for mythical modes of thought and the substitution of discursive for narrative forms of expression.

In a related effort to inquire into the status of narrative and philosophical discourse, James I. Porter turns to a presocratic text by Gorgias of Leontini, the fifth-century Sophist. By examining Gorgias's relations to ancient poetry, Porter provides us with a prehistory of the Platonic rivalry of philosophy and poetry, one which rewrites the mythic origins of philosophy. Shipwrecked on the barge of Platonic dialogues, ancient poetry and rhetoric attest to the presence of traditions that challenge the reduction of philosophy and literature to a dialectical relation. In the case of Gorgias, this other story concerns the breakdown of mythic narrative (the story of Helen) by the conversion of opposing terms through their narrative juxtaposition into "contingent dialectical predicates." This encomium/apology for Helen becomes the locus of the tension between narrative form and dialectical reasoning. As Porter points out, it flaunts the *construction* of Helen's identity as a sum total of her permutations in narrative. These narratives embody different systems of belief, whose comparable plausibility and logical weight unravel the persuasive fabric of this text. Constituted as a figure at the crossroads of myth and dialectics, Gorgias's *Helen* stages the "perplexities of being and saying," of the communicability and interpretability of *logos*.

Porter's essay thus provides us with new insight into Mackey's argument regarding the constitution of philosophy as a dialectical critique of poetry. For Mackey, philosophy brings itself into being as a genre by distinguishing its dialectically ordered discourse from the language of myth. But Porter's essay suggests that Gorgias's strategy renders this distinction impossible. It "demythifies" myth by an appeal, not to dialectics, but to rhetoric: by displaying the strategic character of mythic narrative. And it deactivates narrative by displaying different forms of narration concomitantly, as if they were philosophical arguments. Thus Gorgias's critique of myth in *Helen* suggests that dialectical modes of thought cannot circumscribe the limits of philosophy. Mackey strongly underlines the failure of such an oppositional model to account for the shared complicities and duplicities of philosophy and literature. Porter's essay demonstrates the nature of their "(dis)relationship" (to use Mackey's term) by showing how Gorgias stages the impossibility of philosophy to constitute itself as a proper discourse and genre even as it succeeds in outlining, if only disjunctively, the limits of myth, dialectic, and narrative. Mackey's observation that "what is philosophically interesting about literature is that it is fictive, and what is philosophically interesting about fiction is that it *exists*," makes us realize that, were we to rewrite this statement from a literary perspective, we would have to substitute truth for fiction and thus marvel at the existence of philosophical truth.

1

The Philosophy of Genre and the Genre of Philosophy

Louis Mackey

One of C. S. Lewis's characters describes Aristotle's *Metaphysics* as "a long and difficult book without meter." That the book is long and difficult no one doubts, and anyone who has tried to dope out its meaning has wished that it were both shorter and simpler. That it is without meter is also obvious. But has anyone ever suggested that it should have been written in, say, dactylic hexameter? If there have been complaints of this sort, I have not heard them.

In book 12 of that long, difficult, and prosaic work, Aristotle is discussing the nature of the celestial substances. In the course of this discussion, he makes the following observation *apart*:

> Our forefathers in the most remote ages have handed down to their posterity a tradition, in the form of a myth, that these substances are gods and that the divine encloses the whole of nature. The rest of the tradition has been added later in mythical form with a view to the persuasion of the multitude and to its legal and utilitarian expediency; they say these gods are in the form of men or like some of the other animals, and they say other things consequent on the similar to these which we have mentioned. But if we were to separate the first point from these additions and take it alone—that they thought the first substances to be gods—we must regard this as an inspired utterance, and reflect that, while probably each art and science has often been developed as far as possible and has again perished, these opinions have been preserved like relics until the present. Only thus far, then, is the opinion of our ancestors and our earliest predecessors clear to us.[1]

Aristotle refers in this passage to the mythical cosmogonies produced by the canonical poets of ancient Greece. These poetic accounts of the cosmos (more ancient, no doubt, than those who wrote them down) transmit an important truth: that the celestial substances are divine. The narrative form of these accounts—their *mythos*—Aristotle regards as sugarcoating added for purposes of social control and therefore dispensable without detriment to the truth it makes palatable to the masses.

I am fairly sure the ancients were not such cynical social engineers as Aristotle supposes. But that is not what concerns me. What concerns me is, first, the clear implication that the truth communicated by the cosmogonic myths may be distinguished *simpliciter* from their poetic and narrative form. And, second, the implication, less clear but there nevertheless, that now, in Aristotle's notoriously unmythical and unmetrical essays in first philosophy, that truth is finally communicated in an adequate and appropriate form.

There *is* a truth about the world. In poetry and narrative this truth is expressed in an improper form, a form alien to itself. But in philosophy this same truth is expressed in proper form: truth's own form, the mode of expression demanded by its nature as truth. Content (the content of truth) and form (the mode of expression) are distinguishable, separable, and subject to a certain amount of mixing and matching. One and the same content of truth can be mixed with an improper form, as in narrative, or matched with its proper form, as in philosophical argumentation.

(There is a duplicity here—a double gesture—the first of several I shall note in this essay. On the one hand, form and content are distinguishable and separable, so that a given content of truth may be expressed in a form inappropriate to itself. On the other hand, certain contents demand certain forms. There is a proper form of expression dictated by the essential nature of truth—the form of philosophical discourse—so that philosophy can claim to be the voice of truth itself. Duplicities of this sort will be my recurring preoccupation in the remainder of this discussion.)

But back, for a moment, to Aristotle. In the *Poetics,* also composed without meter, Aristotle explains that poetry is "more philosophical" than history, since poetry tells us not just what did happen but what might have happened or what ideally should have happened. If history is merely true stories and philosophy pure argumentation, then poetry is more philosophical than history because poetry gives us narrative structured by the dialectic of possibility, necessity, and ideality. Poetry approaches truth as it edges away from history (narrative) and snuggles up to philosophy (dialectic).

What we have in these Aristotelian observations is the seed that finally flowers (if that's the word) and perhaps even bears fruit (and here I stop before it runs out of control) in Hegel's *Phenomenology of Spirit.* (Another duplicity, by the way, since for Hegel truth *achieves* its proper dialectical form—*das absolute Wissen* delivered by philosophy—only at the end of a long and tortuous historical narrative.) But of course what Pater said of Plato applies even more aptly to Aristotle. Though he looks primitive to us, he was already quite belated. Ancient in his own time. Not ancient in the sense of primordial or prehistoric, but ancient in the sense of *already very old.* Long before Aristotle the pre-Socratics, who, so far as the historical record may be trusted, originated philosophy, accomplished their intellectual breakthrough by distinguishing their own approach to the world from that of the poets. Some of them, like Xenophanes, were content to call attention to the epistemological errors and moral excesses of the poets. And that, as we know, became the standard philosophical critique of poetry, recited with something like ritual monotony down through the ages: poets tell lies and encourage indecent behavior. More of this later. But the major development in pre-Socratic thought is represented by people like the Milesian physicists. Whether they think all things are water (Thales), air (Anaximenes), or the "unlimited" (Anaximander), they are offering in place of a narrative account of the origin of the world what they take to be a rational explanation of the constitution of nature. Instead of genealogies of the gods, they propose a theory of dialectical transformations by which the multitude of things is alternately separated out from and reabsorbed into a single underlying substance. Heraclitus, for all his obvious and not insignificant differences from the Milesians, does much the same thing—except that in his view the underlying unity imagined by the Milesians as a substance of sorts is identified with the dialectical exchange of opposites. What is symbolized for Heraclitus by fire is apparently the truth that the only stability is the all-pervasiveness of change. Parmenides goes to extremes in the opposite direction. The way of truth proclaimed by the goddess—"Is is and Is-not is not"—proscribes change and narrative development in a way that threatens to deconstruct the poetic vehicle by which it is communicated. The atomistic revision of Eleatic monism explains the cosmos in terms strickly naturalistic and neatly rational—matter and motion—an explanation that still appears to many students of ancient cosmology.

Northrop Frye's *Anatomy of Criticism,* which for many years shaped the minds and methods and curricula of students of literature, supposes that myth is the primordial from of human discourse. That supposition is by no means unexceptionable, as we now know. The originality of myth may be only the myth of originality thrown up by our intolerable belatedness. Nevertheless it is historically (or prehistorically) the case that myth does precede philosophy and the philosophy (historically) begins with a response to myth. Myth is, of course, narrative rather than discursive, and what we have come to think of as philosophy is originally a dialectical critique of myth. Introductory texts in the history of philosophy often tell us that the Greeks discovered reason. Whether they discovered it (as Sutter discovered gold) or invented it (as Alexander Graham Bell invented the telephone) shall remain a disputed question. What is certain is that they invented philosophy. And what they produced (for what other reason do we call them philosophers and begin our histories with an account of their views?) was rational explanations designed to replace mythic narratives. For a long while the narrative form of myth subsists alongside its dialectical counterpart. Plato's dialogues, for example, interweave myth and argument. The logical form of medieval philosophy is qualified by its submission to the canonical narrative of the Scriptures. And so on. But the tendency has been to replace myth altogether with logic, and narrative with discursive modes of exposition. That is the founding gesture of philosophy, and the history of philosophy in the West has been, constitutively, the progressive demythologizing of human consciousness. Contemporary philosophy is pure dialectic, and its literary form, strictly discursive. At least that is the consummation it devoutly wishes and the norm from which it rarely and reluctantly departs.

Philosophy is, foundationally and constitutively, the substitution of dialectical for mythic modes of thought and (equivalently) the substitution of discursive for narrative means of expression.

Now of course the philosophical critique of myth is undertaken—any philosopher will tell you this—in the interest of truth. But what (to coin a phrase) *is* truth? The philosopher replaces myth with dialectic and narrative with discourse in order to get at the truth about the world and (same thing) in order to express that truth in the form demanded by truth itself. Which implies that truth is a system of concepts and judgments that cohere with each other in obedience to the canons of logic and correspond to the structure of reality according to the norms of representational adequation. If philosophy is the dialectical critique of myth for the sake of truth, truth itself is defined in and by the terms of that critique. The philosopher serves a truth that he himself has produced.

The mythographer tells a story. The philosopher (spontaneously generating himself thereby) asks: But is it true? In mythic narrative the question of truth does not arise, because the distinction of true and false is first opened up by the dialectical critique of myth and is expressible only in discursive form. By the time of Aristotle it was already proverbial that "bards tell many a lie." But that proverb is itself sponsored by the philosophically originated conception of truth as the discursive presentation of conceptual formulations achieved through dialectical reflection. In a word: from the beginning truth has meant, in and for philosophy, the prosecution of a dialectical/discursive mode of thought and inscription. What the philosopher declares to the world is: To know the truth you must think as I do, and to tell the truth you must speak as I do. Having thus given birth to truth out of his own innards (like Zeus extruding Athena from his Olympian wetware), it is no wonder the philosopher also proclaims himself her guardian.[2]

The philosopher having constituted himself the parent and guardian of truth, myth and narrative are consequently remanded to literature, a discourse in which (philosophers have always supposed) truth is systematically dissimulated. For every action there is an equal and opposite reaction. Proclaiming itself the native land of truth, philosophy thereby creates "literature": the anarchic domain where ignorance and error run riot, the pseudography of fiction as opposed to the orthography of philosophy—the necessary other-than-philosophy through whose creation philosophy creates itself. And this cleavage between philosophy and literature (opened up by the founding and constituting movement of philosophical reflection) has had two historical consequences that are certainly problematic and quite possibly lamentable.

First, though exiled from philosophy into literature, myth persists in even the most austere dialectic, as a fossil at least, and, more often than not, as a structure displaced from the narrative into the discursive mode and defining covertly the shape of the argument. For instance, the evolutionary philosophers of the late nineteenth and early twentieth centuries were responding to the mythic demand for origins as much as they were generalizing from public and observable data, replacing the discredited myth of Genesis with a respectable myth of science. Or again, the Hegelian-Marxist view of history, recommended as the finest and final achievement of dialectical *Wissenschaft,* displaces and takes the place of—Hegel says it is the meaning and truth of—the Hebraic-Christian myth of redemption. And that, I should suppose, is the source of the power of Marxist rhetoric: it offers an alternative soteriology to a world that desperately feels itself in need of salvation but can no longer invest in the scripturally sponsored economy of redemption. This list could continue indefinitely. What is important, however, is not the persistent intrusion of myth into the structures of dialectic but the fact that philosophy, by defining itself as the dialectical/discursive pursuit of truth (a truth it has itself defined) and by excluding myth and narrative in principle from its precincts, has also systematically obscured from itself the way its logic continues to be nourished by myth and its discourse governed by the demands of narrative form. This self-incurred oblivion to its own roots and resources amounts to a kind of perennial bad faith that troubles the conscience—or at least clouds the consciouness—of Western philosophy throughout its history.

Second, this bad faith of philosophy is matched by a corresponding contamination of self-awareness on the part of the poets. Philosophers have always complained that poets are epistemologically unreliable: they tell tales with no regard for their truth or falsity and retail lying fables at least as enthusiastically and infectiously as they tell true stories. To this charge the poets have replied with their own double gesture. First, they say: You philosophers do not understand the nature of poetry. We are not trying to tell the truth. That's your job. We are only imagining. Everything we say is hypothetical, and therefore our fictions are not subject to judgment by your criteria of truth and falsity. Stories are neither true nor false. They are well written or badly written, that is all. And then they add (here's the second gesture): Anyway, we communicate a higher and deeper truth than any your pedestrian minds can even conceive. We, not you, are the true, albeit unacknowledged, legislators of the world. With this double gesture the poets first attempt to elude the judgment of philosophy and its norms and then resubmit themselves to an escalated interpretation of these same norms. Thus the poets buy back into—or offer to buy back into—the very enterprise of philosophy from which they were in principle excluded. Thus the filiation of philosophy from literature persists unacknowledged by the philosophers, and so the poets attempt to recover the patrimony that the philosophers have alienated.

In the remainder of this discussion I intend to examine these same phenomena from another angle, and—eventually—come to what will have to pass, for the time being, as a conclusion. But first let me insert a bit of intermissionary diversion: a kind of *entr'acte* that may be regarded either as a philosophical narrative or as a piece of narrative philosophy.

It has been necessary over the years for me to participate in departmental discussions of the logic requirement imposed on all philosophy graduate students at my university. Our department actually makes very few specific demands of its graduate students. There are certain area requirements to be met. But these requirements are vaguely stated and may be satisfied by selecting from a wide variety of course offerings. The only course that is required as such of all graduate students is a course in advanced formal logic—and a particular course at that. This requirement is the bane of many graduate students, and from time to time someone proposes to eliminate it or at least to relax it a bit. Such proposals always meet with adamant resistance from the logicians, and the requirement is still in place. Historically, of course, the logic requirement is the last colony of the long-since-dismantled empire of the logical positivists. The logic requirement is for logicians what India was for the British Empire, and as yet philosophy has produced no Gandhis. But the logic requirement is always defended with an argument that goes something like this: If there is one thing all philosophers have to do, it is to argue. Therefore all would-be philosophers must be obliged to master the techniques of sound argumentation, whatever else they may choose to learn. It might be objected that what a student learns in a course in formal logic has virtually nothing to do with most of the actual arguments she or he is likely to examine or to propose, formal logic being no longer an *ars disserendi* but an autonomous and autotelic visual art with (for those who like that sort of thing) its own interest and appeal. Or one might object that there is no such thing as plain vanilla logic, only multiple logics intricately interdependent with the worldviews they organize and the texts they sustain. But such objections would plainly be given no quarter. So I have often reasoned in this way: Arguing is one of the things philosophers have to do but not the only one. They must also read and interpret texts, produce texts of their own, give lectures, and take part in discussions. Therefore they should also be required to take (in addition to logic) courses in literary criticism, expository writing, and rhetoric. At this point, the question is called and the matter decided by an up-or-down vote. With what results you already know.

Take this story as a parable. And take the rest of what I have to say as its explication.

My title suggests, if it does not actually promise, that I will say something about the philosophy of genre and the genre of philosophy. So far I have ignored the one and utterly neglected the other. It's time to make amends.

The status, the legitimacy, and the utility of genre distinctions is a topic of continuing debate among literary theorists. I'm not qualified to intervene in that debate, and I don't want to. In this connection I wish to make just one observation. This one: It was a philosopher who first formulated a *theory* of literary genres. He didn't create them, since they are recognized in the literature long before his *Poetics,* but it was Aristotle in his philosophy of poetry who defined the differences among tragedy, comedy, epic, and the dithyramb. It was also Aristotle who, in the same work, distinguished the super-genus of poetry from the super-genera of history and philosophy, proclaiming poetry more philosophical than history and (presumably) less philosophical than philosophy.

If the philosopher is in a position to define and differentiate the kinds of literary discourse, then philosophy itself must be a superior discourse: a discourse of mastery qualified to judge the claims and achievements of other inferior kinds of discourse, *exempli gratia,* the discourse of poetry. The legislator-judge is not above the law, but he is the authorized interpreter of the law, and by virture of the authority thus vested in him—in which he has thus vested himself—he assesses the legality of subjects and behaviors that fall within his domain. (But of course the fact that he is the author and interpreter of the law implies that he is above it after all. Another duplicity. Be that as it may.) Philosophy, the science of sciences or the super-science, judges all the (other) arts and sciences by reference to the law of which it is the source and privileged arbiter. One thing traditional philosophers have agreed on—almost the only thing they have agreed on—is that philosophy is the custodian of the norms of truth, keeper of the master representations of being by which all (purportedly) lesser representations of reality (e.g., poetry) are to be evaluated. I suspect most philosophers still believe that, though nowadays they tend to whisper it apologetically among themselves rather than proclaim it with authority at interdisciplinary congresses. Once Queen of the Sciences, philosophy is scarcely even a lady any more, and discretion is the better part of a monarch in exile. It has certainly always been clear to the philosopher that philosophy is not poetry, but the guardian of the norms of verity, a kind of universal ontological bureau of standards and a court of epistemological last resort. Philosophy sits upon the rock of truth, on which rock all other representations of reality, truth telling or fictive, are either founded or foundering. In Aristotle's generous verdict, poetry comes off rather well. Better, certainly, than it did in the sterner court of Plato's *Republic.*

This view of philosophy—the philosophers' own view, which I have here only slightly caricatured—one might be inclined to indulge if not actually endorse it, were it not for a couple of disconcerting facts.

One of them is this. Aristotle presumes not only to define poetry and distinguish its kinds. He also distinguishes poetry as a whole from other modes of representation: history and philosophy. We might, as I have suggested, indulge the philosopher's claim to assess the performances of the different kinds of poets. We might even allow him the prerogative of comparing poetry and history. But when he orders history, poetry, and philosophy in a climactic progression that culminates in philosophy, we begin to be a bit suspicious. The judge who passes sentence, however benign, on history and poetry and the kinds of poetry makes a large claim. But the judge who is vindicated before his own tribunal claims at once too much and too little, and his claim is ipso facto questionable. Is philosophy the maker and keeper of the law? Then it cannot fall under the law of which it is the legislator and executor. The norms of representation are not themselves representations to be measured against these norms. As Augustine said of eternal and immutable truth, "non de illa sed secundum illam judicamus." Is philosophy just another system of representations, to be ranked in comparison with things like poetry and history? Then it is not, as such, the repository of the *norms* of representation. The philosopher who presumes (as custodian of the norms) to judge philosophy (as subject to these norms) betrays a duplicitous self-consciousness at least and bad faith at the worst. A philosophy of genre cannot be one of the genres of which it is the philosophy.[3]

But of course philosophy *is* both a genre and the philosophy of genre, and this is the second disconcerting fact. Not only does Aristotle's ranking of history, poetry, and philosophy confess it, the fact is evident also from the circumstance that philosophy itself has a phenomenon, so that it is subject to judgment by the generic norms of history—though it may well be that. More pointedly, if philosophy has a historical point of origin and undergoes a course of historical development, then it forfeits the transcendence required to sustain its authority as the definer of genres and the assessor of generic performances. But philosophy does have an origin. It originates as the dialectical critique of poetry. Does it herewith become a phenomenon or an epiphenomenon of poetry? As an actuality among other actualities, philosophy is subjected to the indicative logic of history. As an event in the devolution of poetry, its preoccupation with necessary truth might seem to be a modally constricted form of the subjunctive or optative logic of poetry, which ranges over all possibilities from the actual to the necessary. In any event, philosophy does originate, and it does have a history, at the end of which (we have been told ever since St. Paul) we now stand. However we may presume to untangle these generic snarls, it is clear that the presumptive position of philosophy, as master of the genres, is hopelessly compromised. The philosophy of genre becomes the genre of philosophy. And this is a difficult identity to preserve intact.

By distinguishing its own dialectally ordered discourse from the language of myth, philosophy brought itself into being as the genre of philosophy. At the same time it created the genre of poetry, conceived as fictional fabulation in distinction from the more primitive conception of poetry as vatic utterance and canonical scripture. There is nothing exceptional or exceptionable in this. New genres, or what are presumed to be new genres, come into being all the time, and by so coming into being alter the whole existing framework of generic conventions. What is exceptional—and perhaps exceptionable—in the case of philosophy is the claim implicit in its founding and constituting gesture and explicitly advocated in the later conception of philosophy as Queen of the Sciences. The claim, namely, that this new genre is not just a genre but the genre of genres: the definer and delimiter of all genres and the arbiter of all merely generic claims and performances. That particular *Selbstbehauptung* on the part of philosophy may well appear an unprecedented and wholly unjustified piece of arrogance.

Of course one might protest that all this is nothing but gratuitous indignation. In the down-to-earth and often refreshing spirit of positivism it might be alleged that the appearance of philosophy in the West, along with all the extravagant claims made on its behalf by its representatives—claims we now all acknowledge to be (at least) overstated—is just a matter of historical fact, not a matter of principle or program, and therefore quite innocent and devoid of ominous implications.

This allegation would be plausible if there *were* such things as mere facts, historical eventualities, empirical coincidences, and the like. But we know there aren't. History is not so guileless as all that. History—which is always the representation of history—is filtered through philosophical presuppositions (not to mention poetic and narrative conventions), so that the allegation itself is not innocent. And so, while there may not be an eternal and immutable system of generic norms—not for our consciousness, at any rate—it is also the case that there are no mere happenings of historical coincidences, either. The constitution of philosophy as a genre and the elevation of that genre by the same act to the status of Master of the Genres was no accident. It was done a'purpose.

Done a'purpose. The deepest desire of philosophy—a desire that comes to full self-consciousness in the philosophy of German idealism—has always been the desire to ground itself, to constitute its own objects and objectives, and to enact its own canons and criteria. Only as self-grounded and self-sustaining—as the self-originating discourse of being itself—can philosophy legitimate its presumptive eminence as master science and master of the sciences. Philosophy is, historically and in its own self-understanding, the discourse of the desire to lay the foundations of truth in a truth it alone possesses, by methods it alone authenticates.

It is this desire to ground itself that finds expression in Kant's critical rejection of all previous philosophy as parasitic on a truth and a reality merely given it to think and not constituted by it. It is this same desire that motivates Hegel's dialectical *Aufhebung* or Kant's doctrine on the *Ding an sich* and the irreducible giveness of intuition.

Or Husserl's determination to locate a presuppositionless starting point for philosophical reflection and the "abyssing" of this determination in *Sein und Zeit*. And so on for pages of examples.

Now of course philosophy does, as I have insisted, found itself and it constitutes itself by breaking away from poetry, which it defines in the same act by which it defines itself. But the coup by which philosophy thus brings itself into being is a gesture of renunciation directed against that which it thereby excludes as its other and on the negative presence of which it thereby confesses itself to depend for its own identity. That philosophy is always only the discourse of the *desire* for self-sufficiency testifies that it is never yet the fulfillment of this desire. And this duplicity—whereby philosophy achieves originality and totality by leaving out that which left out belies its totality and left in betrays its originality—this duplicity, though historical, is no mere historical occurrence but the self-deconstructing moment in the definition of that which by definition is self-defining. The desire of philosophy—perhaps like all desire in this respect—is the desire for that which the failure to possess is the frustration that constitutes its life and the possession of which is the death implicit in its fulfillment.

To illustrate this ambiguous situation of philosophy, and as a relief from these heady abstractions, it may help to recall a phenomenon with which (I am sure) every critic and (I suppose) every philosopher is familiar: the typical course on "philosophy in literature"—or at least the course that used to be (typically) offered under this rubric. Classically conceived as a conjunction of the *dulce* and the *utile,* literature is taken to provide both entertainment and instruction. With regard to the latter, philosophers have thought of literature (at its best) as a kind of popular or popularized philosophy. Though it lacks the self-sustaining truth and the rigorous self-discipline of the real thing (and therefore stands in need of philosophical supervision), literature nonetheless expresses philosophical ideas and discusses philosophical problems, albeit in a nonphilosophical (say lyric or narrative or dramatic) form. Literature presents a philosophical content (a content of truth) in an improper form (the form of fiction). The literary form is the *dulce,* which both recommends and misrepresents the philosophical content—the *utile,* which, insinuated and dissimulated by the *dulce,* can be rescued by the philosopher and reinstalled in its proper form. Thus the syllabus of your typical—or once typical—course in "philosophy *in* literature" (the name says it all) will contain literary works chosen because they express philosophical ideas or discuss philosophical problems that the teacher takes to be important. Russian, German, and French existentialist novels—philosophically garrulous as a rule—are ideal for this purpose. Having read these works, the class, under the guidance of its mentor, will abstract from them their philosophical content and consider that in abstraction from their literary form. Eat the raisin, as it were, and discard the cookie that made it palatable.

However effective such techniques may be in swelling the enrollment of philosophy courses with nonmajors, this is rather obviously an inefficient way to do philosophy and a perverse way to study literature. Literature is not illustrated philosophy, candy-coated philosophy, painless philosophy, or any other kind of philosophy. A novel is not an inferior instance of the philosophic genre. Literature is philosophically interesting, but what is philosophically interesting about literature is not that it contains treatments of philosophical problems or traces of philosophical ideas. What is philosophically interesting about literature is that it is fictive, and what is philisophically interesting about fiction is that it *exists.*

For, the circumstance that there *is* fiction (especially if one recalls that philosophy gave birth to fiction in giving birth to itself) makes philosophical theories about the *relationship between* truth and fiction irredeemably problematic. Suppose, as philosophers have classically thought, that there are norms of truth and that philosophy is charged with administering them. Given its norms of truth, philosophy can (not without difficulty, to be sure) handle simple falsehood: unwitting error or deliberate lie. He who utters a falsehood is either deceived or deceiving. All that sort of thing falls within the province philosophy has marked out as its own. But the person who produces fiction is not deceived—she or he knows the statements are not true—nor does she or he will to deceive—the novelist is not trying to fool you. Do fictions then elude the distinction of true and false, as Sidney thought? The view gives rise to the standard philosophical problem of fictional discourse. Or does the existence of fiction deconstruct the opposition of true and false? If so, that's another problem. Or maybe the same problem in another form.

Take the following two propositions: (1) Fictional discourse is hypothetical discourse—discourse in the mode of "what if"—and therefore neither true nor false; but (2) true and false are contradictories, between which *tertium* (so they say) *non datur.* If the latter proposition is taken to be true (*sic*), then there are no fictions, only falsehoods. But if we take our stand on the former, then the distinction between true and false will not hold firm. Neither of these conclusions is acceptable. No one can seriously deny the existence of fiction as distinct from falsehood. And no one can consistently relinquish or relativize the distinction between true and false.

The second proposition, which excludes a middle between true and false, is the premise of philosophy. The former, which asserts that fiction is the middle so excluded, is the defense of poetry. And the difference between them is one way to characterize the difference between philosophy and literature. But, given the invincible philosophicity of fiction and the equally invincible ficticity of philosophy, that difference itself will not stay where we put it. It is (perhaps) the metastability of this difference that explains (though it could hardly justify) the double gestures by which philosophy and literature struggle to define themselves, each against the other, and the suspicion of bad faith that doggedly pursues them as they work out the historical destinies implied by these self-definitions.

A philosophy is a system of representations that takes itself to be true, a representation (perhaps) of the norms of representation and truth, truthful representation, and representational truth. A fiction is a system of representations that knows itself to be false and is therefore neither deceived nor deceiving—that is to say, not false. But the professional humility of fiction dissembles its commitment (after all) to the norms of truth, just as the pretensions of philosophy dissimulate the ambiguity of its own representations vis-à-vis those same norms. The relation between them is the deconstruction of their difference.

Any representation necessitates reflection on the question: How much of the representation is a representation of the represented? And how much of the represented is an effect of representation? St. Anselm was convinced that the formula "id quo maius cogitari non potest" (which he felt he had received as a revelation) was a form of words (a representation) perfectly transparent to its referent (a representation wholly determined by the represented). His critics have consistently complained that Anselm's "God" is no more than a figment of language. Does the ontological argument give us reality represented in the language of philosophy or the language of philosophy represented as reality? When you look into a mirror—the mirror that art (or is it philosophy?) holds up to nature—do you see *yourself reflected* in the mirror or a *reflection of yourself* in the mirror? Such questions are both decisive and undecidable.

It is no accident that philosophy in the twentieth century has become more and more a metaphysical reflection on the means of representation. By and large, Anglo-American philosophy of language has been a concerted effort to retain at all costs the founding and constituting assumptions of philosophy concerning meaning and reference, whereas recent continental philosophy has systematically distrusted those very assumptions. That, I think, may be the taproot of the misunderstanding that still divides them.

This is no accident. Philosophy was destined, sooner or later, to be brought up against those presuppositions by which from the first it has founded and sustained itself. Nor is it an accident that philosophy, so fried in its own fat, finds itself approaching the condition of that literature that it defined in defining itself and from which it has always distinguished itself. The repressed has returned as it always does, and the problem (or the predicament) of both philosophy and literature has become the problem of language. The medium has displaced, if it has not actually become, the message. The genre of philosophy, constituted as such by philosophy as master of the genres, is a commitment to a particular way of writing (take a position and defend it with arguments) and a particular way of reading (extract the arguments from the text and examine them with a view to accepting or rejecting the position they support). The commitment of philosophy is a commitment to logic as opposed to narrative, and this commitment enshrines a whole system of assumptions about truth and reality—for example, that they are nontemporal and therefore always distorted or lost in narrative representation. But this commitment, with its attendant assumptions, is now seen to be duplicitous, and the genre of philosophy—which also presumes to be the philosophy of genre—can no longer disclaim its inextricable entanglement with and its inevitable contamination by the other it had to exclude in order to become itself.

I hope it is clear that my intention is not to inculpate philosophy nor to compassionate its victim. There are no villains and no victims here. My intention is, rather, and more constructively, to harp on the essential complicity of philosophy and literature—the complicity in their duplicity—and their complex commitment to all the possibilities, powers, problems, perils, and paradoxes of language. The complicity (not quite a unity) underlying the difference (which is really a duplicity) of philosophy and literature is not an external but an internal (dis)relationship, rooted both historically and essentially in that decisive clinamen by which both philosophy and literature have entered upon and acted out their historical essentiality.

By now my goose—or my crow—is pretty thoroughly cooked, and I shall have to eat it. I have spent so much time roasting and basting it that I shall be obliged to gobble it down in great haste. Probably that was no accident either. But before I take that first nibble, let me add just one thing more. Everything I have (however inadequately) done in this essay would have to be done again (and done better) from the side of literature and criticism if we wanted to get the whole picture. Philosophy is not the only suspicious character in this affair. If I have maliciously picked on philosophy, it is perhaps because I am a philosopher of sorts, and it is always more gracious to pick the beam out of your eye than to rail at the mote in your neighbor's. In any case, I know philosophy better—more inwardly—than literature, and my benign neglect of the latter may only betray my lack of that familiarity that inevitably breeds contempt.

So much for justice. I hope (also) that no one will take me to have suggested that philosophy *is* literature and that literature *is* philosophy and that if we just recognize this all our problems will be solved. For one thing, the equations won't wash. Any librarian knows the difference between *Gravity's Rainbow* and *The Critique of Pure Reason*. And any philosopher (ditto any critic) knows that the difference is deeper than Dewey decimal. The thing is to recognize our common duplicity: the difference in our identity and the identity in our difference. Not only are there philosophical narratives (*The Brothers Karamazov* and *Madame Bovary*) and narrative philosophies (Augustine's *Confessions* and Hegel's *Phenomenology*); philosophical dialectic and literary narrative attract and repel each other in every literary and philosophical text. But to recognize this is not to have solved such a problem. It is only to have faced it. That is step one. Whether we then march forward toward a solution or just continue to mark time is something time (perhaps) will tell. In any event, there is no stepping outside or above or beyond the problem. For the philosopher, that means no moving to another department and no ascent to the meta-level from which an impartial view of philosophy, a decisive critique of its follies, and a wholesome reformation of its character might be achieved. True to its destiny, philosophy reappropriates the discourse that would delimit it, and every critique of philosophy is another piece of the problem. Philosophy is a lot like malcontent: you can't complain about it without committing it.

And what about that crow sitting there on the table getting colder and less appetizing the longer I put off munching it? Have I put myself in the position of the philosopher I excoriated earlier, who presumes to lay down the law, to preside over its enforcement, and finally to vindicate himself in his own court? Of course I have. Everything a novelist writes redefines the novel, however minimally. And every act of the philosopher, however perverse, repeats with variations the founding and constituting gesture of philosophy. There is no solution to the problem that does not reconstitute the problem at another level, which of course means that the problem is not a problem but a predicament. I will therefore not be surprised, though I may not be pleased either, when it is pointed out to me that it is also my predicament and that I have not escaped it. The founding and constituting gesture of philosophy is, as I have tried (by repeating it) to point out, a double gesture. I cannot escape the duplicity; I can only acknowledge my complicity in it. To which end, and by way of ending, I appropriate the words of a novelist, Ursula K. LeGuin, reflecting philosophically on her own fictions: "Distrust everything I say. I am telling the truth."

2

Helen and the Rape of Narrative: The Politics of Dissuasion

James I. Porter

I.

According to Nietzsche, the death of Greek poetic forms coincided with the birth of the novel. He illustrates the point with an image, which is brilliantly compressed into a few lines of the *Birth of Tragedy:* "The Platonic dialogue was, as it were, the barge on which the shipwrecked ancient poetry saved herself with all her children: crowded into a narrow space and timidly submitting to the single pilot, Socrates, they now sailed into a new world . . .[1] This new artform, the Platonic dialogue, the fabulous platform of 'dialectical philosophy,' became the model for a surprising offspring, the novel."[2]

The passage, taken whole, contains a welter of contradictions and ironies. Plato did salvage poetry, as a memory; collecting its *disjecta membra,* he brought it back to life, as a monolith, in the name of a self-appointed (and "self-spoken") dialectical philosophy. But the image tells only half the story. On the question of pre-Socratic philosophy, its relations to its sister, ancient poetry, or its rehabilitation at the hands of later philosophers, Nietzsche's emblem remains oddly silent. In what follows I propose to examine a pre-Socratic forerunner of Nietzsche and an anathema to Plato: Gorgias of Leontini, the fifth-century Sophist whose *Encominum of Helen* (of unknown date, presumably long after 441 B.C.), an imaginary defense of Helen, could be viewed in one of two ways, depending on which version of a story we select—either as having fostered and accelerated the "shipwreck" of ancient poetry that Plato would later exploit; or as having merely identified and then exposed the phantasmatic structure of narrative (poetic logic) operative in Homer and in dialectical philosophy alike, the "wreckage" inhabiting all ancient discourse, which no philosopher could hope to commandeer through any amount of Platonizing dialectic, not even by presuming to write the final chapter on poetry in a philosophical fable about poetic forms.[3] On the second view, moreover (one that Nietzsche also foresaw), it is Plato who is revised by his predecessors, and not the reverse; and it is the compulsion of reason that stands *behind* philosophy, driving it forward, to another shipwreck, its own—not with Socrates but with Socrates's *daimonion* (what Nietzsche wished to isolate as the "demonic Socrates") manning the helm.[4]

In what follows, we shall see that for Gorgias narratives and their reception, whether they are about myths or about the world, are fundamentally *cultural* formations that conceal their inner "wreckage." This insight admittedly doesn't cohere with the received view of Gorgias. The author of a recent account of the sophistic movement, representative of the best insights that contemporary scholarship has to offer on the subject, adduces the "modern" concepts of 'ideology' and 'conceptual models,' but warns against their radical imputation to fifth-century thinkers (viz., as conceived by them as operating in the place of any "truths" and "facts" that might be alleged to exist).[5] A view of conceptual models as somehow dissociable from a world of fact is questionable by itself, and Gorgias would no doubt have contested it; but this doesn't invalidate the likelihood that another view of conceptual models, or even of something like what today goes under the name of "ideology," might have been a working part of the sophistic arsenal. There is no reason, moreover, to worry about whether applying these notions to the sophistic critiques of representation would be an abusive anachronism, once we remove a few assumptions from the current picture of Gorgias that tend to diminish the critical force of his writings: namely, that he is chiefly concerned with persuasion (and not with the operations of language generally); that there is some relatively "good" *logos* that can be distilled from the deceptions of all *logoi;* that ancient rhetoric is a technique (or mere exercise) circumscribed by some readily intelligible function; or that its practice is reducible in the end to some modern equivalent like "advertising" or "public relations," and not reducible to precisely a contestation of "public relations" and of public forms of knowledge (often taking the shape of narratives)—forms to which sophistic strategies remain deeply and inseparably tied.[6] The terms *narrative* and *cultural* or *ideological* formations, then, are to be understood, at least for the time being, in their widest possible sense. The latter, in particular, will gather content as we go along, as it only can: there are no universal or universally accepted definitions to which we can appeal; cultural forms and reflexes instead require patient and local specifying—the more so when they are embodied in a discourse such as Gorgias's, whose aim, it will be argued, is to expose cultural assumptions by inhabiting them.

Dialectic, however, requires some immediate elaboration. A roughly historical definition, which we may provisionally accept, gives dialectic as a method that "sets up contradictory predicates for the same subjects,"[7] predicates that must be held synchronously, and, we might add, forcefully together with their subject before awaiting a decision as to their mutual relevance or respective validity (thus, Aristotle calls dialectic the art of "trying" or "testing" [*periastike*]; *Metaphysics* 1004b5; cf. *Rhetoric* 1402a5, with clear reference to Gorgias).[8] Narratives on the other hand will stand, straightforwardly, for arguments governed by a linear logic and a forward progression. From here it follows that a narrative can supply the resolution to a dialectical opposition;[9] but, if so, it is equally true that a dialectical argument can represent a narrative crisis and even the crisis of narrative form itself. Whether the very distinction between narrative and dialectic may itself turn out to be dialectical or to be the product of some concealed narrative makes little difference for present purposes. What matters is that dialectic and narrative, as defined above, are intimately connected: they can contain one another; and they can contain each other's undoing.

If rhetoric can work at cross-purposes with narrative, it can also redefine the meaning of dialectic by interfering with its practice. We can turn to Adorno for help on the relation between these last two terms: "Dialectic—literally: language as the organon of thought—would mean to attempt a critical rescue of the rhetorical element, a mutual approximation of that which is at stake (the *Sache*) and its expression (*Ausdruck*), to the point where the difference fades."[10] First, let us highlight not the fading of the difference, but the limitation implied in the phrase, "to the point where the difference fades." That exquisite point, as I understand it, is one of maximal resistance to a mutual and inevitable indifference, what is indirectly glossed later on by Adorno in the same study as a moment of "presque rien"—the accent falls with equal weight on both halves and bears relevantly upon Gorgias's own bivocal assertion that "nothing is."[11] After Plato, of course, such a rescue operation would be necessary. But in Gorgias's day, and especially in Gorgias's eyes, rhetoric was simply the only form that the manipulation of dialectic could take. Rhetoric—not the formality of substitutions (its most facile understanding) but what Adorno simultaneously calls "the body of language" and "the blemishing stain on thought"[12]—such a rhetoric, institutionalized as sophistic, is the outgrowth and then the palpable reminder of a resistance of knowledge to itself, of the material scandal that no expression can evade (not even Plato's internal monologues and silent thoughts). In the hands of a Gorgias, rhetoric, deployed in the manipulation and inhabiting of positions—if need be, miming (and mining) dialectic and showing itself to be the very unmasterable "organon of thought"—is not so much the source of cognitive uncertainty and embarrassment as it is the very nervousness of cognition itself,[13] just one of the many reminders that recalls thought, negatively and critically—which is to say, on unacceptable terms—to its many more contingencies, determinations, and risks.[14] That Gorgias made a paradoxical use of rhetoric is a well-accepted fact. As a fact, it also carries the weight of a certain indifference. We need to make Gorgias unacceptable again. So much for long-term ambitions.

II.

Gorgias will have been well aware of the intricacies that can obtain between dialectic and narrative. Appearing as he did on the heels of the pre-Socratic revolution, Gorgias was perfectly situated to observe the gradual honing of dialectical argumentation into an increasingly economical and logical instrument[15] and to learn how fraught with tensions the relation between dialectic and its own narrative supports (e.g., inherited or derived mythological frames) could be; this was especially evident in, say, Greek cosmologies, but not only there. For Gorgias, looking upon recent philosophical achievements must have been like watching a building go up, in all its spare lineaments, on the partially demolished foundations of previously existing structures (those of epic, for example). In any case, this was only one of the factors that might account for what I wish to argue is Gorgias's acute sensibility to the constructed, conventional and, *non*-autonomous character of discourse.[16]

A second, historical factor is of a more directly political kind. Gorgias lived during a period of major transformations and, above all, expansions in the social and political domains.[17] One way of viewing these developments in the wake of Pericles at Athens would be to speak of new enfranchisements: of vertical transfers and accessions to power (across aristocracy and *dēmos*); and of horizontal empire-building. From another perspective, we might view in these same developments the "unbridled freedom of [a] democracy" intoxicated with the dizzying prospect of "unlimited possibilities" and new-found power.[18] Even if the second of these accounts may seem a bit overdramatized, the argument can be fairly made that elation and a sense of power attended, virtually as a direct correlate of the new political power, the growth of rational discourse in this expansive world—as did, it has to be added, a concomitant sense of unease and disturbance.[19] Political power could not fail to infect intellectual developments with its own traits. Nor could Gorgias's writings fail to capture (and exploit) both these aspects: both the sheer exhilaration of a rationalism feeling out its furthest limits and, inevitably, the attendant vertigoes and sensations of vacuity. The proliferation of new areas of inquiry at this time, in science, medicine, philology, and elsewhere, richly attests to the exuberant spirit of the age. As a sophist, Gorgias set out to mediate and control many, if not in principle all, of these areas—in his case, by dominating them (the political connotation of this act is never far off) from a critical perspective.[20] Here too, Gorgias, a canny observer of the risk-laden opportunities for rational speculation, must have found an object-lesson in the freshly constructed (and ideology-bound) nature of the discourses around him. His writings, at once shrewd, critical, and opportunistic, have for us, however, not just the value of a reflection on contemporary Greek thinking. They are a part of its symptomatology.

Nowhere is Gorgias's critique of the constitution of thought more in evidence than in the text that has come down to us under the title *The Encomium of Helen*. Here, several branches of contemporary inquiry (ontology, physics, ethics, physiology, and aesthetics, to name just these) flow together, or rather are confronted in a most unpredictable manner. The result, from a literary point of view, is arguably nothing less than the creation of a unique textual object, never seen before, a hybrid that, as a result of its peculiar construction, defies generic definition or even straightforward description. Nevertheless, it is worth the effort to delineate some of the aspects of this textual monstrosity—it is actually an embodiment of critical aporia—precisely for the light that it can throw on the complicities and tensions between narrative form and dialectical reasoning.

III.

We may begin by considering the palpable structure of its argument or, rather, what ought to be regarded as a periphrasis of a nonstructure: for *Helen,* if nothing else, offers up to the beholder a display (*epideixis*) of narratives that is itself an anti-narrative, and ultimately unassimilable to narrative form. On the other hand, in the place of narrative, which provides Gorgias with his raw material, what we do find is a dialectical maneuvering at work, which, as it were, negates and destroys its material. Lifting out this "wreckage," Gorgias sets it on display, not as an obviously visible element or even a residue of his performance, but as its motivating animus, its vital performative element, which is forever tied to its own distortion. Narrative distortion is the substance of Gorgianic narrative, which cannot exist (be legible) except in the form of a flawed display and a defective performance. What one can barely read in his speech is thus not a story but its "plot" of fictions and its unspoken assumptions, which the narrative texture, once exposed in this fashion, cannot, in the end, support. In doing so, Gorgias arguably is extending the well-known critique of his earlier treatise, *On Not-Being or On Nature* (ca. 441 B.C.), which was aimed at unsettling the reigning philosophical paradigms of his day (e.g., those of the Eleatic monists and of the Abderite pluralists), by staging their limits—although to elaborate this last claim would take us directly into another set of texts and deflect us from the task at hand. So rather than confront those texts head on, let us simply follow out Gorgias's argument and stop where he leaves us, at their door.

Now to a schematic and provisional outline of Gorgias's argument in *Helen*. The text opens with a nodding and insincere acceptance of the great values of the day. The outermost frame of *Helen* is thus ethical; within its expository logic we find an innocent exposure (display) of the frame that rivals only that "slippery and uncertain" movement of persuasion itself, to quote Gorgias's words from *Hel.* 11. Whether persuasion ultimately can account for Gorgias's text, as it is usually held to do, is an issue that must be left in suspension for the moment. Gorgias notes that the values of the polis are founded on oppositional structures (*enantia; Hel.* 1): for every orderly virtue (manpower, beauty, wisdom, ethical virtue, truth) there exists an opposed, disorderly attribute. The tendency and force of his argument will be to convert these apparent oppositions, by means of a series of narrative juxtapositions, into much more highly contingent, dialectical predicates, and to show Helen to be the locus of their contradiction, their common subject and point of disjunction.

The sequel may be summarized as follows. In ostensible affirmation of the adornments (or order: *kosmos*) of civic and moral values,[21] Gorgias goes on to give a *logismos* (a rational defense), not of the values per se, but of the story of Helen's abduction by Paris—in explicit refutation of the poets (and their adherents) who were "univocal and unanimous" in their condemnation of Helen on civic and moral grounds. Helen's birth and origins are discussed first; then four competing explanations (*aitiai:* this combines, ambiguously, the senses of "cause," "reason," and "accusation") for her behavior, each with the coherence of a separate narrative, are considered in turn: an explanation is to be sought either (1) in fate (*tychē*), the gods, or necessity,

(2) in force, (3) in persuasion, or (4) in desire; and, in any of these cases, who could blame Helen for falling victim to external compulsion? After these alternatives have been run through and explored at different lengths, Gorgias's exoneration of Helen has, in his own eyes at least, the force of self-evidence, though not yet the character of accepted truth, and it is presented as such, in a rhetorical question put at the end of the speech: "How then can one regard blame of Helen as just, since she is utterly acquitted of all charge, whether she did what she did through falling in love or persuaded by speech or ravished by force or constrained by divine constraint?" (*Hel.* [20]). So ends the acquittal, the ill-effects of one *logos* (a defamation) having been cleansed by means of the good effects of another *logos* (one that is either an encomium or an apology; Gorgias is in fact mixing his genres).[22] The acquittal, at any rate, is followed by a conclusion, which reads, "I wished to write a speech (*logos*) that would be an encomium of Helen and a diversion to myself" (*Hel.* 21).

Diversion, (*paignion,* literally "plaything" or "toy") is the final word of the speech. It is devastating, quite literally so, inasmuch as it scandalously empties out the contents of everything that comes before it. It has also achieved some of what it was intended to do: invite endless speculation. As a result, Gorgias has been accused of everything from nihilism to nominalism.[23] Rather than engage these various labels, which Gorgias no doubt would have shrugged off, provided he got his three minas and could be grudged an encore or two, I would like to save them for the end and, instead, turn back to the speech and its organization. For it is here that the real scandal of Helen occurs.

On a closer look, we can see that Gorgias is manifestly flaunting the *construction* of Helen's identity, which is the sum total of her permutations in narrative, on two levels: in her genealogy, as contained in the twofold story of her birth (this is quietly illustrated by Gorgias through a puzzling syntactical intrication; see below), and in her "pathology," the recounting of her sufferings, by way of the four narrative scenarios named above and their explanation (their etiology). Her mythical birth and origins, exposed in encomiastic fashion in the following passage, are intended to recall the ethical cosmos evoked at the start (*Hel.* 1–2): "Now it is not unclear, not even to a few, that in nature and in blood the woman who is the subject of this speech is preeminent among preeminent men and women. For it is clear that her mother was Leda, and her father was in fact a god, Zeus" (*Hel.* 3). Nature and blood (*physis* and *genesis*) do not exactly amount to virtue and truth, but Gorgias's point is that the latter pair of terms is no less beyond contention or contingent on belief than was, evidently, the first. Divinity, power,[24] rape, and speech are all stated or implied in her pedigree (her mother was Leda, her father Zeus or Tyndareus, depending on whom or what you believe); as it happens, these are also the "causes" that Gorgias will later claim are the unreal source (and exculpating factors) of her blame.

But what matters, ultimately, is not just what you believe, but how you believe: belief is structured, and structures are revealing. So the "what" of Helen's origins already contain and forecast the structural attributes that she is to acquire, as victim, in Gorgias's text; and these, symptomatically, are double, that is, dialectical, ensnared in the perplexities of being and saying or, if we choose to translate somewhat more literally, of being and becoming (*physis* and *genesis*): "For it is clear that her mother was Leda, and her father *was* [*genomenos*] a god, but *allegedly* [*legomenos*] a mortal, Tyndareus and Zeus [and here the crucial contamination of an assertion with its own rhetoric comes in], of whom the one [Zeus], just because he *was* [*dia to einai*], *appeared* [*edoxen*] the father, and the other [Tyndareus], just because he was *claimed* [or himself claimed] to be [*dia to phanai*], was disproved [*ēlegchthē*] to be the father; and the one was the most powerful of men and the other the lord of all."[25]

Language and reality falter into contact with one another at the point where language, like being, appears and at the point where being recedes by appearing, only to take with itself something from language (that point is marked syntactically by a chiasmus and ironized as being "self-evident": *dēlon,* "it is clear").[26] Being proves nothing; but if language can only apparently prove being, it *cannot also prove the reality of appearance.* One further trap laid by Gorgias, aimed at complicating beyond telling the story of Helen.[27] But in Gorgias's own words, this is just a "beginning" (cf. *Hel.* 5, 21; also below).

Helen has already begun to lapse into an enumeration. The subject of predication, she is herself an effect of attribution, "ek toioutōn genomenē" (*Hel.* 4), "a resultant being" or "the result of such (contradictory) circumstances"—a singular plurality. In Greek, she is ta prōta tōn prōtōn (*Hel.* 3), "the first things among first men and women" (the translation "preeminent" glosses over the potential nuances of this idiom, which it pays to render literally) before she is called a singular "woman."[28] The account of Helen's plural identity is strategic. Here, for comparison's sake, we might take a side-glance at Gorgias's other preserved set piece, the *Defense of Palamedes* (roughly contemporaneous with *Helen*). The latter speech consists entirely in a verbal reconstruction of what the defendant, Palamedes (the inventor of games and a few letters of the alphabet, cf. [DK 82B11a(30)]) claims to be a nonevent (*"to mē genomenon"* [DK 82B11a(5)]; cf. DK 82B11a(11)]), something that never happened but that nonetheless furnishes the substance of a criminal accusation leveled against him by Odysseus. *Palamedes* is, in essence, a proof of not-being as is *Helen* itself, which begins by "showing," through a series of negations, that a nonevent took place and which ends by showing, as I hope is becoming clear, that Helen herself is that nonevent. A figure to be read, Helen becomes the motivation and projection of the very ideologies that her behavior was said or supposed to have threatened (Helen giving rise to ambitious designs: social achievement, honor, prowess, the exercise of knowledge are all implicated): "Her *one body* was the cause of bringing together *many bodies* of men thinking great thoughts for great goals, of whom some had greatness of wealth, some the glory of ancient nobility, some the vigor of personal agility, some command of acquired knowledge" (*Hel.*, 4) (compare the virtues tallied up in *Hel.* 1: manpower, beauty, wisdom, virtue, truth, and generally, "praiseworthy things").

Helen hinges and unhinges the logic of the one and the many. The last-mentioned of the motivations, "the command (*dynamis;* literally, "force" or "power") of acquired knowledge (*sophia;* literally, "wisdom" or "cleverness")," contains a reference to the cognitive embarrassment that Helen's "one body" (*hen sōma*) occasions (be this for philosophy, morals, or aesthetics) and continues to occasion, now that this odd juxtaposition of body as stimulus for mind has been brought out into the open and has acquired a textual fixity in Gorgias's treatise (contrast the more orderly and conventional distinction given earlier between the two sets of complements: "What is becoming . . . to a body [*sōma*] is beauty [*kallos*], to a soul, wisdom [*sophia*]").[29] The further embarrassment is of course that Helen, here, is just the idea of a body and the embodiment of an idea, not a body in any defensible sense.

A figure to be written, Helen, like the object of Palamedes's apology, is the sum of the (here) four alternative scenarios about her that are retailed by Gorgias in order to absolve her from all responsibility and guilt (another sense of *aitia;* cf. *Hel.* 2); and these, in turn, are so many vain projections upon a blank, prior screen and a *tauto legein* (tautologism). The status of the tautology is perhaps governed by one of Gorgias's philosophical masks, as an argument from *On Not-Being* implies: perceptions of "the same thing" will vary and so will its descriptions.[30] Taken to the limit, the critique of identity issues in a critique of self-identity, where nothing can be said to be the "same" as itself.[31] But this is an ulterior echo and the product of another strategy of containment. Let us explore the perspectival projection of Helen—this fugitive coincidence that Helen somehow "is"—just briefly.

At one level, which is induced and corroborated by textual associations, Helen has the exact status of the iconic image depicted in the following passage:

"Whenever painters perfectly create a *single* figure [literally, "one body," a *hen sōma,* as she was called above] and form [a *schēma,* or "figure"] from *many* colors and bodies [*sōmata*], they delight the sight" (*Hel.* 18). A composite figure, she is, at another level, not what she is, but both more and less: for the perception of the poetic process and workmanship (*poiēsis* and *ergasia*), we learn in the continuation of the above passage, brings an aesthetic gratification no less intense than the pleasures afforded by illusion, but one that is no more certain either. In sheer narrative terms, Helen embodies her own self-difference: she is a not-one marked out by a many or, rather, a manifold of possible negations: a technical disjunction—a poetic effect—that merely completes the logic of the simulacrum, in strategic narrative terms. Completes, but does not exhaust or arrest, for a closer look shows that the cumulative strategy of *Helen* is to negate, in turn, these negations, that is, their self-standing identity. Through a recessed logic of entailments and verbal repetitions, Gorgias manages to equate without quite conflating necessity, violence, persuasion, and desire, by "showing," in effect, that each of the terms in the series is an aspect of the remaining terms: all are in a sense reducible to force or to persuasion or to desire or to a higher necessity or higher fate.[32] The repeated exposures of Helen only intensify the effect of her reduction to a simulacrum, but now one that exceeds the bounds of poetry and its aesthetic gratifications, in the way that poetry exceeds itself. Helen is a locus that is traversed by multiple codes that have been forced or seduced into a wavering and disquieting identity.

We may consider just enough examples to make the point graphic. It will be intuitively obvious that metaphysical compulsion, for instance (fate, the gods, or necessity), cannot be neatly separated from force, the topic of the next *aitia;* for "it is the nature of things . . . for the weaker to be ruled and drawn by the stronger, and god is stronger *in force* and in wisdom and in other ways (*Hel.* 6)." Nor can persuasion be considered apart from metaphysical compulsions, for we learn two paragraphs later that "speech is a powerful lord, a *dynastēs megas,* which by means of the finest and most invisible body [*sōma,* possibly modeled after the atomistic hypothesis of particles and corporeal porosity] effects the *divinest* works."[33] Needless to say, the incantations of persuasive speech are "sacred" (*entheoi;* literally, "full of the god") (*Hel.* 10, ad init.). In view of *Hel.* 12, ad fin., a hopelessly corrupt passage,[34] the forces of persuasion and that of necessity at the very least have the same quality or power (*dynamis*): "The persuader, *like* one who compels [literally, "necessitates"], does the wrong, and the persuaded one [Helen], *like* one compelled [necessitated], in speech is wrongly charged." An ambiguous particle, *hōs,* creates a precise confusion in the italicized portions: the logics of analogy ("like") and causality ("since") appear to overlap, in their discontinuity. Language in its effects is, moreover, a kind of rape: in *Hel.* 12 "under the influence of speech" (or "song;" *hymnos*), Helen's fate was to be "just as if *ravished* by the force of the mighty (*hōsper ei biatērion biai hērpasthē*]."[35] Through the violence of language, divinely masterful persuasion approximates seduction, the last of the *aitiai.*[36]

Here Gorgias is specifying the physiology by and through which language is presumed to operate (a subject to which we will come back below). But the immediate question is why Gorgias, having gone through all the trouble of setting up contradictory predicates for his dialectical subject, simultaneously seeks to resolve them in a series of approximations and analogies. There are a number of possible replies.

IV.

One answer to the question about Gorgias's methods and their apparent incongruence might be called a "narrative solution" to the problem of mythical identity. Gorgias is simply displaying the limitless powers of *logos* within its own realm: its powers are plastic; it can create and dissolve realities at its user's will,[37] in this case by narrativizing them. This would accord well with other of Gorgias's pronouncements on language and reality. There have indeed been attempts by scholars in the past to link up the logic of *Helen* with Gorgias's theory of language, particularly as it is laid out in the remains of *On Not-Being,* for example, the claim that language is self-contained and can convey nothing of what exists outside itself, but only itself: we do not hear vision; we cannot communicate *pragmata,* sensible realities about which we boast our language to be and to which it is in fact irreducible; we are condemned to linguistic tautologies, to a communication of and through words, hence, to deception and distortion.[38] From this it seems to follow that language exists in an autonomous domain (at least, so the argument runs); and the same will hold for the psychological reality that it governs, which must be granted an existence that rivals, even supersedes, sensible reality.[39] Hence, Gorgias can be credited with the view that "persuasion was sovereign because there was no truth over and above what a man could be persuaded to believe."[40]

Such a solution, which also happens to be the going theory about him, suffers from one potential failing: it is imprisoned in a narrative of persuasion.[41] So little is at stake with the truth of Helen's fate, we might believe Gorgias's insistent pleas in *Helen* about the inordinate power of persuasion, but why should we when we will disbelieve everything else (all the rhetorical promotions and supports) save, perhaps, the claim (or its insistence) itself?[42] But apart from the formal question of belief, there are logical residues as well. Paradoxically, instead of locating linguistic autonomy in some comprehensible way, the link with persuasion opens up the question of its status all over again. The real problem with all such readings of Gorgias is that they sacrifice their own genuine rigor. For if language is truly autonomous, self-enclosed, autarchic, self-sufficient, it will also be autonomous from its psychic effects.[43] Restore Gorgias's conception in all of its radical stringency, and we must imagine a *logos* without effects (perhaps parallel to a body without organs), a *logos* that knows no distortion (but is knowable only through and as distortion [*apatē*], deception [*doxa*]), a *logos* that is not reducible to *peithō* (although it is only through persuasion that such a *logos* will find expression); but also a *logos* that is not reducible to *logismos* (reasoning). How else are we to make sense of the repeated statements that both persuasion and reason are explicitly said to be *superadded* to *logos,* as in *Hel.* 2: "by introducing (*dous;* literally, "imparting") some reasoning (*logismos*) into my speech/the story (*logos*)"; and in *Hel.* 13: "persuasion (*peithō*), *when added to* (*prosiousa;* literally, "when it comes toward") *speech* (*logos*),"[44] just as in *Hel.* 9, poetry is defined as "*logos* plus (literally, "having") meter";[45] and in *Hel.* 8, *logos* is not strictly reducible to the *sōma* (body) it activates (whether as its instrument or its locus)—though no one pays any heed to these warnings.[46]

Logos has thus to be severed from its materializations (its predications); these, in effect, can only falsify its substance and identity. At this point of maximal abstractness, assumed in the full rigor of the conception, *logos* begins to take on the aspect of Parmenidean Being: one, indivisible, imperishable (in the sense of not being contingent on an *archē*),[47] inaccessible to the mind and the senses (being incorporeal).[48] If so, then all that Gorgias has succeeded in doing is displacing but not dismantling the Parmenidean principle of identity. Grant unlimited autonomy to *logos* and the consequence that follows few commentators of Gorgias have had the courage to admit: *logos* will be remystified, reinvested with all the attributes of an onto-theological precept with which Gorgias has indeed strewn his discourse (as in *Hel.* 8–10) and against which, it has always been assumed, that discourse is pitched.[49] Is this approximation with the object of his critique the sign of a crisis or of a capitulation? Is Helen, indeed, the Parmenidean goddess of revealed truth?

With this, we reach an intolerable impasse: we can celebrate with Gorgias the powers of the logos, and we will be marveling at nothing. This is the point. *Logos,* so construed, is equivalent to nothing. The *logos* we have described is not an analogue of Parmenidean Being, despite the apparent overlap of attributes, but its negation: it mimes the attributes of self-identical Being in every way but ontologically. Such a *logos* has no identity, only a nonidentity that is not stable and autonomous but contingent upon negated identities: it is a *logos* that is not-persuasion, not-reasoning, not-self-identical but only contingently different. A material negation and not a material identity, *logos* is a construct that negates, dialectically, its own constitutive elements of identity (just as Gorgias's concessions everywhere in *Helen* border on self-damaging evidence for his own special pleading).[50] Gorgias's logic from *On Not-Being,* if it is to be discovered elsewhere (e.g., in *Helen*), must be followed out to its radical conclusion—to the logical incompatibility of autonomy. His dialectic as it unfolds in *On Not-Being or On Nature* is more than a critical commentary on Parmenidean identity. In a sense, Gorgias is merely drawing out some of the still disputed implications of Parmenides's poem, the inevitable consequence that Parmenides knew and sought to evade ("the ladder which must be thrown away")[51] or else knew but failed, in Gorgias's eyes, to expose sufficiently, in all its painful aporia, namely, the realization that autonomy is logically self-refuting.[52]

Logos may enjoy a certain autonomy, but not sovereignty or lack of contingency; it is not a totalizing construct, it cannot sweep in its train the world of *pragmata* (sensible objects) through the bare assertion of its epistemological irreducibility to them. (Nor does Gorgias ever allow the four competing *aitiai* of *Helen* to reduce simply to any single factor like persuasion; they remain mutually irreducible, and this too is in keeping with Gorgias's claims from *On Not-Being* where Gorgias argued for the irreducibility of the various senses, of thought, and of language to each other.) The problem of irreducibility is only heightened by the realization that *logos* is itself a *pragma,* endowed with sonorous and other forms of material consistency, though it is not just these features either.[53] In the process, Gorgias is merely closing the gap that Parmenides had already opened by inviting speculation on the relation between truth and persuasion (for the true way of Being is that of Persuasion, who "attends upon" Truth; DK 28B2).

So it is wrong to state that Gorgias's *logos* is completely severed from its materializations. On the contrary, *logos* is nothing outside of its materializations—like Helen herself. *Logos* has no being, only the attributes of being, which derive from the contrast between "the *logos* that is not" and "the *logos* that this *logos* is not." If *logos* can't communicate the contents of an outer reality, this is not just because the two realities are incommensurable, as it is standardly assumed, but because *logos can only fail to communicate the inner reality of its very own contents,* since in the final analysis *logos* has no measurable relationship to its own material expression, namely, distortion. Compare the following: "for it is not at all [sound] or color [or any phenomenal object] but *logos* that is communicated; with the result that it is not possible to think color, but [only] to see [it], nor [to think] noise, but [only] to hear [it]."[54] So Gorgias is not yet committed to anything like Parmenidean ontology. Nor is the solution to the problem to be sought, so to speak, in a phenomenological reduction of all *logoi* to one *Logos;* rather, it is to be sought in the critical reduction of all *logoi* to themselves. And such a reduction brings to light nothing, beyond a multiplicity of self-specifying negations: the door is thus open to a self-critical investigation of the claims of reason.

The thrust of Gorgias's logic (as I understand it) is in a direction away from the values of identity and autonomy, which are metaphysical desiderata, and toward a more critical notion of specificity, which is to say, toward a specification of alienated meaning—the series of silent negations by which meaning is predicated and sustained, and which has its analogue in the ways in which *logos* is circumscribed, delimited, and *limited* by the spheres of sensation, and by the material or discursive contingencies that shape its contours. Thus, even the pristine, rarified *logos* reconstructed or inferred just above must be construed in terms of its possible negations, or in the resistances it sets in motion, but only doubtfully as a pure positivity. It is a material deposit, a leftover, a *paralipomenon* of discourse, which reveals its contingency upon language and thought (and their objects), even as it requires their fatal disjunction: like the process of the inscription of sight described, or rather narrated, in *Hel.* 15–17, analogous to the imprints of persuasive language in *Hel.* 13–14. Let us turn, then, to these passages and to Gorgias's physiological description of language.

V.

In our analysis above, we mentioned "the finest and most invisible body [*sōma*]" that Gorgias posits as the efficient cause or locus of persuasive effects (*Hel.* 8). To the particle theory of linguistic and/or psychic matter, we must add a theory of "impressions" (*typoi*), which gives an account of the imprints of *peithō* (persuasion) on the psychic disposition of the hearer (as in *Hel.* 13): "persuasion impresses [*typōsato*] the soul as it wishes"), impinging itself directly on the *taxis* (arrangement, structure, condition) of the soul: "The power [*dynamis*] of speech [*logos*] relative to the *taxis* of the soul is comparable to [literally, "has the same *logos* as"] the *taxis* [prescription/arrangement] of drugs relative to the nature of bodies" (*Hel.* 14). "Directly" is a most uncertain commentary on the passage: it fails to reckon with Gorgias's careful avoidance, evident in his choice of terms, of anything resembling a close formal correspondence between the two structures (*taxeis*) of cause and effect, which is to say, between variously incommensurable materialities. Commentators have long been embarrassed by the surplus of repeated terms in this sentence.[55] Formally, the repetition of *taxis* reinforces a balanced chiasmus; logically, it creates an imbalance that is not easily redressed.[56] Part of the problem lies in the "near miss" of the trope *dynamis/taxis::taxis/physis,* suggesting the imperfect fit of the "power" of logos, the taxis *is* allegedly affects (in the soul) and the taxis to which it is likened (of drugs working on the "nature" of the body). We can perform a massive conflation of all the terms (*taxis* = *physis* = *dynamis*), but then the exact material character of words, the chief burden of the comparison, will depend for its definition on a flimsy analogy (the burden subsequently devolves upon a metaphor, establishing nothing: words "drug" the soul). But this is not all. To "taxis" should be added the more troubling persistence of "logos," which figures twice, once in the *definiendum* (the logos in question) and once in the *definiens* (the logos governing, analogically, the various terms). Circularity looms near,[57] and we are no closer to an understanding than we were when we started out.

Clearly, the details of this scheme cannot be taken very far, thanks to their incompleteness; Gorgias simply fails to give us enough information to reconstruct his theory of language and of linguistic affect in a coherent way. But are we even entitled to assume that that theory, so manifestly incomplete, is also intended to be coherent? Or is it not rather that the theory's truth, the logic of the homology (or rather, simile), resides in a tropological hiatus, in the blank space crossed out by the *X* of the chiasmus (recalling the doubtful locus of origins from *Hel.* 3)? At the very least, Gorgias's physiological argument would appear to define the general receptivity of the soul, and if we still hope to put some flesh on the rudiments of his psychology there are other places to which to turn.

As in the case of persuasive language, for instance, visual effects are said literally to "inscribe" themselves in the form of iconic images (*eikonas*) impressed (*typoutai*) on the mind (*Hel.* 15–17). This second passage deserves some attention, as it sheds a (negative) ray of light on the first. The context is overtly defined by the overwhelming powers of visual seduction, such as those that rendered Helen a helpless victim of Paris's beauty, although curiously, the example chosen is of fearful impressions. Gorgias is preparing a further conflation, of force, desire, divine compulsion (for eros is a god [*Hel.* 19]), and persuasion;

he is ultimately preparing a disabling finishing stroke to his previous arguments about the powers of logos: "It has happened that people, after having seen frightening sights, have also lost presence of mind [literally, "are driven from their present thought"] for the present moment; in this way, fear extinguishes and excludes [literally, "drives out"] thought [*noēma*] (*Hel.* 17).

The impingement of vision requires the desertion of the light of reason. In *Hel.* 15, for example, visual perception is not willed but contingent: "for the things we see have not the nature that we wish them to have, but the nature that each actually has." Described in both passages is a moment of mutual approximation (of thought and sensation) but also of mutual inversion: an ecstatic invasion in which thought is driven out so as to accommodate the inscription of sight (yielding a condition of *agnoēma psychēs* [thoughtlessness]; *Hel.* 19).[58] Once again, the potency of language is being reduced to a minimum:[59] echoes with the foregoing (especially the theory of impressions, verbal in *Hel.* 13 and visual in *Hel.* 15) do less to reinforce than to hold apart the two radicals of "psychology." The soul is "impressionable," to be sure; but Gorgias offers us only competing (and incomplete) explanations of how these impressions come into existence, and these impressions do not share anything in common beyond the weakest of analogies and a synonymous nomenclature (*typousthai*). And according to Sextus's report, visual objects and words, to the extent that they can be said to exist at all, are the most incommensurable of all things (DK 82B3[86]).

All of this, of course, goes directly against the celebrated claims made in (and consequently for) *Helen* about the inordinate psychagogic powers of poetic (and rhetorical) language, their capacity to impinge unmediatedly their form and content (or perhaps just their form) on the makeup of the mind. Perhaps these claims stand in need of revision. The "merging" (*sugginesthai*) of the power of incantation with opinion in the soul, foreseen in *Hel.* 10, must be referred to a passage like *Hel.* 14 and all its complications before being taken at face value. The description of the effects of poetry on the hearer in *Hel.* 9 is equally problematic for similar reasons; this too presumes, rather facilely, a psychological identification (*idion ti pathēma*) based on a radical alterity (*ep' allotriōn te pragmatōn kai sōmatōn*)—the very sort of identificatory process that the whole of *Helen* unsparingly attacks, not least of all by posing as its subject a projected image (an icon) representing everything to all admirers and detractors alike and, consequently, representing nothing but a reader's desire.

The exclusive focus on the powers of logos in *Helen* tends to distract us from the defining contours of that same logos, its frames and its limits. The question of logos can, and perhaps should, be put in different ways. Possibly, Gorgias is describing the paralipomena of language, its empirical effects (even if through the transparently vitiated comparisons with sensory impacts)—but this is still not yet to describe language per se. Just as possibly, language as we know it is itself a paralipomenon of the world, a fragmentary remains, as unfathomable as any sensation; but, if so, then Gorgias leaves us with the paradox that we cannot even properly "sense" language (cf. again DK 82B3[86]: logos is received through an organ different from either hearing or sight).[60] The indecision between these, I would suggest, is irresolvable, a stubborn deposit of Gorgias's dialectical construction, which is achieved (though never "completed") not so much by way of a reduction as by way of a *resistance* to language and its effects. Nor is Gorgias exempt from his own critique. Needless to say, Gorgias's claims suffer the same fate as befalls those that constructed Helen's prison of fame (*Hel.* 2): all but total dissolution through the invitation to analysis.

And yet, far from heralding a physiology of language forsworn of all corporeality and of all contact with externality (a physiology without body or matter), Gorgias's "theory," such as it is, does imply connections with the world that it regards, circumspectly, to be sure, and at some distance.[61] Disjunctive relation is relation nonetheless—even if it is a disjunction that aggravates rather than evaporates the problem of the material, outer world (*ektos;* DK 82B3[84]), precisely by bringing the problems of exteriority to the interior of linguistic functioning itself (in an interior fold within language that language, needless to say, cannot touch or unfold). Noncoincidence of language with itself assures, rather than just making problematic, its contingency (and physical "contact") vis-à-vis the world (which is just one further untouchable surface). Isn't this also the shockingly plain lesson of Saussurian linguistics? "No linguistic item [*fragment de langue*] can ever be based, ultimately, upon anything other than its non-coincidence with the rest."[62] By "the rest" is to be understood everything that falls outside the system and heterogeneously to it: a gulf of otherness on which, it follows, all intralingual differences are in fact premised as well. Such noncoincidence is precisely the very condition of possibility for any contact-making at all, just as the promised autonomy and power of a faculty (such as language) in its "proper" domain can be measured only against its deficiencies relative to other powers in other domains, or to the heterogeneities it cannot control even in its own.

This, I take it, is the meaning behind Gorgias's twin claims (in Sextus's summary) about the *dependencies* that obtain between language and "the rest."[63] First, "For logos [he says] is compounded [*synistatai*] from the *pragmata* that befall us [*prospiptontōn;* literally, "strike us"] from without, namely, from the objects of perception and sensation [*aisthētōn*]" (DK 82B3[85]). Gorgias's thesis is not that sensations make on us a determinable impact, for which lanugage then acts as the registry. It is not even clear that Gorgias has in his sights *language* in some abstract and rarified sense, but only language as we invent it and as its concept is thrust upon us by the stern and impassive obstinacies of the world. Nor does Gorgias have in mind any obscurer sort of causalities, as the following mistakenly might suggest: "From the incursion of taste there arises within us the expression that concerns [or "is predicated of"] that quality, *ho kata tautēs tēs poiotētos ekpheromenos* (and likewise for color)." Clearly, our words gesture vaguely toward their objects, just as the process by which words come into existence is left half lit by Gorgias's description.[64] Gorgias's logos is a composite "of" sensations, in the sense that it is the composite of these things conceived of as radically different from language (as noncoincident with and radically irretrievable in language); logos is emphatically not a direct sum of the effects of *pragmata:* rather, it is (like Helen) a not-one marked out by a not-many. As the collective body of language, logos is an incomplete summation of what it is not. Second, "If this is so," the report continues, "then logos isn't exhibitory [*parastatikos*] of the outside; the outside is revelatory [*mēnutikon*] of logos." Language—as construed here by Gorgias, that is, as a construct built out of the heterogeneous materials of experience and one that barely holds together, besides—exhibits not that which lies outside of language but that which belies language itself, namely, its defining deficiency. Hence the significance of Gorgias's reversal: the outside is *revelatory* of that deficiency.[65] Language is defined not autonomously from but as dependent upon that which limits and delimits its sphere of operations. Take away the "outside," and language vanishes too (the way being and appearance are mutually dependent, DK 82B26).[66]

Gorgias is not disavowing the possibility of communicating, only of communicating reality.[67] And for the same reasons that language fails to "contain" and transmit externalities (being radically heterogeneous to them), it is incommensurable with any of its alleged effects. Neither is it Gorgias's thesis in *Helen* that language precipitates psychic or corporal effects, if that means simply reversing (or mirroring) the flow of impingements from external sensations. He is giving an aporectic analysis of the neat causalities that such a view commonly presupposes (cf. *aporiai,* MXG 980b20, which I take to be the equivalent of *paignion* in *Hel.* 21). Words or thoughts may be so responsible; but we will always be a priori debarred from a cognition of this fact.[68]

VI.

This, finally, gives us a dialectical solution to the problem posed earlier. It is not intended to displace so much as to complicate the narrative of persuasion mentioned above. "Solution" is probably misleading. "Provocation" comes closer to the truth, and it is to be connected back up with the impetus to specificity which we detected in Gorgias above. The near conflation of the four strands of the *mythos* of Helen are required to expose the various, constructed character of that *mythos* and of mythmaking in general. Their irreducible difference (desire is not persuasion, though desire persuades, and persuasion desires) is required to expose the space in which a minimum of intelligibility, traversed by a dialectical movement, can occur: the mutual negations (of the four *aitiai*) are all contingent at some level, not autonomous; they describe, not nothing, but *"presque rien."* Specifying this *presque rien,* reducing it to a further minimum, a smaller point of (even greater) resistance, is the paradoxical driving mechanism of Gorgias's logos. Posturing as Helen, while ravaged by the implacable counterlogic she represents, Gorgias's narrative can no longer be held in focus but only analyzed, critiqued, or made into the grounds of a much larger critique—the critique of cultural practices and formations, of the powerful grip of oppositional structures, of the motors of power and desire, and so on.

Gorgias's own discourse in *Helen* is by direct implication party to the crimes it narrates; it thus comes to dwell uncomfortably (and symptomatically) on the ambiguity of its own origins, in the end: "I have observed the procedure that I set up at the beginning [*en archēi*] of the speech," Gorgias declares in summation (*Hel.* 21). But which beginning? At *Hel.* 5 Gorgias announced, in mystifying tautologies, "Having now gone beyond the time once set for my speech, I shall go on to the beginning (*tēn archēn*) of my future speech." We could look to several things to derive Gorgias's *archē* for him: to the professed aim in *Hel.* 2 of injecting some *logismos* (rationality), into the logos (either: his speech or the story circulating around Helen); or to the invocation of probability in *Hel.* 5, which governs the four *aitiai* narratives or, rather, their defeasance; or to the oppositional structures announced at the outset, upon which the reversal of Helen's shame is grounded. We might read this invocation of an *archē* as another proof within a Parmenidean induction: to be a *genomenon* (lapsed event), is to have a determinate *archē;* speech has none; therefore is not an event but is more like the nonevent of Being, an *einai.*[69] But as we saw above, such a being for Gorgias can only have a phantasmagorical status.

VII.

I have neglected to mention perhaps the most interesting aspect of *Helen,* which also happens to be its most tacit feature. Gorgias's play of narratives seems in fact to be premised on two strands of the myth of Helen, which it juxtaposes in a *non*-narrative (though no longer clearly dialectical) fashion, much like a nonintuitive reading of body and void (the one that Leucippus and Democritus gave to these items), conceived less as strict antitheses than as the shifting conditions of each others' identities (for void "is," but no more and no less [*ouden mallon*] than body "is": void, in effect, *is* where body is not, and vice-versa):[70] (1) the rape of Helen, known from Homer; and (2) the rape of a phantom (the shadow-image [*eidōlon*], of Helen, which was taken to Troy in her place), known from Stesichorus.[71] Lesky, in his *History of Greek Literature,* states that Gorgias pulls off his stunt, his defense of Helen, "without availing himself" of this alternative myth.[72] Other scholars simply ignore the possibility that Gorgias's Helen might be the incorporation of a phantom, a being that is not. But Helen qualifies as an exemplary not-being just by virtue of being mythical. It makes no difference that Gorgias's entire speech is overtly premised on her sailing off to Troy, as in *Hel.* 5: "I will lay out the causes [motivations, explanations, accusations] through which it was reasonable [probably or likely] for Helen's voyage to Troy to occur [*genesthai*]." Statements like this address only the logic of Helen's abduction; they tell us nothing about Gorgias's endorsement of that logic, and if anything they suggest his distance from it.[73] Then again, he is speaking to an audience who "know what they know" *Hel.* 5—traditionally, a wink from the poets and a sign of irony.

But what does one "know"? In *On Not-Being,* Gorgias takes the extreme position—which he also *performs*—that knowledge is the source of intolerable aporia. In *Helen,* he suggests that knowledge of what is and is not is its own kind of mythology and an exertion of power; it is the construction and negation of a phantasmal other. Gorgias is exhibiting an insight, not only into the phantasms of power, but into their frailty; and rhetoric is a synonym not for this power, but for its phantasm. Gorgias's rhetorical display is simultaneously a display of a phantom: it mimes the attributes of power, the structures of desire that motivate power, and the structures of belief that sustain it. But naming this phantom "Helen," by turning her active powers into passions wrought against her, Gorgias turns power, allegorically, against itself. Power is further circumscribed by the disparity of its accounts and the uncertainty of its effects. Here, too, Gorgias's own rhetoric is an analogon for the power it claims to wield (the power of persuasive tactics); how odd that its activity should consist chiefly in the limitations it puts on itself and in the freedom (to gainsay, to disbelieve) it grants to its audience.

Gorgias's starting assumption, which he everywhere advertises, is that to take a stance is to occupy a position, to enter—complicitously—into a game (*paignion*) and to risk control over its stakes. The stakes are culturally defined, like the positions that Gorgias sketches in; but by rhetorically inhabiting these positions, and by flaunting this occupancy, Gorgias directs attention to the logic of their relations and to their reversibility. It is tempting to look upon this process as a commentary on the ideological makeup of fifth-century Athens and as a form of cultural critique, just as Gorgias's own discourse, by virtue of occupying a position relative to the field of discourse it pretends to govern—in relation to (and not autonomous from) a public realm of experience—is implicitly an expression of an ideological field.

However intriguing and valid this possibility may be, determining its implications will require an investigation into other materials, of a historical kind, and will call for a larger framework than has been adopted in the present paper, which has sought to explore some of the unsuspected intricacies of Gorgias's best preserved writings. Any cultural reflexes that might be found in Gorgianic rhetoric will reveal positions not readily masterable by individuals, because they do not define autonomous domains,[74] nor can they be dismissed, refuted, or simply waved away. Tied deeply to social values and beliefs, ideologies can never be fully demystified, but only identified, in turns, as positions and negations within a field saturated by narratives and their wreckage. Gorgias's writings in effect put on display these positions and negations. Persuasion seems strangely out of place here, on this account of him, though demystification continues to apply. What kind of authority does Gorgias's logos command? Here we might call upon a critic of ideology, Althusser, who usefully reminds us that, "those who take recourse in an ideology as they would in a mere instrument of action, like a tool, find themselves caught in its toils, and absorbed by it at the very moment that they make use of it, convinced all the while that they are its arbitrary masters."[75]

Although they are not reducible to one another, we might easily substitute "logos" for "ideology" here and still arrive at a valid description of Gorgias's project. Logos can no more be grasped or controlled than can the ideologies and the cultural coordinates that may turn out to define its positions. In marked contrast to some of Gorgias's pretenses and misleading seductions, Gorgias's discourse is not at all aimed at positive persuasion or self-standing validity. Still less is it a sophistic celebration of persuasion. Its power is conceptual, not psychological, and it lies in the recognition of its own impotence. It works by subtraction, and is the negation of persuasion. It is a form of cultural *dissuasion.*

This is its own peculiar from of seduction and truth. Any conclusions we draw about the precise nature of Gorgias's stakes in a cultural criticism may have to be confined to speculation or put off for a future date. At the very least, Gorgias is illustrating the fragilities, contingencies, and complicities of any rationalizations of power. But no discussion of *Helen* in particular should ignore the equivocal, possibly ambivalent, possibly ideologically critical role of sophistic rhetoric in Athenian public discourse, as represented by one of its major practitioners.

Part 2

The Poetic and the Political: Martin Heidegger

Until recently it has been common to discuss the work of Heidegger in relative abstraction from his personal politics. The Heidegger "case" is of rather recent vintage. Not that there had been any lack of ascriptions and accusations from the very start. His Rectorial address (1933), after all, was public property. But since the appearance of Victor Farias's book, whatever its limitations, and other revelations of Heidegger's continued relationship to the National Socialist movement, it has become virtually impossible to consider his work at any length without at least implicit reference to the matter of his political involvement.

The essays in this section are no exception. Indeed, given that each treats of philosophy and poetics in the broad sense, it is not surprising that two of them make explicit mention of the somewhat analogous case of Paul de Man. In both instances it is a question of the degree to which the "poetic" way of dwelling that the later Heidegger in particular introduces and advocates absolves him from responsibility for the appalling political and social consequences of the movement he seems never to have repudiated. It is this issue that frames the following discussion, even when the explicit topic is the relation between philosophy and the poetic way of dwelling in the world.

Graeme Nicholson observes a profound duality in Heidegger's thought between the pastoral and the political. The former, which characterizes his later work, is rooted in his peasant background with its profound respect for the earth and its distrust of the technological, its sense of thankfulness and of "letting be" (*Gelassenheit*), rather than of resoluteness and control. The pastoral face of Heidegger, he insists against Farias, Marxists, and others, could have no politics. It is in Heidegger's other face, the one turned toward the future, toward the individualizing and authenticating appropriation of being-unto-death, that Nicholson reads the vision of struggle and drive associated with the fascist movement. The way each face is related to the other constitutes the theme and thesis of Nicholson's article. It forms the subtext for the other essays as well.

The study by Herman Rapaport moves Paul de Man to center stage. The occasion is de Man's "correction" of William Barrett's widely read "existentializing" of Heidegger's thought. To the dismay of many of his followers, Heidegger is popularly listed among the leaders of the existentialist movement in this century along with Sartre and de Beauvoir. Barrett's books played no small part in this process in the English-speaking world. But in "setting Barrett straight," Rapaport claims, de Man misreads Heidegger's concept of authenticity, separating it from the French emphases that would raise the very issues of resoluteness and direct action that Nicholson connects with Heidegger's political face. Rapaport sees operative in de Man's "transvaluation" of

Heidegger's authentic/inauthentic dichotomy both a dialectics of purification from the political undertones of Heidegger's thought and an "arche-trace of deconstruction" whereby this dialectical sublation is shown to require its own failure. De Man's misreading, in other words, is tactical. Rapaport continues the conversation in the first essay by alluding to conceptual aporias of our own tradition that repeat themselves in the de Man affair.

Matthias Konzett takes issue with critics like de Man who focus on the ontic, structural dimension of modernist poetics, overlooking its constructive side. Concluding that poetry "will not tolerate the discovery of its nature in any other manner than the poetic itself," he reads the later Heidegger from the perspective of Wallace Stevens and conversely. Employing a distinction between abstraction and empathy to capture the inner dialectic that characterizes "poetic" dwelling for both Heidegger and Stevens, Konzett undertakes a thematic as well as formal analysis of the latter's "The Poem that Took the Place of a Mountain" in order to reveal the lived, totalizing, and "disclosive" nature of the poetic act.

In a note, Konzett refers to Heidegger's "problematic political involvements" and subscribes to Lacoue-Labarthe's recommendation to concentrate on "the question which the age poses through Heidegger" rather than focus on short-lived polemics. In turning away from the "political" face toward the "pastoral," he admits with Nicholson that literature "offers no answers to politics." But could it not be that their interrelation is at least integral to the question that the age poses through Heidegger? In other words, that the meaning of being resonates with freedom such that totalitarian politics would be *eo ipso* inauthentic?

Dennis J. Schmidt completes this circle of essays in both directions at once by his version of Lacoue-Labarthe's theme of the passage from the specular to the audible or acoustic (temporal) in postmodern thinking and, secondly, by defending the thesis that this move toward the aural favors the apolitical both in Nietzsche and in Heidegger. It could be argued that what distinguishes postmodern thought from its predecessor is the demise of the ocular paradigm for explanation and understanding in philosophy and literature. If, as Schmidt argues, the question of music is *the* question of postmodernity, its relation to the political is likewise of crucial contemporary interest (Heidegger's two faces again). For Nietzsche claims and Heidegger implies that as music goes, so goes the polis. Schmidt concludes that our current "society of repetition" (Attali), by debasing temporality and music, has likewise undermined the political and that the *Satz,* which Heidegger described in musical terms as propelling us into postmodernity, is equally a "leap to a new social basis for the work of art."

3

Two Faces of Heidegger

Graeme Nicholson

I

A major theme in the critical writing about Heidegger is the matter of provincialism. Recently we see the theme renewed in Farias's book *Heidegger et le Nazisme*.[1] Tracing the boy and young man from his pious, obscure family, through the dour Catholicism of his schooling, through the rustic ceremonies around an old preacher, Abraham a Sancta Clara, up to the Jesuit novitiate, Farias gives us a man who will be determined through and through to stand in resistance against modernity and democracy. We have already seen this slant on Heidegger in the writings of Robert Minder, Paul Huehnerfeld, and Karl Löwith. Habermas, too, speaks of the Heideggerian *Provinz* that came to be urbanized by Gadamer. There is truth in this picture, and it will certainly be confirmed by a reading of the poems and belles-lettres assembled in vol. 13 of Heidegger's *Gesamtausgabe*. I want to call this one of Heidegger's faces, yet I think it has to be supplemented by an account of a very different face, a very different theme in his thought. I am far from wishing to criticize this first aspect of Heidegger. So instead of calling it by a negative name like "rustic," "nostalgic," *or* "provincial," I call it "pastoral"—I want to invoke a literary category rather than a sociological one. The pastoral face of Heidegger was most beautifully expressed in the *Letter on Humanism,* from which I shall quote later on.

Where Farias, Minder and other critics go wrong, I believe, is in tracing Heidegger's political commitment to the Nazis in the 1930s to this pastoral side, this "rusticity," as they would call it. I think it was a contrary tendency altogether that led him to the Nazis.

The early poetry is all in the pastoral mode—in fact, all the poems Heidegger published are in some sense pastoral. A striking piece of this type is the well-known piece of 1933, "Why Are We Staying in the *Provinz*?" in which he expresses his resistance to the imperative forces now running the Reich from Berlin. To this mode also belong the 1950 meditations on the thing and its place between earth and sky, mortals and immortals. Writing like this brings before us the lay of the land in Messkirch and into the landscape around Messkirch—for instance, in Heidegger's memories of the *Feldweg,* the path he followed daily in his studious walks when he was nineteen or twenty, and in his memories of the church tower of Messkirch with its intricate system of bells; or it traces his experience of Freiburg and the Black Forest, the depth of stoniness in the mountains, the fall of snow on tree branches, the *Holzwege,* and the forest clearings.

First, anyone who explores a territory like a Black Forest mountain will have to *respond* to its heights, its depths, and its contours. And to follow a path, a *Feldweg,* is to be *led* to the discoveries that it harbors for us. It is by taking our place within the encompassing environment that we become climbers or travelers. What we are, our being, is prompted by the lay of the land. And there is a sense in which the land speaks to us—our thoughts are stirred and awakened by its promptings, too. Both our being and our thinking answer to the land: both are our way of belonging within the province, the region.

Second, when we take the trouble to climb the hills, we discover how the clouds drift above the mountain tops, how the trees cling to the rock, and where the spring water begins its downward path. All these elements have had their own harmonious interplay for untold thousands of years. And yet when the climber finds them, they are in a curious way renewed. Yes, their harmony was achieved without the climber, but his perception, his discovery, his thought, his words bring something of value. A poem captures the beauty of a scene: the poem does not *add to* its beauty, for that was complete; but to express what we saw does magnify it. Such translation into word, thought, poetry, or picture convinces Heidegger that we are *needed.* Yes, the world's elements have their own interplay, and yet only *Dasein* discloses the world. We have this special destiny, and that is in accord with the so-called difference between beings and being, or between world and being.

There is no pastoral writing in *Being and Time.* But the *ontological point* or *meaning* of the pastoral writing is there even though somewhat overshadowed. It is one of the central aspects of *Dasein* to be attuned, affected, or pervaded by world. This element in our very being is called *die Befindlichkeit*—untranslatable, alas, but perhaps we may approach it with circumlocutions: the posture that we take on through being in an environment, subject to being pervaded by influence from the environment.

Another document of this ontology is Heidegger's description of the world of work with its thousand connections and interconnections, giving every element in the environment its own significance *(Bedeutsamkeit).*

There is no doubt that Heidegger is telling us that we must belong in a world, indeed always in one specific environment, though of course that theme is overshadowed by another theme, to which I shall come in a moment. Our being and our thinking are dependent upon our posture. But above all it is the *Letter on Humanism* that expresses our belonging together with being in a series of pastoral images that expresses the first face of Heidegger.

On account of its richness of theme, a striking wealth of images, and the complexity of its references to philosophical literature, the *Letter on Humanism* defies summary. But for my present use, it is enough to remark that it begins with questions concerning *human action* and then leads the discussion into the complex involvements among *thinking, language,* and *being.* I intend to pick out some images that bear upon the involvements of these three.

1. *The Farm.* As he approaches the end of the essay, Heidegger is contending with questions of the *language of thought:* how the thinker can avoid the high-flying abstractions of metaphysics and learn to dwell in a humbler and simpler mode. Thought will also need to learn some new way of dwelling in its language. "When thinking comes to utterance, it traces tiny furrows through the language. They are even more inconspicuous than the furrows that the farmers lays, as he moves slow of step through the field." Furrows in the language are all the thinker leaves. Their inconspicuousness is due to the weight, the depth, and the vastness of that ground and element over which thinking moves and upon which it dwells.

2. *The Clouds.* Just prior to those closing sentences, Heidegger offers another image, not entirely consistent with "the farm," perhaps, and yet surely drawn from the same storehouse of pastoral poetry. Here too he insists on the weight and dignity of language, to which a thinker must submit. But this is an image expressing the relationship between *language* and *being:* "Language is the language of being in the way that the clouds are the clouds of the sky." Clouds are sustained in the vast open dimension of the sky. They hover in it, and it is not contained in or encompassed by them. And yet they do gather and concentrate into a visible form: the vapors that pervade the sky. Just as the furrows in the earth are not only sustained by the hidden depths below but also show us something of those depths, the clouds do in a way illustrate the sky. In the clouds, and so in language, lies the domus in which the vast dimension, the ethereal,

becomes accessible to us in a gathered form and, one must say, in a determinate form.

3. *The House.* Turning now to the beginning of the essay, we come to the image that has become more famous than any other. Like "the clouds," it is an image for the relationship between *language* and *being,* though in the concentrated prose of these opening paragraphs, all the themes of the essay are playing together. Heidegger calls language "the house of being." In the first place, this involves a double relationship between ourselves and our language. He says that this is the house in which we live. But he adds that poets and thinkers are the guardians and watchmen of the house. They tend it, and while they do so they also live in it. Occupying the house is a condition for renovating it: renovation is a form of dwelling. This also means that language can never become completely an object for us.

But the image insists that language is the house *of being:* while it does *afford* us housing, it is not the house *of* human beings. This does not mean that being also "lives" there. It means that those who do have their habitation there are able to experience the approach and the presence of being. This image draws upon the biblical narratives about the house of God. The tabernacle and the temple were by no means God's dwelling, but rather the place where he would draw near to those assembled there.

4. *The Fish.* A little later on Heidegger invokes an image for the relationship that particularly concerns us here, that between *thinking* and *being.* He is saying that the "technical" view of thought, which he traces back to the Greeks, seeks to measure its powers for solving problems. But this view has lost sight of the native element proper to thinking, which is being:

> One judges thinking according to a measure that is inappropriate to it. Such a judgment is like a procedure that seeks to estimate the nature and powers of a fish by seeing how well it is able to live on the dry land. For a long time now, all too long, thought has been sitting on the dry land.[2]

The element native to the fish is the vastness of the open sea. It has given life to the fish; it affords it food and breathing; it encompasses it behind and before; it yields before the fish, giving it mobility, so the fish may explore its dimension in pathways ever new. The sea brings light to the eye of the fish and discloses the forms of life and rock that also have their being in the sea element. The fish can never take the measure of the sea, and it is content. Those who live on the dry land, however, and snare the fish think they can take measure of the sea element and of every element. They are quite deceived.

II

Now I propose to sketch a second face of Heidegger and to do so by drawing upon some passages from *Being and Time* and the Rectorial address. This is the political face—the pastoral Heidegger had no politics and could have none. The second face was the product, not of his childhood, but of his adult experience, a product of the war that broke out when he was twenty-five and of that cockpit of struggle, the Weimar Republic, which endured throughout his thirties. It was when he was exactly forty and newly returned to Freiburg that the Depression began, and he began to draw certain firm political conclusions.

Let me give a preliminary name, and a preliminary identification, to the element I am contrasting with the pastoral. It is the theme of struggle, or strife, or drive (*der Kampf, der Streit, der Drang*). This is an element in every adult life. We can describe it in a general way as something well known both to Heidegger and to all of us, and then we can begin to understand the ontological meaning that he in particular assigns to it.

Struggle and drive are experienced in institutions where contending parties compete. Universities, for instance, prove to be like that once one is within them, even though they do not always look like that to dreamy freshmen or to the world outside. But beyond this normal contentiousness of everyday institutions and economic structures, there is the armed struggle of national armies, inconceivable *vast* in modern war, inconceivably *disastrous* in result. But Heidegger believed that the ontological meaning of struggle showed up in the way an individual existed in struggle. The armed soldier, more than anyone, formed an explicit relation to death, a being-towards-death whose most intense form was a walking or running forward right into its jaws: *Vorlaufen in den Tod*. It is by resoluteness, indeed, that we advance into death, and this quality, resoluteness, is the inner struggle or strife that is manifest in the most extreme case. As struggle is inwardly lived, it is the explicit assumption of anxiety: you do not evade it, it pervades you. A still deeper analysis discloses to Heidegger that the hour of one's death is in a way the actual revelation of one's being or life. Death is the possibility that not only makes us serious but also it singles us out, each one of us in his or her uniqueness.

At a deeper level still, this point (the bond of death with each one's unique being) reveals that it is not only my death that is on its way toward me. My very being too is still en route to me, still held back, still withheld from me, still belonging to the future, not simply given to me, not really here in present time. The inner meaning of struggle, then, is this futurity. For us to exist is to be stretched out towards a coming death and therefore always ahead of ourselves, never resting in a stable condition. We exist only by an exit from self toward our being that remains withheld. We are temporal to such a degree: our being is a self-displacement into time, a time whose very heart is futurity, a futurity that beckons but can never complete its arrival except at the point where we are not—where we die. To accept the law that existence brings such self-externalization and such unrest is human authenticity.

Now this is the cycle of thoughts that turns up in a political interpretation of the Rectorial address. I shall pick up only two aspects of the address to illustrate this.

First, according to the address, the self-assertion of the university is the radical insistence upon its own vocation and essence; by an insistence upon its destiny, it earns the right to self-government. But it is only by the radical projection of this essence upon the future that its vocation will come to it. A mere survey of its past circumstances is in no way a clue to its essence. Will to science, which is the essence of a self-asserting university, is the self-exposure to uncertainty, danger, and darkness. Study and thought are not just attuned and responsive to that which is; they pose a challenge to the world to meet the questions we pose to it.

Second, the role of the university is to awaken the sense of this dangerous world among its own faculty and students, a training that must involve the capacity to be hard on one another and, of course, to be hard on oneself. It is by the disciplined hardness of science that the student body becomes fit to lead the people. *The destiny of the German people is to be a community of struggle as surely as the university is a people prepared to march into a threatening future.* Both the educational program of the address and its broader political implications draw upon the themes of self-projection, struggle, authenticity, and, above all, the temporality that has its primary sense in the future.

III

To distinguish these two faces is by no means the end of our task in this study. Rather, we have to ask about the ways in which the two are related to one another: Is one a *mask* for the other? Is one the face of youth, the other of age? Do the two gaze into each other with recognition? Of course these two faces enter into a relationship! To call Heidegger a thinker or a philosopher is to grant that the effort of achieving stable order among his "ideas" and his "faces" is taken as the primary task of his lifetime. The relationship between one "face" and the other, however, seems to me to have changed as decade followed decade and work followed work. Let me speak first about *Being and Time.*

It is the second face that overshadows the first one in the text of 1927. Clearly the theme of *Befindlichkeit* and the account of the world of work give concrete testimony to *Dasein's* responsiveness to world, being-in and belonging-to-the-world. Nevertheless, in the structure of our being, it is the self-projecting character of our life that takes priority. In the fusion between *existentiality* and *facticity,* or between *Verstehen* and *Befindlichkeit,* the former takes a clear priority. The task of the book is above all to convince us of the urgency of our self-projection into the darkness of the future. It is the priority of the future among the three ecstases of temporality that undergirds this choice decisively. Now any thinker wants to account for the elements that he is engaged in suppressing and subordinating. And so the 1927 book expresses Heidegger's victory over his own pastoral heritage. It is not absent—it is absorbed in a secondary role.

In the Rectorial address, the projection of a collective or social being into the future is carried forth to an astounding degree. There is no recognition of a social past, no recognition of a social present, only the urgent demand that the *Volk* resolve to enter a future with resoluteness—the same as the demand that the address poses to the smaller-scale academic community. I will not conceal my belief that the address suffers terribly just because of the radicalism and insistence with which the pastoral face has been suppressed; very likely the lyrical pastoral essay of 1933, "Why do we stay in the *Provinz*?" was a cry of release of a violated face.

Another text begun in 1930 and worked over for many years is "On the Essence of Truth." Indeed, it is a work of great depth and power, and that is due in part, I believe, to the means it has found for bringing disparate things together. This essay manages to achieve a relationship between darkness and light, between truth, on the one hand, and two contending forms of untruth (namely, concealment and error), on the other hand. This may afford us the deepest insight into the way the faces of Heidegger come together.

First, the suppression of the pastoral by the futural cannot be true and cannot be allowed to continue! And yet, to one who has eyes to see, the modern world appears to have conquered every vestige of the pastoral, relegating it to the domain of the dreams we retain of childhood, dreams that are rarely true even of actual childhood. But where untruth belongs to the essence of truth, we may well surmise that the denying function of the futural project, the radicalism of the Right, is necessary to it, constituting the concealment that continues along with the errancy that accompanies any political project.

Second, at the same time, the essay reminds us that any pastoral symphony like *Das Ding* must *likewise* harbor within it a mighty cargo of concealment, specifically of the radical-activist self-projection that came into its own in *Being and Time* and the Rectorial address.

Serious criticism of Heidegger's Rectorial address must be at once philosophical and political. In this paper, I have sought to reply to one of the lines of critique that stress its political content. Critics of a Marxist bent have usually brought to the text their disdain for the pastoral mode. They are urban by conviction, regarding what stands against urbanism as reactionary. For this reason, they are disposed to link the Nazi impulse of Heidegger to this peasant heritage. But my belief is that the Marxist critique tends to cast into the shadows the hardness, the radicalism, the futurism, that actually animated Heidegger in his period of serious political action. And when we seek to look more deeply into the *philosophical* character of this address, what we find, I think, is another, deeper element of suppression that accompanies the suppression of the pastoral face. The central issue here is the structure of time. So convinced is Heidegger here of the supremacy of the futural mode of human temporality that he is prepared to speak of a people (*Volk*) as finding its being only in the future that awaits it, just as *Being and Time* argues this for the individual. *It is this that cannot work!* While there is some possibility of construing the temporality of each individual as being shaped by the future more than by the past or by the present, this cannot work once we have turned our attention to the community. The futural mode of politics is a utopia without content and, hence, without the slightest chance of succeeding. Marx was right, and he was not alone, in urging us to grasp the detail of the synchronic character of the economy if we want to practice politics: to know that which is, the *present*. He was also right along with others in teaching the necessity of grasping the long, deep *history* of every nation and every institution. Heidegger, believing that national temporality, like individual temporality, came solely out of the future, neglected even to study the history of the cause and the party to which he so recklessly committed himself.

One of the faults of the book by Farias is that it gives us no new insight into the actual nature of National Socialism. This too is a phenomenon of many faces, but the literature on the case of Heidegger is usually content with a one-dimensional presentation of the phenomenon. I have tried to show that it was anything but a pastoral nostalgia that led Heidegger into the party. Whether there were others drawn in by folkloric elements is a question I cannot really answer: perhaps there was a pastoral face to Nazism, along with other faces. But *Heidegger's* interest in it was surely well expressed by Heidegger himself when he said in the *Introduction to Metaphysics* that the inner truth and greatness of it was the encounter between modern man and the essence of technology. That thrusting and modern sensibility was fully on display in the Rectorial address.

We today are able to see that a racial doctrine—especially anti-Semitism—was at the very heart of the Hitler movement. It was, so to speak, the stone around which other materials gathered. Moreover, we see above all the result this doctrine brought—in Auschwitz and Treblinka. We also have access to the writings of Rosenberg, Krieck, and others who fought their way into positions of ideological leadership. It is not necessary, however, to see the difference between Heidegger and some of these other Nazis. He did commit himself to the movement, but the interesting thing, from a philosophical point of view, is that his writings in the twenties and thirties actually developed a devastating critique of the ideas that became central in the years of Nazi rule. Heidegger worked out a thorough critique of biologism, as he called it, or of vitalism, as we might call it—a doctrine that was invoked by people like Rosenberg to offer foundations for a Nazi worldview. Heidegger's fate has the irony that, while he gave his open support to the party, his actual philosophy completely undermined the ideas that the Nazis invoked to justify their policy. Biologism was the intellectual underpinning for racism.

In this respect, Heidegger's fate appears to be the exact opposite of the fate of Nietzsche. Nothing is more clear to the reader of Nietzsche than his scorn for the racism, chauvinism, and especially anti-Semitism that he took to be the telltale vulgarity of Bismarck's countrymen in the Second Reich. And yet, while Nietzsche lent the force of his pen to ridicule the movements that were the prototype of Nazism, his actual philosophy can only be seen as lending support to a biological doctrine of man, a perspectival account of truth, and a conception of history as the struggle for power. These are just the themes that Heidegger undertook to attack in his writings of the later thirties.

4

Repositioning Heidegger

Herman Rapaport

It was during the 1960s that Heidegger began to emerge in the United States as a major philosopher whose influence would be very significant for literary critical theory. Considered by many to be a brilliant but shadowy thinker with a politically objectionable past, Heidegger underwent an important critical revaluation due in large part to the efforts of W. J. Richardson, who, in *Heidegger: Through Phenomenology to Thought,* provided a reliable outline of Heidegger's philosophy; John Macquarrie and Edward Robinson, who, in their painstaking translation of *Sein und Zeit,* made Heidegger's major early achievement available to English readers; and figures like William Barrett, who reinterpreted Heidegger in the postwar philosophical context of French existentialism.[1] Given that literary critics were very interested in appropriating both existential and phenomenological analyses for the interpretation of literature, we should not be surprised that Heidegger aroused considerable curiosity in literary circles.

In "Heidegger Reconsidered," a review of William Barrett's *What is Existentialism?* the literary critic Paul de Man clearly sees that the historical moment has come in which to reposition Heidegger's philosophy.[2] In fact, de Man is farsighted enough to look beyond the existential appropriation of Heidegger to something else—what for us has come to pass in a so-called linguistic turn. Already in the early 1960s de Man anticipated that such a turn in the human sciences would create enough cultural and historical distance to allow a figure as politically objectionable as Heidegger to be forgotten or, at least, bracketed. In fact, such a forgetting was already achieved by 1965, when J. Hillis Miller published a key critical study entitled *Poets of Reality,* which performed an impressive Heideggerian reading of Wallace Stevens.[3] But where critics like Miller were content simply to forget a certain prewar Heidegger, Paul de Man had the conviction that such a forgetting could come only at the cost of dismantling a revisionist existential interpretation that rehabilitated Heidegger's thought in the light of postwar French philosophy. This conviction led to the curious result that just as de Man announced a linguistic reading of Heidegger that conveniently left behind an objectionable ideology, de Man, in that very gesture, recollected or brought back into view the very disturbing aspects of Heidegger that we have been encouraged to forget.

In "Heidegger Reconsidered" de Man challenged the existential reading of Heidegger in the following way:

> For nothing is more remote from Heidegger than this confusion between the pathos of direct experience and the knowing of this experience—a confusion that, ironically, has become associated with so-called existential thought, mainly because of Sartre's famous and unfortunate phrase about the precedence of existence over essence. One could rather describe *Being and Time* as the most thoroughgoing attempt to cleanse our thought from the confusion not only in language, but in the philosophical project as a whole.[4]

De Man, then, is arguing that Heidegger had been perversely appropriated by a French existential contingent and that, in opposition to this group, Heidegger believed that one could "understand our own subjectivity by transforming it into language and, ultimately, by seeing it exactly as it is, in the pure language of true philosophy." While the French existentialists had confused pathos and knowledge, Heidegger, according to de Man, had not only purged feeling but cleansed language. Hence, de Man argues that in Heidegger the word *existential* does not refer to any kind of "visceral response," such as the pathos of direct experience, as William Barrett claims. Rather, the term *existential* refers to "philosophically conscious knowledge as opposed to immediate, intuitive, experienced knowledge." In Heidegger, therefore, the existential refers to an awareness of experience purified of Cartesian subjectivity or, as de Man also says, of an "undifferentiated and opaque mass of direct actions."[5]

De Man presumes that Barrett's misreading of existentialism in Heidegger is mediated by Jean-Paul Sartre, who, in 1944, linked the concept to direct action. "Since existentialism defines man by action," Sartre wrote in 1944,

> it is evident that this philosophy is not a quietism. In fact, man cannot help acting; his thoughts are projects and commitments, his feelings are undertakings, he is nothing other than his life, and his life is the unity of his behavior.[6]

Indeed, this unity of behavior is characterized by certain emotions that are the enabling conditions for action; they include anguish, despair, optimism, and what Sartre calls "a sense of responsibility." De Man, for his part, suggests the authenticity of such enabling emotional conditions are Barrett's focus and that consequently Barrett has profoundly misconstrued Heidegger.

In contrast, de Man argues that Heidegger's *Being and Time* stresses an inauthentic and partial relation to things in precisely the place where interpreters like Barrett have missed it:

> Heidegger's aim in this book is primarily to show how the possibility of an inauthentic and partial relationship towards things inheres in the very nature of the human makeup along with the intent to overcome it. The entire organization of *Being and Time* is determined by this theme.[7]

This is a rather sweeping evaluation of so complex a treatise; however, the passage de Man has in mind occurs in a section entitled "Existential Projection of an Authentic Being-towards-Death," where Heidegger asks how Dasein's potentiality for Being is considered as the possibility of an authentic existence. Heidegger remarks that we must acknowledge an anticipatory disclosure so that a "pure understanding [*zum reinen Verstehen*] of that ownmost possibility [occurs] which is non-relational and not to be outstripped—which is certain and, as such, indefinite." Heidegger continues, "Here it can become manifest to Dasein that in this distinctive possibility of its own self, it has been wrenched away from the 'they . . .' The ownmost possibility is *non-relational* [*unüberholbar*]."[8] Therefore, the possibility of Dasein's existential projection is inherently different from the "they."

De Man interprets this to mean that Dasein's own self is inauthentic to the extent that it cannot be identified with any pregiven or already established notion of selfhood but exists, rather, as an existential projection that is characterized as nonrelational [*unüberholbar*]. However, de Man strategically overlooks the fact that Heidegger is considering nonrelationality in terms of Dasein's being laid claim to by death. Heidegger writes,

> The non-relational character of death, as understood in anticipation, individualizes Dasein down to itself . . . It makes manifest that all Being alongside the things with which we concern ourselves, and all Being with others, will fail us when our ownmost potentiality for Being is the issue. Dasein can be *authentically itself* only if it makes this possible.[9]

De Man intentionally misconstrues these remarks to mean that Dasein can be authentically itself only to the extent it relinquishes an authentic understanding of death and the potentiality for Being. This, however, is not what Heidegger was literally saying. Rather, as Graeme Nicholson has aptly put it, Heidegger is arguing that "Death is the possibility that not only makes us serious—it singles us out, each one of us in his or her uniqueness."[10] It is this interpretation that de Man not only violates but argues against in order to pull asunder the proximity of Heidegger to French existentialism as well as to put distance between his review and Barrett. Whereas French existentialism can be said to have assumed a relationality among subjects through which authenticity can be conceptually established, Heidegger, from de Man's perspective, is made to stress a nonrelationality that bears on what de Man is calling "inauthenticity." However, in pointing to this estrangement from French existentialism, de Man praises Barrett for noticing the possibility of a German/French rupture at the end of *What is Existentialism?* between "Sartre's basically unphilosophical undertaking" and Heidegger's much more rigorous and purified project.

In turning to Heidegger's later work, de Man writes that Heidegger "has occasionally adopted the oracular tone—but this is perhaps an understandable human weakness in someone who may feel he is not correctly understood."[11] According to de Man, Heidegger betrayed the philosophical distance of the early work by a tonal shift to the oracular. This is a human weakness that makes possible the reintroduction of a pathos that Heidegger had before successfully purged. De Man suggests that the later Heidegger lapsed into the kind of existentialism that he should have resisted, an existentialism in which the philosopher's life comes to appearance as an emotional authenticating tone. Yet, de Man credits Heidegger's later work for having taken a literary turn. "Poetic language interests Heidegger because it is not less but more rigorous than the philosopher's, having a clearer consciousness of its own interpretative function."[12] Here, once more, purification in its relation to language is at issue, though purification occurs not for the sake of establishing a more genuine consciousness; on the contrary, it occurs as a part of a critical activity that calls the authentic into question. Here the late Heidegger is considered to reinforce the early Heidegger.

At the end of the review, de Man credits Barrett as well as the English translation of *Being and Time* with ushering in a "new period . . . in this country's attitude towards Heidegger." This new period, de Man says, "will do much to further a correct understanding of an intellectual movement that has been much maligned, as well as much admired, for the wrong reasons."[13] This abrupt ending is curious. After all, de Man has both complimented and deprecated Barrett in a way that thoroughly undermines our confidence in the American reception of Heidegger. Then, quite ironically, de Man ends the essay by suggesting that the English translation of *Being and Time* in conjunction with studies like Barrett's *What is Existentialism?* will usher in a new understanding of Heidegger's thought and will lead us away from that which has been both maligned and admired for the wrong reasons. But how will a study like Barrett's, itself quite ill conceived, according to de Man, deliver us from a misunderstanding of Heidegger?

Apparently, Barrett's study, for all its flaws and intellectual misalignments, does not dwell on Heidegger's politics and therefore initiates a tactical forgetting through which an authentic or real appreciation of Heidegger can take place. In other words, through the inauthenticity of the American reception of Heidegger, we are ironically capable of achieving a much more authentic reading of Heidegger's work, and particularly *Being and Time.* Thanks to this irony, a transvaluation of the authentic/inauthentic dichotomy has occurred in which what once was called "inauthentic" is now considered to be authentic. De Man makes this move by suggesting that it would be incorrect to read Heidegger in the superficially authentic context of European culture—that is, German fascism—and that one would do better to study Heidegger in a way that is culturally and politically inauthentic or estranged, which is to say, by way of a dispassionate American academy. Only by way of such indirection do we come to achieve a sublated authenticity that is not reducible to the term's prior characteristics. Although de Man's review reflects little genuine admiration for an American approach towards European culture, he ironically suggests that such cultural indirection, far from being inappropriate, allows enough distance to prevent us from plunging into the impure, "undifferentiated and opaque mass of direct actions, feelings, or emotions" that would characterize the naively authentic reading of Heidegger in a cultural and historical context. De Man, therefore, is implicitly championing a reading of Heidegger that is purged or purified of pathos and cleansed of an unsublated notion of the authentic characteristic of certain objectionable political ideologies. Such a reading would, to recall de Man's remarks on *Being and Time,* take distance from the "they," in this case, from an objectionable collective appropriation of Heidegger under the aegis of an always already known subject or self—for example, a naively authentic politicized self, such as that referred to by Victor Farias. It is this appropriation of an "authentic" Heidegger that de Man is referring to when he points to what was maligned and appreciated in Heidegger for the wrong reasons.

Yet if such distance from an objectionable ideology is established by means of a dialectical or Hegelian reading of Heidegger's dichotomy of authenticity and inauthenticity, there is, at the same time, a countermovement in de Man that adopts a more radical Heideggerian notion of a nonrelationality with the "they"—the "they," in this case, pertaining to the dialectical opposition of the authentic and the inauthentic itself. As we can see in retrospect, given our familiarity with Derridean deconstruction, in "Heidegger Reconsidered" de Man is manipulating the authenticity/inauthenticity thematic in a way that anticipates Derrida's treatment of the voice/writing distinction in *Of Grammatology*. Although undecidability and deconstruction are not yet explicitly on de Man's theoretical horizon, the potentially very radical Heideggerian notion of nonrelationality and indefiniteness already inheres in de Man's understanding of the distinction between authenticity and inauthenticity. This nonrelationality, moreover, appears in nothing less than the indeterminateness of the cultural or political interface between the European and American receptions of Heidegger. It is here that the reciprocal or dialectical relationship between the authentic and the inauthentic will be demolition even as the terms imply a dialectical transvaluation. We might say that for those who care to look, an arche-trace of deconstruction has come to appear momentarily in de Man's text against the backdrop of dialectics.

Yet, if one can begin to intuit the coming into proximity of two such hermeneutical formations—the one dialectical and the other proto-deconstructive—one should caution that each of these formations resists the other. And in this conflict, I maintain, one can already see a conflict of political allegiances that should not escape notice. In the dialectical argument, we can appreciate how a politically debased notion of authenticity and direct action is sublated by a notion of authenticity that draws from what Heidegger called the "inauthentic"—the "partial relationship towards things [that] inheres in the very nature of the human makeup along with the intent to overcome it." In this dialectic between the partial relationship and what de Man calls "visceral response" (predicated upon a naive vitalistic notion of authentic experiential fulfillment), we can see the overcoming of an existential perspective that Herbert Marcuse had already identified with Nazism in the 1930s. Indeed, as if to emphasize the extent to which Heidegger's philosophy takes its distance from an objectionable politics, de Man emphasizes terms relating to a sublated rhetoric of purification. Reference to a dialectically purified philosophical language or to the purgation of pathos is meant to show, by means of an appeal to the inauthentic, how estranged Heideggerian thinking is from crude ideologies, such as fascism, that privilege existential immediacy.

At the same time, however, de Man turns away from a dialectics of purification by introducing what I have called a "proto-deconstruction" of the authentic/inauthentic antinomy. This turn is complex and concerns de Man's perception of the new era in the reception of Heidegger initiated by an inauthentic American understanding. Even here, of course, the dialectics of transvaluation is initially staged so that we are asked to believe that Barrett's inauthentic or blind study opens onto an insightful or sublated authenticity in which a more genuine Heidegger is revealed. Yet, at the same time, this dialectics is resisted by the fact that Barrett is so thoroughly discredited that we have come to understand the American reception of Heidegger as an extraordinarily nonrelational or partial correspondence that utterly conceals or forgets Heidegger in his European contexts even as these contexts are being appropriated. What we have is not a transvaluation of an objectionable ideology but rather the coming to pass of an indeterminate relation between American and European cultures, a relation that ambivalently, perhaps even undecidably, does and does not appropriate Heidegger. Dialectical transvaluation is resisted, then, and a nonengagement is introduced that more or less conceals even as it sanctions politically unacceptable ideas. This resistance to the dialectics of transvaluation, however, is not entirely of de Man's making, for, as de Man realizes, it is a consequence of history itself as a politics of concealing and revealing, of forgetting and remembering. That is, with the arrival of an American reception of Heidegger that is inevitably nonrelational or indefinite, an objectionable politics has been forgotten and hence left intact as a latent order of conceptual relationships. De Man treats this interface both in terms of forgetting and recollecting what is objectionable in Heidegger.

This forgetting and recollecting is itself in de Man's rhetoric of purification, which invokes a rather sophisticated overcoming of an ideology of authenticity even as it can be read in terms of a reductive metaphysics. We can easily hear the latter, with all its dubious ideological trappings, in de Man's statement that "*Being and Time* [is] the most thoroughgoing attempt to *cleanse* our thought." Moreover, resonances of this statement carry over into his reference to Heidegger's interest in a "pure language of philosophy," "a clearer consciousness," or the "true poet."[14] These latter remarks, of course, are all subordinated to the perception that Heidegger wants to cleanse our thought by means of turning to the question of language. Although the rhetoric of purification belongs to a dialectical overcoming of a naive notion of authenticity, it is accompanied by tonalities that do not encourage dialectical transvaluation. As if to acknowledge this, de Man sarcastically writes, "One was willing to see Heidegger replaced and bypassed by the younger French existentialists whose politics were much more appealing."[15] That is, intellectuals were eager to forget a politically unappealing Heidegger; yet, de Man cautions, it is this politically unappealing person who ought to be remembered. In fact, it is the politically unappealing itself that de Man will allow to resonate even as it is being transvalued. And, of course, such unappealing sonorities can be heard not only in the rhetoric of purification, but in the invocation of an inauthentic experience, the kind of experience which reminds one of fascist desensitization.[16]

Like the wartime writings in *Le Soir,* de Man's "Heidegger Reconsidered" is characterized by delicate contradictions and tonal splittings. And here, of course, we become alert to the question of politics as a division of correspondences, tonalities, or conceptual allegiances that both risk and resist transvaluation. Ideology, in other words, is constituted in terms of the proximity of positions that are the consequence of an elision of the difference between the inauthentic and the authentic even as that difference is being affirmed. But to what end, we might ask, is such a parcelling out achieved? In papers presented at the Fourteenth Annual International Association for Philosophy and Literature convention, Professors Graeme Nicholson, Massimo Verdicchio, Steven Ungar, and Tom Keenan are all in general agreement that the main fallacy committed by those who have so harshly criticized Heidegger and de Man is nothing less than the attempt to reduce these figures to an authentic politics that is homogeneous and stable, a politics present to itself which can be claimed as fundamental for an understanding of these figures. Not only Victor Farias and Philippe Lacoue-Labarthe on Heidegger, but Zev Sternhell and John Wiener on Paul de Man would like nothing better than a stable and authentic target for their criticisms. However, such a desire for authenticity leads only to yet another rhetoric of purification, to the very politics of law and order to which these critics are so fundamentally opposed. De Man, I think, is painfully aware of this trap. But he is aware of something else, too, which is the possibility that an invocation of the inauthentic is similarly fated to engage an objectionable politics. In part, this is why de Man's rhetoric of purification is allowed so many ironic sonorities. What de Man teaches us is that we may not be able to gain anything like an authentic distance from what was historically unappealing as long as one is hemmed in by the dichotomy of the authentic and its opposite. In short, we cannot divest ourselves of even weak links with fascist ideology by simply trying to take direct polemical action by means of taking up sides, making bold choices, or erecting stable targets. Indeed, if fascism were that easy to overcome, it would never have achieved such a powerful and deadly force. What de Man teaches us, then, is that fascism is more than an evil thing that one can simply reject or avoid, because it comes to appearance from within conceptual aporias that, given a Western tradition, we are philosophically unprepared to dismantle. The irony, of course, is that if we are to deconstitute such aporias, we may have to traffic with precisely those thinkers once linked to a politics we may prefer to reject altogether.

But if this is the lesson of "Heidegger Reconsidered," why is it that one senses, even against one's better judgment, that de Manian catharsis is not entirely interested in taking the kind of distance I have invoked from what is euphemistically called "the politically unappealing?" Is it that such distance taking is not, as de Man's text suggests, a philosophically viable option? That we cannot, in fact, establish our difference from what we find most appalling? Or is this a much more simple issue, one of a psychological attachment, say, or of a refusal to entirely foreclose on prior allegiances? It is here, of course, that the wartime writings become most bothersome, since their existence serves as reasonable cause for suspicion. That we need not put ourselves in the position of having to choose between philosophical sophistication and psychological motivation goes without saying. In fact, were we to do so, we would once more find ourselves in the pincers of the authentic/inauthentic dichotomy. Still, the possibility that psychological attachments and resistances may well accompany a sophisticated dismantling of ideological constructions is a conjunction that may well dismantle our own ability to take sides on what has been called "the de Man affair."

5

Stevens, Heidegger, and the Dialectics of Abstraction and Empathy in Poetic Language

Matthias Konzett

In "A Collect of Philosophy," the common project of philosophy and poetry is characterized by Stevens as that of "creating confidence world."[1] Contemporary critical perspectives, while being faithful to this common project in act, have, however, departed from its spirit. This departure can be found already in the thought of Sartre and his conversion of the contingency of being-in-itself into a ground of nothingness and negation, its being-for-itself. What Sartre may have seen as a necessary effort to complete Heidegger's ontology in a critical fashion is now taken as a legitimate project of persistent doubt. Sartre, in trying to resist Heidegger's large claims concerning the freedom of a particular Dasein, reads the concept backward, that is, from the contingent level of the in-itself of an existence, its material facticity, towards the level of freedom, the for-itself of an existence. The realm of freedom is thus found to be inauthentic by nature as it denies the facticity of its foundation and as it conflicts with the freedom of the other. For Sartre, the inauthenticity of all consciousness lies with its immaterial nature that prevents it from becoming an absolute in-itself and from achieving substantiality.

Following Sartre's better-known positions, recent critics of poetry establish themselves almost exclusively on this speculative level of negativity, focusing on the ontic giveness of the world as it prevents and cancels out any ontological appropriation of it. De Man, for example, speaks of the poet's desire for a language that originates naturally like a flower, for in natural objects such as flowers "there is no wavering in the status of their existence: existence and essence coincide in them at all times"[2] However, as de Man claims, the poet eventually discovers that his language originates unlike flowers, that is, metaphorically rather than naturally:

> Poetic language can do nothing but originate anew over and over again; it is always constitutive, able to posit regardless of presence but, by the same token, unable to give foundation to what it posits except as an intent of consciousness.[3]

Adopting Sartre's critique of consciousness, de Man extends it to poetic language as an inauthentic structure by which poetic consciousness fails to establish its own foundation other than in the form of an intent or objectification of the world. With critics such as de Man, the study of poetry has come to focus primarily on the structure of poetic form as the contingent level on which poetry erects its world. By means of rhetorical or structural analysis, the freedom of poetic expression is now shown to be illusory and reducible to mechanisms of typification in language and communication either as positive structures of conventional practice (structuralism, historicism) or as negative structures of self-deception (deconstruction, Freudian critiques). A partial recovery of a lost constructive side in modernist poetics, one suspended since the rise of a hermeneutics of suspicion, requires therefore a careful reconsideration of its premises as articulated in both its philosophy and poetry. For the purpose of such a clarification, I would like to engage the poetry of Stevens in a dialogue with the poetic investigations of the late Heidegger[4] so as restore from within poetic language a reflective world still viable and relevant for our communicative self-understanding.

In his late work, Heidegger completes and transcends his earlier philosophical analysis of the reflective conditions of human existence by focusing on the medium that articulates its concerns most adequately, namely poetic language. In *Being and Time,* the projection and self-staging of human Dasein was first explored on the concrete level of everyday practical involvements as its preliminary horizon of intelligibility. As drawn primarily from the world of practical involvement, however, Dasein still retains subjective and anthropological characteristics that make the project of an existential hermeneutics a deviation from Heidegger's main project, the understanding of Being as Being. Thus, starting with *Holzwege,* Heidegger begins to give increasing attention to the work of art as a reflective activity that preserves an essential openness and proximity to Being as an event that cannot be entirely subsumed by human praxis. The enterprise of philosophy itself is in fact for Heidegger no longer conceivable in any other environment that in the neighborhood of poetry.[5] This neighborhood of thinking and poetry has been equally acknowledged by modern poets such as Valéry, Rilke, Eliot, and Wallace Stevens who similarly seek to strike a more adequate balance between form of human design (abstraction) and forms of experience (empathy).[6] The work of art, as the articulated ground of man's freedom and design from within experience, figures thereby as the symbolic stage of our self-appropriation in and through Being. "Poetry," writes Heidegger, "is authentic or inauthentic according to the degree of this appropriation"; for "man is capable of poetry . . . only to the degree which his being is appropriate to that which itself has a liking for man and therefore needs his presence."[7]

"The Origin of the Work of Art" is Heidegger's first major effort to clarify and understand the nature of art as constitutive of forms of expression and reflection that contribute to the significance of life. As in *Being and Time,* Heidegger begins with the material facticity of thing and work that superficially characterize the work of art as embedded in and defined by the pragmatic context of craftsmanship. Heidegger establishes artistic form (the material of the work of art, its "thing" character) as inseparable from the activity that constitutes its purpose and definition in its use and making (its "work" character). The traditional notion of aesthetics that form somehow subsists or extends into content—materials give shape to form and consequently to content (representationalism)—is therefore held by Heidegger as misleading, since it ignores that the interfusion of form and content is controlled beforehand by a particular set of purposes, a totality of work assignments. The work of art as equipmental in its nature, an object founded and signified in its use, thus would take a "peculiar position intermediate between [manufactured] thing and [freely created] work."[8] Harold Bloom's study of tropology in poetry can be said to interpret the work of art on such a preliminary practical level by identifying the poetic work, its figuration, with a particular set of rhetorical purposes—namely the Freudian mechanisms of defense—as the clarifying context of its symbolic structure. In a slightly different manner, structuralist critics have tried to account for a symbolic order of poetic figuration in a theoretical fashion by subsuming rhetoric under a linguistic structure of sign production, metaphor (substitution), and metonymy (combination) and thereby identify structural equivalences relative to a given conventionalized cultural practice of linguistic codification. Even though Heidegger would agree with Bloom and the structuralists that it is indeed language that speaks in poetry—"Man first speaks when, and only when, he responds to language by listening to its appeal"—he makes it clear "that [this] is not to say, ever, that in any word-meaning picked up at will language supplies us, straight away and definitely, with the transparent nature of the matter as if it were an object ready for use."[9] Both Bloom's and the structuralist's approach to poetry therefore suffer from having typified the work of art as tool (ready-to-hand object) or tool structure (present-at-hand object). While both approaches offer complex analyses of poetic texts, they fail, due to their formalized and therefore unpoetic presuppositions, to arrive at a proper poetic understanding. Poetry, it appears, will not tolerate the discovery of its nature in any other manner than the poetic itself.

In trying to preserve the work of art as such, Heidegger is not satisfied with merely establishing pragmatic goals or conventional use as the ultimate horizon for the work's entire range of activities prior to and apart from its founding activity: "We must . . . avoid making thing and work prematurely into subspecies of equipment."[10] The purpose of art, as it is clarified by Heidegger, lies not so much in bringing its activities to bear in a world of praxis and convention, thereby losing its reflective orientation in a task at hand, as in elucidating its fundamentally free and interpretive activity prior to any formalization in connection with certain practical goals. The work of art, in its effort to escape any formalization and alienation of human practices, is therefore said to direct its attention to the immediate encounter with existence itself, "the disclosure of a particular being in its being."[11] Stevens similarly states that a "poem is a particular of life thought of for so long that one's thought has become an inseparable part of it or a particular life so intensely felt that the feeling has entered into it."[12] The work of art thus holds that the entirety of life, rather than any formalized segment of it, is the only natural whole worthwhile to be reflected upon as that which can be authentically lived and shared in artistic expression. In discussing Heidegger and Stevens, Paul Bové focuses similarly on this fundamental connection between life and art in which the latter can no longer be separated or extricated from the burden of existence:

> Since the poet is free to blast away the 'aesthetic' interpretations in language by 'rethinking' the 'centers' and revealing their Being as fiction, he performs and discloses movements which are possible only in the medium of life and not in art.[13]

Poetic thinking, as underlying all the arts, can thus be understood as a reflective activity constantly investigating the conditions of its possibility as the condition of a reflective life shared with others. Or as

Stevens simply writes: "The theory of poetry is the theory of life."[14] In Stevens's conception of poetic thinking, the conditions of the possibility of people making and the reflective laying out of the possibilities of Being are thus one and the same.

With this preliminary definition of poetry in mind, one would naturally want to inquire as to how the freedom of its activity, if truly given, manifests itself in poetic form. How can one understand formal configurations in poetry as something other than the result of a conventionalized linguistic use or tropology? To clarify this question, it is best to follow and reenact the discoveries of a poet who has himself tried to clarify the relation between abstraction and empathy, between form as structure and form as expressive totality. In entering the discussion of Stevens's poetry and its figurative operations, however, it is necessary first to conceive adequately of the activity that motivates these operations. We must begin therefore with a clarification of what Stevens calls "the poem of the mind in the act of finding / What will suffice" so as to be able to conceive properly of its manifestation in poetic form.[15] For without a preliminary understanding of Stevens's poetic context, a formal analysis would lack all meaningful ground.

Stevens's *Notes Towards a Supreme Fiction* marks a major breakthrough in his work by establishing explicitly for the first time a poetics that was only implicitly given in his earlier poetry. Poetry is consequently thematized as the subject of poetry in a more elaborate and systematic fashion as opposed to previous and more narrow reflections on its nature. In continuity with his earlier works, these explorations into the nature of poetry are still articulated entirely from within the poetic idiom. Heidegger parallels Stevens's endeavor by insisting that one must necessarily undergo an experience with poetry if one is to understand its ground properly, that is, poetically. Theoretical knowledge or presuppositions of any kind thus are said to stand in the way of poetry. Stevens, in fact, advises the poet-novice or ephebe to "become an ignorant man again" if he is to understand at all the origin of poetry, "the poem is the cry of its occasion."[16] This search for a pretheoretical realm of understanding and intelligibility can indeed be found with many of the premodernist philosophers. Nietzsche thus links the knowledge of the Apollonian directly to the Dionysian rapture. Bergson's realm of pure duration, Husserl's "urdoxa" or original belief, Cassirer's symbolic forms and Santayana's notion of animal faith likewise point to a conception of prerational, primitive, or narrative understanding as poetic or pure knowledge. Even Heidegger goes as far as characterizing the work of art as "the happening of truth" on a preconceptual level. In modern art, a return to primitivism is similarly found in the works of Picasso, Ernst, and Giacometti. Unlike the attempt to enchant and bewitch the world magically, however, as found in primitive ritualistic practices, modern art radicalizes primitivism down to the level of a poetic construction that is founded only in its activity. Tangible objects are thus not sought to be known in and of themselves, or manipulated in their objectivity, but serve merely as clues signifying the manner of their poetic appropriation. Discussing one of Picasso's primitive sculptures from this point of view, Rosalind Krauss writes:

> Meaning does not precede experience but occurs in the process of experience itself. It is on the surface of the work that two senses of process coincide—there the externalization of gesture meets with the imprint of the artist's act as he shapes the work.[17]

While the artistic imagination thus releases itself to the world in externalizing its invisible activity in the object (empathy), it equally abstains from any physical appropriation of this world other than in the form of a legible sign (abstraction). The fundamental unity of subject and object thus occurs as a language, a structure inherent in the distension and condensation of act and object, signifier and signified. Abstraction and empathy thereby mutually transcend the confines of subject and object and join them in their fundamental unity.

In Stevens, the unity of the abstract and empathetic motivation of the poetic sign is clearly and unmistakably stated in his *Notes,* which insist that the poem "Must Be Abstract" and "Must Give Pleasure" alike:

> It must be visible or invisible,
> Invisible or visible or both:
> A seeing and unseeing in the eye.
>
> . . . .
>
> But the difficultest rigor is forthwith,
> On the image of what we see, to catch from that
>
> Irrational moment its unreasoning,
> As when the sun comes rising, when the sea
> Clears deeply, when the moon hangs on the wall
>
> Of heaven-haven. These are not things transformed.
> Yet we are shaken by them as if they were.
> We reason about them with a later reason.[18]

Abstraction, for Stevens, marks the return to the "First Idea," the "belief in an immaculate beginning."[19] The poem "brings back a power again / That gives a candid kind to everything."[20] The poem thus always speaks from beyond the visible with an invisible sight that preserves the irrational moment of its activity in the visible aspects of its projected world. Or, as Heidegger writes, "poetic images are imaginings . . . that are visible inclusions of the alien in the sight of the familiar."[21] The resulting pleasure of the poem is to have reasoned and not reasoned at all, to be shaken or moved by things as if they were transformed by the meanings that we ascribe to them. Here, Stevens clearly follows his mentor Santayana who defines aesthetic pleasure as being "disinterested" to the extent that it does not seek to impose on its occasion nor rationalize its activity: "Every real pleasure . . . is not sought with ulterior motives, and what fills the mind is no calculation, but the image of an object or event, suffused with emotion."[22]

This immersion of the poet in the active movement of life where subject and event become inseparable from one another points to yet another tenet in Stevens's *Notes,* namely that the poem "Must Change" continually so as to preserve the spontaneity of a lived activity, of "the fluctuations of certainty, the change / Of degrees of perception in the scholar's dark."[23] The temporality of reflection thereby opens up the space for the poetic enactment of life as an existential project. Thus, the necessary changes and determinations of nature are experienced in the equally changing light of the poet's determinations of freedom and appropriations of life as meaningful existence:

> There was a project for the sun and is.
> There is a project for the sun. The sun
> Must bear no name, gold flourisher, but be
> In the difficulty of what it is to be.[24]

Being, "the difficulty of what it is to be," as it is understood in Stevens's appropriation of Plato's parable of the sun, must be approached properly in its own right, that is, poetically. Plato similarly describes the cave dweller's ascent to knowledge, the sun, in his "Allegory of the Cave" as one in which he must not impose upon the purity of the experience of coming to knowledge and undergo a necessary "conversion of the soul": "Last of all he will be able to see the sun, and not mere reflections of him in the water, but he will see him in his own proper place, and not in another; and he will contemplate him as he is."[25] Stevens, less idealistic than Plato in his search for pure and legitimate forms of reflection, simply urges the poet-novice to "see the sun again with an ignorant eye / And see it clearly in the idea of it."[26] The core of all Being lies with the "inconceivable idea of the sun," with "perceiving the idea / Of . . . this invented world."[27] In Stevens, unlike in Plato, Being emanates, not from privileged forms of Being, *ideae*, articulated as a rationale or sufficient reason for its origin, but from a poetic project that seeks to express the "strong exhilaration / Of what we feel from what we think" as the project of a reflective laying out of life being inseparable from its fulfilled pleasure and excitation.[28]

In summary, Stevens's preservation of abstract and empathetic projections as unified experience grounded in reflection allows for a poetic conception of the world, one that Heidegger characterizes as the letting be of Being in contradistinction to the impositions of technological thinking and its subordination of the world to human practices. Poetry thus emerges as a creative conception of the world grounded in the satisfaction of having simply lived, that is, lived deeply from within its immediate reflective horizons such as birth, death, suffering, and compassion that are pushed aside in our everyday concerns. In this respect, poetry falls nothing short of a venture in which its only certainty can be found with its own single fulfillment of life: "It is a world of words to the end of it, / In which nothing solid is its solid self."[29] Or as Stevens speaks elsewhere of "the poem of the mind in the act of finding / What will suffice":

> It has to be living, to learn the speech of the place.
> It has to face the men of the time and to meet
> The women of the time. It has to think about war
> And it has to find what will suffice. It has
> To construct a new stage. It has to be on that stage
> And, like an insatiable actor, slowly and
> With meditation, speak words that in the ear,
> In the delicatest ear of the mind, repeat,
> Exactly, that which it wants to hear, at the sound
> Of which, an invisible audience listens,
> Not to the play, but to itself, expressed
> In an emotion as of two people, as of two
> Emotions becoming one.[30]

Poetry, in order to speak of that which "will suffice," Stevens insists, must begin to speak from its own ground, "to learn the speech of the place." It has to construct a world negotiable as one truly shared with others. Its expressed exhilaration or pain found in adversity profoundly reflects the need for communication as the need to see our lives continued in others. To the extent that this reciprocity is refused or covered up, one is condemned to live unpoetically and inauthentically. The poet, therefore, as the heroic and "insatiable actor" is the figure that seeks to restore the primal unity of the experiences that we share when we share our lives reflectively. As we begin to listen to others as a part of our shared horizon of what it is to live and to die together, we begin to listen to ourselves in a manner more truly and more strange, in a manner approximating life at "the central of our being."[31]

Up to this point in this discussion, Stevens's and Heidegger's poetics have been shown to be compatible in their concern with a reflective laying out of Being and its appropriation in the articulations of poetic language. Having established the dynamics of abstraction and empathy as a tentative interpretive framework for the understanding of what is at stake in poetic discourse, namely, nothing less than a sense of sufficiency and adequateness of life found in poetic reflection, I shall now turn to the question of figuration and its operation in poetry. As was stressed earlier, an exclusively formal analysis endangers the status of poetry by reducing beforehand its foundational operations to schemata to which the reflective activity of poetry is subordinated. A conventional formal analysis thus offers instrumental figures (synecdoche, metonymy, and metaphor) without conclusively clarifying the larger contexts of their organization. The meaning of the poetic texts, as deconstructive critics have rightly pointed out, seems to disappear as it emerges as a relational unit within a formal system with no clear and indicative limits. This is not to say that a formal analysis is altogether impossible. If subordinated properly to the activity and horizon of poetic reflection, one may begin to conceive more adequately of the context that motivates poetic form and thereby understand its peculiar configurations. For the sake of such a tentative analysis, I will discuss Stevens's "The Poem that Took the Place of a Mountain" and try to relate its figuration back to the poetic context as the communicative and reflective horizon from within which poetic figuration operates.

Stevens's "Poem that Took the Place of a Mountain," in the light of a Heideggerian reading, dramatizes the unity of the poetic world that dwells in the proximity of the fourfold horizons of earth, sky, immortality, and mortality. As a reflective vortex, these horizons open and light up the poet's world as a lived and thought totality. The poem in its total integration of setting and voice draws the poet into the proximity of his being as a dwelling or abiding that is facilitated by the poem. The mountain, as one might mistakenly infer from the title, is not sought to be replaced entirely by the poem. Rather, its presence is interpreted as a vital and manifest horizon, the earth, that lends support and visibility to invisible voice that animates the poem. In this respect, the poem resembles the visionary landscapes of allegorical fiction in which a *potentia* or supernatural power disclosed itself to the poet in a visionary setting. In clear distinction to traditional allegories, however, the *potentia* in Stevens's poem is the poem itself as a possible lifeworld found in poetic reflection:

> There it was, word for word,
> The poem that took the place of a mountain.
>
> He breathed its oxygen,
> Even when the book lay turned in the dust of his table.[32]

From its beginning, the presence of the poem discloses itself as the natural ambience in which the poet moves reflectively. Even in the temporary abandonment of his poetic vocation, the poet draws his vitality from the poem and breathes its vital oxygen. The mountain representing the intersection of the horizon of earth and sky offers the promise of the transcendence of common human experience. This transcendence is not to be confused with the aspiration of metaphysics: while reaching towards heaven, the mountain is equally anchored in the earth and therefore rooted in the reality of human experience. Transcendence is found precisely at the site where it occurs, not in heaven or in nature, but at the threshold or horizon that leads one both beyond and back to experience. This horizon is constituted by the poem, not the written poem on a page, but the actual movement of life itself that sustains the poet's dwelling on earth:

> It reminded him how he had needed
> A place to go in his own direction
>
> How he had recomposed the pines,
> Shifted the rocks and picked his way among clouds,
>
> For the outlook that would be right,
> Where he would be complete in an unexplained completion.[33]

The poem as the movement of life urges the poet forward towards his reflective limit where he will find himself in "unexplained completion." The limit the poet approximates in his activity of shifting and readjusting perspectives is that of his mortality which makes a lived perspective possible. As the limit of all human projects, it allows for a closure of life and the reflective recovery of a meaningful whole, "the outlook that would be right," from the accidental and fragmentary circumstantial to life. In this outlook, the poet recovers and remembers that which he had anticipated as completion, his origin or reflective birth:

> The exact rock where his inexactnesses
> Would discover, at last, the view toward which they had edged,
>
> Where he could lie and, gazing down at the sea,
> Recognize his unique and solitary home.[34]

The poet's reflective anticipation of a relation that would restore him to his world in a lived completion resolves in a moment of elevation, a privileged perspective, in which he recognizes and rediscovers that which he already possesses, the "Being that has a liking for man," as Heidegger would say. Of this Being or "exactness amidst inexactness" the poet gains reassurance and certainty in his deliberate poetic advances towards the view or horizon pointing beyond the mountain's edge. The sea, as the place of the poet's reflective birth, lies beyond this edge in an abyss. Only as the poet dares to advance towards this limit and learns to live within the venture of his mortal condition, can he live like an immortal, that is, in the absolute certainty of having lived at all in the exacting exactness of Being.

Having established the general thrust of the poem's thematics, the rejoining of life in the life of poetic composition, I shall now turn to a tentative formal analysis. In reading the poem poetically, we have discovered its repeated emphasis on completion or a whole as always already given and continually embodied in its partial configurations. The poem thus opens with a dramatic exclamation: "there it was." Its world is given in its entirety, "word for word." Its partial manifestations (recomposing, shifting) are guided beforehand by the desire for unity and completion. Figuratively, this union emerges as the total blending of the code of setting and the code of voice or persona and comes about in the partially spontaneous and deliberate intersection of two metonymic chains, trains of association, which in their overlapping constitute a metaphorical or reflective level of substitution. The intersecting layers thereby establish human activities and their ambience (building, dwelling, thinking) as intrinsically connected to the natural realm. The natural life can thus no longer be clearly separated from the reflective life since it comes into its being as it is recomposed and rearranged by the artist. The poem would therefore appear to possess an abstract quality in its appropriation of nature as a semiotic design or abstract language. This abstract design, however, is equally embedded in the concrete voice or rhythmic animation of the poem. As such, the poetic vision is centered in the movement of living speech that provides the context for the figurative level. Sonority and rhythm contribute to an enhanced presentation of the poem's empathetic embrace of nature and break down the formal structural design (metaphoric pole of equivalence superimposed on the metonymic pole of dissimilarity and contiguity) to the level of poetic speech as spontaneous act: "To write poetry is measure-taking, understood in the strict sense of the word, by which man first receives the breadth of his being."[35] For Heidegger, the rhythm of poetic speech points to more than merely a formal measure in prosody, namely to form as a form of life:

> Rhythm, rhusmos, does not mean flux and flowing, but rather form. Rhythm is what is at rest within itself. Rhythm bestows rest.[36]

In Stevens's poem, the dwelling within the poetic activity is made clear by the deliberate and meditative rhythm with which poetic reflection proceeds. Long drawn lines, deliberate pauses, vocalic length and unvoiced sibilants (recomposed, pines, gazing, recognize) contribute to a lulling and halting tone. This axis of rhythmic homogeneity is superimposed onto an axis of discontinuity and abrupt breaks in rhythm. Thus a few terse statements are interspersed (there it was, at last) to accelerate the rhythm and lend the poem dramatic tension. Plosives (ro*c*k, too*k*, pi*ck*ed, exa*c*t) and voiced sibilants (inexactne*ss*e*s*, di*s*cover, *s*ea, *s*olitary) contrast with the mellifluous tone of the poem and form the background for the foregrounding of continuity in rhythm. Rhythm thus enhances the notion of poetic dwelling as a rest amidst the ceaseless flux of events. As a linguistic correlative, it communicates the temporality of the poetic reflection that animates the poem. In this late work of Stevens, the poem's tonality reflects the assured relaxation of the mature master, the poet who has learned to write in what Heidegger would call a state of "Gelassenheit." In this particular state of mind, Being or existence is allowed to enter fully one's reflective horizon and concern and is thereby encountered on its own ground.

In this analysis, we have seen that the synthetic activity of poetic consciousness permeates all levels of poetic construction ranging from the material (phonic, rhythmic) to the figurative and abstract design of the poem (syntactic-semantic). The context and spontaneity of the poem, however, rest with the unified and projected lifeworld communicated through poetic speech. As the negotiable and immediate world that is shared in our encounter with one another—Being-in for Heidegger is a Being-with others—its horizons cannot be formalized, if their viable relation is to be reserved. Poetic speech invites poetic reflection and ultimately withholds its revelations in a purely theoretical treatment. Stevens's "The Poem that Took the Place of the Mountain," for example, offers in many ways a more adequate understanding of Cézanne's painterly visions of Mont Saint-Victoire than a traditional descriptive analysis could accomplish. Stevens, who knew Cézanne's work well and claimed to have read much that was written on the artist, expresses more vividly and immediately in his poem the shared aspiration of making art and nature the same where, in the words of Cézanne, "the landscape thinks itself in me and I am its consciousness."[37] Cézanne's concern with the "lived perspective," the actual realization of one's sensations (*réaliser mes sensations*) rather than their reproduction, coincides with Stevens' search for a poetic vision that constitutes a landscape or region of the spirit. Cézanne, often called "the father of modern art," claims that he "wrote in painting what had never yet been painted, and turned it into painting once and for all."[38] Painting for the modern artist thus becomes the language that expresses and realizes the uniqueness of one's experiences, the "happening" or event in which the "art work opens up in its own way the Being of beings."[39]

The interpenetration of setting and the life that is lived within this setting characterizes the modern poetics of Stevens and Heidegger as well as the painterly poetics of Cézanne. Of the latter Merleau-Ponty writes:

> What motivates the painter's movement can never be simply perspective or geometry or the laws governing color, or, for that matter, particular knowledge. Motivating all the movements from which a picture gradually emerges there can be only one thing: the landscape in its totality and its absolute fullness, precisely what Cézanne called a 'motif.'[40]

The emergence of the totality (whole) and its structural differentiation (parts) in the painterly vision is, according to Merleau-Ponty, inseparably joined in the motif. As such, structural analysis can never give sufficient insight by itself unless it is related to the context that informs the work of art. This context, as has been pointed out, is that of the lived perspective in Cézanne, or what Stevens refers to in *The Rock* as the "poem as icon," "the fiction of the leaves" as the "imaginative transcripts" of the life lived in the poetic appropriation of the ground of Being:

> It is not enough to cover the rock with leaves.
> We must be cured of it by a cure of the ground
> Or a cure of ourselves, that is equal to a cure
> Of the ground, a cure beyond forgetfulness.
> And yet the leaves, if they broke into bud,
> If they broke into bloom, if they bore fruit,
> And if we ate the incipient colorings
> Of their fresh culls might be a cure of the ground.
> The fiction of the leaves is the icon
> Of the poem, the figuration of blessedness,
> And the icon is the man.[42]

The poem that places us beyond ourselves, beyond subjectivity, as well as beyond the ground of objectivity, potentially offers a ground on its own terms, that of being the icon or figuration of the life that it mirrors and conceives in its search for the human element in the wilderness of the landscape:

> These leaves are the poem, the icon and the man.
> These are a cure of the ground and of ourselves,
> In the predicate that there is nothing else.
> They bud and bloom and bear the fruit without change.
> They are more than leaves that cover the barren rock.
>
> . . . .
>
> They bloom as man loves, as he lives in love.
> They bear their fruit so that the year is known,
> As if its understanding was brown skin,
> The honey in its pulp, the final found,
> The plenty of the year and of the world.
> In this plenty, the poem makes meanings of the rock,
> Of such mixed motion and imagery
> That its barrenness becomes a thousand things
> And so exists no more. This is the cure
> Of leaves and of the ground and of ourselves.
> His words are both the icon and the man.[42]

The barren landscape becomes humanized not because it speaks of ourselves, not because of the facticity that we may ascribe to it, and not even as the result of a fictive covering of the leaves. Its human voice is that of the poem that brings man closer to himself as the being that continually perishes in the fulfillment of his Being and thus becomes a landscape unto himself, an icon of the movement of life. Or as Heidegger writes: "Only man dies—and indeed continually, so long as he stays on this earth, so long as he dwells. His dwelling, however, rests in the poetic."[43] Like Heidegger's exemplary poet Hölderlin, Stevens "sees the nature of the 'poetic' in the taking of the measure by which the measure-taking of human being is accomplished."[44] Poetry, in this respect, stands as the abode and shelter for human dwelling as the ground of all Being, as its ownmost icon or "language of Being."

As was pointed out, the poetic concern of both Stevens and Heidegger rests with the human need for constant self-alienation and recovery of a vital relation to one's Being found in the impulse of sharing it poetically in the strangeness of human encounter and love. To advance and promote this vital insight, a discussion of the relation of abstraction and empathy was meant to clarify the manner in which figuration operates both poetically and structurally. It was considered necessary that a strict apophantic or theoretical discussion (a mere showing) had to be abandoned for the sake of a tentative poetic hermeneutics in which showing becomes inseparable from an appropriation and reactivation of vital ideas akin to the manner in which they were put forward. If such a procedure may appear as an irrational transgression of the limits of criticism, two answers may be given in response. As I have shown, poetic reflection proceeds not without its own rationality, a vital reason, so to speak, that derives its orientation from the repeated investigation as to the possibility of its own ground and thereby reaches a level of reflectiveness by which it can measure and evaluate its own discoveries. A more simple response I take from Stevens himself, who equally urged the recovery of poetic reflection by promoting a "fiction that results from feeling":

> They will get it straight one day at the Sorbonne.
> We shall return at twilight from the lecture
> Pleased that the irrational is rational.[45]

6

Acoustics: Heidegger and Nietzsche on Words and Music

Dennis J. Schmidt

> Every silence is composed of nothing but unspoken words. Perhaps that is why I became a musician. Someone had to express this silence, make it render up all the sadness it contained, make it sing as it were. Someone had to use not words, which are always too precise not to be cruel, but simply music.
>
> Marguerite Yourcenar, *Alexis*

> Understanding a sentence is much more akin to understanding a theme in music than one might think.
>
> Ludwig Wittgenstein, *Philosophical Grammar*

> Almost cruelly, we can contrast the communicative wealth of the musical with the waste motions of the verbal.
>
> George Steiner, *Real Presences*

> Music is surrounded by groping colloquies that never cease, though they are no means of comprehension.
>
> Ernst Bloch, *Philosophy of Music*

In the eleventh hour of Heidegger's lecture course dedicated to a thought that he calls one of the leitmotives of modernity, namely, *"der*

Staz vom Grund" (a thought only inadequately translated by the translations to which we have become habituated: "the principle of ground" and "the principle of reason"), Heidegger turns his attention to describing the emergence of the limits of that thought and so of modernity. It is a gesture dedicated to clearing a way for the appearance of what Heidegger takes to be the summons of thinking today, a call from the future that he always argues has only been heard as the faintest of echoes. But his particular concern at this point in the lecture is to establish the limits of the notion of the subject and to show how the notion of the subject loses the preeminent place it had won in the course of modernity as an account of the essence of human being. Once the notion of the subject is dislodged as both the principle and the ground for thinking, Heidegger claims that the principle of ground itself is called into question, thereby opening the way for another kind of thinking, one that does not submit in advance to either principles or grounds. Characterizing the culmination of modernity as the end of a thinking that followed the dual guidelines provided by the principle of reason and the notion of the certifiable subject, Heidegger then alludes to the different style of thinking that is heralded by history at a juncture such as ours: "Understanding being means that man stands in the open projection of being according to his essence . . . Through the understanding of being that is experienced and thought in that manner, the representation of human being as a subject is, to speak with Hegel, set aside. Only insofar as man stands in the clearing of being, according to his essence, is he a thinking being."[1] The point of course is that history has now readied thinking for the end of the representation of human being and that with the collapse of such representations thinking needs to ready itself for a different, presumably more original, experience of human being as the being of history and language, the being exposed to the destiny of being itself. Almost casually, and with great rapidity, Heidegger then compresses the entire remaining difficulty of modernity, the congealed residue of all that is to be set aside and surmounted by thinking today, into one word: *dialectic.* He then argues that a certain language of thinking is played out in the dialectic, a call (*Geheiss*) and countercall (*Entsprechung*), which, he contends with unswerving persistence, remains wooden, ultimately calcified and too frozen ever to touch upon and speak out what is most alive. The dialectic stands, for Heidegger, as the last refuge of a thinking that lives, not from time and history—that is, from a response to the finite destiny of being—but from static images that prop up a system of representations, principles, and reasons. Against the dialectical conception of history, ever the foil for Heidegger from the final pages of *Being and Time* to the texts of his final years, Heidegger suggests that an appreciation of a certain "leap," one too agile for any dialectical movement, is requisite for a thinking that is capable of comprehending the present, culminating juncture of history and so touching upon its own truth: "the history of Western thinking shows itself first of all and only as the destiny of being when we look back upon the whole of Western thinking *from out of the leap* and that whole is to be thoughtfully preserved as the destiny of being that has happened."[2] Finally, Heidegger advises his listeners that a new sensitivity to tone is requisite for the full appreciation of the leap to be made today, that leap that permits this "look back" and thoughtful preservation of "the destiny of being" as "whole" and that is to prepare for the arrival of "post"-modernity: "the leap out of the principle of reason . . . concealed itself behind the change in tonality of that same principle."[3] Sharpening that point, and yet rendering it even more puzzling, Heidegger then says that "if we fully think through the polysemic word *Satz* not only as 'statement,' not only as 'utterance,' not only as 'leap,' but at the same time *in the musical sense,* then we arrive at the complete connection to the principal of reason."[4] The movement here is from *Satz* to *Satz*—from, finally, language to music. Or so it seems.

The movement of Heidegger's text is especially difficult at this point, and the claim in which it culminates is quite curious; that *Satz*—sentence, statement, utterance, proposition, principle—a word that names all that inclines toward language and, above all, toward the syntax of the dialectic, when taken to its radical truth, its deepest moment, exposes its musical sense. Almost imperceptibly, Heidegger takes his distance from Hegel, who jeers at "musical thinking which is no more than the formless jingling of bells or a warm misty feeling that never arrives at the concept."[5] At the end of modernity then, at the limits of the dialectic, at the moment when we hear the "resonance between being and ground resounding,"[6] music appears.

That is a claim that sounds more commensurate with what one might expect from Nietzsche than from Heidegger. There is, or so it seems, a striking absence of any serious reflection on music in Heidegger's work. One finds powerful images of painterly works—who does not associate van Gogh's painting of peasant shoes with Heidegger's meditation on the work of art?—as well as images of architecture and sculpture. Above all, one cannot read Heidegger without taking to heart the key role that meditation upon poetry and certain specific poems plays in his work. The recovery of the finite experience of language, especially language at the moment of its greatest concentration and density, namely language in the poem, seems to command the movement aimed at overcoming the metaphysics of subjectivity that is the trademark of modernity. Heidegger is not alone in his dedication to this recovery; Foucault put the point of this turn to language clearly when he wrote:

> 'I speak' runs counter to 'I think.' 'I think' led to the indubitable certainty of the 'I' and its existence; 'I speak,' on the other hand, distances, disperses, effaces that existence and lets only its empty emplacement appear . . . No doubt that is why Western thought took so long to think the being of language: as if it had a premonition of the danger that the naked experience of language poses for the self-evidence of the 'I think.'[7]

Language then, this "repetition of what continually murmurs outside,"[8] has been the leading theme of work that has followed in Heidegger's wake. It has finally earned its name as the "house of being" and so one reads—without interruption—that "being that can be understood is language."[9] And yet there remain these haunting references to music and the arresting fact that despite the acknowledgement that tonality and musicality play a keynote role in the move beyond modernity. Nonetheless, despite Heidegger's clear predilection for musical language ("ringing," "sounding," "pealing," "fugue," "tonality," "resonance," "song," "echo," "rhythm"—the list could easily be continued), one never, or so it seems, finds extended reflections upon the musical work in Heidegger.[10] While the Greek temple perches dramatically on a cliff overlooking the raging sea below, one finds Beethoven's quartets languishing "like potatoes in the cellar."[11]

But then there is Nietzsche who stands between those bookends of modernity—Hegel and Heidegger—and who speaks both on behalf of a thinking that listens to music and quite pointedly against that view of the privilege of language in experience so strongly held today by those working in a context shaped by Heidegger. So, for instance, Nietzsche claims in *Twilight of the Idols* that "[o]ur real experiences are anything but loquacious . . . They don't have the power of speech. What we can express with words is what we have passed beyond. Whatever we have words for that we have already got beyond. In all talk there is a grain of contempt."[12] Or in *Birth of Tragedy* he says: "Language, as the organ and symbol of appearance, can never reach the deep interior of music from without, but . . . remains only in external contact with it."[13] Where word picks up we have reached a second order of experience, the other side of an echo. For Nietzsche, the threshold of language is not, as it is for Heidegger, the threshold of all thresholds, the threshold without a before, an outside, or other. Rather, language, for Nietzsche, is the afterthought or reproduction of the more original experience that is best characterized as musical. In language the closest approximation to that experience is the language of tragedy, the highest expression that language can bear of the conflicted nature of the will. That is a decision about the relation of language and ruin that Heidegger too might make (his admirations for Hölderlin's translations of Sophocles provide ample testimony for that claim), but however close Heidegger might come to Nietzsche on this point, it remains the case for Nietzsche that even tragedy, born out of the spirit of music, does not embody the antagonisms and agonies of the will as well, as profoundly, as music. For Nietzsche, even the well-chosen word, the word that has poetic power, inevitably falls short of the power of the note in motion and relation. In the end, we speak at all only because ours is a world in which music is possible. One confesses then that "it may well be that man is man, and that man 'borders on' limitations of a peculiar and open 'otherness,' because he can produce and be possessed by music."[14] Music makes language possible, and language that reaches beyond the limits of representation pays homage to that debt. At the outset of *Twilight of the Idols* we are reminded that this point is all important to our time of passage.

What about music then? What about this appeal to tonality and this leap (*Satz*) that is to be thought as a musical movement (*Satz*) and that Heidegger calls the "requirement of thinking that still lives today"? To ask about music in the context of a concern with following Heidegger's effort to push thinking beyond the presumptions it assumed in modernity is not a matter of posing a question intended to extend something like "Heidegger's aesthetics" into a delimited field of artistic performance. Far from it. Such a question is, it should be clear from the outset, thoroughly remote from any such project, especially since one of the guiding efforts of Heidegger's approach to the work of art is to remove it from its metaphysical ghettoization in what has come to be called "aesthetics"—a word that among the legacies of modernity has most thoroughly saturated thinking today. It is not a matter of presuming in advance to know what Heidegger means when he speaks of "tonality" and a "musical sense" but of asking what these words might mean today. To what degree can we say that the enigmas of thinking today, the obstacles it confronts and the topics it is consigned, are exposed and repeated in the enigmas of music? More precisely, it is a matter of asking a very simple, if initially bizarre, question; namely, is there music? If there is music, then what might it take to hear music today?

I believe that, in the end, this question of music becomes massive, moving far beyond one's initial expectations and opening a tangle of issues one might never suspect on the basis of Heidegger's passing reference to the question. Lacoue-Labarthe has already indicated one of the largest dimensions upon which it touches:

> The interesting thing about the phenomenon at which it aims, as we can easily see, is that it should make possible to return, by basing the analysis initially on the intraphilosophical distinction between the visible (the theoretical, the eidetic, and the scopic, etc.) and the audible (or the acoustic, and I do not say the verbal), to the *hither side* of the "theoretical threshold" itself. It should make it possible to return to the place where the *theory of the subject* (but perhaps also *the subject of theory*) would see itself, if I may say so, obliged to put into question its privileged apparatus, its instrument, which, from Plato to Lacan, is a specular instrument, And a *speculative* apparatus.[15]

My intention in what follows is not to broach the largest significance of the question of music for the movement between modernity and postmodernity, nor is it even to deal with the full question of music as it might be pursued in either Heidegger or Nietzsche. Rather, my specific intention is simply to raise, and then try to formulate, the question of the relation of words and music in the context of that relation as it is thought by both Heidegger and Nietzsche, but to raise that question first of all as a question itself rendered problematic, perhaps even preempted, by virtue of the relation pertaining between music and technological reproducibility. How far can we speak of the "refusal of clarification and assimilation into frameworks of meaning"[16] that is discovery of every reflected experience of language without being drawn into the question of the relation of language and music if for no other reason than the astonishing fact that tonality, tempo, and rhythm—the elements of music—belong to any possible clarification and meaning of language. Might one need to think the refusal of the word together with the refusal of music? How far can the question of poetry be put before it is compelled to confront its own truth as song,[17] eventually coming to ask about what Mendelssohn described as "songs without words"? But, even before that question can be asked today, we need to take seriously the difficulty of any talk of music if not always then at least for today. It is that difficulty of questioning today that Heidegger drove home so insistently, a difficulty that Nietzsche naively passed by. In other words, in what follows I propose to begin to pose a question that one finds recommended by both Heidegger and Nietzsche as a question of special urgency for this historical moment at the culmination of modernity, in order to ask whether that very same question has been closed off by virtue of precisely this historical moment. Has music made an appearance as an issue for thinking only in the mode of its disappearance?

Is there music then? Of course it still remains Nietzsche rather than Heidegger who is possessed by this question, and it is Nietzsche who first links this question to the question put to us by our age, thereby rendering it ineluctable. It is striking just how deeply Nietzsche defines the question of history at the end of modernity as a question pinned to the thought of music. Equally striking is how remote the question of music has become even in our reading of Nietzsche.[18] His claim is clear: music is, he contends, "a woman"[19] and without it "life would be an error."[20] At least that is what he says shortly before unmasking the "four great errors,"[21] those metaphysical delusions that first emerge and show their hitherto hidden truth against the cool blue backdrop of the peculiar historical twilight that marks our age. Nietzsche's own sense, never unshadowed by a certain "untimely" ambivalence, is that he comes, in the apt words of Hölderlin before him, both "too late" and "too early,"[22] but always "after" those errors have been unveiled as such. Like Heidegger, Nietzsche finds it both continually necessary and impossible to place himself with respect to history by virtue of a separation from what Nietzsche characterizes as the high philosophical noon of metaphysics, namely, the era of such errors. For Nietzsche, it is a separation announced with the approach of twilight and night. But, more than a mere separation, Nietzsche claims that thinking today can be characterized only by a radical transformation, a reversal and countermovement, since he claims that beginning with him the direction of thought will no longer be best described as an ascent to bright lights, such as the curious ascent described by Socrates in the seventh book of the *Republic.* It is rather to be experienced as a time of passage through dark times, one through which we need to negotiate our way by new means and without the old idols that were the stars by which thought once took its own measure. It is that need for a new measure for thinking to which Zarathustra is answering when he says that "with the approach of midnight things are heard that by day may not be made loud."[23] Consequently, in order to grope our way through these turbulent times that define us as "after" metaphysics (a notion that we now need to define in order to defy), we who think out of this time of passage—a "we" dislocated and thoroughly problematized along with the thought of "life," as "error" or otherwise—we need to move away from our habitual speculative reliance upon seeing, upon *theoria* as defined in the Greek world, to a new relation to listening. The passage from noon to midnight is, as Lacoue-Labarthe has claimed, equally the passage from the visual to the aural. Music then plays the keynote role in the awakening of these times. Likewise, our historical place bears a special relation to music. To think our time, the passage and destiny that it marks, we need to listen to the music of the night. If not for such music, "life would be an error." More to the point: if life can be said to make a point, then we hear it in music; quite simply then, without music life would simply be pointless. Understanding such a point, Bloch finds it possible to speak of "the good fortune of the blind."[24]

Some of Nietzsche's claims about music seem clear at first: "Music," he says, is "deeper than dreams" and the Apollonian world of the eye and its plastic arts;[25] it is the real voice of, and answer to, the pain and contradiction of life that gets plastered over by the comforting so-called truths of religion and philosophy. In music, like childbirth, "*pain* is pronounced holy."[26] That "great pain, that slow pain in which we are burned with green wood . . . pain which takes its time [and which I might add *is* the pain *of* time] pain that forces . . . us to descend into our darkest depths."[27] As such, music is the "language of the will in its immediacy."[28] It is the discourse of the will unconstrained by the limited discourse of words. In an aphorism Nietzsche claims that "we have art lest we perish of the truth," but to think through that aphorism it must be acknowledged that music is art par excellence, its deepest, most articulate moment.[29] It is the truth that dislodges the truth that is the error from which we would otherwise perish. Music, of course, is what metaphysics always lacked and failed to hear, and so it is music that forms the countermovement to the decadence of the tradition; it guides us in the dark passage between twilight and dawn, it primes us for the future. The old center could not hold, but now Nietzsche seems to be saying that the future is melocentric, that is, if it has a center at all. The stakes could not be higher since everything for Nietzsche—the body, will, time and return, language and tragedy, pain and violence, every countermovement to nihilism—unfolds along an axis that is articulated by what Nietzsche calls "music."

But the most obvious remark one can make about music simultaneously draws it closer to Heidegger's avowed concerns and hammers home the difficulty of thinking it in the context of these large concerns: music itself, the key to our time, needs to be thought as a certain relation to time. Music not only marks our time in a special manner, but also raises the question of time itself as its own special question. So music is doubly important insofar as it raises the question of time as the preeminent question of our time (for Nietzsche it appears most sharply as the thought of the eternal return; for Heidegger, initially at least, as the finite time of Dasein) and insofar as it is emblematic of the tropological passage between the times that Nietzsche himself marks—the time between Hegel, and the claim of the perfection of metaphysics, and today as the time calling for the overcoming of metaphysics. Nietzsche's historical place, like the place opened up by music, is best thought as pure passage that destroys itself in the movement that is its own happening. It is such passage that Heidegger referred to as demanding a "leap."

But the question that Heidegger leads us to ask today is this: what about this possibility of being "without" music, how real is this subjunctive that says life "would be" an error? What does it mean that we must mark our time as a musical passage and even as a catacoustic moment out of tune with what preceded it, as a time of noise? Even Nietzsche, ever confident in the potency of music, concedes the difficulty: "After the song of the wanderer and shadow, the cave all at once became full of noise and laughter."[30] The question is: how far can we go toward thinking music in our time at all? To what extent does music itself remain captive, even prohibited, by our time? According to Nietzsche, music should speak to our time just as it once spoke with a special excellence as the spirit of that time giving birth to tragedy. But does it? Or does the riddle of our time as a time of twilight and transformation preempt the question of music as Nietzsche thought it, as redemption from "error"? Are there elements of "our time" that displace the possibility of its own truth?

To raise that question one must focus on its political significance. I believe that this decision to politicize the question of music, to draw it forward into the question of social practices and political economies, is not arbitrary but covertly recommended by Nietzsche himself when he says that only through music can we understand the joy in the annihilation of the individual, and that this "Dionysian dissolution of the chains of individuality is . . . the basis of every political instinct" and the "fabric of community."[31] To understand the stakes of the question of music one needs to bear in mind that for Nietzsche, music, properly thought, defines the possibility of the polis as well as the dissolution of its borders. Music, for Nietzsche, has the power to overcome the individuation of the body and the distance that lives in the visual world: it has the power to draw us instead into the deep community of reciprocity, to the point of our true, our mutual, permeability. The polis in the time of twilight and transition, at the site beyond good and evil, understands music and is guided by it.

If there is music, that is. If the polis is possible. It is the despair of that possibility, the impossibility of political life today that shadows Heidegger and to which he gives voice when he sighs that "only a god can save us." The question of music is not far removed.

Adorno raised a preemptive question in his essay "On the Fetish Character of Music"; namely, must all music today sound like Parsifal did to Nietzsche's ears?[32] In other words: are we already too late for the truth of our time? Is it now the case that music has become one more vehicle of escape and not a path of revelation? Is Jacques Attali right when he claims that "music is illustrative of the evolution of our entire society: deritualize a social form, repress an activity of the body, specialize its practice, see it as a spectacle, generalize its consumption, then see to it that it is stockpiled until it loses its meaning. Today, music heralds . . . the establishment of a society of repetition in which nothing will happen any more."[33] Have "the times" overtaken music, obliterating its truth?

Of course, the idea that music generates feelings of community, that among the arts it is the most immediately political, is not a new idea. Plato already knew the political power of music and its relation to order and disorder; he was quite sensitive to this power when he made the question of musical harmony one of the first issues to be addressed in the formation of the polis.[34] Aristotle, who discusses music in the context of his politics, acknowledged that power as well.[35] But the contemporary question about the relation of music and political life adds a new twist to that idea. It is a serious, and to Nietzsche a potentially devastating, charge that says that the potentials of music do not guide, but are undermined and guided by, its relation to political economy. More precisely, the claim is that the peculiarities of music's mode of reproducibility—its readiness to be frozen mathematically in the digital recording and its capacity to have its violence on the vinyl of the analogue recording—that those mathematical and violent elements of music now exposed by the modes of its reproducibility have left the situation of music today in such a regressive state that it all now can only sound like Parsifal, the threat of our time praised and celebrated. Social dynamics have married the technological imperative and in the process swallowed the possibility of music. Today, "even the performance sounds like its own phono recording."[36]

This readiness for the recording reveals what Adorno calls the "Egyptian quality" of music—a quality Nietzsche, writing at the very moment that the first recordings were being made, does not acknowledge.[37] But we must acknowledge that in the recording, time on the move, time that denies the emptiness of eternal duration by being perpetual movement and arrest, time that again and again affirms the ephemeral and incandescent, is *immobilized and paralyzed.* Precisely at the point that history and time emerge as worthy of thought, the technological reproducibility of the musical work of art seems to have frozen and stockpiled time and set history adrift. Given that revelation, can we speak of music with innocence today? Can music speak to us any longer? Can "we" ask the question of music without asking about its relation to such reproduction? Benjamin has already raised the question: "the work of art is always fundamentally reproducible. What had been made by men could always be imitated by men . . . But technical reproducibility of works of art is something new."[38] Benjamin defined that "something new" first of all as a "withering of the aura of the work of art."[39] If music severs itself from its own auratic character, if it severs its relation to ritual by lending itself to such immobilization, then what does that mean for Nietzsche's claims? If music is immune to that paralysis, then it seems that we must concede that "up to now, we have not really known what music itself is called and who music is."[40] This time of twilight is the time of music's approach. But it is also a time in which technology has sharpened the difficulty of any "musical sense" by challenging the very meaning and possibility of music.[41] Does the "leap" (*Satz*) that Heidegger contends is required by history today, a leap needing a "musical sense," go limp and lose its life in the age of technological reproducibility? Has modernity so sedimented itself in the form of modern technology, which like aesthetics is one of the enduring legacies of the modernity now said to be drawing to a close, and so invaded the times that music can only appear in muffled and mummified form today? Benjamin argued that the withering of the aura is the condition for the emancipation of the work of art from its "parasitical dependence upon ritual"; it is from that point of emancipation that one can begin to understand why Heidegger spoke of the movement between modernity and postmodernity as a musical movement, as a *Satz* that is equally a leap to a new basis for the work of art.

The specific challenge to Nietzsche's claims about music is clear: what kind of music can Nietzsche point to that resists such Egyptian potentials? It is simply too easy, too vague, to answer "Dionysian." Is the Dionysian found in Beethoven's "Ode to Joy"—music with words—listened to on the stereo or rigid according to the etiquette of the concert hall? Or is it only for one who can play music or compose? Can we sit serenely listening to such music of one primal will? Can it be written? Or does Beethoven, deaf at the end, conducting but unable to hear the orchestra playing his Ninth Symphony, does Beethoven, reading the score, conducting by his bones, have one perfect relation to music, the ideal set of ears? Mahler proposed an answer when he said that the most important part of the music is not in the notes.[42]

Or do such questions simply displace the real issue of music? Does Heidegger's suggestive remark about a requisite "musical sense" today move in some altogether other direction? Is it appropriate to try to localize, to identify, music in such ways? If not, then how are we to draw near to the inner secret of music as Nietzsche understands it? Especially when—in a passage that echoes Heidegger's most urgent claim about all art—he claims that "music is not at all to be judged according to the category of beauty," and that it runs far deeper than the world of "feelings" and "effects."[43] The enigma of music only deepens once we recognize that need to think it freed from the claims of beauty if we are to think it at all. The summons of music today is a call to questions only begun to be asked. Simply put: what happens in music when we recover it from its ghettoization in "aesthetics"? If we can recover it that far at all. What does it take to develop this "musical sense" to which Heidegger refers thinking today?

In the *Twilight of the Idols* Nietzsche writes that "all rhythm still appeals to our muscles."[44] Significantly, that remark occurs in the context of criticizing that "kind" of music that no longer leads us back to the body, music that specializes itself "at the expense of those faculties which are most closely related to it," and that, when touched upon, allow us to "enter into any skin."[45] That is one of the many remarks that point us to the direction music is to be thought; namely, that music shows itself "on the passionately moved human body."[46] Music elaborates itself on—if not as—the human body.

But then that is ultimately no surprise, since the body is the locus of the self-elaboration of every truth in Nietzsche. Everything confesses itself in some relation to the body. One sees for instance the work of metaphysics in the posture and gait of our bodies. One sees such confession too in the bodies of *Zarathustra:* dwarfs, cripples, eunuchs, hunchbacks, "eunuchs" before the "harem" of history, those who "hobble" and "limp" into the twilight. Bodies incapable of any sort of "leap."

Of course, nothing escapes our being a body, a *this* in the utmost. Or, as Heidegger put it in writing of Nietzsche: "wir leben insofern wir leiben."[47] Speech too is a bodily act. In *The Gay Science* Nietzsche claims that language emerged to protect the body that speaks it out. But its relation to the body not withstanding, language never reaches and unfolds in the deep and dark places of music, and the reason explains Nietzsche's insistence that the reach of music outstrips that of language. Nietzsche's contention is that languages—always found only in the plural, always only what Bakhtin named "heteroglossia"—differentiate and divide, working along the fault lines of the principle of individuation. But that music, as having its essential, its tonal subsoil rooted in the body *that we are all said to share,* possesses the potential to dissolve and annihilate the principle that individuates. This means of course that Nietzsche regards the body in its truth as gender-neutral; it is not so much the sexual body but the anatomical body that we share. The body in question is anybody's body. Everybody belongs to the body that Nietzsche speaks about.

Obviously a problematic claim at best since, in the end, the link between the body and the annihilation of the individual can be fully understood only if we understand the body as the sexual body, not as the body defined by the borders of the skin, but as the ecstatic body, the body that affirms itself in the other of its skin. Death is always mine, it is always the mortality of *this* body, not "the" body which gives it force. In *Being and Time* Heidegger tried to think the "*Jemeinigkeit*" into which death delivers each of us such that every act can be understood only as an act of putting one's ownmost singularity on the line; yet, he did that without reference to the sexuality of body. But death cannot be understood as a matter of anybody's body. It is only in this regard that one can see why Nietzsche says that music has always had the body as its subject, and it does so by taking us out of ourselves and setting us into question with the possibility of any fundamental relation at all—either in love or death. Relationality then, like the body, belongs to the essence of music, and that is what sets music apart from all else, giving it a potency greater than that found in the word. The word alone can make sense, it can speak and lay claim to being language, but the isolated note can never be called "musical" since in every note there is the resonance of another. A great musical work is thus, in Attali's phrase, "always a model of amorous relations, a model of relations with the other, of eternally recommenceable exaltation and appeasement, an exceptional figure of represented or repeated sexual relations."[48] Once we begin to understand the darkness and thirst of music we discover that music has special relations with the erotic, but it also bears an equally deep affinity with death: "what touches or moves me in music, then, is my own mourning."[49] When properly understood, music emerges as binding love and death, joy and mourning, and that is why "the more joyful the joy, the purer the mourning slumbering within it."[50]

The point Nietzsche wants to make is that the body understood as universally shared unites and that it is the basis of our belonging together, of our universality and communal life. But what Nietzsche tends to forget precisely at this politically all-important point is that even when thought as the ecstatic sexual body, it also keeps us apart and names our distance. As the site of pain and death—something that along with pleasure and birth defines the sexual body in equal measure—the body radically ruptures and forever unravels the prior community of our lived permeability that Heidegger called the "with world." What Nietzsche understates is that the body, though it belongs to that community, though it too has and is a shared language, ultimately remains, along with our mortality, that which individuates us to the hilt. One might say that the body is the name and locus of our mortality. By this body, not by the idea of body, but by this one, I am pulled back, ambiguously placed in community, left mysterious, dark, and hidden from all probing and uninterrupted union. Even the sexual body cannot escape or overcome its fundamental "this-ness," its being torn between its this-ness and ecstasy.

Taking the body—too often the anatomical body stripped of both gender and sexuality—as the basis of community, localizing and universalizing the political at the conflicted side of the body but refusing to problematize that conflct, is the reason that Nietzsche's politics are finally marked by a basic apoliticism, as well as by an incapacity to cope with the radical divides that belong to the nature of any community. It is, I would argue, precisely this apolitical politicism that Heidegger latches onto in his Rectorial address, and it is this attachment that let him be hunted by the thought that "Nietzsche hat mich kaputt gemacht."[51]

But the full question of how Heidegger picks up and pushes themes emerging from his reading of Nietzsche is much more complex than I have indicated. What is important to note is that, in the end, Heidegger's sense of language in referring us to language in the poem moves within the same horizon of concerns as the one in which one finds Nietzsche's discussion of music moving. It would be thoroughly misguided—a double travesty—if one proposed the question of the relation between language and music, a question awkwardly raised by both Heidegger and Nietzsche, as a matter of privilege, hierarchy, or priority. It is a matter not of competition that emerges here but of a peculiar difficulty, a yearning and a cry too easily forgotten and effaced. A matter of relations and community still without clear formulation. In turning to language that folds back upon itself, attentive to rhythm, time, tone, and gesture, Heidegger brings us always back to language that, like music, prevails in what Hölderlin described as "a mode of relation and thematics," to language as a mode of song.[52] In other words, language in Heidegger might have very much to do with the relationality that draws Nietzsche to music, singling it out, distinguishing it "as the most original manifestation, under which is to be understood all becoming."[53]

That remark brings us back to the most obvious issue in music—one of the principle issues challenged and transformed by the special mode of capture at work in music's reproducibility—namely, music as a mode of time: of relation, return, repetition, even, one might argue, of the redemption and revenge of time against itself. Music, having the body as its subject, the will as its immediate object, remains nonetheless always time made loud. It is our mode of communication with the movement of time, with all of the ambiguities hinted at by the word *with.* But Nietzsche remains strangely silent on this point of the relation between time and music, tending to slip into the unproblematized remark that music is a matter of "becoming." Of course it is becoming, but it is also equally dissolution and the play of resolution and relentless dissolution. It is the struggle of the harmonic.

The "becoming" that is heard in music is essentially dissonance, the inner secret and truth of harmony, and of this dissonance Nietzsche says:

> The primordial phenomenon of Dionysian art is difficult to grasp, and there is only *one direct way* to make it intelligible and grasp it immediately: through the wonderful significance of *musical dissonance*... only music can give us an idea of what is meant by the justification of the world as an aesthetic phenomenon.... [In it] we recognize a Dionysian phenomenon: it reveals to us the playful construction and destruction of the individual world as the overflow of a primordial delight. Thus the dark Heraclitus compares the world-building force to a playing child placing stones here and there and building sand hills only to overthrow them again.[54]

The reference to Heraclitus is crucial: all of the Heraclitean fragments speak from out of the riddle of dissonance understood as the truth about harmony, the fact that dissolution cannot be felt without union. The playfulness of play, the play-space of time from which music lives and thrives, is this infinitely compressed infinity between union and dissolution, the real locus of becoming and locality of music. At that point of tension and openness—the point of dissonance and harmony alike—the instant is most fully alive. Held in the grip of music one relates to time as pure self-destruction and passage—the present is no longer infinitely compressed between a merely deferred memory or hope. In music there is no time for such deferral. In music we learn that dissonance is not a destructive force but a mode of love and affirmation, a redemptive creative act.

Another way of making the same point is to say that the sort of music that Nietzsche wants to affirm, music that understands the struggle and secret dissonance of harmony, has nothing nostalgic about it. It suffers no "revenge" against time. In Dionysian music—music that moves with the uninhibited will—there is no time to bemoan paths not taken, there are no "meanwhiles" teleologically pegged to something still remote, no dead movements, no moments outside the play-space of becoming, no moments not rich enough to return eternally. Of course, saying that does not obliterate the full force of dissolution, of the loss that belongs to becoming. Such music is not the music of contentment, but always of joy and mourning *at once,* of fullness and loss *at once.* Baudelaire's remark will always remain true: "Nothing can restore to the world the fragrance it has lost." The struggle of harmony is the struggle of death itself, the pain of dissolution, and insofar as it is felt on the "passionately moved human body" it is felt as the body in pieces, the body torn and in spasm. Music moves us and does so always with the power both to tear us apart and to bring us to the point of real communion. The temporality of musical *dissonance* is as much about pain and mortality as it is love and affirmation. That is why music has an essential relation to mourning and lamentation as well as celebration. In the end, music stands as the most powerful reminder that time is not so much about the so-called moments of time, about the ossification of the confrontation with the course of time into past/present/future, as it is about dissonance. Heidegger, of course, is the one who dedicated himself to thinking precisely such dissonance.

Real participation in music draws us into the dissonant body and into the full instance at once, and it does so (so says Nietzsche at least) more fully and profoundly than words can ever communicate. Music places us, body and soul, at the site of dissonance, the very site of the pain and contradiction of life that get plastered over by the so-called truths of religion and philosophy. Religion and philosophy, having effaced the body and denied time, are incapable of thinking and affirming the profound pain, equally the deep joy, that issues out of the contradiction of being at all. The "musical sense" that Heidegger finds requisite today carries with it a receptivity to precisely what has been effaced by a thinking guided by the images of onto-theology, a thinking modeled after an infinite and omnipresent mind that has no body and suffers neither pain nor death.

Nothing touches and binds time and the body more directly than music, and that is why Nietzsche says: "music never *can* become a means; one may push, screw, torture it; as tone, as roll of the drum, in its crudest and simplest stages, it still defeats poetry and abases the later to its reflection."[55] Nothing outstrips its potential as "the language of the will in its immediacy." Language, as Nietzsche understands it, has a liability, a tendency to objectify time, that music, living as it does from dissonance, does not. One might argue with and for Nietzsche, as Blanchot does, that Nietzsche's conception of language does not match his practice, that in his fragmentary writing, his aphorisms and the perpetual recoil of interruptions in his texts, Nietzsche writes dissonance. That, to some extent, is quite true, but, as Nietzsche knew, the liability of language, its propensity to metaphysics, will never be lifted so long as language has its grammars: "I fear we will believe in God so long as we have grammar."[56] Dissonance can never be made obedient to grammar. Captured by grammar, speech risks paralyzing the temporality of radical dissonance. Frozen on that page, writing risks effacing dissonance—carried in gesture and tone—even further. Or, as Heidegger put it: "In script the scream is easily smothered."[57]

Heidegger's rather abrupt reference to a "musical sense" summoned by the end of the metaphysics of modernity might have the appearance of a casual gesture, but, like most such abrupt flashes in Heidegger's texts, it has nothing casual about it. But, even if deliberate and calculated in its appearance, the meaning of that gesture itself, which opens a cut to the heart of the issue of the lecture, remains opaque at best. My intention here has simply been to suggest some of the lines that need to be pursued if that cut is to be followed through on its own terms. It has also been to open up an avenue of inquiry into Nietzsche that Heidegger himself does not take but that nonetheless exposes a productive line of issues for both Heidegger and Nietzsche. There is then a serious question put to us by the thought of music today, one that Adorno seems to have raised with more directness than either Heidegger or Nietzsche. It is a question that draws together the seemingly divergent concerns of language, body and technology. A question, in the end perhaps, of what Heidegger called "the *Gestell.*"

Most of all, it is a question concerned with far more than drawing an inarticulate line marking the unmarkable limits of language. It is important that we widen our view of just what that question is asking. The point is that music—which has always raised, then redoubled, the questions of reproduction and repetition in the move from score to performance to recording—has today been drawn into the contemporary mutations of such questions, into what Heidegger thought under the name *Gestell.* Such questions of modern technology and its own peculiar political economics and imperatives lead, as Benjamin pointed out, to questions of fascism. Taking up the question of technology, even the transformation of music in the age of its technological reproducibility, demands that the political meaning of that transformation be addressed. Linked to technological reproduction it seems that in these times music is in danger of severing its roots in ritual, sacrifice, and celebration. Its original meaning, which Nietzsche believed would teach us about the transformations necessary in ourselves to meet the demands of our times, is in the process of being transformed.

Part 3

Contesting Modernities

If the debates about modernity and postmodernity have clarified something, it is less the status of these terms in relation to each other than their shared complicity as contesting modernities. The difficulty is that discussions about postmodernity invariably raise the specter of modernity, invoking the necessity for its interpretation and thus foregoing the need to question it as more than yet another belated modernity. Thus while postmodernity may be in question, it is modernity that is under the siege of competing critiques that attempt to elucidate its character by invoking terms such as *rationalization, secularization, subjectivity,* and *representation.* It is not merely the meaning of these terms that is under dispute but also their narrative exposition as dialectical structures and forms of legitimation.

For Fred Dallmayr the state of siege that "modernity" finds itself in today reflects doubts already expressed in relation to particular features of modernity. More specifically, modernity is at issue as a product of the Enlightenment undergoing the Weberian process of "rationalization," including intellectual secularization, disenchantment from nature, political reorganization in terms of rational-administrative efficiency, and economic industrialization. The question of a vantage point from which to critique modernity leads to challenges of its historical character (as bearer of the legacy of the Enlightenment), as well as of the fate of reason and its impact on the discourse of philosophy. The major figures of these debates, Kant and Nietzsche, mark each in their own way the turning points in a drama, whose meaning Dallmayr explores as a function of different discursive typologies. He institutes a dialogue where Strauss, Rosen, Habermas, Foucault, and Connolly are set into debate with sometimes overlapping but ultimately mutually exclusive results. This unfolding drama stages concurrent and competing discourses that result either in the denunciation of modernity (Strauss and Rosen) or its recovery as an unfinished project (Habermas). Allying himself with Foucault and Connolly, Dallmayr identifies his conception of postmodernity as "an internal critique of modernity," that is, a field of strategic contestations. Signifying a farewell to the "metanarratives" of metaphysics (an invocation of Lyotard's critique), Dallmayr's interpretation of postmodernity calls upon a "radical relationism," in the effort to make philosophy politically responsible.

In his essay on modernity, Cascardi turns to the Weberian terms of "secularization" and "disenchantment with the world" in order to critique the Heideggerian account of the emergence of modernity. Heidegger's emphasis on notions of subjectivity and representation conceals, according to Cascardi, the problem of secularization by masking the social and historical forces that shaped their emergence. Cascardi seeks to address the tension between history and theory, which he interprets in "the form of a conflict between ideals and norms." By transposing philosophical questions into an examination of structures of belief, Cascardi resituates the specificity of history in the realm of cultural pragmatism. Relying on Blumemberg's distinction between "a language of belief" and a "normalizing language of critical enlightenment," Cascardi suggests a return to concepts of agency that reinstate in a secular mode the subject of belief.

Foucault's archeology of the human sciences, *The Order of Things,* is a text whose richness sustains and rewards a variety of readings. Stephen David Ross construes this work as the odyssey of representation across modernity. He sees a persistent division at work wherever language is confined to its representative function. This struggle between representation and language, between order and disorder, is intensified when representation attempts to represent itself, as in the case of Foucault's analysis of Velasquez's *Las Meninas.* What Ross adds to this rather well known story is its implicit political dimension as elaborated by Hobbes in *Leviathan,* an aspect of representation that seems to have eluded Foucault at the time. The division that infects every attempt at full and comprehensive representation undermines the unity and identity of the person, and thus of sovereignty, at the very threshold of modernity. For the two architects of political modernity, Machiavelli and Hobbes, the public as the space of appearing to the collective other relies on the fictiveness of representation, on its mis-representing. Meditating on a profound albeit enigmatic phrase of Foucault's in which he refers to a "middle region" where in every culture there is the "pure experience of order and its modes of being," Ross concludes that this middle region, the locus of representation as transgression and otherness, lies between truth and untruth, not beyond praxis and art.

Candace Lang returns to the question of modernity and postmodernity through a discussion of the status of dialectic and narrative in historical discourse. Taking as her point of departure Frederick Jameson's and Hayden White's impassioned debate about the inherently dialectical character of narrative, Lang explores the meaning and possibility of narration in a postmodern context. Using Lyotard's and Thébaud's *Just Gaming* as a background, she suggests that the confusion of prescriptive and descriptive propositions, with no relation of logical implication, undermines the possibility of a totalizing theory or master-narrative of legitimation. Instead of functioning as ground and motive for political action, dialectic and narrative thus emerge as local strategies, reducing the field itself to a site of contested authorities. This pluralization of narrative does not imply, however, its negation.

It merely shifts our attention to the dependence of verisimilitude on the norms that define plausibility (Genette). Identifying Jameson as a practitioner of motivated narrative, Lang contends that his rediscovery of the freedom to narrate represents a step beyond irony, into humor. Lang's understanding of the role of humor, not as a state of mind, but as a strategy, opens up the question of modernity from the vantage of a post-ironic (the longer self-reflective moment of negation in the Hegelian dialect), that is, postmodern perspective.

7

Modernity and Postmodernity

Fred Dallmayr

Something curious is happening in the midst of our modern (Western) civilization: "modernity" is under siege today. To speak with Gallie, Alasdair MacIntyre and others, modernity has become a "contested concept."[1] This is not entirely a new development. From its inception, the direction and achievements of modernity have been surrounded by uneasiness and doubt—although such doubt was typically directed at certain features and only rarely at modernity as an epoch or paradigmatic framework. Before proceeding further, let me suggest a rough sense of the term: by 'modernity' or 'modern culture' I mean a culture or way of life that is the product of Western Enlightenment and that has undergone the Weberian process of "rationalization" in every domain, including intellectual secularization, disenchantment from nature, political reorganization in the direction of rational-administrative efficiency, and economic industrialization. Problematization of this way of life, in the form of a pervasive malaise, emerged first in *fin de siècle* Europe (prototypically in Vienna and Berlin). The malaise gathered momentum during the interbellum period, particularly in Weimar Germany, with its progressive polarization of intellectual life. During the Second World War, the unease found expression in a major document written by two intellectuals in exile: Horkheimer's and Adorno's *Dialectic of Enlightenment,* which remains one of the most gripping and penetrating texts on the glory and pitfalls of Western modernity.[2]

After the war, cultural and intellectual issues were at first overshadowed by the emerging East-West confrontation, that is, the conflict of the superpowers—which in essence was a dispute over which side represented or embodied more genuinely the aspirations of modernity. Only after the Cold War settled into a conventional routine did the issue of modernity itself resurface again—on a broad front and with almost unprecedented intensity. It was only then that the controversy surrounding modernity gathered into a genuine philosophical and intellectual debate. Under such rubrics as the "modern project," the "age of technology" or the "age of the worldview," the strengths and weaknesses of modern (Western) culture were placed in the limelight of public scrutiny. It was also then that modernity was specifically defended by philosophers against its detractors, for example, in Hans Bluemberg's *The Legitimacy of the Modern Age*.[3] It was during the same period that the term *postmodernity* or *postmodernism* began to come into vogue, first in architecture and art, and then in philosophy, literature, and cultural analyses in general. One should probably not forget that these intellectual discussions were and are silhouetted against a changing global background: specifically, the emergence of non-Western societies and cultures in Africa and Asia—societies whose presence on the world stage for the first time calls into question the primacy or preeminence of Western culture and modernity. My presentation in what follows proceeds in three steps: First, I give an overview of the dispute surrounding modernity and its contested status; next, I highlight some particularly prominent or salient features of this dispute; and, finally, I indicate possible directions or meanings of postmodernity (and especially the meaning that seems most plausible to me).

I

If one surveys the debate or controversy surrounding modernity, one can probably sort out three major avenues or positions: one that critiques modernity from the vantage of a way of life and mode of rationality that preceded modern culture (and from which that culture departed to its detriment); next, an approach that, while acknowledging historical irreversibility, attempts an internal or immanent (postmodern) critique of key features of modern life; and, finally, a position that seeks to vindicate modernity against both its premodern and postmodern detractors. To be sure, in concrete arguments, these postures are never neatly segregated, and there is room for multiple overlaps and reciprocal borrowings. Nevertheless, there may be an advantage in surveying the terrain along these broad, ideal-typical lines.

The first alternative was prominently articulated (if not inaugurated) by Leo Strauss in his critical assessment of the "modern project." According to Strauss, this modern project basically involved a shift from reason to will and desire, and thus a lowering of the standards of rationality established by the ancients. As he wrote in 1964:

> According to that modern project, philosophy or science was no longer understood as essentially contemplative, but as active. It was to be in the service of the relief of man's estate, to use Bacon's beautiful phrase. It was to be cultivated for the sake of human power . . . Philosophy or science, which was originally the same thing, should make possible progress toward an ever greater prosperity.[4]

In one of his earlier works, Strauss claimed that the instigator of the modern project was Thomas Hobbes, but he later modified this claim and located the rupture with the past in Machiavelli. Basically, Strauss's critique of modernity was a deliberate attempt to renew the "battle of the books," that is, the *querelle des anciens et des modernes.* In this battle, he resolutely sided with the ancients. To quote him again:

> The inadequacy of the modern project, which has now become a matter of general knowledge and of general concern, compels us to entertain the thought that this new kind of society, our society, must be animated by a spirit other than that which has animated it from the beginning.[5]

We have to think, he added, of the:

> restoration of (classical) political-philosophy . . . Such a return to classical political philosophy is both necessary and tentative or experimental. Not in spite, but because it is tentative, it must be carried out seriously; that is to say, without squinting at our present-day predicament.[6]

From a slightly different perspective (though one not incompatible with that of Strauss), Stanley Rosen has formulated the modern predicament in terms of a rift between formal reason and will—a rift deriving from the abandonment of classical substantive (or holistic) rationality. As he writes in one of his recent books, *Hermeneutics as Politics:* "Kant is the paradigm of the internal incoherence of the Enlightenment," namely, of the "conflict between mathematics and Newtonian science on the one hand and the desire for individual and political freedom on the other."[7] In Rosen's view, Kant's paradigm illustrates both the incoherence of the Enlightenment and the collapse of reason into unreason (or arbitrary choice). In his words:

> Reason is itself constituted, or let us say constitutes itself, in accordance with the will to freedom. The upshot is that freedom both grounds, and is grounded by, reason . . . Judged by the canons of traditional logic, which Kant accepts, his argument is invalid.[8]

Since Kant's time, rationality has been further eroded by the steadily intensified stress on imagination and spontaneity. The entire development, according to Rosen, highlights the two chief trouble spots of modern Enlightenment: "the self-destruction of an exclusively or predominantly formalist rationalism, and the celebration of freedom as spontaneity." The emphasis on spontaneity, in particular, makes reason "unreasonable because arbitrary," which leads to the consequence that reason is seen as "an artifact of history," which is the reverse of the earlier view that "history is an artifact of reason."[9]

As presented in *Hermeneutics and Politics,* the path of modernity reaches its culmination in Nietzsche and his abandonment of objective-rational standards in favor of the will to power: "We thus come directly to the late-modern view, made dominant by Nietzsche and today accepted among postmodernist thinkers without prominent exception: To reason is to interpret, because reason itself is an interpretation."[10] Translated into political terms, the infatuation with interpretation (or hermeneutics) is said to lead ultimately to Maoism or anarchism, in any case to some type of nihilism. A case in point is Michel Foucault, on whom Rosen lavishes some of his more eloquent polemical passages:

> As a decadent product of the Enlightenment, Foucault's "value-free" commitment to a suitably modified scientism and his complicity in the attempt to tear down "rationalist" or bourgeois power structures do not constitute a serious political position but rather amount to, or serve, a romantic identification with the outcasts and the oppressed. Archeological science is replaced by a genealogical transvaluation of values, or a paradoxical, but today almost obligatory, left-wing Nietzscheanism.[11]

The same proclivities are exacerbated in Derrida's work and especially in his celebration of "*différance.*" Derrida, Rosen notes:

> radicalizes Kantian spontaneity and entirely detaches it from concepts or rules. Spontaneity qua *différance* is not the transcendental ego but the primordial writer that produces signifiers rather than rules. The spontaneous Derridean signifiers themselves signify *other* signifiers—exactly as in the case of Jacques Lacan.[12]

Together with Strauss, Rosen does not place much hope in an internal or immanent critique of the Enlightenment and modern liberalism. There is for him no liberal solution to the aporia of the Enlightenment, because, he states, "liberalism (and *a fortiori* socialism) is itself the crystallization of that aporia."[13]

These comments are addressed both to advocates of modernity and to their postmodern critics. Regarding the former, the leading and most articulate spokesman in our time is undeniably Jürgen Habermas. From Habermas's perspective, modernity is a condition that can be neither retrogressively undone nor radically transcended. As he insisted in 1980 when receiving the Adorno prize, modernity is far from exhausted but rather an ongoing and inexhaustible enterprise, indeed an "incomplete project" awaiting further development. Appealing specifically to the *querelle des anciens et des modernes,* he argued that the term *modern* in earlier times was always linked with the model of antiquity. However, the spell cast by the ancient world was "dissolved with the ideals of the French Enlightenment." What emerged at that time was a notion of modernity wedded to the belief, inspired by modern science, in the "infinite progress of knowledge and in the infinite advance towards social and moral betterment." What Habermas calls "the project of modernity" or "the project of Enlightenment" is basically a three-pronged departure from tradition and movement toward emancipation. Formulated first by the philosophers of the Enlightenment, the project consisted in the effort "to develop objective science, universal morality and law, and autonomous art according to their inner logic." At the same time, Enlightenment philosophers sought to utilize or unleash the cognitive potential of these spheres for the enrichment of everyday life—that is to say, "for the rational organization of everyday social life."[14]

More recently, in his *The Philosophical Discourse of Modernity* (1985), Habermas has fleshed out in greater detail the intellectual scenario of the modern age. Going beyond broad synoptic assessments, the study presents the Enlightenment and its aftermath as a series of philosophical discourses (or modes of agument) and corresponding counter-discourses and anti-discourses. A central trademark of modernity is again located in the differentiation of "autonomous" cultural spheres—science, morality, and art and their respective validity claims—together with the resulting rationalization of the domains of everyday life or the "lifeworld." In Habermas's words:

> The specific dignity of cultural modernity consists in what Max Weber called the relentless differentiation of 'value spheres' . . . For now questions of truth, of justice and of taste can be treated and unfolded in accord with their own types of inner logic.[15]

Regarding the life-world, *The Theory of Communicative Action* (1981) has pinpointed its role as a background reservoir of cultural meanings, while simultaneously outlining its transformation under the impact of progressive rationalization and differentiation (of value spheres).[16]

As can readily be seen, the Weberian-Habermassian tripartition of value spheres is a derivation from and quasi-canonization of Kant's three Critiques (whose division was precisely pinpointed by Rosen as the dilemma of modernity). In the meantime, the canonical schema of modernity has been challenged by many writers or thinkers as an intellectual straitjacket whose "foundations" have become dubious. If it is granted that the schema involves basically three types of subject-centered relations—subject-object (science), ego-alter (morality and law), and subject to itself (art)—then its structure can be traced to the modern paradigm of "subjectivity" (or philosophy of consciousness) whose ground has been eroded by the combined impact of language philosophy and poststructuralism. This erosion provides the occasion for an internal or immanent critique or "deconstruction" of modernity that is the hallmark of postmodernism; as is well known, the leading figures in this deconstructive enterprise are Heidegger, Derrida, and Foucault. For present purposes I want to highlight the approach of immanent critique by turning to a political theorist, William Connolly, and particularly to his recent book entitled *Political Theory and Modernity*. In Connolly's presentation, modernity or the modern project is rooted in human subjectivity and revolves around the Baconian equation of knowledge and power. In modernity, he claims, the insistence upon "taking charge of the world" comes into its own. Nature, he writes:

> becomes a set of laws susceptible to human knowledge, a deposit of resources for potential use or a set of vistas for aesthetic appreciation . . . Human and non-human nature become material to work on.[17]

As he adds, modernity involves a relentless process of modernization—which has its own inner momentum and its own dialectic: the drive to mastery entails or intensifies the subordination of nonmasters, "and recurrent encounters with the limits to mastery make even masters feel constrained and confined. These experiences in turn accelerate drives to change, control, free, organize, produce, correct, order, empower, rationalize, liberate, improve and revolutionize selves and institutions."[18]

While linked with perpetual modernization, however, modernity for Connolly is not a completely open-ended enterprise or an unfinished project but rather a paradigm or discursive framework whose contours can by now be more or less clearly discerned and hence critically assessed. Looking back over the period roughly from Hobbes to Nietzsche, he perceives a distinctive though not monolithic gestalt. "Modernity, then," he writes:

> is an epoch in which a set of contending understandings of self, responsibility, knowledge, rationality, nature, freedom and legitimacy have established sufficient presence to shuffle other possible perspectives out of active consideration. The room to maneuver allotted to each of the terms in this lexicon helps to demarcate the space within which the others may vary.[19]

Mapping this lexicon or discursive gestalt, however, is already a first step toward transcending it or at least toward bending some of its constitutive ingredients out of shape—a move bound to be resented and resisted by champions of canonical modernity. Thus, Connolly continues:

> if one seeks to rethink radically dominant theories of the self, one is called into court for failing to live up to established theories of freedom or responsibility; if one seeks to rethink dominant understandings of nature, those thoughts are jeopardized by the effects they engender for established understandings of the modern self as subject.[20]

Small wonder, then, that postmodern thinkers have been treated as outcasts not only by defenders of the "great tradition" (of classical thought) but also by devout modernists concerned about the erosion of the pillars of modern Western society. The latter are bound to "condemn efforts to extend thought in this way as 'unthinkable,' 'self-contradictory,' 'self-defeating,' 'perverse' or 'mad' "—accusations that occasionally may "indicate the limits of the thinkable as such" but in other respects "may also disclose, darkly and imperfectly, boundaries within which modern discourse is contained."[21] Undaunted by such accusations, Connolly in any event takes up the cause of the outcasts, that is, of critical-experimental thought, particularly as an antidote to the disciplinary conformism of our age. "In troubled times," he states:

> it may be imperative to try to push thought to the edge of these boundaries that give its form. It may be important, however unlikely it is that the attempt will meet with complete success, to try to rethink the conceptions of self, truth, nature and freedom which bound modern discourse.[22]

II

Before proceeding, it may be desirable to glance back briefly over the terrain of the preceding discussion. As should have become clear, the issue of modernity coalesces today into a multifaceted debate, into a kind of second-order discourse about the discursive structure of modernity. All the participants in the debate assume such a second-order stance—since already to thematize the "discourse of modernity" is not to be completely enmeshed but to stand at an angle to it. As one will also note, despite strong contrasts, disagreement among the contestants is not complete. Connolly agrees with Rosen at least regarding the paradoxical or dilemmatic character of modernity. Rosen in turn concurs with Habermas in the defense of "rationality" and in the strong distaste for all forms of postmodernism. Connolly finally agrees with Habermas at least on the point that modernity is irreversible and cannot be cancelled *post hoc.* These concordances, of course, are only the reverse side of their conflicts. Rosen wishes a "pox" on both modernism and postmodernism; he goes so far as to claim that both are the same ("the distinction between postmodernism and modernism is absurd").[23] His strongest invectives are reserved for postmodern thinkers like Foucault and Derrida, but he is not particularly mellow on modernists either. "The doctrines of Habermas, like those of his colleague K.-O. Apel," he writes:

> are a fashionable and well-meaning attempt to circumvent the exhaustion of modern philosophies of subjectivity and thereby to continue with the goals of the Enlightenment in a coherent, self-consistent manner. Their method is a friendly eclecticism that sacrifices nothing. Unfortunately, this amiability leads to the loss of everything.[24]

Habermas pronounces a similarly acerbic verdict on both Straussian "premodernists" and deconstructive postmodernists, occasionally subsuming both (and other critics of modernity) under the summary label of "young conservatives."[25] Connolly for his part silhouettes both modernity and postmodernity against the backdrop of premodern visions of "order" (which cannot be retrieved). In a statement that resembles Rosen's view, he sees a continuity between modernity and postmodernity: "The aspiration to become postmodern is one of the paradigmatic ways to become modern." However, the continuity here is also marked by rupture and internal contestation.[26]

One telling gauge of the controversy—a kind of litmus test or *experimentum crucis*—is the status assigned to Nietzsche (and post-Nietzscheans like Foucault and Derrida). For Rosen, Nietzsche is the harbinger of nihilism and anarchism; he is the first to cross the bridge from rational knowledge to the chaos of interpretation. As previously indicated, Foucault is presented as a "decadent product of the Enlightenment"—thought not nearly as decadent as Derrida. "As he comes closer to Nietzsche," Rosen states:

> Foucault also moves closer to the romantic and largely negative version of Maoism . . . But at no stage of his career does Foucault illustrate the speculative madness of Nietzsche, whereas this is perhaps Derrida's outstanding feature.[27]

In this assessment Rosen joins ranks with Habermas, for whom Nietzsche is basically the pacemaker of archaic regression and primitivism. In *The Philosophical Discourse of Modernity,* Nietzsche occupies the position of a "turntable" (*Drehscheibe*) separating the Enlightenment discourse of Kant and Hegel from the headlong plunge into the abyss of irrationalism and irresponsibility. In his function as turntable, Nietzsche represents the "dark writer" (or *bête noire*) of the bourgeois age, opening the gates to a host of equally dark or sinister figures (like Heidegger, Derrida, and Foucault).[28] A very different outlook pervades Connolly's work. Nietzsche there emerges as *Grenzgänger* (marginalist) of modernity who, for this very reason, can address probing and unsettling questions to the modern project. "Friedrich Nietzsche," Connolly writes (and the statement can be extended to post-Nietzscheans):

> sought to interrogate modernity from the perspective of imaginary points in the future, and he developed a set of rhetorical strategies designed to loosen the aura of necessity and sanctity surrounding categories of the present.[29]

In Connolly's presentation, Nietzsche aspired to call modernity into question without either lapsing into nostalgia for past modes of life or postulating a future utopia where we could finally reach a "home in the world." As he adds, Nietzsche "fosters thinking, for those who do not ward him off before thought can proceed."[30]

Another, closely related litmus test has to do with the status assigned to the Enlightenment tradition. In Strauss's view, Enlightenment is a deeply problematical and ultimately misguided endeavor because it weans the indiscriminate spreading of light where the latter cannot really penetrate, that is, the erasure of the divide separating Plato's cave from the sunlight of truth. Harshly put: Enlightenment signifies the artificial electrification of the cave. For Rosen, Enlightenment is no less problematical. As indicated, he finds the Enlightenment project basically incoherent, or at least rent by an internal rift: the rift between mathematical or scientific reason and political emancipation (guided by human will). As a result of this rift, modern Enlightenment is said to "self-destruct" in the end, crushed between the millstones of an "exclusively or predominantly formalist rationalism" and the "celebration of freedom as spontaneity.[31] This view is entirely at odds with that held by Habermas, who, as mentioned, regards Enlightenment as an inexhausted and basically inexhaustible enterprise, as an "incomplete project" calling for further expansion. From this vantage, there cannot be an end to the spreading of light, a light cast by human inquiry and rationality; eventually all corners of the cave of this world are to be illuminated or spotlighted—in Weber's terms, they are destined to be "rationalized" (or "disenchanted"). As indicated, modernity for Habermas is wedded to the belief in the "infinite progress of knowledge and the infinite advance towards social and moral betterment." As presented in *The Philosophical Discourse of Modernity,* the Enlightenment project was inaugurated by French thinkers from Descartes to Voltaire and then crystallized in German Idealism from Kant to Hegel. In Kantian thought, enlightenment signaled the emergence of mankind from a condition of self-induced tutelage. For both Kant and Hegel, modernization or the achievement of modernity meant the progressive refinement of consciousness and subjectivity, specifically in the domains of science, ethical freedom, and aesthetic judgment. During the nineteenth century the Enlightenment project was further developed by Hegel's heirs, especially by the Left-Hegelians whose perspective—in Habermas's view—is still the dominant guidepost in our time.[32]

Habermas's belief in the continuity of the Enlightenment project is not shared by poststructuralist (or postmodern) thinkers—at least not along the same unidirectional lines. Shortly before his death, Foucault wrote an essay entitled "What is Enlightenment?" which was meant as a tribute to Kant (who wrote an essay with the same title two hundred years earlier). The tribute, however, was complex and multifaceted. In the opening section of the essay, Foucault accepted Kant's definition of Enlightenment as the effort to awaken mankind from self-induced tutelage or immaturity, where *immaturity* means "a certain state of our will that makes us accept someone else's authority to lead us in areas where the use of reason is called for."[33] In reflecting on what was happening in his own age—the eve of the French Revolution—Kant included a historical dimension in his own critical enterprise; by considering the import of "today" for philosophical thought, he adoped the "attitude of modernity."[34] For Foucault, however, paying homage to Kant was by no means a matter of simply celebrating the accomplishments of "*the* Enlightenment" or of imitating the Kantian outlook or style of inquiry. Rather, Enlightenment as a critique of immaturity and authority had also to be turned into a critique of the authority of "Enlightenment." As Foucault wrote, the ethos of modernity "implies, first, the refusal of what I like to call the 'blackmail' of the Enlightenment."[35] Recognition of the achievements of the classical Enlightenment, and of Kant's philosophy in particular, should not lead to a simple submissiveness to the past: such recognition, he observed:

> Does not mean that one has to be 'for' or 'against' the Enlightenment. It even means precisely that one has to refuse everything that might present itself in the form of a simplistic and authoritarian alternative: you either accept the Enlightenment and remain within the tradition of its rationalism . . . or else you criticize the Enlightenment and then try to escape from its principles of rationality.[36]

For Foucault, it was particularly important to free or extricate the continuing relevance of Enlightenment as critique from the historical accretion of "humanism" and anthropocentrism (i.e., the focus on modern subjectivity); in his view, Enlightenment and such humanism were far from synonymous but rather in a state of tension. In our own time, it was important to relegate this humanist accretion to the past:

> Just as we must free ourselves from the intellectual blackmail of 'being for or against the Enlightenment,' we must escape from the historical and moral confusionism that mixes the theme of humanism with the question of the Enlightenment.[37]

According to Foucault, the Enlightenment ushered in an attitude of critique, but this critique now has to be concretized and sharpened into a critique of all preconceptions, including those bequeathed by the Enlightenment. The required philosophical ethos, he wrote, "may be characterized as a *limit-attitude* . . . We have to move beyond the ouside-inside alternative; we have to be at the frontiers. Criticism indeed consists of analyzing and reflecting upon limits."[38] In exemplary fashion, Kant reflected on the rational limits of knowledge or the knowable; but this was no longer enough:

> the critical question today has to be turned back into a positive one: in what is given to us as universal, necessary, obligatory, what place is occupied by whatever is singular, contingent, and the product of arbitrary constraints? The point, in brief, is to transform the critique conducted in the form of necessary limitation into a practical critique that takes the form of a possible transgression.[39]

For Foucault, this point entailed as a consequence that criticism is

> no longer going to be practiced in the search for formal structures with universal value, but rather as a historical investigation into the events that have led us to constitute ourselves and to recognize ourselves as subjects of what we are doing, thinking, saying.[40]

In that sense, and in contrast with Kant, contemporary criticism is "not transcendental, and its goal is not that of making a metaphysics possible: it is genealogical in its design and archaeological in its method."[41]

Commenting on Foucault's essay, Habermas (in a memorial paper written after the former's death) mistook its tenor as simply a tribute to Kant and Enlightenment philosophy, ignoring the complex multivocity of the text. Seen as a tribute to, and endorsement of, the Enlightenment, the essay, for Habermas, was in conflict with the rest of Foucault's opus:

> Up to now [until 1984], Foucault traced this [critical] will-to-knowledge in modern power-formations only to denounce it. Now, however, he presents it in a completely different light, as the critical impulse worthy of preservation and in need of renewal. This connects his own thinking to the beginnings of modernity.[42]

In his earlier work, Foucault allegedly contrasted the critique of power with the rational "analysis of truth" in such a fashion "that former becomes deprived of the normative yardsticks that it would have to borrow from the latter. Perhaps the force of this contradiction caught up with Foucault in this last of his texts."[43] Habermas's reading or misreading can readily be challenged, and it has been challenged by numerous writers, including Hubert Dreyfus and Paul Rabinow. Focusing on the escape from immaturity promoted by Enlightenment, Dreyfus and Rabinow compare and contrast the Kantian, Habermasian, and Foucauldian conceptions of maturity. In Habermas's reading, according to Dreyfus and Rabinow, Kant's maturity consisted in "showing us how to save the critical and transcendental power of reason and thus the triumph of reason over superstition, custom, and despotism—the great achievement of the Enlightenment.[44] From Habermas's own vantage, maturity is the discovery of the "quasi-transcendental basis of community as all we have and all we need, for philosophy, and human dignity."[45] For Foucault, however, our critical task today is different: "On Foucault's reading, Kant was modern but not (fully) mature. He heroically faced the loss of the grounding of human action in a metaphysical reality, but he sought to reground it in epistemology."[46] Habermas in turn seeks to find this grounding in a transcendental language-community. Foucault resisted both of these universalizing positions. Instead of relying on abstract principles, he counseled an experimental testing of limits, a "limit-attitude" always ready to transgress "universal" categories or "necessary limitations." His work thus fostered a practical ethos that respects difference and otherness without subduing them to a universal formula.[47]

III

At this point it may be time—perhaps high time—for me to drop the mask of *rapporteur* or bystander and disclose my own leanings. This can readily be done. In the debate as sketched (and without intimating a complete consensus), my own sympathies are basically with Foucault's and Connolly's position, that is, with a conception of postmodernity as an internal critique of modernity. In my own view, the prefix *post* in the term *postmodernism* designates not simply a temporal annex or succession but rather an internal happening. Differently phrased, the prefix has the significance more of a dash or incision, revealing the inner complexity and ambiguity of modern consciousness and rationality. As an incision, the prefix also has the connotation of a wound or an affliction undergone by contemporary experience; in Hegelian language one might say that postmodernism is a marker along the "highway of despair" of modern consciousness. This notion of incision or internal critique undergirded some of my earlier writings that attempted a subdued deconstruction of key categories of modern thought (though without ever exiting completely from the Hegelian confines of "determinate negation" and "sublation" or *Aufhebung*). Thus, *Twilight of Subjectivity* (1981) probed the implications of an imaginary decentering of modern "subjectivity" in a number of domains, specifically the domains of inter-subjectivity, man-nature relations, social development, and ethics. Building on this exploration, *Polis and Praxis* (1984) pursued the same kind of decentering or eclipse into more overtly political terrain: by focusing on the notions of political action (or praxis), of political "power" and human "freedom," and finally on the enterprise of political theory or philosophy itself. A companion volume, entitled *Language and Politics* (1984), linked the eclipse of the *cogito* with the contemporary "linguistic turn," tracing the repercussions of the latter on the conception of man as a "languaging creature" (*zoon logon ekhon*) and as a "political animal." More recently, my concern has been with the meaning of modernity, with the prospect of global politics (between development and underdevelopment), and with the status of democracy.[48]

As forays into *terra incognita,* those studies—like those of other "postmodern" explorers—cannot possibly claim conclusiveness or pretend to settle the course and significance of postmodernity. In fact, contrary to the summary condemnations pronounced by Habermas and Rosen, its adepts are far from constituting a uniform phalanx; congruent with the acceptance of ambiguity, the postmodern terrain is itself a field of contestation. To highlight this last point I want to turn briefly to one of the most prominent advocates of postmodernism whose work actually gave broad currency to the term itself: Jean-François Lyotard. By way of conclusion I then want to indicate my disagreement with his approach (which will be seen to revolve again around the issue of determinate negation). In *The Postmodern Condition,* Lyotard portrays postmodernity as the disintegration or dismantling of the great "metanarratives" of the past, that is, of the stories assigning a holistic meaning or purpose to Western culture and its evolution. In Lyotard's usage, metanarrative or metadiscourse refers to "some grand narrative, such as the dialectics of Spirit, the hermeneutics of meaning, the emancipation of the rational or working subject, or the creation of wealth."[49] These grand stories, in his view, are in the process of being dispersed into heterogeneous language games, into "clouds of narrative language elements." In lieu of comprehensive-unifying schemes, postmodernism is said to tolerate only a "pragmatics of language particles" and socially or politically only an institutionalization "in patches—local determinism."[50] Critiquing totalizing models of social life, including Habermas's model of communicative consensus, Lyotard insists: "Such consensus does violence to the heterogeneity of language games. And invention is always born of dissension."[51] Employing Nietzschean imagery concerning a perpetual struggle for power, he presents speech acts and actions in general as "moves" within a game—where move signifies a combative strategy or challenge. This, he writes, "brings us to the first principle underlying our method as a whole: to speak is to fight, in the sense of playing, and speech acts fall within the domain of a *general agonistics.*"[52]

Lyotard's perspective on speech acts and language games is amplified into a broader theory of social and political life—always with an edge against integrative or harmonizing visions or frameworks. The chief target of his deconstructive effort is the view—shared by idealists and functionalists alike—that society is "a unified totality, a 'unicity' " (a view that Lyotard in a more recent work calls "totalitarism").[53] Departing from such unifying schemes, our age (our postmodern age) is said to witness the " 'atomization' of the social into flexible networks of language games"—with each speaker or participant being located at particular "nodal points" of competing communication circuits.[54] Instead of being submerged in social harmony, the "atoms" of society are perceived as operating at the crossroads of pragmatic relationships and involved in perpetual "moves" and "countermoves." "What is needed," Lyotard asserts, "if we are to understand social relations in this manner, on whatever scale we choose, is not only a theory of communication but a theory of games which accepts agonistics as a founding principle."[55] According to a more recent work, entitled *Le Différend,* postmodernity denotes the radical "decline of universalistic discourses," a process giving rise instead to "thought in dispersal" (or thinking in the mode of diaspora).[56]

I do not wish to prolong unduly this discussion of Lyotard; the general strategy of his argument seems fairly evident. In his presentation modernity relates to postmodernity in a similar way as does homogeneity to heterogeneity, unity to multiplicity, universalism to particularism, and harmony to dissensus or contestation. While I share Lyotard's apprehensions regarding unity and uniformity, I cannot entirely concur with his emphases. My reservations extend to several dimensions of his argument. First of all, I distrust radical reversals or substitutions, especially if they are meant to offer an exit route from the metanarratives of modernity or "foundational" metaphysics. In my view, the move from metaphysics to post-metaphysics is more difficult to accomplish than is often assumed (by postmodernists). Generally speaking, metaphysics can scarcely be "overcome" by inverting its premises or priorities: particularly by turning from holism to dispersal, from consensus to dissensus, from "paradigm" to "paralogy," or from harmony to agonistic contests. What these reversals neglect is the complex interlacing of the paired opposites and the ambivalent status of their meaning; they also tend to cloud or obscure the continuing import of metaphysical teachings—and the hazards involved in their abandonment without replacement.[57]

More importantly, Lyotard's reversals (I am afraid) restore "foundationalism" in a new guise: namely, the foundational status of particulars, of language-particles, of separated agonistic contestants or contending antagonists. In the absence of mutual bonds or constitutive relationships, the contending parties are liable to lapse into self-centeredness and unrelated fixity, that is, into the very kind of self-enclosure (or egocentrism) that deconstruction is supposed to undermine. This point does not necessarily vindicate traditional holism or "totalitarism," to the extent that such holism involves a restrictive enclosure and a barrier against "otherness" (or difference). After the experiences with totalitarianism in our century, there can be no intellectually viable road leading back to this kind of holism. In this sense, postmodernism excludes a restorative path or the path of a simple "homecoming"—a fact that does not transform it into nihilism or a "cultural death-wish" (except insofar as death, of sorts, is always part of a genuine renewal and transformation). In my own view, postmodernity signifies indeed a farewell to the grand "metanarratives" of metaphysics. But precisely the abandonment of all fixed foundations does not lead to chaos or a general "war of all against all" but rather to a radical relationism in which no part can claim absolute primacy or supremacy. In this respect, I believe, post-metaphysics seems congruent with the outlook and requirements of social democracy. In more philosophical (Hegelian) terms, one might say that the "absolute" is relational or relationship, or that relationship is what "being" in the end is all about.[58]

8

Secularization and the Disenchantment of the World

A. J. Cascardi

In an essay entitled "The Age of the World Picture," Heidegger proposed a theory of representation that has since provided the accepted view of the relationship between the subject and the modern age.[1] In Heidegger's account, the invention of subjectivity is coextensive with the emergence of a "modern worldview"; the position of transcendental reflection as established in the philosophy of Descartes marks the transformation of the world from an all-embracing cosmos into an objective representation, picture, or "view." When faced with the historical question of whether the origins of modernity may be explained with reference to any other age, Heidegger responds that the world picture does not change from an ancient or medieval one into a modern one; he argues instead that the fact that the world becomes a picture at all is what distinguishes modernity. As a result of this process, Heidegger argues, the cosmos is transformed into a world of represented objects, and truth, as well as the discourses that follow from claims to truth (e.g., morality), come to be measured in terms of their adequacy to a subject who stands over against the world. In Heidegger's view it is this, the self-proclaimed priority of the subject in its transcendental stance, that validates the historical self-assertion of the modern age. Its profound ambivalence is made visible in, among other ways, the replacement of the striving toward transcendent ideals by a normative concept of progress as the immanent development of human powers and aims:

> The newness in this event by no means consists in the fact that now the position of man . . . is an entirely different one in contrast to that of medi-

> eval and ancient man. What is decisive is that man himself expressly takes up this position as one constituted by himself, that he intentionally maintains it as that taken up by himself, and that he makes it secure as the solid footing for a possible development of humanity.[2]

To speak in terms of inner-worldly progress and self-improvement rather than perfection and, therefore, to invoke a concept of the world as a finite totality, as the possible object of transformation, presupposes the existence of a secular social and historical realm in a way that speech about the "cosmos" (for antiquity, the Middle Ages, or the Renaissance) or the fate of Being (for the postmodern thinker who claims to have "overcome" history) does not.[3] In the most rigorous sense, "representation" is a form of world-construction that is dependent on the belief that there are no intelligible essences, no preordained qualities, and no "auratic" presences in the world. The disappearance of such qualities yields a vision of the world as potentially open to transformation from within, but it also raises fears that the world may be governed by no authoritative perspective or controlling point of view. As Descartes says graphically in a crucial moment of the *Meditations,* "it feels as if I have fallen unexpectedly into a deep whirlpool which tumbles me around so that I can neither stand on the bottom nor swim up to the top."[4] If we probe behind Heidegger's interpretation of Descartes to uncover the drama of skepticism and reason played out in the Cartesian texts, we can see that for Descartes it is the disorienting experience provoked by the loss of natural forms that in turn precipitates the search for a "transcendental" position from which to evaluate competing points of view. As the anti-skeptical arguments of the Cartesian tests reveal, the disconcerting multiplicity of perspectives may be stabilized through the formation of a transcendental subject and a corresponding "worldview"; but this requires that we accept a division of reason, and a displacement of the subject, into two separate and sometimes conflicting domains, the empirical and the transcendental. Thus, while it may be possible to compensate for the disappearance of natural qualities from the world and to stabilize the diversity of perspectives within the world, by placing the subject in a position of true knowledge *above* the world, it could also be said that the problem of reason is thus reduced to that form that is amendable to the discourse of modern science.

The Cartesian account of subjectivity (which Heidegger radically foreshortens into the theory of representation) in turn conceals the problem of secularization by masking the social and historical processes through which the subject of modernity was shaped. Indeed, to speak of the invention of subjectivity in relation to the loss of "natural qualities," as in the shorthand usage of the paragraphs above, is to conceal the social forms in which the idea of the "natural" may be contained and expressed. If the standard Cartesian and Heideggerian accounts of subjectivity are thus speculative and abstract, this is because they cover the fact that the modern subject was fashioned in response to the secularization of the world. As we shall see in the pages to follow, the emergence of a secular subject reflects the process by which the transcendent authority of religious ideals came to be replaced by a series of increasingly normative social practices, bound together by the newly formed transcendental subject of rational discourse. As a consequence of this process, the dualisms of the Judeo-Christian tradition (the divisions, for instance, between the temporal and the eternal, the here and hereafter, that had come to replace what Weber described as the original, "this-worldly" orientation of archaic religious beliefs) were refashioned into a division of the world along empirical and transcendental lines. In this way, the transformation of the world into a representation, angled and framed by the subject, became the source of a series of antinomies located within the subject-position itself. For instance, while the modern subject is committed to the denial of all preexistent essences, so too is the subject committed rationally to transcending this condition, in an attempt to provide a grounding for inner-worldly practices and norms. And while the modernizing interests of the subject may rely on the rejection of natural qualities in order to produce a world that would be open to the exercises of human freedom and control, the claims to truth of modern philosophical discourse depend on the subject's ability to transcend the world-shattering doubts that the loss of such qualities would entail. The disappearance of intelligible essences may be regarded as a positive development insofar as it allows for the infinite transformation of the world and for the openness of discursive contexts to endless reconfiguration from within. But whereas religion once provided a means to view the political and social transformations of the world either as motivated and willed by God, or as merely temporary and therefore as inconsequential, the modern subject's openness to inner-worldly transformation demands that the subject itself determine which contexts will enlarge its transformative capabilities and which are less likely to be open to transformation from within. For a thinker like Descartes, the demand to regulate the possible transformations of the world can best be met if we invoke the "transcendental" imperative of reason to render the world fully accessible to prediction and control.

As we shall see in somewhat greater detail below, the division within the subject between empirical and transcendental modes of discourse is the source of an unproductive conflict between norms or routines and transcendent ideals. It originates with the institution by the subject of a "transcendental" point of view that serves to transform transcendent ideals into rationally accessible norms. The formation of the subject thus marks a crucial moment in the process that Max Weber described in terms of the progressive rationalization of the world. To be sure, the normalization of ideals is the source of the hope that we may be able to institute modes of authority whose motives might be transparent and accessible to us all. Yet it seems that the subject of such progressive rationalization is bound to incur one of two fates: either ideals become so fully rationalized that they no longer serve to exert any critical pressure on our normative contexts and routines; or else ideals are so dissociated from rational norms that they become the mystified and inaccessible sources of "value" in their own right. In either case, the normalization of ideals or the idealization of norms leads to the closure of contexts and the reduction of opportunities for social change. Whether one interprets the process of rationalization, with Descartes, Hobbes, and Habermas, as representing a rise in the level of reason and a heightening in the rationality of social institutions, or whether one regards it, along with Horkheimer and Adorno, as the source of the increasing reification of social relationships, the result is the same—a denial of the tensions within the subject, based on the assumption that the rationalization process is universal and complete.

For Heidegger, by contrast, such questions do not arise, because the disappearance of intelligible essences does not indicate a shift in our philosophical perspective on the world or an historical transformation of the world but rather signals the moment of God's withdrawal from the world. The result is a secularization process that is seen to occur independent of the agents who suffer its effects. Thus, despite the fact that Heidegger is widely regarded as one of the preeminent critics of metaphysics and of the position of the subject, he tends to regard the invention of subjectivity and the origins of the modern age as events occurring within the history of metaphysics; in Heidegger's formulation, modernity is a metaphysical phenomenon: "metaphysics grounds an age."[5] He accepts unquestioned the priority of the philosophical foundations of modernity over its social, historical, political, or aesthetic roots, even as he proposes to call those same foundations into question. More important, he regards as untransformable the same contexts whose contingency he also asserts.[6]

Unlike the concepts of 'subjectivity' and 'representation,' however, *secularization* is a term that carries with it a recognition of the fact that the world is the sum of certain historical and social processes plus the conceptual categories in which these are articulated and framed, rather than a pure construction of the subject or the product of a metaphysical process to be described in terms of the abstract and inscrutable workings of Geist. Phrased in other terms, it can be said that the secularization thesis—that the "rational" institutions of modernity are not in fact autonomous, that the secularization process was not complete—directs us toward the tensions, for any description of modernity, between history and theory, a tension that I would suggest is carried forward in the form of a conflict between ideals and norms. On the one hand, a recognition of the world as secularized rules out the possibility of adopting any purely speculative ideals, for the concept of secularization makes sense only insofar as ideals have lost their religious aura and have come to be transformed into social and historical norms. Yet, on the other hand, secularization represents a positive development in the process by which the world has been rendered increasingly rational and real. To conceive of existence within a secularized realm thus raises the expectations that contexts may be transformable by agents and that actions will have a certain intelligibility and normativity within the world in a way that talk about the "history of Being" does not. As Hegel showed in his critique of "speculative" thought, ideals without norms lack the content that would render them relevant to the world and so cannot exert any pressure on the course of concrete events. The speculative thinker may have beliefs but will be unable to sustain convictions. Stated in more formal terms, it can be said that speculation does have a specific content and that this is the history of philosophy, whose primary aim has been a description of the shape and conditions of rationality as they obtain independent of any particular practice or institution. Habermas's critique of modernity is a speculative critique in just this sense; the theory of communicative action he proposes as an alternative to subjective reason is not the product of any existing historical institutions or practices but rather is derived from the universal principles of intelligibility and communicability themselves.

When Heidegger describes the origins of modernity as the metaphysical process by which the world became normalized as a "picture," he implicitly rejects the meaning of secularization as a social and historical term. Having deliberately removed himself from the realm of inner-worldly practices and institutions, however, he is subsequently unable to exert any critical pressure on the world. To be sure, the notion of "world" was central to the first section of *Being and Time* and to Heidegger's effort in that volume to provide a framework in which the nature of the human being (Dasein) might be made clear against a background of inner-worldly practices and beliefs. In Heidegger's "reversal" of Descartes, it is not the subject who first assumes relationships with and pre-positions itself toward the world but rather the world itself, as a collection of secular practices, that establishes the horizon within which entities can be encountered and understood. But, phrased in other terms, it can be said that the "world" absorbs and nullifies the difference between the secular subject and transcendent ideals by rejecting rather than seeking to reconstruct the relationship between norms and ideals as a function specific to the *social* world. By seeking to reveal a more fundamental and archaic "difference" than any of those the secular subject might disclose, Heidegger comes to posit the notion of a world that stands, as an "ungrounded ground," on nothingness and that asserts itself as prior to the beginnings who relate themselves cognitively and pragmatically to objects within it. Not unsurprisingly, Heidegger's understanding of "world" leads him to posit the vanishing of the social in its conventional guise and the disappearance of the subject-self ; he follows Pascal to the extent that he describes the self as that entity that, among all others, cannot possibly be "come across" in the world. And while it would seem that Heidegger's "world" might itself provide a certain content for human actions and afford the intelligibility and normativity that they demand, it turns out that the human being is so interwoven with the context-shaping processes of the world-disclosure that Heidegger can characterize its attitude only in terms of a passive releasing or "letting be" (*Gelassenheit*) toward everything within the world. As a result, Dasein is deprived of any potential for critical analysis or idealization and is led to accept as untransformable the horizons of its world. Thus, while Heidegger's contextualist notion of "world" is meant to set us free from all those (false) forms of transcendence that have historically held us hostage, in return for the revelation of a more fundamental difference, the idea of returning any positive powers to the critical self is virtually unimaginable within the framework that Heidegger provides. Indeed, Heidegger conceives of the self as a context that has the capacity of being without any content; as a result, it leaves the world in which it moves both radically contextualizes and untransformed.

To reinterpret the concepts of 'subjectivity' and 'representation' in terms of the secularization of the world is to acknowledge the fact that the modern world is itself the sum of certain historical and social transformations, rather than a pure construction of the subject. It is, furthermore, to see in these transformations a refashioning of the relationship between norms and ideals. For Heidegger, however, the death of God and the corresponding emergence of the secular subject describe the plot of the history of metaphysics as the story of the forgetfulness of Being. Even if we regard belief from a fully "disenchanted" point of view, not as an expression of the unity of fact and value, or of norm and ideal, but instead as a mode of being in adherence to objects that are given only indistinctly or not at all, then clearly belief could be seen to manifest itself as the way in which consciousness survives the fundamental forgetfulness, the ever-present absence that pervades the world. Is Heidegger's theory of the forgetting of Being then an attempt to desecularize the world? And is his interpretation of Dasein to be read as a venture toward reestablishing the grounds for belief? Perhaps the answers are to be found in the fact that Heidegger reincorporates the process of secularization, as the gradual movement of God's withdrawal from the world, within the history of metaphysics, which in modernity has grown up independent of belief. In Heidegger's account, modernity is a wholly metaphysical phenomenon ("metaphysics grounds an age"), one that can be successfully recounted from the perspective of the enlightened thinker surveying a history of forgetfulness and loss. Thus, while Habermas has not incorrectly observed that Heidegger reinterprets Hegel's confidence in the significance of the history of philosophy in terms of the unimpeachable authority of metaphysics for the modern age ("through it the philosopher masters the sources from which each epoch fatefully receives its own light"[7]), it would seem more important to say that despite the fact that Heidegger is widely regarded as one of the preeminent critics of metaphysics and of the position of the subject, his critique of subjectivity remains within the bounds of that same metaphysics. But whereas the Derridean critique of Heidegger, which makes a related point, seeks a still broader indictment of "Western metaphysics" as a whole, I would suggest that the problem of *merely* subsuming Heidegger within the history of Western metaphysics is that it blinds us to certain facts that bear more precisely on the configuration of the modern age.

This point can be fleshed out in the following terms. As a thinker who remains unwittingly faithful to the modern heritage, Heidegger does not desecularize the world or reestablish the conditions for belief. On the contrary, Heidegger is drawn toward a form of idolatry insofar as he regards as untransformable the very same contexts whose contingency he also asserts.[8] The story of the abandonment of the world by Being, or of the forgetfulness or refusal of Being, encourages Heidegger to identify the secular history of the world, and the meaning of practices within that world, not as expressions of (historical, social, temporal, or interpersonal) norms in tension with a transcendent ideal or, conversely, as ideals that have been only partially and imperfectly (because humanly) achieved, but rather as products of an abstract and inscrutable process whose historical origins are displaced from the early modern period and are subsumed within "Western metaphysics" as a whole. Already for figures like Descartes, Hobbes, and Pascal, nature was no longer intelligible in terms of the principle of the firstness of Being but rather by the potential for anxiety, isolation, and fear of disaggregated subject-selves. The historically contingent and socially specific nature of these views are nonetheless refashioned by Heidegger into the more radical claim that Being has been withdrawn. Indeed, Heidegger claims that what we as moderns have come to call "religion" is not an expression of the shifting tensions between norms and ideals at all but, rather, symptomatic of a metaphysical "disenchantment" or *Entgötterung:*

> only through that loss is the relation to the gods changed into mere 'religious experience.' When this occurs, then the gods have fled. The resultant void is compensated for by means of historiographical and psychological investigations of myth.[9]

Such criticisms are nonetheless prone to be self-validating insofar as they presume the veracity of their own conclusions in advance. And as Hegel showed in his critique of "speculative" thought, they are bound to be abstract. Since the abstract lacks the means to render its judgments relevant to the world, it cannot exert any pressure on the history of concrete events. The speculative thinker may thus have beliefs, but he will be unable to sustain convictions. Stated in more formal terms, it can be said that while speculation may have a specific content, this will be nothing other than the history of philosophy, which Heidegger here reconstructs as the history of the forgetting or refusal of Being.

Notwithstanding his indictment of "Western metaphysics," Heidegger remains within the sphere of the Enlightenment to the extent that he registers the cultural loss created by the Enlightenment's demystification of religion, together with the wish to overcome that loss through a critique of precisely those categories through which religion had been demystified—in terms of the passage just quoted, through the critique of "historiographical and psychological investigations of myth." And yet Habermas interprets Heidegger less as the epiphenomenon of an Enlightenment in the process of transcending and canceling itself than as the advocate of a staunchly anti-Enlightenment stance. Of all the critics of modernity, Habermas says:

> only Heidegger vaporized this concrete need [for religion] by ontologizing it and foundationalizing it into a Being that is withdrawn from beings. Through this shift, Heidegger makes unrecognizable not only the source

> of this need in the pathologies of an ambiguously rationalized lifeworld but also a resolutely subjectivistic art as the experiential background for the radicalized critique of reason.[10]

To be sure, Habermas resists mystification by Heidegger's talk of "forgetfulness" and "Being," but he fails to see that his position and Heidegger's are equally "disenchanted." This is because Habermas fails to recognize the contradictory nature of the secular culture of the Enlightenment and, indeed, the incompleteness of the secularization process in eradicating the authority of religion from modern culture in the West. When Habermas claims that "the deformations of a one-sidedly rationalized everyday practice" evoke the need for something like religion, Habermas formulates the problem of modernity in such a way as to allow the theory of communicative action to confirm the very process of secularization required for its justification; by positioning "communicative action" as a wholly secular alternative to the philosophy of transcendental subjectivity, he insures the further rationalization of ideals and precludes the very processes of world-transformation he hopes to foment. In principle, communicative reason is meant to regulate the multiplicity of perspectives present within discourse by invoking a standard of intelligibility that must apply to discourse as a whole. To the extent that this standard is in turn derived from within the field of discourse and not from a transcendent revelation or intuition that might break through and transform that field, the descriptive claims it has been used to support are manifestly true, but they are remarkably empty as well. Habermas seeks, for instance, to derive norms from what he describes as "the performative attitude of participants in interaction, who coordinate their plans for action by coming to an understanding about something in the world."[11] As Stanley Rosen has wryly pointed out, the proliferation of such "theories" is symptomatic of a decadent exuberance and of an overproductiveness that are themselves the products of a fully disenchanted world;[12] in the case of Habermas, I would say that the wish to theorize the obvious represents a symptomatic response to the reduction of ideals to discursive norms.

How may the stunning vacuity of Habermas's theory be explained? It is clear enough that the theory of communicative reason is thoroughly dependent on a diagnosis of the problem of modernity as one of societal rationalization and on a reading of the process of disenchantment from the perspective of the secular subject who has "overcome" the origins of its rational capacities in the "mystifications" of archaic religious beliefs. Insofar as reification and rationalization require "liberal" solutions to the problem of modernity—solutions that can in principle be normalized and made accesible to all—they must not rely on the truths of revelation, which may be transmitted only to the chosen few. Indeed, Enlightenment has frequently been seen as an inherently problematic concept precisely because of its exoteric dimension; the achievement of Enlightenment is made possible by the process of demystification and secularization but, in turn, permits the indiscriminate dissemination of light, even into those religions that might be left to intuition or the powers of revelation.[13]

To return to Heidegger, the concept of "world" delineates the horizon within which entities are manifested to the human beings who existentially choose to enter into a relationship with it. And yet Heidegger cannot at the same time deny that this "contextualist" definition of the world is dependent on a notion, traceable to figures like Milton and Pascal, of a hidden or absent God. For Milton, the withdrawal of God occurs at the archaic moment of the Fall, and it separates us forever from a truth we continuously but vainly struggle to find:

> Truth indeed came once into the world with her divine Master, and was a perfect shape, most glorious to look on; but when he ascended . . . then strait arose a wicked race of deceivers, who . . . took the virgin Truth, hewed her lovely form into a thousand pieces.[14]

For those who regard the Fall as a deprivation, rather than as a source of human empowerment, the thankless task of human history will be to restore the form of Truth, "gathering limb by limb" her fragments wherever they are found. "We have not found them all," says Milton, "nor even shall doe, till her Master's second coming." Seen from this angle, it will appear that only a reintroduction of some transcendent principle could provide for the recuperation of the form of Truth and all this would imply—the reconciliation of social differences, the reintegration of norms and ideals, and the recovery of beauty in what Schiller might describe as the "Aesthetic State." Seen from another point of view, however, the Fall may be regarded as the source of human empowerment precisely because it allows perspectives to multiply and so keeps us from settling into forms that unnecessarily blinker our perception. As Stanley Fish said of Milton:

> in order to see further we must always be in the process of unsettling and moving away from the ways of seeing that now offer themselves to us . . . The entire process is named by Milton 'knowledge in the making' and the 'constituting of human virtue,' and it will not be completed, he acknowledges, until our 'Master's second coming.' Meanwhile we must

> be ever on guard against the danger of freezing knowledge in its present form and making it into an idolatry.[15]

As Fish goes on to explain, one would expect a politics of liberal tolerance to emerge from this skeptical epistemology. Indeed, Milton himself argued that:

> if it comes to prohibiting there is not ought more likely to be prohibited than truth itself; whose first appearance to our eyes blear'd and dimm'd with prejudice and custom is more unsightly and unplausible than many errors.[16]

If this is the case, then it is incumbent upon us to make no exclusions "but to welcome each and every voice which together, if in a different tone, will form so many 'brotherly dissimilitudes' and 'neighboring differences'."[17] So seen, difference becomes the source of our connectedness with a transcendent ideal and a form of empowerment, rather than a site for the struggle of competing ideals; and the social in turn becomes not the realm in which individual differences are subsumed under the image of an overarching whole but rather the place in which the limiting condition of difference is itself perceived as the (partial) manifestation of a transcendent ideal. This, in the estimation of Fish, is why Milton's insistence "that we not pitch our tents *here,* on the campgrounds of any orthodoxy," is qualified by a future hope:

> 'till all visions will be one and indistinguishable from the vision of deity' [Milton]. Difference then is only a temporary and regrettable condition, but one, paradoxically, that we must take advantage of it we are to transcend it.[18]

And yet Milton's final aim, like Hobbes's, is to reintroduce a figure of transcendence in order to temporalize, relativize, and finally transform secular difference in the image of a transcendent ideal. Precisely because MIlton posits a secularization process that he then seeks to overcome, he remains a crucial figure in the history of subjectivity in the West.

The examples of Milton and Heidegger help reveal that the social conflict between norms and ideals visible in the process of secularization has implications for any account of modernity as both an historical and theoretical paradigm. We can, for instance, see that a purely speculative interpretation of the process of secularization is bound to deprive the subject of its powers as agent in linking the differences generated by historical contexts with trans-historical ideals. By the same token, the emergence of a purely historicist stance with regard to the rational ambitions of modernity may be seen as a reflex of conditions in which ideals have been drastically routinized and their transformative powers correspondingly reduced. In either case, the goals of the subject in establishing modes of authority that would link norms and ideals could not possibly be met; indeed, in a fully rationalized world there would be no ideals available for authority to invoke, for all ideals would have become norms. But if the "disenchantment of the world" and the invention of subjectivity are not episodes in the history of metaphysics, and if reference to such speculative processes itself represents a denial of the powers of the subject as agent in linking norms and ideals, what then might these be? Max Weber provides one response in the thesis about the "disenchantment of the world" as a process of social change. To be sure, the Weberian thesis may be read as itself a product of the secularizing logic that it proclaims to diagnose. And, as we shall see in a moment, Weber's development of an ethics of responsibility may explain the peculiar "disenchantment" with which his theoretical position is expressed. For some, however, Weber's thesis is evidence of a positivistic social science, secure both in its method and its value-neutral stance. The result would be a theory that transposes metaphysics into scientific terms, one that would allow us to rationalize the secularization process, transforming Heidegger's "withdrawal of the gods" and related statements into a series of concrete social phenomena that would better be described in practical terms—as the gradual loss of faith of communities of believers, for instance, or as the shrinking parishes in the countryside. For others, Weber's focus on the ethical implications of religious beliefs and his struggle to locate a language of conviction that, in the absence of belief, would be compatible with an ethics of responsibility toward the world, is based on a refusal of the religious principles in terms of which an ethical position might be framed.

And yet it remains equally clear that Weber cannot be so easily read as attempting to accomplish either one of these things. With regard to the first of the claims announced above—namely, that the secularization theorem represents the conclusion of a positive social science and the triumph of the position of a "detached observer" over the objects of his analysis—it may, for instance, be noted that Weber regards even the theistic content of religious belief as a reflex of normative needs and, thus, as reflecting a demand for social organization, not as a statement of theological doctrine or of a positive social fact. Indeed, even Hans Blumenberg was forced to recognize that the central thesis of *The Protestant Ethic*—that the capitalist valorization of success in business is the secularization of the "certainty of salvation" in the context of the Reformation doctrine of predestination—represented something vastly more ambitious than an "objective" sociological claim. For Blumenberg, Weber's book presented a model of the secularization theorem, for in it a specific social phenomenon was explained as the transformation of another, more original one preceding it. From Blumenberg's point of view, the problem with Weber's thesis lay neither in its sociological content—that inner-worldly asceticism may represent the de-originating transformation of an earlier saintliness—nor in his social-science stance but in the hidden threat that it, as an historiographical phenomenon, seemed to pose to the autonomy of the modern age:

> what is meant [by secularization] is not only the qualitative disappearance of features having a sacred or ecclesiastical derivation but also type of transformation of this realm of derivation itself, that is, an 'alteration in the social form of religion' in the direction of a 'cultural religious' function, and thus 'a tendency towards the inner "secularization" ' of religious institutions themselves.[19]

In Weber, as in others, this process is said to occur "in such a way that the asserted transformation of the one into the other is neither an intensification nor a clarification but rather *an alienation from its original meaning and function*."[20]

For Blumenberg, the secularization theorem places at risk modernity's crucial distinction between a language of belief, however tenuous, secondary, or inaccessible, and a normalizing language of critical Enlightenment, embodied not only in philosophy and science but also in the historiographical modes through which the story of modernity is itself told. If the process of "secularization" somehow makes de-originating figures out of all historical transpositions from one realm to the other, then any instance of the rhetoric of "secularization" would threaten to reveal the inauthenticity of the connections between a secular modern historical consciousness and the archaic ideals underlying it. In this context Blumenberg took Karl Löwith's *Meaning in History* as the paradigmatic "misreading" of modern historical narrative, whose concept of progress Löwith claimed was derivative of the eschatological patterns of Christian and Jewish salvational history.

Still more radically conceived, the secularization theorem is premised not on the persistence and authority of the past but rather on the failure of the secular to fulfill its own expectations for the complete absorption of the sacred. As in the work of Harold Bloom, modern (mis)reading never becomes a fully transumptive trope of the original;

it remains always haunted, mysteriously possessed (and thus secretly energized) by various "daemonized" forms of the precursor culture. The transformation of a failed secularization process into the dynamics of modern literary history represents for Bloom a way for literature to deflect the damaging implications that the failure of secularization would otherwise have for modern culture as a whole. But because Bloom in fact adopts a negative version of the Enlightenment's secularization theorem, he must attempt to reverse the rhetoric of secularization by taking "misreading" not just as confirming evidence of the fear that no proper work remains for us as moderns to accomplish but as an ideal for the creation of the modern self. Thus it must be said that for Bloom secularization is no longer the symptom of a pattern of misreading at all. The very notions of trope and figure and, finally, of misreading as such, demonstrate the contradictory status of ideals within modernity itself.

Seen in Weberian terms, norms have their archaic roots in charismatic forms of authority, that is, in forms that we approach with the ambivalence characteristic of terror and obedience. Indeed, the normative foundations of social life are certain to remain incomprehensible if one interprets them only from the perspective of what they achieve for the perpetuation of existing social systems or of what they are able to satisfy in the way of reason's demands.[21] Thus, for Weber, the process of "secularization" reflects a struggle to contain the disorientation effects of religious and charismatic ideals, in order to legitimate their authority for society as a whole. "By its very nature, the existence of charismatic authority is specifically unstable," Weber writes, for:

> The charismatic authority does not deduce his authority from codes and statutes . . . nor does he deduce his authority from traditional custom or feudal vows of faith, as is the case with patrimonial power. The charismatic leader gains and maintains authority solely by providing his strength in life. If he wants to be a prophet, he must perform miracles; if he wants to be a war lord, he must perform heroic deeds. Above all, however, his divine mission must "prove" itself in that those who faithfully surrender to him must fare well. If they do not fare well, he is obviously not the master sent by the gods.[22]

Read against his background, secularization is the process by which the instability inherent in the charismatic authority of prophets and priests can be stabilized and contained. Secularization is thus a social function that is meant to account for the authority of collective practices in normalizing the forces of ideals; and while its contradictory effects may be "rationalized" in the form of a developmental history, the process of "secularization" does not necessarily make reference either to the content of those practices or to the historical schema according to which changes from the sacred to the secular might be assumed to take place. For instance, the presence of a body of theological doctrine, along with the institutional organization of the medieval monastery, are for Weber evidence of an attempt to transform other worldly ideals into a series of inner-worldly goals. In Weber's view:

> the monk is the first human being who lives rationally, who works methodically and by rational means toward a goal, namely the future of life. Only for him did the clock strike, only for him were the hours of the day divided."[23]

Conversely, one of the paradoxes of Weber's view is that the rational forms of modern asceticism brought with them not a decrease but a redoubled intensity of the religious dimension of life. If we understand the large-scale effect of secularization in terms of the attempt to transform ideals into norms, then it may be possible to understand the paradoxical fact that the inner-worldly asceticism diagnosed as crucial to the "Protestant spirit" brought a dramatic *enlargement* of the space over which religion could have control. But this was a transformed concept of religion, to say the least. Since a primary mechanism for the process of rationalization was the subjectification of ideals as moral and rational norms, the space over which religion could have force was in principle infinite, since it was identical to the "inward" space of conscience itself. The result, which makes the success of a poem like *Paradise Lost* directly dependent on its effects in the reader's conscience, was a condition not unlike the one that Milton describes in *The Christian Doctrine* as "Christian Liberty," namely, a state in which we are (transcendentally) free but bound to give ourselves over to a series of stringent internal rules:

> So far from a less degree of perfection being exacted from Christians, it is expected of them that they should be more perfect than those who were under the law . . . The only difference is that Moses imposed the letter, or external law, even on those who are not willing to receive it; whereas Christ writes of the inward law God by his Spirit on the hearts of his followers, and leads them as willing followers.[24]

In Weber's terms, Protestantism is a concealed and ultimately unsuccessful expression of the need to relocate and "normalize" a series of transcendent ideals within the framework of modern secular life. To regard modernity as a secularized realm is not on this account to contemplate the eventual recovery of what is lost or hidden within it, for that recovery would remain impossible until the history of secularization is reversed and the subject redeemed by our "Master's second coming." Instead, Weber remits us to a series of ethical stances whose validity asks to be appraised internally in terms of the ways in which these attempt to balance a series of competing needs within a context in which religion has become, in Hegel's terms, "positive," and the world has become autonomous and abstract. In view of the world's autonomy, the subject must answer the question of what should determine an ethical stance—science, which is oriented toward an action's outcome, or belief, which is concerned with an act's intrinsic worth. These twin prospects, which despite their incompatibility are conjoined within the subject of the modern age, represent the possibilities that Lukács described in *The Theory of the Novel* as available to the subject—to "normative man," who has achieved "freedom in his relationship to God."[25] Whereas the ethic of responsibility adjusts to the secularizing logic of modernity and to its effects upon the world, the ethic of conviction rejects this process and remains committed to the principle of an act's intrinsic worth. And whereas the ethic of responsibility, in an effort to transform the value-neutrality of the subject into value-pluralism for society as a whole, seeks to generalize the principle of inner freedom as the freedom of conscience for all, the ethic of conviction must remain quixotically committed to the irrationality of society and the world.[26]

Weber's interest in the language of conviction—however "disenchanted" this language may itself have become—was substantiated by a desire to preserve the authoritative function that religion once supplied for social life. The secularized subject is nonetheless caught up in the oppositions of transcendental freedom and inner constraint, of capital accumulation and ascetic self-denial, of world adjustment and world flight. These divisions in turn lead Weber to seek in the ethic of responsibility an appropriate response to the conditions of existence in a disenchanted world. Weber's work may be seen as a product of the very process he was attempting to diagnose, to the extent that his attempt to reconcile conviction and responsibility in essays like "Politics as a Vocation" and "Science as a Vocation" provides evidence of the instability of the rationalization process itself. In Weber, the relationship between belief and science mirrors the conflict among the value-spheres as it is found in the disenchanted world. As one of Weber's best critics, Wolfgang Schluchter, explains:

> In the disenchanted world you must reckon not only with the dualism between value and reality, but also with a value of pluralism, with the

> fact that a person can find different 'gods' and be obedient to them. The ethic of responsibility can effect a reconciliation neither among the various value positions and reality nor among the different values themselves. It can only establish the preconditions for facing up to and for arranging a rational confrontation.[27]

Weber failed to justify the responsibility of value-freedom as that position most appropriate to the conditions of a disenchanted world and he failed likewise to reestablish a language of belief. For Weber, there is no possibility of a recuperative or redemptive critique of religion that would be compatible with the normative social science stance and, conversely, no normative science able to reproduce in us the convictions of religious ideals. Weber may be thus cited as an example of someone who holds convictions that no longer flow from beliefs. In this same sense, his ethical pronouncements read like the after-effects of convictions; they serve nonetheless to help us recall what it might be like to behave in concert with belief.

9

Modernity and the Misrepresentation of Representation

Stephen David Ross

One way to read *Les mots et les choses*—translated more felicitously for our purposes here as *The Order of Things*—is as an epic history of modernity whose heroine is language, engaged in a great voyage, beset by dangers on all sides, especially by villains who seek to regulate her plenitude and excess. Among these villains is classical—that is, modern—representation. Foucault follows that theme in Heidegger in which *alētheia's* excess is contrasted with the orderliness of representation.

> Philosophy is metaphysics. Metaphysics thinks beings as a whole—the world, man, God—with respect to Being, with respect to the belonging together of beings in Being. Metaphysics thinks beings as being in the manner of representational thinking which give reasons.[1]
>
> What characterizes metaphysical thinking which grounds the ground for beings is the fact that metaphysical thinking, starting from what is present, represents it in its presence and thus exhibits it as grounded by its ground.[2]
>
> . . . we must acknowledge the fact that *alētheia,* unconcealment in the sense of the opening of presence, was originally experienced only as *orthotēs,* as the correctness of representations and statements.[3]

Heidegger, following Nietzsche, takes this dominance of the correctness of representation to begin with the Greeks. Foucault regards it instead as typical of the Enlightenment:

> So signs are now set free from that teeming world throughout which the Renaissance had distributed them. They are lodged henceforth within the confines of representation, in the interstices of ideas, in that narrow space in which they interact with themselves in a perpetual state of decomposition and recomposition.[4]

This story culminates in the famous passages at the end of *The Order of Things* in which the human sciences constitute themselves in the shadow of representation, thereby also constituting the figure of "Man":

> . . . man for the human sciences is not that living being with a very particular form (a somewhat special physiology and an almost unique autonomy); he is that living being who, from within the life to which he entirely belongs and by which he is traversed in his whole being, constitutes representations by means of which he lives, and on the basis of which he possesses that strange capacity of being able to represent to himself precisely that life.[5]
>
> The object of the human sciences is not language (though it is spoken by men alone); it is that being which, from the interior of the language by which he is surrounded, represents to himself, by speaking, the sense of the words or propositions he utters, and finally provides himself with a representation of language itself.[6]

The close of this epoch, ruled by the human sciences, is the end of both "Man" and the confinement of language within its representation:

> Man had been a figure occurring between two modes of language; or, rather, he was constituted only when language, having been situated within representation and, as it were, dissolved in it, freed itself from that situation at the cost of its own fragmentation: man composed his own figure in the interstices of that fragmented language.[7]

There is another way to read *The Order of Things,* another theme within its epic movement. The confinement of language within classical representation is the regulation of the excess of language by a certain view of its truth: correctness, correspondence, and re-presentation. The figure of "Literature" appears as the excess of language within classical representation.[8] Although Foucault does not pursue its implications, this framing of excess is a continuation of what Socrates calls the "ancient quarrel between philosophy and poetry."[9] I would insist that Plato's own mimetic forms, the dialogues and storytelling, speak against—or, at least, speak in a divided way about—the superiority of propositional truth. For the voice in which the lyric poets may justly speak, when they make their case to return to the polis, is *poiētic* rather than propositional.[10] Socrates himself utilizes a *poiētic* voice only seven pages later, in the myth of Er.

The quarrel between philosophy and poetry passes in *The Order of Things* into a struggle between representation and language: order and disorder. Yet just as *mimēsis* appears in a more divided form in Plato then the quarrel can represent, the relationship between representation and language appears both in Foucault and throughout modernity as far more divided than the story told above. With the demise of the classical representation of representation, representation reappears, in *The Order of Things,* in the form of excess and transgression. It reappears in the fragmented, divided form that it has always worn, however mutely and obscurely.

I will return to *The Order of Things* to pursue this point. But I wish to foreshadow it first by pointing out that representation has seldom been represented in quite so unbroken a way as Heidegger frequently suggests and that metaphysics has also been far more divided than its representation as ontotheology. The voice of Enlightenment modernity I will consider is that of Hobbes, for whom representation is fundamentally political, while its representation is transgression.[11]

"Of Persons, Authors, and Things Personated," chapter 16, in *Leviathan,* marks the end of part 1, "Of Man," and precedes part 2, "Of Commonwealth." It is where Hobbes makes his transition from human beings to politics. He discusses sovereignty and power entirely in terms of representation:

> A person is he whose words and action are considered either as his own or as representing the words or actions of another man, or of any other thing, to whom they are attributed, whether truly or by fiction.[12]

Many of the ideas here would repay close examination, especially ownership, attribution, and the representation by one's actions of a thing rather than another person. The fundamental notions for our purposes, however, are those of an artificial person and of representation by fiction:

> When they are considered as his own, then is he called a *natural person;* and when they are considered as representing the words and actions of another, then he is a *feigned* or *artificial person.*[13]

The idea of a person involves action as representation, including misrepresentation as well as reproduction. Otherness belongs to the ideas of both representation and being a person, while the latter is inseparable from representation: that is, divided by it. There is no fundamental unity to the idea of person, not even that embodied in the idea of sovereignty.

Representation in Hobbes is inseparable from fiction as well as truth, artifice as well as nature. The circularity of representation opens a space for misrepresentation and untruth, for pretense, fraud, and deceit, while the idea of a person occupies that fraudulent, fragmentary space, rests profoundly on misrepresentation and deception. The idea of action at the center of Hobbes's theory of practice is that of the stage: representation as performance, deception, illusion. Within the idea of a person lies the idea of representation as misrepresentation, of performance behind a mask, in disguise. What a person does is to "personate" or represent a person, himself or another, where personation is impersonation:

> The word *person* is Latin . . . which signifies the *face,* as *persona* in Latin signifies the *disguise,* or *outward appearance* of a man, counterfeited on the stage; and sometimes more particularly that part of it which disguises the face, as a mask or vizard . . . So that a *person* is the same that an *actor* is, both on the stage and in common conversation; and to *personate* is to *act,* or *represent* himself, or another.[14]

The idea of a person is one of portrayal behind a mask because personation is representation as misrepresentation. To represent is to perform on the stage, where every movement suggests deceit, including both self-representation and self-deception. The truth of performance is the truth of deception. *Poiēsis* is its own counterfeit.[15]

This dividedness of representation is the site on which Hobbes defines his view of sovereignty: the sovereign is the representative of the people, whether they agree or not, whether or not he consults them or is concerned with their desires. He exercises their authority. At the center of the discussion is the notion of authority and how it can be transferred as well as implemented, in both cases by (mis)representation. The question of power in collective human life is a question of representative authority, of how a person or an institution can stand for—act and speak for—another person or thing. This absent presence is the heart of both representation and public life. Behind the idea of politics lies the dividedness of the powers and representations that constitute a public. The movement from the state of nature to a commonwealth in Hobbes is from natural powers without representation to powers embodied in representation: performance and portrayal, personation and impersonation, truth inseparable from its counterfeit—*poiēsis.*

In Hobbes's extraordinary analysis, authority is unintelligible apart from the identity of representation and misrepresentation. We can discern a similar view in Machiavelli, though falling short of Hobbes's:

> When it happens that some one does something extraordinary, either good or evil, in civil life, he must find such means of rewarding or punishing him which will be much talked about. And above all a prince must endeavour in every action to obtain fame for being great and excellent.[16]

What is important—essential to civil life—is being talked about, obtaining fame: that is, representations of greatness and excellence. The public life is one of representation: representation and power are inseparable.

A similar view of the public is found in Arendt:

> The term "public" signifies two closely interrelated but not altogether identical phenomena:
>
> It means, first, that everything that appears in public can be seen and heard by everybody and has the widest possible publicity. For us, appearance—something that is being seen and heard by others as well as by ourselves—constitutes reality.[17]

> Second, the term "public" signifies the world itself, insofar as it is common to all of us and distinguished from our privately owned place in it. This world, however, is not identical with the earth or with nature, as the limited space for the movement of men and the general condition of organic life. It is related, rather, to the human artifact, the fabrication of human hands, as well as to affairs which go on among those who inhabit the man-made world together. To live together in the world means essentially that a world of things is between those who have it in common, as a table is located between those who sit around it; the world, like every in-between, relates and separates men at the same time.[18]

The public world is constituted by appearance: by representation *as* a public, by the making of artifacts, by fabrication. Being seen and being heard—in a public, human space constituted by fabrication—transpire as representation. Showing remarkable prescience, Arendt defines this representational public as an "in-between," at once separating and relating, same and other.

> Under the conditions of a common world, reality is not guaranteed primarily by the "common nature" of all men who constitute it, but rather by the fact that, differences of position and the resulting variety of perspectives notwithstanding, everybody is always concerned with the same object . . . The end of the common world has come when it is seen only under one aspect and is permitted to present itself in only one perspective.[19]

The "same order" is a public representation defined by its differences. The presence of "one" perspective destroys it. A common public, it is fabricated as an artifact and shared as difference. Arendt has a powerful sense of what "commonality" can mean in relation to otherness, in virtue of representation and definitive of sovereignty. What she does not do as profoundly as Hobbes is to emphasize the fictiveness of representation and thus the inseparability of the misrepresentative side of public life. Hobbes's view that authority is a fictitious creature surpasses both Machiavelli's and Arendt's.

The dividedness of personal authority pertains to representation "itself," not just to words and deeds. Representation inhabits the space where authority is constituted and divides that space in ways that resist any undivided presence. Once words are words, the authority that surrounds them becomes institutional, historical, dispersed. Representation is public as well as private. It is always both public and private, reciprocally. One of the few ways in which Arendt's powerful sense of the public quality of representation falls short is that she defines the public exclusively in relation to representation and appearance, leaving the realm of the private to fall outside representation:

> To live an entirely private life means above all to be deprived of things essential to a truly human life: to be deprived of the reality that comes from being seen and heard by others, to be deprived of an 'objective' relationship with them that comes from being related to and separated from them through the intermediary of a common world of things, to be deprived of the possibility of achieving something more permanent than life itself.[20]

The private realm falls away from representation, although the shelter it requires from the harsh glare of public representation requires another (mis)representation. Arendt maintains a Kantian distinction between the "objective" and "subjective" that passes into her view of public and private, a distinction overthrown when representation circles back upon itself. In the public nature of words and acts, authority ceases to belong exclusively to subjects and is located at once everywhere and nowhere. A public space is always representational in the doubly divided sense of meaning and authority. In a public world with an unknown future, no one can own his words; no one can own his deeds. Representation marks this negativity positively.

We may return to Foucault. Where modernity in Hobbes is defined by calculating reason but belied by the misrepresentations in representation, modernity in Foucault, after Kant, is defined by the unthought. The human sciences, even within modernity, seek to regulate the unthought within their empirico-transcendental circularity.

The circle here is an aporia. The aporia of representation is what *The Order of Things* defines historically. It defines it as misrepresentation—more precisely, it defines the space in which representation misrepresents itself.

> Order is, at one and the same time, that which is given in things as their inner law, the hidden network that determines the way they confront one another, and also that which has no existence except in the grid created by a glance, an examination, a language; and it is only in the blank spaces of this grid that order manifests itself in depth as though already there, waiting in silence for the moment of its expression.[21]

The space of representation, understood transgressively, is where sign and symbol, word and thing, are the same yet other, where the great domination of the same faces itself at the limit. The inescapable prepositions that follow representation—"of," "by," "through," and "for"—haunt every representation, especially "in" (another preposition) the representation of representation. In this space of representation folding back onto representation there lies a middle region between ordered and known truth, in which representation as order exceeds itself.

> Thus, between the already "encoded" eye and reflexive knowledge there is a middle region which liberates order itself . . . This middle region, then, in so far as it makes manifest the modes of being of order, can be posited as the most fundamental of all: anterior to words, perceptions, and gestures . . . Thus, in every culture, between the use of what one might call the ordering codes and reflections upon order itself, there is the pure experience of order and of its modes of being.[22]

The middle region is the in-between where limit and transgression are to be found. This middle region "liberates order *itself*." It is *"most fundamental"* and is where we find the possibility of a "*pure* experience of order and of its modes of being" (my emphases). These primacies and purifications are aporias within representation and order, where disorder is indistinguishable from order, where representation is identical with misrepresentation.

Order both belongs to things as their inner law and exists "only" in representation. Representation both presupposes order and comprises it. Representation and order are the same and different. At the point at which they meet, order is disorder as representation is misrepresentation. In this play of otherness within the same lies the transgression of their limits. In the invisibilities that surround representation lie the "only" representation we may find of "pure" representation: transgression.[23]

> [In *Las Meninas*] representation undertakes to represent itself here in all its elements, with its images, the eyes to which it is offered, the faces it makes visible, the gestures that call it into being. But there, in the midst of this dispersion which it is simultaneously grouping together and spreading out before us, indicated compellingly from every side, is an essential void: the necessary disappearance of that which is its foundation—of the person it resembles and the person in whose eyes it is only a resemblance. This very subject—which is the same—has been elided. And representation, freed finally from the relation that was impeding it, can offer itself as representation in its pure form.[24]

This "pure" representation is representation "itself," freed from its classical bonds to both its subject and object, freed to disrupt and violate itself. Representation can represent itself "only" by representing what exceeds it. The "pure" form of representation must be heard in Foucault, not as the origin of representation, but as transgression, at the limit, where representation represents itself by (mis)representing its limits, where the representation of limitation is the same as the limitation of representation—the same in virtue of their difference.[25]

The conjunction of representation with itself as both speaking for and speaking of and by has been criticized by Gayatri Spivak, who notes that in German the distinction is marked by two different words, *vertreten* and *darstellen*.[26] Her critique is that to confuse speaking for and speaking about is to reinstate the Subject (European and male). In Deleuze, for example, she claims:

> Two senses of representation are being run together: representation as 'speaking for,' as in politics, and representation as 're-presentation,' as in art or philosophy.[27]
>
> In the guise of a post-Marxist description of the scene of power, we thus encounter a much older debate: between representation or rhetoric as tropology and as persuasion. *Darstellen* belongs to the first constellation, *vertreten*—with stronger connotations of substitution—to the second. Again, they are related, but running them together, especially in order to say that beyond both is where oppressed subjects speak, act, and know *for themselves,* leads to an essentialist, utopian politics.[28]

Spivak associates the sites of "purity" in Foucault—"pure" madness, "pure" representation, order "itself"—with the pure presence of an oppressed subject. Political praxis is overwhelmed by too much talk of talk. Where the subaltern is third world and female, there is no point from which she can speak *for herself.* To think there is is to name an undivided Other which, by a reverse movement, reinstates the European Subject. Rather, Spivak suggests, we may consider the site of oppression to call forth unrelenting critique and that the European's task is neither to speak *for* the other nor to *let* the other speak but to speak for himself from within the dividedness of his representations. The masculine pronouns are explicit.

That the white, male, middle-class philosopher may speak "only" from within a divided representation of his representational standpoint does not belie its limits or transgressions. The representation of representation within oppression and privilege may represent—"know"—itself as divided, even while reinstating privilege, which is itself divided. This divided representation disrupts the privilege of one standpoint over another, disrupts representation through its own misrepresentations. To see the "of" in representation "only" as a conjunction of speaking for and speaking about in which oppressed people are oppressed once more is to represent it as a synthesis blind to its own misrepresentations. The passages from Hobbes indicate that the play between power and representation can shatter the relationship in classical representation between signifier and signified as the duplicity of the latter can shatter the naming of privilege within the authority of political representation. The single word *representation* marks not a unitary presence but a fragmented site of disruption. Here misrepresentation belongs to representation as untruth belongs to truth.

The story told in *The Order of Things* is the epic voyage of language from its dispersion throughout the world's mirrors to imprisonment within the confines of modern discourse, then to freedom in a new dispersion. Language is the site at which excess meets finitude—not just the finitude of death, though surely enfolded among its transgressions, but the finitude that knows itself to be transgression.

> Perhaps there exists in speech an essential affinity between death, endless striving, and the self-representation of language. Perhaps the figure of a mirror to infinity erected against the black wall of death is fundamental for any language from the moment it determines to leave a trace of its passage.[29]

The possibility we have considered is that the transgression of language, in which it both enfolds and disrupts itself, extends to representation as well as to power and desire. Here, as language exceeds representation, representation exceeds itself. For if the vast play of being that is its appearance and disappearance appears "only" in language, are we not in danger of another centering in which langage controls its own profusion?

> The whole curiosity of our thought now resides in the question: What is language, how can we find a way round it in order to make it appear in itself, in all its plenitude?[30]

> The dispersion of language is linked, in fact, in a fundamental way, with the archeological event we may designate as the disappearance of Discourse. To discover the vast play of language contained once more within a single space might be just as decisive a leap towards a wholly new form of thought as to draw to a close a mode of knowing constituted during the previous century.[31]

Perhaps the modernity whose close is represented in the pages of Foucault as the vast play of language, and in Derrida as the play of signs, or "arche-writing," becomes ultramodernity—others call it "postmodernity"—when the movement whereby language recaptures its enigmatic liberty is seen to be a figure that belongs to representation, mirrored both in its repetitions and departures, and in the nonspaces of the differences between language and representation, desire and representation, and representation and power. What Foucault says about language's reciprocity is true about representation, but also about power, desire, history, and truth:

> It is possible that in every work language is superimposed upon itself in a secret verticality, where the double is exactly the same as the thin space between . . . A work of language is the body of language crossed by death in order to open this infinite space where doubles reverberate.[32]

Modernity is the moment where doubling is excess. Ultramodernity is the moment where doubling doubles back to exceed itself. In this circle of circles, in their transgressions, representation is caught up both as prisoner and as sovereign. We may recall, within the journey of language to itself, the figure that represents representation:

> let us, if we may, look for the previously existing law of that interplay in the painting of *Las Meninas,* in which representation is represented at every point . . . All the interior lines of the painting, and above all those that come from the central reflection, point towards the very thing that is represented, but absent.[33]

This absent subject/object, the sovereign represented by absence—nonrepresentation but also misrepresentation—is, of course, "Man": "a quite recent creature, which the demiurge of knowledge fabricated with its own hands less than two hundred years ago."[34] "Man" is the creature fabricated in the representation of representation, manifesting sovereignty. The power that fabricates "Man" is the power that, turned back on itself, destroys him. The figure here is Nietzsche's:

> humanity . . . proceeds from domination to domination . . . [allowing] violence to be inflicted on violence and the resurgence of new forces that are sufficiently strong to dominate those in power.[35]

Power is transgression "only" where it includes resistance within itself, against itself, where domination does violence to domination, where violence turns back on violence, but also, within the rule of representation and "Man," where sovereignty turns back on itself, establishing as sovereign in place of representation, to be succeeded by a shift of power in which representation reestablishes sovereignty in a different form:

> man appears in his ambiguous position as an object of knowledge and as a subject that knows: enslaved sovereign, observed spectator, he appears in the place belonging to the king, which was assigned to him in advance by *Las Meninas,* but from which his real presence has for so long been excluded.[36]

In this figure of the captive sovereign lies the reciprocity of domination and violence that ultramodern representation needs to disrupt itself. In *Las Meninas,* "Man" appears in a form of representation that is not language and that exceeds language. Similarly, the visibility whereby "Men" are disciplined, made to appear in their criminality, is a bodily representation that also exceeds language. Representation exceeds language as language exceeds representation, as both are exceeded by being and exceed being, as power and desire exceed each other and both language and representation, as each exceeds itself, as they all exceed the body and are exceeded by it. All these excesses are at the limit, where excess is transgression. The most prominent form of such transgression is where power and representation dismantle themselves, where the dispossessed can neither represent themselves nor escape representation by others.

By any name, be it *mimēsis,* judgment, knowledge, or meaning, representation is in the middle, between truth and being, knowledge and experience, rulers and ruled, circling back upon itself and the others. This midpoint, despite every representation of representation as repetition, is at the limit, where representation is transgression. Turning back on itself, representation both accommodates and disrupts itself, is both patient with its achievements and violent toward them. In this circularity, representation tears itself asunder in a violence for which transgression is both acquiescence and truth. Within philosophy, transgression is aporia. Within practice, it is sacrifice, the inescapability of destruction. Within art, it is itself. Art *is* transgression, except that in this identity we efface the transgressiveness of both practice and truth, lose both failure and untruth: above all, we lose misrepresentation.

In his travels, Gulliver comes to the island of Lagado, where it is proposed in the Academy to stop using words for things, with all their confusions, and carry things themselves about: things both being and representing things. The excess of words over things passes into the excess of things over themselves. The story appears to suggest that such excess, the other at the limit, arrives with language. The trouble is with the idea of the arrival of language, as if it had an origin. Rather, while things do not always mark themselves, they cannot simply "be" themselves, without excess. The truth is that being is its own excess and transgression. This truth is itself at the limit, and exceeds itself in its untruth. An ultramodern, local metaphysics may be situated at this limit-point of excess, where not only language, representation, and untruth, but also being and metaphysics, are themselves at their limit, exceeded by the excesses that define and divide them. In such transgression, reality is inseparable from unreality, truth from untruth, representation from misrepresentation. This inseparability is where pararepresentation—simulation—meets ultrareality. Metaphysics here is ultrametaphysics: another site of transgression.

The middle region where representation is transgression is not a region of truth "alone," even with untruth; falls within praxis and art. The middle region is between truth and untruth but also between rulers and ruled, rules and caprice, necessity and freedom. All ideas of sovereignty and power, governance and rule, occupy the midpoint where representation is represented, since no power can be effective without implementation, where the latter is representation. We speak of unrepresentative government, as if "only" certain forms of governance were representative, as if "only" certain forms of judgment were representation. Where these *onlys* define the terrain of thought, they move away from the limit. Where these *onlys* define the terrain of practice, they place practice far from transgression, defining it by rule, under the same. The capacity of representation to circle back to destroy itself is where the same finds itself divided by an other that at once defines, defies, and defiles it. This defilement of the same within is both oppression and the challenge posed to it by the fragmentation within the representation of representation. The representation of representation, both sovereign and significant, is its misrepresentation. The challenge ultramodernity poses to modernity is to represent the misrepresentation within representation, an inexhaustible task, represented within the global economy as the resistance of the unspoken other who can neither speak nor be spoken for, but who exists as a "mis-" within every representation.

10

Narrative, Dialectic, and Irony in Jameson and White

Candace D. Lang

It is a commonplace to affirm that both narrative and dialectic were prime targets for post-'68 French critical theory, which identified them as the ideological tools of a repressive political authority. Dialectical thinking was condemned for its ruthless sublation of all differences; narrative was stigmatized as dialectic's accomplice, the means by which authority represents itself to its subjects in a story whose internal coherence gives it all the apparent inevitability of natural causality, at the same time writing those subjects into that story so as to make their position in the social hierarchy seem as natural and inevitable as the logic governing the narrative. This critique of what Lyotard termed the "master-narratives" of legitimation (foremost among them the Marxist narrative of world history, born of Hegelian dialectics) entailed the simultaneous rejection of traditional "realist" (i.e., linear, continuous) historiography and fiction in favor of the fragmented, discontinuous forms adopted by the *Annales* historians or the New Novelists.

Also incriminated was the concept of irony, equated by philosophers with the self-reflective moment of negation in the Hegelian dialectic and thus, ultimately, with the all-comprehensive, synthesizing authority of an "absolute spirit"–type observer who judges history from the outside. In literature, irony was identified as a trait shared by the omniscient narrator, the self-reflective romantic (an incarnation of Hegel's "beautiful soul"), and other descendants of the autonomous self-knowing, self-observing Cartesian subject, whose disappearance from the modern novel (already well under way before the sixties) marked the demise of the traditional "full" character.

This is the background against which I will be considering Fredric Jameson's and Hayden White's relative positions on the status of narrative, dialectic, and irony. For both, narrative is inherently dialectical in that it imposes a unity and a finality on an apparent chaos of elements. Both also affirm that history is accessible only in textual form, although for neither does this constitute a denial of history's reality. Yet in Jameson, those are the presuppositions of an impassioned defense of narrative and dialectic, whereas for White, they are grounds for a questioning of narrative's hegemony in historiography and fiction.

Thus Jameson approves of White's critique of the naive empiricism of nineteenth-century historiographers in the latter's *Metahistory*, which argues that each historian's interpretation of the relationships among events corresponds to the internal structure of one of the four major tropes—metaphor, metonymy, synecdoche, and irony—and that none can be said to constitute a more accurate representation of reality as it "really" was. Jameson concludes, however, that White's essentially synchronic tropological readings repudiate "genuinely historical [read dialectical] thinking," and that diachrony, like any repressed, returns in another form—this time as cyclical or mythical thinking.[1] The four tropes correspond to moments of a history of histories in which the Enlightenment's ironic skepticism about the adequacy of historical representation is followed by periods of (more or less naive) metaphoric, metonymic, and synecdochic historiography, only to return as a renewed metahistorical self-awareness, the still-prevalent ironic perception (shared by White) of the figural nature of all historical writing. While recognizing the role of irony as the negation leading to *Aufhebung* in authentic dialectical thinking, Jameson holds that White's ironic moment is not dialectical and can only usher in another metaphorical stage and so on. Now, cyclical thinking is anathema to Jameson because it makes the human subject the hapless victim of Necessity or contingency. The Marxist master narrative, on the other hand, is a genuine dialectic moving toward a positive conclusion, because it frees the subject by making him or her an active agent in history with the ability to bring about in the future the fulfillment of the promise of the past (more about *how* later). According to Jameson, then, the decline of narrative is the sign of a sick, decadent creature.

White's own conception of where his thinking will lead us next is not entirely clear. He does condemn his own ironic perspective (and that of contemporary historiography in general) as a form of radical skepticism that makes all political action absurd but maintains that "the recognition of this Ironic perspective provides the grounds of a transcendence of it." Ironically, he suggests that beyond irony lies the freedom for historians and philosophers of history to narrate "in whatever modality of consciousness is most consistent with their own moral and aesthetic aspirations"[2]—a claim that might, after all, be construed as a confirmation of Jameson's analysis.

That such is not the case, however, is made quite clear by White's essay on Jameson's *The Political Unconscious*,[3] in which he criticizes Jameson's allegiance to narrative and responds to his critique of *Metahistory*. After remarking that there is a repressed tropology in Jameson, he goes on, in a passage that has a distinct French post-Marxist ring, to emphasize the repressive aspect of the Marxist master narrative:

> The crucial problem from the perspective of political struggle is not whose story is the best or truest but who has the power to make his story stick as the one that others will choose to live by or in. It may well be that the decline of narrative reflects less a condition of decadence than sickness unto death with the stories that representatives of official culture are always invoking to justify the sacrifices and sufferings of the citizenry.[4]

He further suggests in his conclusion that the "death of 'History,' politics, and narrative" and the advent of

> modernism in the arts may be less a regression to a pseudo-mythic condition of consciousness than an impulse to get beyond the myth-history distinction, which has served as the theoretical basis for politics that has outlived its usefulness.[5]

We must return to the French arena for a more thorough elaboration of the kind of post-ironic phase White seems to be trying unsuccessfully to imagine. In the sixties, Gilles Deleuze drew a distinction between the tired and timeworn self-reflective negativity of irony and an affirmative Nietzschean humor that manifested itself in the nondialectical thinking and nonnarrative writing characteristic of postmodernity (still called "modernity" in those days).[6] Jean-François Lyotard appropriated the term as a label for the kind of post-Marxist rhetorical strategy and political theory he was seeking to work out in his writings.

In *Au juste* (*Just Gaming*),[7] published in French in 1979, or two years before Jameson's *Political Unconscious* (six years after *Metahistory*), Lyotard and Jean-Loup Thébaud seek through dialogue to elaborate a humorous notion of justice—that is, to understand how and why we can act justly in a postmodern[8] context defined precisely by the absence of all criteria for action. In other words, they are asking what kind of politics is possible when there are no ontological grounds for any prescriptions, given that "all politics implies the prescription of doing something . . . that will transform reality."[9] The principle notions or strategies mobilized in the dialogue are narrative and dialectics—but not, in principle, of the Jamesonian ilk.

The crux of the problem, and of Lyotard's argument, is that one cannot derive an *ought* or prescriptive statement, from an *is*, or denotative, descriptive statement.[10] Western political tradition has relied on the belief that a denotative, or narrative, statement can logically imply certain prescriptions—that is, on the Platonic notion that a definition of justice can provide a theoretical model on the basis of which to act in order to produce a just society. Hence, we have clung to the possibility of a totalizing theory or grand narrative of legitimation, which can provide a stable ground for political action. However, the recognition that the descriptive and prescriptive are two different language games with no relation of logical implication results in our being obliged to judge without (absolute) criteria—or, rather, to invent our own criteria, or little nonauthoritative legitimating narratives, on a purely local and pragmatic basis.

In this respect, the postmodern condition is analogous to the pagan polytheistic world of Greek mythology, populated by gods whose laws are no more stable than their mutable selves and by mortals who are constantly trying to match wits with these capricious incarnations of fate by, as it were, manipulating the narratives into which the gods have written humans.[11] This situation is reflected in the texts of certain Greek Sophists and rhetoricians, for whom all prescriptions are subject to discussion,[12] which, for them, means to rhetorical confrontations in which there is no pretense of appeal to ontological grounds, so that it is always the cleverest or most convincing argument, not the rightest or truest, that prevails. This kind of agonistic exchange, leading to a judgment founded on opinion alone, is a "pagan" (or "good," for Lyotard) dialectics, one that does not produce models or truth but merely "allows the judge to judge case by case."[13] The Hegelian dialectic is to be rejected because it legitimates repressive political power by not respecting the multiplicity of orders of discourse but hierarchizing them and ultimately reducing them all to ontology, which is in fact but one language game among others.

To clarify the still-vague notion of just how we do judge on a case-by-case basis, Lyotard summons the Sophists and Kant to form a curious alliance based on their shared belief that "there is no reason of history" and no knowledge in matters of ethics or politics. These assumptions underlie what Lyotard sees as the theoretical predicament of the contemporary European intelligentsia:

> One cannot put oneself in a position of holding a discourse on the society; there are contingencies; the social web is made up of a multitude of en-

> counters between interlocutors caught up in different pragmatics . . . it is not true that a political decision can be derived from a reason of history. That is what the debacle of the Marxist narrative . . . means specifically.[14]

Sophistic thought has the merit of replacing truth by opinion, so that the just is simply what has always been agreed upon as such; in a word, the verisimilar (*vraisemblable*, sometimes translated as "plausible"). The drawback to this conventionalism is that it could be used to justify as unacceptable a politics as that of Nazism. So Lyotard brings in the Kantian Idea, defined as a "reflective use of judgment . . . , a maximization of concepts outside of any knowledge of reality,"[15] in order to give Sophist conventionalism a creative dimension, to free it from its total dependence on the past, or tradition, by introducing the possibility of foreseeing the use to which it will be put in the future.[16] This Kantian version of Sophistry is exemplified in Aristotle's account of the rhetorician Corax's defense of a physically strong client accused of battering a weak person. When the victim's lawyer argued on the grounds of verisimilitude (received opinion) that it was obvious that the stronger had beaten the weaker, Corax responded with the claim that his client foresaw that he would be inculpated by his great strength, and precisely for that reason did *not* beat the weak man. Thus the Sophist maximized not the concept but opinion, in fact effecting in it a reversal, or negative logical transformation such that the formerly implausible is dialectically rendered plausible in a conceivable future. So functions the dialectics of opinion when implemented by the Idea.

There remains the problem that Kant's Idea—the finality that regulates judgment—is that of a totality of reasonable beings,[17] an Idea unacceptable in a postmodern context; for it we must substitute a notion of multiplicity, plurality, or divergence. This leads to Lyotard's conclusion that justice consists in respecting the plurality of language games, that any political act that denies or represses that diversity must be judged unjust. This means of course that we must maintain the plurality of narratives that transmit the prescriptions governing the different language games.

Surely Lyotard's cynical, pragmatic use of "pagan" narrative and dialectics is at the farthest remove from Jameson's unwavering fidelity to the Marxist versions of them. The latter declares unequivocally that the Marxist grand narrative subsumes all others and that this Idea of finality is one of Totality. However, despite his defense of "realist" (versus "modern") fiction, Jameson's argument for the Marxist narrative makes no appeal to a naive doctrine of realism as an adequate representation of reality or of history. Jameson is quite emphatic about the inaccessibility of the Real in itself, or History, which is experienced, he says, only as Necessity, or "the inexorable *form* of events."[18]

Necessity is an oddly ambiguous word in this context. It has both the sense of the inevitable, fate, or natural law (that over which humans have no power)—which, from the human perspective (and what other perspective is there?), is also contingency or at least the experience of our contingency. To further confuse the issue, we have just read on the preceding page that "the 'emotion' of great historiographic form can then always be seen as ... the powerful reorganization of otherwise inert chronological and 'linear' data in the form of Necessity: why what happened ... had to happen the way it did."[19] Here Necessity is clearly the product of the historiographer's art, a causality (a Necessity, or meta-Necessity?) s/he writes into history. However, Jameson further remarks that "from this perspective ... causality is only one of the possible tropes by which this formal restructuration can be achieved, although it has obviously been a privileged and historically significant one."[20] It is hard to imagine what, other than causality (or the illusion of it), could structure a narrative acceptable to Jameson, who condemns the radical contingencies and discontinuities of modern fiction as a means of "distorting and representing reality"[21]—unless perhaps it is Jameson's own version of the historiographer's work, which Hayden White has termed "narratological causality."[22] Here the word *causality* should not distract us from the fact that this is a distinctly different animal from the three other forms of causality—mechanistic, expressive, and structured—which Jameson has sketched out and rejected one by one, for it entails structuring events from the point of view of the present through a kind of "willing backward in time." As White puts it: "willing backward occurs when we rearrange accounts of events ... in order to endow them with a different meaning or to draw from the new emplotment reasons for acting differently in the future"; it "places emphasis on the actions of living human beings in choosing a past as the particular set of possibilities that they will labor to realize or fulfill in their own future."[23] Insofar as this "willing backward" transforms a brute past into something we desire and can use for positive action, we may describe narratological causation with a term Jameson himself uses in referring to his own dialectical method of fitting parts of everyone else's theories into his own: "mak[ing] a virtue out of necessity."[24] On the other hand, the future that we must work to realize also constitutes the moral of the story, since it is what White calls the "closure to which every narrative aspires"—in this case, the prospect of a unified human community, which Christianity and Marxism "envision as a moral necessity."[25] Seen from the perspective of its telos, narratological causality consists in making a narrative out of a prescription, an *is* (or *was*, or *will be*) out of an *ought*—in other words, in making a necessity out of a virtue.

Now a detour through narrative theory may show that this is not so contradictory and that we can (or even *must*) have it both ways. In an essay entitled "Vraisemblance et motivation" (Verisimilitude [or Plausibility] and Motivation), Gérard Genette performs an analysis of narrative logic that results in the following typology: (1) The *récit vraisemblable*, or verisimilar (plausible) narrative, in which events seem to follow one another in an absolutely necessary sequence, as though determined by a natural causality, and therefore need no explanation or justification (the effect being a powerful illusion of "realism"); (2) the *récit motivé*, or motivated narrative, characterized by frequent authorial or narratorial interventions serving to justify the plausibility of the actions (the archetypal example of this is the Balzacian narrative, crammed with maxims and psychological laws constituting what Genette calls an "artificial verisimilitude" that functions as a built-in theory of Balzac's narrative practice); (3) the *récit arbitraire*, or arbitrary narrative, which seems to follow no logic whatsoever and makes no excuses for it (here we may cautiously classify the "modern" novel).[26]

If the first kind of narrative seems so "realist" or "natural," it is because the characters' actions correspond to the readership's notion of verisimilitude, which, Genette points out, has nothing to do with "reality."[27] The verisimilar is based solely on opinion—not about what *is*, but about what *ought* to be. The implausible is what *ought not* to happen in a story, a violation of both natural and moral law—or, more accurately, it is perceived as a violation of "natural" law precisely because it transgresses moral codes (the natural being nothing but the moral in disguise). To write a plausible narrative, then, one cannot simply borrow from reality, one must make what is conform to what ought to be (in the reader's opinion)—that is, make a virtue out of necessity. At the same time, given the fact that, from the point of view of the author, the whole sequence of events is structured backwards from the projected ending, or moral of the story,[28] and yet must also appear perfectly "natural," then the work of narration consists in making a necessity (the reader's verisimilitude, or "ought") out of a virtue (the author's finality, or "moral"). The production of "realist" narrative thus entails a dual operation: first, that of taking received opinion, or the plausible, as the criteria for narrative reality, or necessity, and second (but also simultaneously), taking the elements of this narrative necessity (or received version of what ought to be) and concatenating them in such a way as to produce "logically" the desired end—which might in and of itself, without benefit of narrative, have appeared totally implausible, like Corax's client's being innocent.

To return to Jameson, then, what I am suggesting is that his "narratological causality" is remarkably similar to Lyotard's Corax's pagan dialectics. Narration, by Jameson's account, is an act by means of which the human subject, from the point of view of present historical conjecture, and with the Idea of a desirable future, constructs a plausible version of his past (that is, one in conformity with opinion in that it mimics "natural," linear causality and makes no claims to ontological authority), at the same time articulating the elements of the narrative chain so as to result in a denouement that seems perfectly logical in the context of the narrative, even though absolutely implausible in the light of the past. Only this version (my narrative) of Jameson's grand narrative of the "human adventure"[29] can make sense of how, after insisting ruthlessly on the fact that "history is what hurts, it is what refuses desire" and that all the great realist historiographers of the past have represented Necessity "in the form of the inexorable logic involved in the determinate failure of all the revolutions that have taken place in human history,"[30] he can still believe in the possibility of a happy ending. Jameson has often been accused of great naïveté for his quasi-religious faith in Marxism, but what if he were just *rusé* (not deceitful, but artful, wily—or cunning, like Hegel's history)? Lyotard would say that if he were *really rusé*, it would be impossible to tell.[31] Jameson is certainly aware of the singularity of his stance, however that stance may be labeled, which may explain why, were we to try to classify his own writings (calling them "narratives" for the sake of the argument) according to Genette's typology, we would have to place him alongside Balzac as a practitioner of the "motivated" narrative, because of the immense theoretical scaffolding he erects to support his version of literary history. Can anyone who has ever read Jameson repress a smile upon reading in his review of *Metahistory* that White's "bristling conceptual apparatus . . . tends to provoke the annoyance we feel when heavy artillery is rolled out to dispatch a gnat"?[32] Jameson's theories, like Balzac's, seem to attest to a strong sense that what he is trying to prove does not conform to contemporary received opinion. White says as much in his defense of Jameson's theorizing (and of all literary theory):

> This is the function of theory in general—that is to say, to provide justification of a stance vis-à-vis the materials being dealt with that can render it plausible. Indeed the function of theory is to justify a notion of plausibility itself. Without such justification, criticism especially is left with nothing but 'common sense' to fall back on.[33]

This brings us back to White, and to my conclusion, which is merely a hypothesis: Perhaps Jameson himself, right under White's very nose, has surreptitiously taken the step beyond irony and rediscovered the freedom to narrate that seemed such a utopian possibility in *Metahistory*. Jameson may be the only *humorous* Marxist critic writing today.[34]

Part 4

Legitimacy and Truth

The *post*modern, as its name implies, is parasitical upon the modern. Its identity is linked to that of its counterconcept. It defines itself primarily in terms of what it is not. Hence the renewed interest of late in the nature and limits of "modernity." One of the major authors to address this topic is the German philosopher Hans Blumenberg, whose works, especially *The Legitimacy of the Modern Age, The Genesis of the Copernican World,* and *Work on Myth,* deal with modernity, not in terms of its Nietzschean overcoming, as do most "postmodern" treatments, but from the perspective of its relation to the metaphysical and theological controversies of classical antiquity and the Middle Ages. His belief in modernity's necessary and inevitable "progress" in solving problems left unresolved in prior epochs leaves Blumenberg open to criticisms of naive evolutionism and/or absolutism with regard to the criteria for assessing this advance. Both David Ingram and Robert Wallace address this issue in its broader context of truth and relativism, reason and human finitude, the context within which Lambert Zuidervaart writes as well.

If we take for defining characteristics of (Enlightenment) modernity the autonomy and "self-assertion" of reason—Kant's *sapere aude*—it seems that the modern age must defend both its radical difference from the preceding epoch and its right to replace the onto-theological (Heidegger) account of history with one of its own. Such, at least, has been the prevailing Romantic view. It has likewise been argued by philosophers like Karl Löwith, Martin Heidegger, and Carl Schmidt that the distinction between the modern and the premodern is at best one of degree, not of kind, and that the modern is but a secularization of Christian, medieval culture. Blumenberg undertakes his defense of modernity by substituting the notion of "reoccupation" for that of "secularization" to describe the relation between these epochs. The term denotes the filling of "answer positions" that had become vacant in an earlier epoch, but whose corresponding questions could not be eliminated. It is the questions that are perennial, their answers are epoch-specific. Thus the persistent Gnostic problem of making sense of an imperfect and corrupt world, to take a favorite example of his, is addressed in the modern epoch by the assertive control of nature. By acknowledging a functional similarity across a substantial difference, Blumenberg hopes to defend the superiority of modernity without anachronism or teleology—a weakness Wallace observes in the Habermasian case for the values of the modern age.

After a sympathetic defense of Blumenberg against accusations of naive progressivism and a sober account of his case for the persistence of myth in our disenchanted world (our existential desires for meaning and happiness are simply not met by scientific or technological progress), Ingram points out several difficulties with the reoccupation thesis as Blumenberg expounds it. He then turns from *The Legitimacy of the Modern Age* to the later *Work on Myth* to assess Blumenberg's subsequent attempt to legitimate modern institutions as successful solutions to perennial problems. The field of inquiry shifts from intellectual history to philosophical anthropology. Ingram seems to agree with Wallace that Blumenberg "splits the difference between Habermas and Gadamer" by arguing that the evolution of tradition is itself rationally motivated in a way that *limits* the modern demand for rational foundations. These limits are circumscribed by mythopoeic thought. But this complementarity thesis regarding myth and reason appears to contradict the historical account provided by *The Legitimacy of the Modern Age* and renders doubtful Blumenberg's original thesis about legitimating the modern age. If we can speak of such legitimizing any longer, Ingram concludes, it will have to be in *post*modern terms, namely, in a manner that is forward-looking but nonfoundationalist as well as respectful of the role played by "myths and parochial narratives" in giving meaning to our quotidian lives.

Wallace defends the thesis that Blumenberg affords us a middle way between the hermeneutics of Gadamer and the "universal pragmatics" of Habermas. Blumenberg's method respects tradition in that it allows "Institutions" such as common sense, myths, and social practices the benefit of the doubt based on their successful social functions, but without slipping into a traditionalism that would honor no reason for correcting or even abolishing the same. In other words, Blumenberg's "Darwinism of culture" employs a true analogue to natural selection, namely, the survival power of certain Institutions, while reserving a place and criteria for critical evaluation of these Institutions—a task for which Wallace believes that Gadamer fails to provide. This method likewise confers a unity and a legitimacy on the modern age by means of the thesis of reoccupation without subscribing to a universal teleology of reason. As Wallace insists, unity is achieved by the *terminus a quo*, the enduring questions, not by the *terminus ad quem*, some ideal consequence, as Habermas would have it. This "Darwinism of culture" likewise yields a middle ground between hermeneutical relativism, admittedly a disputed reading of Gadamer's position, and pragmatic rationalism by means of a concept of scientific truth that is both historical (epoch-specific) and transsubjective.

The debate over modernity and pre- or postmodernity is as much about truth and rationality as about legitimacy. Lambert Zuidervaart underscores this point in his assessment of Albrecht Wellmer's reading of what the latter calls Adorno's "aesthetic redemption of modernity." As the aesthetician of the Frankfurt School, Adorno was critical of bourgeois rationalism and favored an aesthetic reconciliation of what atomistic scientism had divided and multiplied. Especially in his *Aesthetic Theory,* Adorno develops a concept of artistic truth that is philosophical though nonpropositional, without being existentialist or pragmatist. Assuming that artistic truth is metaphorical, Wellmer softens considerably the force of Adorno's claims, revealing a certain rationalistic bias on his own part in the process. Zuidervaart argues against Wellmer that philosophical ascriptions of truth to art are not merely metaphorical, indeed, that the very meaning that philosophers give to "truth" is informed in part by the philosophical truth claims they make about art. Though Adorno would scarcely appreciate the association, Heideggerian "truth as disclosure" seems a prime example of such a relation between truth and art. Yet this could hardly be construed as a "redemption," not even an "aesthetic" redemption, of modernity.

11

Reflections on the Anthropocentric Limits of Scientific Realism: Blumenberg on Myth, Reason, and the Legitimacy of the Modern Age

David Ingram

> Men make their own history, but they do not make it just as they please; they do not make it under circumstances chosen by themselves, but under circumstances directly encountered, given and transmitted from the past.
>
> —Karl Marx

However one chooses to look at it, the modern age is problematic in a manner unique to it. We moderns are conscious of the demands that universal humanism and scientific rationalism place on us, demands that continually call forth renewed efforts at self-justification and legitimation. No one understands this better than Hans Blumenberg, whose voluminous treatises attempt to legitimize our legitimizing. The logical regression implicit in this formulation states the problem admirably: "The problem of legitimacy is latent in the modern age's claim to carry out a radical break with tradition, and in the incongruity between this claim and the reality of history, which can never begin entirely anew."[1] Descartes exemplifies the circularity (or self-referentiality) implicit in legitimizing legitimizing in his rationalist attempt to ground knowledge of self and world in intuitive certainty (freedom from prejudice). Philosophers of history from Voltaire to Marx exemplify it in their equation of Enlightenment and progress.

Today's enlightened historians reject the Enlightenment's prejudice against prejudices—its realism, if you will—thereby undercutting the foundationalist and progressivist assumptions that fuel the legitimist's project.[2] Modernity, they claim, is legitimized by the Judeo-Christian tradition it secularizes or not at all. If the former, then modernity remains—at least, according to its own foundationalist and progressivist criteria—illegitimate. Blumenberg, on the contrary, thinks that the modern age can be legitimized without appeal to teleological theories.[3] His strategy involves showing how it resolved the crisis of high scholasticism in a way that permitted the two antipodes of the Middle Ages—the infinitude of God and the finitude of man—to be reinscribed in a new scientific system that has proven highly adaptive. If we can no longer speak of absolute progress, we *can* speak of limited progress relative to preceding problems. In particular, we can say that scientific humanism "reoccupied" a place in the functional system of life that had been vacated by medieval Christianity. By solving Christianity's metaphysical crisis in a manner commensurate with the latter's own criteria of success, it filled a role that was necessary, progressive, and, by implication, legitimate.

The preceding formula, however, captures only one side of Blumenberg's thought. Blumenberg realizes that the new age is not legitimated *solely* by the criteria of success presupposed by its predecessor. Exponents of the new age redefine these criteria even as they appeal to them, thereby changing the problem originally posed. No common standard exists to establish a simple base of comparison; therefore, even judgments of relative progress are rendered problematic.

I shall argue that Blumenberg's ambivalence about the possibility of legitimation stems from unresolved tensions inherent in modernity. I have already mentioned one of them: the tension between rational self-grounding (modernity legitimated in light of its own criteria) and rational progress (modernity legitimated in light of its predecessor's criteria). Another concerns the tension between justification claiming objective validity (based on scientific realism) and justification claiming subjective validity (based on anthropocentric idealism).

In this essay I focus on the latter tension. I characterize it as a tension because Blumenberg, like so many others in the German and French tradition, holds that the two extremes are complementary: what he calls "self-assertion" culminates in the objectifying quantification of space, time, and matter definitive of scientific realism.[4] Of course, realism of this sort is incompatible with the practical and moral side of modern self-assertion, which endows collective subjects with the freedom to constitute reality through the imposition of meaning and value. Hence the tension.

I hope to show that Blumenberg's own legitimation of modernity vacillates between these poles. His use of natural selection to legitimate cultural institutions supposedly dispenses with teleological assumptions. However, his insight into the history of reversals leading up to and continuing beyond the Copernican revolution shows the danger implicit in this realist account. Ultimately, Blumenberg's own use of natural selection for purposes of legitimation remains burdened with progressivist and teleological residues. Indeed, it renders his philosophical anthropology serviceable for the type of rationalization associated with myth—albeit under conditions that exhaust that peculiar form.

I

Blumenberg's defense of modernity is laid out principally in the intellectual history traversed by *The Legitimacy of the Modern Age* (1976 [1966]). His analysis of the dialectical tensions implicit in it, however, is developed in anthropological and philosophical speculations contained in *The Genesis of the Copernican World* (1975) and *Work on Myth* (1979). In keeping with the logical order of Blumenberg's own reflections, I will begin by addressing problems raised by the former of these texts.

The Legitimacy of the Modern Age argues that modernity is a legitimate, that is, necessary and progressive, response to problems generated by medieval Christianity. On this reading, it would be simplifying matters considerably to say that the scientific humanism that climaxed the Renaissance emerged in stark opposition to the predominant theology, as an explosive residue left over from the pagan, worldly values of ancient philosophy. Such humanism was not a mere repetition of naturalistic attitudes and civic ideals rooted in classical antiquity. This is not to deny, of course, that the retrieval of classical thought during the Renaissance stimulated the development of modern attitudes toward scientific observation, measurement, and mathematization. However, as Blumenberg points out, the reflexive curiosity that informs the *unrestricted* appetite for knowledge in the modern age is no direct descendent of classical *bios theoretikos,* but is mediated and provoked by a dualism inherent in medieval Christianity.

The classical model of knowledge presupposes a teleological metaphysics in which contemplative rest and fulfillment are the norm. Just as the cognitive faculty naturally seeks to possess and become its object in thoughtful imitation, so nature strives for intuitive disclosure and completion in knowledge (*LM*:286). Underlying this model, then, is an implicit monism in which subject and object are united in a state of maximum self-realization.

Now, it is precisely this identification of knowledge, virtue, and happiness that lent impetus to the negative assessment of theoretical curiosity so characteristic of Hellenism (*LM*:243). The idea of an indefinite striving for and progressive accumulation of knowledge is foreign to the classical model of cognition, which postulates the possible attainment of an absolute and final truth. This is particularly evident in Platonism, the most extreme example of classical monism. As Blumenberg notes, the identification of knowledge and self-fulfillment implicit in the classical model cannot but lead to the subordination of empirical learning to ethical self-reflection. Of course, the Socratic equation of knowledge and virtue does not unambiguously terminate in the cessation of self-questioning. However, in Plato's objective idealism not only is sensory observation—now judged illusory—replaced by self-reflection as the true path of knowledge, but self-reflection comes to mean the purely rational intuition of an immutable, supersensible "nature" (*LM*:246–55). Plato's realism—if we can call it that—remains undeveloped. It hasn't yet problematized the relationship between a finite knower (subject) and an infinite known (object), namely, the latter is still conceived idealistically (or anthropocentrically) in terms of final ends.

One might object that the Socratic/Platonic devaluation of empirical observation is hardly characteristic of classical epistemology. Indeed, both Skepticism and Stoicism stressed the importance of natural observation, and they did so in a manner that seemed to imply a radical incommensurability between human cognition and divine truth. Both reversed the Platonic hierarchy by equating knowledge with immediate sensation. Yet neither developed a realist metaphysics.

Stoicism and Skepticism advocated withholding judgment regarding the existence or nonexistence of objects outside the mind in favor of allowing the subject perfect freedom to determine the condition of his own inner states (*LM*:257–77). Despite their apparent reversal of the Platonic hierarchy, these philosophies continued to equate true knowledge with self-reflection in the service of a higher, therapeutic goal—that of nonsuffering (*agatheia*) and self-sufficiency in harmony with nature. Nature—reality—is still regarded as an intrinsically rational, purposive cosmos. Thus, Hellenistic philosophy never achieved a realist perspective requiring endless cognitive adaptation to a wholly infinite "other." Ultimately, it conceived of self-knowledge as a defense against the sort of endless questioning and worldly dispersion that leads beyond the circle of internal integrity and salvation.

But how are we to understand the "progressive" materialism of the atomistic theories of antiquity, if not as a denial of classical monism? The Epicurean variety of atomism that later found wide acceptance during the Middle Ages and Renaissance seems to challenge classical monism in its postulation of a plurality of atomically constituted worlds whose configurations are governed by chance. Here, final knowledge of eternal truths appears to be ruled out by metaphysical contingency. Yet, as Blumenberg goes on to argue, such is not the case. Once again, the atomists' therapeutic aims—the achievement of happiness through indifference—presupposed a deeper knowledge of cosmic lawfulness. Indifference still required faith in the cyclical constitution and disintegration of complex configurations out of *finite* atomic forms (*LM*:154–59).

The radical questioning characteristic of scientific humanism is incompatible with the epistemological and metaphysical monism—and antirealism—of Greek philosophy. It would take more than the atomists' postulation of a *finite* plurality of *actual* worlds to undermine the secure unity of knowing subject and known object. It would take the nominalists' doctrine of an *infinite* plurality of *possible* worlds. But this doctrine would have to await medieval Christianity's accession to the utter groundlessness of being previously postulated by the Gnostic heresy of irrational creation.

According to Blumenberg, both the modern age and the age preceding it were responses to crises. The crisis that led to the decline of classical cosmology and its replacement by nonnaturalistic—ultimately nominalistic—theocentrism was provoked by the monistic tendencies of the former. However, it was the *dualism* implicit in medieval Christianity's own efforts to resolve this earlier crisis that later provoked the rise of scientific realism.

The failure of fourth-century Neoplatonism to explain matter (evil) as an emanation from pure form (the One) contributed to the rise of a Gnostic heresy vesting creation and salvation in two distinct Gods (*LM*:128). In combatting this dualistic heresy, early Christianity, largely under the influence of Augustine, returned to the monistic cosmology of antiquity, which united first and final causes in one principle. Accordingly, Augustine redeemed matter by tracing its origin to divine creation. This accomodation to Neoplatonism, however, could be achieved only by introducing Gnosticism through the back door. Evil must be attributed to human freedom (original sin), so that whatever divinely preordained suffering is inflicted on the seemingly innocent can be interpreted as "just punishment" within a perfect order (*LM*:129–36).

Augustine's response to Gnosticism is also revealing in its epistemological implications. On the one hand, Augustine continued to legitimate his position by appeal to assumptions derived from classical epistemology. Like the gnostics, he defended recollection as the rightful path for knowing God and used philosophical methods of disputation to defend the lawfulness of divine creation that had been denied by them. On the other hand, he criticized Gnostic attempts to achieve salvation through recollection alone (*LM*:314–20). In equating these attempts with vain curiosity, he allied himself with an absolutist theology that was radically opposed to classical epistemology. Iranaeus, Tertullian, and other Patristic authors had already criticized Gnosticism for its "naturalism." They denied that recollective knowledge could reunite the knower with a transcendent origin from which he was separated by an infinite duration. Moreover, they condemned such knowledge for being an illegitimate appropriation of secrets that only God had the right to reveal.

The contrast between the metaphor of divine ownership (linking truth and divine revelation) and the classical metaphor (linking truth and visible light) could not have been greater (*LM*:291–304). Nature now appeared less familiar. Not alien, to be sure—that would come later with modern science. But as a book of divine symbolism, nature required endless interpretation. Ultimately, Augustine's denunciation of the cognitive drive as a product of original sin would later provoke a nominalist reaction in which worldly curiosity—now shorn of its eschatological pretensions—would become legitimate.

In Blumenberg's opinion, Augustine's invocation of divine omnipotence and omniscience was certainly not the only solution to the problem of evil available to early Christianity. The doctrine of original sin, Blumenberg tells us, must be thought as a "spontaneous generation," (or mutation, to use the language of natural selection) that proved particularly enduring owing to its successful fulfillment of a function previously fufilled by classical antiquity. It is tempting to think that the durability of Augustine's doctrine is a function of its responding successfully to a universal question: the problem of suffering. But as Blumenberg reminds us, the continuity is not one of *meanings*. "Questions do not always precede their answers." And whenever "great questions" are retrospectively adduced to legitimate new answers, they are invariably reinterpretations of older questions. Augustine appropriated the classical heritage in a manner that redefined its notions of cosmos and knowledge to the extreme point of surpassing them altogether. To cite Blumenberg, "an ingrained traditional mode of activity has lost its motivating content of ideas and thus also its intelligibility, so that the schema of the activity is available for a retrospective interpretation and integration into a new context of meaning, which in the process makes use of and secures, above all, its sanctioned status as something that is beyond questioning" (*LM*:78). Elsewhere Blumenberg makes the same point with reference to the metaphorical nature of functional reoccupations.

"Carryings over," metaphorical functions, again and again play an essential role here. Alexander conceives his historical project by reversing Xerxes' march across the Hellespont. The God of the Old Testament transfers his sovereignty in history by means of a covenant. The citizens of the National Convention, in the French Revolution, take metaphors of the Roman Republic literally, in their costume and speech.[5]

I shall have more to say below about the importance of myth and metaphor for understanding legitimation. More pertinent to our present concern is the way in which Augustine's metaphoric continuation of the Gnostic myth opened up an unbridgeable gap between finite and infinite that later proved decisive for the rise of scientific realism. According to Blumenberg, Augustine's precarious defense of an omniscient, omnipotent, and perfectly benevolent deity opened up a new dualism. The widening gap between infinite deity and finite humanity—Christianity's reoccupation of Gnostic dualism—eventually led nominalists to abandon the quest for divine knowledge (truth) in favor of a more modest enterprise: prediction of observable appearances.

Once it is conceded that God's will is limited only by the law of contradiction, the actual world no longer retains the status of a rational cosmos, or singular vessel in which His creative powers, indeed all possibilities, are exhausted. Bishop Tempier's condemnation in 1277 of the Aristotelian conception of God as an intelligible first principle makes sense in this context. Creation loses its inherent reasonableness in light of the infinitely many worlds God could have chosen. Lacking a *ratio creandi* upon which to direct its contemplative search for universal essences, human reason is necessarily thrown back upon its own (not God's) principle of order and economy (Ockham's Razor).

Modern self-assertion (*Selbstbehauptung*)—by which Blumenberg means existential openness toward possibilties and not mere self-preservation—is thus born of epistemic uncertainty and ontological contingency (*LM*:138–40). The contradiction between cosmic perfection (determinism) and divine omnipotence (freedom) or between divine benevolence and worldly suffering inevitably provoked a humanistic reaction (*LM*:198). Cognitive adaptation to a creation presumed to be objectively meaningful and rational gives way to worldy *curiosity* about contingent forces whose prediction might further the interests of humanity. As Blumenberg so felicitously puts it, "because theology meant to defend God's absolute interest it allowed and caused man's interest in himself to become absolute" (*LM*:197).

The ascent from Ockham's nominalism to Descartes' rationalism is described in painstaking detail by Blumenberg. What concerns us here is the ambiguous way in which Blumenberg describes modern attitudes as these are reflected in the philosophies of Cusa, Bruno, and Copernicus. Modern self-assertion is realistic and objectifying in its approach to nature—and hence is anti-anthropomorphic, anti-teleological, and anti-humanistic in orientation. At the same time, it is highly skeptical, assured of its own contingency, and all too cognizant of the subjective and otherwise "intentional," interpretative, metaphoric, and purposive nature of its knowledge.

Nicholas of Cusa and Giordano Bruno are the epochal figures in Blumenberg's account of this dialectic—the former having glimpsed the summit of modernity from the far side of the Copernican divide, the latter, on this side, having almost reached it. Cusa developed the humanistic implications of nominalism in a decidedly anti-anthropomorphic direction. His doctrine of learned ignorance emphasized the limits of discursive reasoning with respect to divine knowledge even as it praised the human spirit as the highest and most perfect reflection of God (*LM*:357). This led him to conceive the use of static proportions in mathematics and geometry as a replicable, proto-scientific procedure for *approximating* truth. Most importantly, however, his conceptualization of the earth as a center in motion contributed to relativizing the anthropocentric standpoint (*LM*:491–513).

The destruction of anthropocentrism is certainly one of the important *consequences* of the Copernican revolution. However, it is Copernicus's anthropocentrism that explains his modern, scientific realism. Blumenberg notes that Copernicus's defense of heliocentrism is far less significant for the establishment of modern attitudes than is his methodological success in transforming astronomy into a science comprising more than a mere art of hypothesis and prediction. Copernicus's realism grew out of his vision of a unified science. In this respect, his homogenization of terrestrial and celestial realms merely realized what was already implicit in the nominalist relativization of space/time, form/matter distinctions with respect to divine intuition. Copernicus also believed that such a unified knowledge was also available to man, albeit by means of theory rather than intuition.[6]

As Blumenberg notes, it is one of the profound ironies of Copernican realism that its humanistic supposition of an objective standpoint shared by God and man alike would provoke an idealistic *reversal*. On the one hand, scientific realism will found its theories on mathematical principles that seem remote from anthropocentric purposes. On the other hand, the denigration of the anthropocentric (or commonsense) viewpoint, which views the earth as the static center of the universe, will give rise to a new anthropocentrism. In German idealism from Kant to Nietzsche, even scientific knowledge will appear (in comparison to some God's-eye point of view) subjective, perspectival, and merely hypothetical.

Blumenberg's treatment of realism is admittedly ambivalent. He agrees with Nietzsche that a teleological residue survives in realistic conceptions of science that regard knowledge as a theoretical and practical adaptation to pregiven nature (*LM*:140). Yet he defends realism as a regulative idea indispensable for scientific progress. Indeed, his own historiography, which attempts to legitimate modern institutions on the basis of a nonteleological theory of natural selection, commits him to a realistic conception of adaptation. On the other hand, he repeatedly emphasizes that reality is only known indirectly, through symbolic constructs.

The ever-growing gap between a lifeworld intuitively revealed through sense perception and an abstract nature indirectly disclosed through scientific theory contributes to a perspectivalism wherein all knowing is conceived as interpretative (*GCW*:622–43).[7] The Book of Nature and its biblical cipher lose their timeless singularity once they are interpreted by the Book of History (as in Spinoza's *Tractatus theologico-politicus*). Similarly the Book of History loses its natural objectivity once it is interpreted by the poetic activity of human speakers (as in Vico's *New Science*).[8] Gnosticism thus returns with a vengeance: the Augustinian opposition between finite (subjective) understanding and infinite (objective) knowledge culminates in the anthropocentric idealism peculiar to post-Kantian thought, in which the realistic achievements of modern reason are now conceived as products of a Promethean, transcendental subject. As we shall see, Blumenberg, like Vico and Nietzsche before him, will regard the metaphorical (mythopoetic) and rhetorical nature of symbolic understanding as an anthropological constant no longer restricted in scope to the historical appropriation of ideas.

The anthropocentric implications of modern realism are further explored in Blumenberg's discussion of the importance of scientific method in constituting humanity as a universal subject of progress. Writing in the wake of the Copernican revolution, Giordano Bruno was already in a position to grant human self-assertion the kind of creative power later bestowed on it by Nietzsche. By ceasing to regard the earth as a fixed center—on the Ptolemaic model it was the heaviest and innermost of the celestial spheres and hence the least affected by the circular motion introduced into the system through divine self-contemplation—Bruno stripped matter of its finitude and inertia. Endowed with intrinsic motion, nature—with man its pinnacle—became divine (*LM*:561–95).

The Promethean conception of humanity, as a collective subject who progressively orders an infinite, disenchanted nature in accordance with its own needs, received its first methodological articulation in the writings of Francis Bacon. As Blumenberg points out, Bacon's belief in the power of experimentation and his understanding of the link between knowledge and self-assertion captures the spirit of the modern age better than Galileo's faith in observation and Descartes' insistence on metaphysically grounded method (*LM*:384–90). [9]

Here again, we find evidence of Blumenberg's ambivalence with respect to realism. Faith in observation and methodological foundationalism are aspects of modern, scientific realism that fulfill metaphysical functions. Observation fulfills the teleological function inherent in monistic cosmology, which assumes the natural adaptability of cognition to a pregiven reality; methodological foundationalism fulfills the genetic function inherent in theocentric cosmology, which assumes the legitimizing force of origins and absolute beginnings. At the same time, faith in observation and methodological foundationalism represent aspects of modern self-assertion that break with traditional assumptions. Galileo's discovery of the telescope contributed enormously to the destruction of the old faith in the natural reliability of immediate intuition (vision) as a means for directly achieving complete and final identification with reality. The method of analysis and deduction (resolution and composition) that he and Descartes deployed not only endowed predictive science with greater mathematical precision; it also defined it as a replicable procedure of quantification and measurement enabling something like unlimited, infinite progress (*LM*:371–72). Together, these aspects of scientific method constituted a community of research—a universal historical subject—that progressively shapes its reality in accordance with realistic assumptions (*LM*:353).

II

The key to understanding the legitimacy of the modern age resides in "our" belief that a universal culture stressing scientific problem solving and individual autonomy (self-assertion) progressed beyond a metaphysical worldview based on unquestioned authority, resignation, and complacency. From Descartes through Habermas, defenders of Enlightenment have grounded this culture in rational insight alone; its claim to progress is ostensibly legitimated by its emancipation from traditional prejudice.

Secularization theorists from Hegel through Heidegger, however, have argued that modern institutions are not *sui generis*. Reason itself is a secularization of Judeo-Christian dogma, so that justification for the modern age must be retrospective. Blumenberg, too, is sympathetic to this criticism—up to a point. Scientific rationalism and existential self-assertion are incompatible with teleological conceptions of historical progress—hence, secularization theories of the Hegelian variety are inherently suspect. Modern institutions cannot be legitimated as embodiments of some ultimate end; at most they can be legitimated as progressive relative to premodern institutions. In particular, he argues that "the concept of the legitimacy of the modern age is not derived from the accomplishments of reason, but from the necessity of those accomplishments" (*LM*:99).

Critics of Blumenberg often ignore his insistence on "the separation of cognitive achievement and the production of happiness" (*LM*:404).[10] His discussion of myth, to which I shall turn shortly, emphatically underscores the nihilistic implications of scientific rationalism and self-assertion in a manner that can leave no doubt as to the limits of modernity in solving humanity's most pressing existential problem: the search for value and meaning. This accords with Blumenberg's own gnosticism: the modern alienation of subjectively meaningful lifeworld from objectively disenchanted universe reinscribes the Christian dualism of finite and infinite.

Despite this ultrarealist position (or rather because of it), Blumenberg talks about historical progress in a way that lends credence to the critics' contention that he is more interested in the accomplishments of reason than in their necessity. This becomes apparent when we examine Blumenberg's remarks about the kind of necessity inhabiting the link between medieval Christianity and modernity. At first blush, these remarks suggest a nondialectical necessity. It is precisely because their legitimacy is dependent on some notion of progress that modern reason and self-assertion are not—contrary to secularization theorists—reducible to, or implicit within, premodern attitudes. Yet progress in comparison to some prior set of beliefs presupposes a common frame of reference. This common frame of reference consists of "questions [that are] relatively constant in comparison to answers" to specific problems as well as a "constant matrix" of expectations and needs.

At this juncture we must take note of an important ambiguity in Blumenberg's account of the kind of nonreductive identity linking modernity and premodernity. In the aforementioned citation Blumenberg claims that modernity's progress is registered in novel answers it gives to questions posed by medieval Christianity. According to him, "a program of self-assertion against transcendental uncertainties, rejecting every kind of resignation, had become necessary" in the face of "difficulties on which the medieval/Scholastic system was to run aground" (*LM*:468). In a nutshell, the scholastic system sought to answer the question of salvation by appealing to a philosophy of history invoking the notion of an absolute beginning and end. This answer proved unsatisfactory in light of the contradictions animating late scholasticism. Modern science, by contrast, offered hope of a lesser, more worldly salvation through self-assertion. However, it could not legitimate itself without also offering an answer to the metaphysical question.

> Thus, as we know, the modern age found it impossible to decline to answer questions about the totality of history. To that extent the philosophy of history is an attempt to answer a medieval question with the means available to a post-medieval age. In this process, the idea of progress is driven to a level of generality that overextends its original, regionally circumscribed and objectively limited range as assertion. (*LM*:48–49)

Unlike its scholastic counterpart, the scientific notion of infinite progress designates a negative, *limit* concept marking resignation in the face of the indefinite, meaningless task by which humanity, not the individual, asserts its right to self-preservation (*LM*:83–85). In order for the modern project to justify itself as a meaningful vehicle of salvation—indeed, as a better instrument of redemption than Christian faith—it had to clothe itself in the mantle of Christian apologetics by assuming the mythical guise of universal history. The same can be said for the foundationalist and realist aspects of modernity. They are legitimate insofar as they constitute "necessary"—and perhaps better—responses to problems engendered by scholasticism. However, they are illegitimate insofar as they overreach (or regress behind) the anthropocentric standpoint of modern self-assertion, which emphasizes the contingency and perspectival relativity of human thought. The same, of course, can be said of modern humanism when it opposes science in the name of (objectivistically undefiled) subjective experience (see note 7). Thus, for Blumenberg, "lifeworld" and "reality" denote regulative ideas that delimit a human condition lacking positive (subjective or objective) foundation.

There is no easy way to resolve the problem of illegitimate reoccupation, since the legitimacy of modern subjectivism is impugned by modern objectivism, and vice versa. Indeed, even illegitimate reoccupations can be understood as necessary and progressive. Blumenberg's other account of historical reoccupation invokes a notion of continuity (identity) that ostensibly avoids this problem. On this new account, it would no longer make sense to distinguish legitimate from illegitimate reoccupations. Instead, any organization of thought that proved durable (adaptable) could be regarded *prima facie* as legitimate.

Before discussing this second account of reoccupation, it will be helpful to examine another interpretation of the kind of commonality linking otherwise incommensurate systems of thought. One of the shortcomings of the different-answers-to-similar-questions interpretation of historical continuity is that it sneaks teleology in through the back door. Comparing epochal shifts as both necessary and progressive leads us to view epochal change as "irreversible," moving "in a single, unambiguous direction" (*LM*:468). Blumenberg's other interpretation of historical continuity can avoid this result but—as I shall show—only at the cost of undermining the concept of historical progress undergirding modernity's claim to legitimacy.

On the new interpretation, the common frame of reference "is not one of contents but one of functions" in which "totally heterogenoeus contents . . . take on identical functions in specific positions in the system of man's interpretation of the world and himself" (*LM*:64). "In the new organization," Blumenberg notes, "certain questions are no longer posed" (*LM*:467). More specifically, the old questions are radically reinterpreted by the new system, so that it no longer makes sense to talk about old and new worldviews providing different answers to identical questions.

Recall what was said about Augustine's retrospective and highly metaphoric reinterpretation of the Gnostic problem of suffering. The problem is framed no longer in terms of recollection and return to pristine origins but in terms of future redemption from original sin. Once we accept the notion that modern responses are only functional reoccupations of premodern positions, we can no longer privilege scientific self-assertion over medieval resignation as a superior response to *identical* problems. The modern and medieval organizations of knowledge would be incommensurable in the Kuhnian sense of the term.[11]

Although incommensurability does not—indeed, cannot—rule out all cognitive comparison, the possibility for radical translation on, say, a Davidsonian, Quinean, or Gadamerian model hardly refutes Blumenberg's claim that Christian and modern worldviews are responses to different sets of problems.[12] The interpreter of a totally unfamiliar language must assume that (s)he mostly agrees with the speaker on the basic facts of the world in order for interpretation to proceed. Nevertheless, the principle of charity (as Davidson understands it) allows for large disagreement as well.[13]

The *partial* intertranslatability of modern and premodern systems of meaning, then, does not effect their *local* incommensurablity (as Kuhn puts it) with respect to certain core terms that remain semantically determined by context-specific practices. Since modern conceptual schemes, attitudes, and so forth are no longer conceivable as better responses to medieval problems, they can no longer be legitimated by standards of progress. Of course, they might still be legitimated by standards of necessity. But 'historical necessity' is a notoriously elusive concept, whose deterministic connotations clash with the new strategy of legitimation proposed by Blumenberg in *Work on Myth.* It therefore remains to be seen whether the theory of natural selection advanced there can succeed where *The Legitimacy of the Modern Age* fails.

III

Like *The Legitimacy of the Modern Age, Work on Myth* attempts to legitimate modern attitudes and institutions by showing that they are successful solutions to antecedent problems. But now the emphasis shifts from intellectual history to philosophical anthropology. Modern rationality can be justified, but—as Copernican reflections on the remote possibility of intelligent extra-terrestrial life imply—"reason would not be the summit of nature's accomplishments . . . [but] would be a risky way around a lack of adaptation; a substitute adaptation; a makeshift agency to deal with the failure of previously reassuring functional arrangements and long-term constant specializations for stable environments" (*GCW*:683).

Blumenberg's appeal to natural selection as a legitimizing principle is motivated by the following objection (which we can imagine a rationalist like Habermas posing): If reason, or modern self-assertion, is justified only as a response to problems immanent in prerational tradition, then its claim to legitimacy would be dependent on criteria that ultimately rest on dogmatic authority or prejudices (*Vorurteile*), as Gadamer puts it. In other words, the evolution of tradition culminating in modern self-assertion would not itself be rationally motivated. The theory of natural selection meets this objection by arguing that the evolution of tradition is itself rationally motivated and—what's especially important—motivated in a way that limits the modern demand for legitimation, understood as a demand for rational *foundations.* In this way, Blumenberg hopes to split the difference between Habermas and Gadamer.

Foundational reasoning is, of course, an essential aspect of modern forms of legitimation, albeit one whose own legitimacy must be carefully circumscribed. As a quest for absolute beginnings and endings it represents the sort of illegitimate reoccupation of metaphysical positions that Blumenberg criticizes. As an "endless task" (Husserl) it represents an undertaking worthy of philosophers and scientists in their disinterested search for truth. But this model of progressive enlightenment—of radical questioning—cannot be extended to the domain of everyday practice without undermining the habits, customs, and "institutions" (Gehlen) that provide the preconditions and resources for understanding and acting. Demand for rational justification in this context is legitimate only when it is selectively aimed at specific traditions whose problem-solving capacity is placed in doubt: "What the heading 'institutions' covers is, above all, a distribution of burdens of proof. Where an institution exists, the question of its rational foundation is not, of itself, urgent, and the burden of proof always lies on the person who objects to the arrangement the institution carries with it."[14]

This is where Blumenberg's "Darwinism of words" makes its entry. The durability of tradition is itself ample justification in support of its adaptability, where adaptability implies successful problem solving. According to Blumenberg, culture is an adaptive response to a biological shortcoming:

> Man's deficiency in specific dispositions for reactive behavior vis-à-vis reality—that is, his poverty of instincts—is the starting point for the central anthropological question as to how this creature is able to exist in spite of his lack of fixed biological dispositions. The answer can be reduced to the formula: by not dealing with this reality directly. The human relation to reality is indirect, circumstantial, delayed, selective, and above all metaphorical.[15]

The "absolutism of reality" confronts the deficient human with a mass of undifferentiated stimulii whose chaotic power is checked by symbolic constructs that serve to name, differentiate, limit, and control (*WM*:3–4).

Judging from Blumenberg's account, such mythopoeticizing is largely metaphorical in the way described by Vico; the symbolic constructs of mind and spirit are metaphors for the body—a body, Merleau-Ponty would later add, that experiences itself as unity prior to thematic reflection.[16] In this respect, myth no less than reason is "a piece of high-carat 'work of logos'" (*WM*:12). Indeed, if we accept Blumenberg's claim that "reason means just being able to deal with something," then even dogmatic forms of tradition are rational (*WM*:63).

Blumenberg's use of myth to illustrate the legitimacy and rationality of *unfounded* institutions appears to contradict the historical account of *The Legitimacy of the Modern Age,* which stakes its defense of modernity on the historiographical necessity of drawing epochal boundaries. This reversal is frought with positive and negative implications. By redefining reason in terms of successful adaptation, he is able to argue that the foundationalist and realist demands of *modern* rationality are derivative aspects of reason that find their limit in reason. In doing so, however, he seems to commit the same mistake secularization theorists like Heidegger and Adorno make: blurring the distinction between premodernity and modernity, myth, and reason, by reducing rational self-assertion to some universal, anthropological disposition for self-preservation.

Blumenberg would doubtless reply that the originality of modern self-assertion is compatible with its origin in myth. Citing the Gadamer-inspired *Rezeptionsästhetik* of Wolfgang Iser and Hans Jauss, he argues that a necessary condition for myth's durability and continued reception is its adaptability to changing contexts. Just as myth is a metaphorical interpretation of and compensation for the body, so reason is a metaphorical interpretation of and compensation for myth. Therefore, the meaning of reason and myth, as well as the meaning of specific myths and types of reason, does not remain constant. What does is the functional (successful) reoccupation of a basic place (or the satisfaction of a basic need) in the system of life. Myth and reason complement each other: the former survives because it fulfills a need that neither objectifying science nor subjectifying morality can satisfy: the need for some higher meaning and purpose.

Perhaps this explains why the Book of Nature metaphor continues to haunt modern biology, where RNA molecules are said to "read" genetic codes written in the DNA alphabet, and why the myth of eternal recurrence survives in the death instinct postulated by Freudian psychoanalysis and the second law of thermodynamics (the principle of entropy) postulated by physics (*LW*:381–403). If so, it might also explain why Blumenberg's rationalistic appeal to natural selection succeeds in legitimating reason (narrowly and broadly conceived) only to the extent that it incorporates a rational account of progress embedded in a mythic account of recurrent and originary struggle—a feature it shares with Marx's historical materialism.[17]

Today, myth is overshadowed by reason, so that work on myth, that is, the reception of myth, labors under the imperative of finality. Mythicizing that "brings myth to an end" and "fully exploits and exhausts" the form of a given myth through extreme deformations of its "original figure" functions to "present the subject's responsibility to himself and for himself," but in a manner that liberates the decision to act from temporizing rationalization and future uncertainty (*WM*:266).[18] The Prometheus myth has furnished today's existentialists with the heroic model requisite for the modern age; the reincarnation and recurrence myths in Schopenhauer and Nietzsche offer a kind of metaphysical ground (and comfort) for the otherwise contingent and indefinite strivings of the will. Blumenberg's myth of adaptation and progress merely reinstantiates these themes at the level of science.

I will return to the importance of myth for legitimation at the conclusion of my paper. By way of getting there I would like to take up the related problem of legitimating modernity by appeal to natural selection. Blumenberg insists that the natural selection of culture implies that "there is objective progress" and that "history, whatever else it might be, is also a process of optimization" (*WM*:165). Two problems arise here. The first concerns the standard for determining progress. As we saw above, one cannot assume that the questions (problems, needs) addressed by a "new" organization are the same ones addressed by the "old" organization. In some sense, the new system reinterprets the old problems by integrating them into a different problem context. Thus the problem of spiritual and physical survival we moderns "inherited" from antiquity and medieval Christianity is really our problem, not theirs. The same applies to our needs; adaptation and self-preservation are relative to cultural values that change with the organization of life.

A realist, of course, would reject this view. And Blumenberg *does* sound like a realist when he claims that *optimization* establishes "a definite distribution of burdens of proof for what wants to give itself out as rationality" (*WM*:166). Thus according to Blumenberg, we are entitled to assume that the durability of an institution is a sign that it satisfies real needs that conform to the objective and universal conditions of optimal living.

To be sure, the mere fact that a given institution satisfies the *subjective* needs of a particular society is no sign that it is advancing that society's true well-being, since members of a society can be deluded on this score. Indeed, if optimization implied satisfaction of only subjective needs, it could not blunt rational questioning in the way Blumenberg thinks. Most people believe they are served well by scientific specialization. Yet, as Blumenberg himself notes, in order to recognize that history is a process of optimization "one does not have to deny that there can be inconsistencies in the system of the objectifications produced by selection, inconsistencies that impair the overall result. They are due precisely to the isolation and rendering autonomous of partial subsystems in the historical process; the history of science and technology—both severed from the continuity of life as a result of unavoidable specialization—is an example of this" (*WM*:165–66).

The question arises: when do such inconsistencies render a system nonoptimal? When does scientific objectivism "progress" to the point where it becomes regressive, or illegitimate from the standpoint of modern, "subjective" demands for self-determination? To pose this question *as* a question of legitimation, namely, as a "modern" demand for rational justification, we would have to possess an objective standard of need satisfaction, either a realist conception of human nature or, more plausibly, an evolutionary theory possessing normative import. Habermas, who explicitly addresses Blumenberg's concerns regarding the splitting off of elite subcultures and the colonization of the lifeworld by technologically oriented economic and administrative subsystems, takes the latter route.

Teleological theories—including those that assume the modest form of reconstructive logic—are incapable of satisfying their own rationality requirements. Even if one could develop a *testable,* normative theory of moral development for individual and society—a prospect that seems doomed from the outset—the abstractness of formal-rational competencies whose superiority is to be demonstrated would render them indeterminate with respect to the kinds of global evaluations requisite for determining the superiority of whole systems of thought. Habermas himself concedes as much.[19]

In the final analysis, natural selection can explain neither the necessity nor optimality of cultural institutions.[20] Seen from this Darwinian standpoint, modern rationality emerged as a random mutation that proved successful at solving certain problems—period. Whether it was the only solution possible at the time and whether it presently conduces to the optimal well-being (survival) of society cannot be answered: success is no substitute for self-realization and fulfillment. This conclusion is echoed by Stephen Jay Gould, who has devoted much effort in documenting the often discontinuous and nonprogressive nature of adaptive change in the realm of biology.[21]

If we can still speak of legitimating the modern age—and there is considerable doubt whether even Blumenberg thinks we can—it would have to be a postmodern legitimation. Such a mode of legitimation, to paraphrase Jean-Francois Lyotard, would accept the forward-looking (progressivist) idealism of the Enlightenment heritage minus its foundationalism (universalism).[22] At the same time, it would acknowledge the role that *petit recits*—myths and parochial narratives—play in lending purpose and meaning, in short, legitimacy, to our lives.

The conjunction of modern self-assertion, which opens up an indefinite space for innovative questioning vis-à-vis the possible, and parochial tradition and habit, which stabilize and delimit the range of the possible, is not, to be sure, a consistent or harmonious mix. Indeed, it's far from obvious what this *pastiche* of modern and premodern narratives concretely achieves. Lyotard relishes the schizophrenic dissolution of the modern subject implicit in the conflictual politics of the everday. Blumenberg, on the contrary, thinks that "final myths" provide a kind of regularity and groundedness to our lives that enables us to accept the ideal—but empty—demands of modern self-determination. Uprooted from the past and shorn of higher purpose, modernity cannot be legitimated. At best, its "legitimacy" would depend on encouraging the dissent, heterogeneity, and novelty necessary for solving its own problems.

12

Blumenberg's Third Way: Between Habermas and Gadamer

Robert M. Wallace

In this essay I want to show, very briefly and schematically, how certain of Hans Blumenberg's key ideas about rationality, science, and human life differ from the better-known positions of both Jürgen Habermas and Hans-Georg Gadamer on these topics in ways that could enable us to get beyond the chronic conflict, which Habermas and Gadamer typify, between rationalism and (what rationalists describe as) relativism. Blumenberg does not, in general, address Habermas's or Gadamer's positions directly, and neither Habermas nor Gadamer has commented (to my knowledge) on the key Blumenbergian ideas that I will lay out, so the dialectical connections that I will suggest are not yet widely appreciated. But a careful reading of Blumenberg makes it obvious that they are not at all accidental.

I will begin by outlining Habermas's rationalist project. Since his well-known debate with Gadamer in the late 1960s,[1] Habermas has been engaged in developing a program under the rubrics of "universal pragmatics" and a theory of "communicative action," which would establish the universal significance and validity of modern scientific and moral/practical rationality against what he sees as the relativistic implications of hermeneutics. His central concept in this effort has been that of 'communicative competence,' a universal human goal that Habermas wants to analyze in a manner paralleling Chomsky's account of linguistic competence, Piaget's of cognitive development, and Kohlberg's of moral development; and Habermas imagines that when we understand this goal state and the process of development that leads up to it, we will be able to reconstruct the history of the human species as aiming at it in the same way that the history of each normal individual does. And insofar as modernity exhibits this kind of "species competence,"[2] more clearly than any other cultural formation does, modernity's universal validity, for the species, will be evident.

It is obvious that this ambitious program bears a definite resemblance to the great modern "philosophies of history," from Voltaire and Condorcet through Kant, Hegel, Compte, and Marx. Habermas of course claims that his theory differs from some of these in that it is not an a priori one but is capable of being falsified by its possible failure to conform (in the case of individual development) to the great majority of the intuitions of competent subjects and (in the case of history) to the historical data. Whatever one may think about the former case, in the case of history there is certainly room for skepticism about the results of such testing, because the uniqueness of the sequence of the species's (supposed) "development"—the fact that it has only happened once—makes it difficult to know how to distinguish its essential features from its accidental ones, so as to compare the process to whatever we decide is essential to the developing competence of individuals. In which case, the difference between Habermas's program and the classical philosophies of history may be less clear than he would like it to be.[3]

However that may be, another noteworthy thing about Habermas's model, beyond its awe-inspiring ambition as a "research program," is how conventional and unsurprising its basic content sounds. Unlike the antipositivist theses of some of his earlier work (*Knowledge and Human Interests*, in particular), the antirelativist thesis of this recent work is absolutely in line with mainstream modern thinking, from the eighteenth century onwards, about the nature and significance of science and other modern undertakings. What it does do, however, is to articulate assumptions that are not always stated so clearly in the twentieth-century versions of this type of thinking. In particular, the conception of the history of the species as a goal-directed process, in which we moderns have arrived at the goal or are closer to arriving at it than anyone else, is less often stated (now that explicit "philosophies of history" have fallen into disrepute) than it is (probably) taken for granted as an unspoken premise.

When it is stated, however, it is not easy to reconcile with other, equally basic modern assumptions. Blumenberg suggests this when, in a discussion of the way this attitude influences writing about the history of science, he calls it "temporally 'nostrocentric'" (us-centered); thus putting it in the same class as the "geocentric," "anthropocentric," and "ethnocentric" views that we think we have overcome since Copernicus, Darwin, and (say) Ruth Benedict.[4] Identifying our own attitudes as those that the whole history of mankind aimed at bringing about *is* a bit presumptuous, when you look at it that way. Besides being presumptuous, however, viewing history as having an inherent goal at all conflicts, on the face of it, with the suspicion of teleology, which has been a continuous theme of modern scientific thinking since Descartes and Bacon. And, finally, as Kant himself came close to noticing and as Blumenberg emphasizes, the idea that the species's moral and intellectual "competence" develops in the course of its history, so that earlier generations are in principle incapable of the *Mündigkeit,* the full adult responsibility that we think we have arrived at, requires us to deny those generations the full respect that Kant taught us is due to fellow free moral agents. "Thought-structures of the 'education of the human race' type," Blumenberg writes, "defend the idea that history has a meaning [or: a direction] at the cost of those who were born too early to be able already to be 'well-educated.'"[5]

"Well, you may have a point," I can imagine Habermas responding, "but how can we have an objective critique of evils like systematically distorted communication if we have no normative ideal of human competence, or (which amounts to the same thing) if we assume a priori that all cultures are equal in their ability to implement it? Won't this lead in practice to a relativism in which human values and decisions are ultimately arbitrary and irrational?" This was Habermas's essential objection to Gadamer's hermeneutics, and the avoidance of this, as the supposed alternative, is his strongest argument for the whole universal-pragmatic project.

However, Blumenberg shows a way between the horns of this rationalist/relativist dilemma by providing an analysis of the relation between tradition and critique, human finitude and rationality, which is more complex and convincing than what either Gadamer or Habermas is able to provide, in two crucial ways. First, Blumenberg proposes a type of unifying historical interpretation that can make modernity comprehensible and legitimate (as Habermas, very reasonably, wants to do) but without having recourse to the "nostrocentric" teleology that Habermas (like the great modern philosophers of history) employs for this purpose. In this way, Blumenberg gives an account of the human metaphysical/biological condition—a "philosophical anthropology"—that enables us to understand the necessary dialectic of tradition and rational criticism, in human life, in a way that (again) neither Habermas nor Gadamer enables us to do. Thus the rationalist/relativist crux by which thought has been bedeviled since the time of Romanticism appears to be avoidable, after all, if reason can comprehend its own finitude in the way Blumenberg suggests.[6]

Let us look at the first aspect—Blumenberg's historical legitimation of modernity. It has generally been assumed that if one could understand the genesis of modernity as unambiguous progress, by some universally valid standard (as Habermas and his predecessors in the philosophy of history do), then there would be no adequate reason for our commitment to it and that commitment would have to be felt as essentially random and arbitrary (unless— still worse—it were part of some process of inevitable decline). Habermas's insistence, in his criticisms of Gadamer, on the extralinguistic constraints of reality and of our pragmatic dealings with it and on the possible "objectivity" of critique can be understood as an insistence that our commitment to modernity is not arbitrary in this way but is based on a universally valid "learning process" (as progress is described in his "Reconstruction of Historical Materialism").[7]

Now, what Blumenberg does in *The Legitimacy of the Modern Age* is to show how it is possible to understand the genesis of modernity as a compelling and legitimate process without understanding it as a progress toward something universally valid (such as final human "competence"). For Blumenberg, modernity is legitimated not by a goal but by a preceding problem: the problem of "theological absolutism," the late medieval and Reformation inscrutability of the divine will and impotence of human effort in matters of faith and salvation. Blumenberg argues that given nominalism's theologically motivated destruction of the notion of an inherently orderly cosmos, the only alternative left to man in this situation was to seek epistemic and technical control of the world—as modern man has done. But the crucial thing to notice, for our present purposes, is that we seek this control of the world, not because reality, rationality, or human nature ("competence") dictates such an attitude, but because a previous way of being in the world has come to constitute an insoluble problem for us, to which the move to modernity constituted the nearest thing to a solution that was available. That is, Blumenberg's explanation and legitimation of modernity is in terms not of teleological goal, a *terminus ad quem*, but of a preceding problem—a *terminus a quo*. This is only one case, as we will see, in which this kind of shift is crucial to Blumenberg's thinking.

Of course, however convincing it may be as an historical interpretation, this kind of account will never really satisfy a universalist like Habermas. Even when it is filled in with comparable accounts of the preceding epochs—the genesis of Christianity itself as the nearest thing to a solution to the problems of ancient thought in their ultimate radicalized form in Gnosticism; and the genesis of ancient cosmic metaphysics as the nearest thing to a solution of the problems left by myth—

Blumenberg's story will always leave the rationalist unsatisfied feeling that his modern mode of existence is being "justified" by its relation to other historical phenomena that are themselves (as he sees them) "arbitrary," not dictated by reality, rationality, or human nature as such.[8] Modernity is being justified as, in effect, a way of "coping" with human problems, rather than as a fully "competent," *mündig* way of dealing with reality—and thus it may not provide a basis for the kind of (ultimately) objective "critique" (of forms of consciousness and communication) that Habermas wants to defend. However, given the way the latter ambitions lead, at least in Habermas's case, to modes of thought that themselves appear to conflict with basic modern precepts like suspicion of teleology, and universal respect for fellow human beings (irrespective of contingent circumstances like their particular location in history), the case for considering Blumenberg's more modest alternative seems strong.

It is time to turn to the second aspect of Blumenberg's solution to the dilemma of rationalism versus relativism. What I want to show is how Blumenberg not only gives us a more acceptable interpretation of the nature and status of modernity and its form of rationality than Habermas can provide, but also gives us an account of the human condition that legitimizes "tradition" and clarifies its relation to critical reason in ways that go beyond what either Habermas or Gadamer has been able to provide.

In his *Die Lesbarkeit der Welt* (1981), Blumenberg takes pains to distinguish his own attitude to language and reality from the one suggested by Gadamer's doctrine, in *Truth and Method*, that "Being that can be understood is language."[9] Blumenberg apparently would not object to the proposition that language is a *precondition* of understanding anything, but he suspects that "the metaphorical linguistification of Being [itself] is aesthetic," and "is entirely in the service of a concept of 'Being' that is directed against the ideal of scientific objectivization."[10] As one who argues for the "legitimacy of the modern age," Blumenberg can hardly endorse such a project.

But of course from the fact that Blumenberg agrees with Habermas in this kind of criticism of the antiscientific tendency that Gadamer (despite his protestations to the contrary) has inherited from Heidegger, it does not follow that Blumenberg will interpret the role of the "ideal of scientific objectivization" in human life in the same way that Habermas does. A key passage in which Blumenberg's difference from Habermas on this subject emerges is the following, from his *Work on Myth*:

> Rationality is all too ready to engage in destruction when it fails to recognize the rationality of things for which no rational foundation is given,

> and it believes it can afford to get carried away by the process of establishing rational foundations . . . One does not need to be conservative . . . to see that the demand for "critical" destruction, and then for a final rational foundation, leads to burdens of proof that, if they were really accepted and undertaken as seriously as they are asserted and demanded, would no longer leave room for what is supposed to be gained, by this process, for the intelligent movement of existence . . . There is an extravagant attitude toward the establishment of rational foundations that assumes from the beginning, or at least accepts, that only those who are professionally commissioned or self-commissioned to carry it out can afford to engage in it. If, however, enlightenment allows thought to be legitimated only by the fact that everyone does it himself and for himself, then thought is the only thing that has to be excepted from the human capacity to delegate actions. From that, in turn, it follows that something that everyone unavoidably has to do himself and for himself simply must not be an 'endless task.' As such it stands in indissoluble contradiction to the meager finitude of the life that the thinker-for-himself has disposition over. Reason . . . must then reach some accommodation with this fundamental condition of our existence . . . Philosophy has to keep this antinomy of life and thought in mind in connection with all the self-addressed demands for rationality that spring from its own womb.[11]

By emphasizing the Enlightenment theme of thinking for oneself (the "sapere aude" of Kant's essay "What is Enlightenment?") as the key to emancipation, Blumenberg draws attention to the ambiguity of Critical Theory, which wants to promote this kind of emancipation by means of an objective-scientific "critique" that (given what we know by now about the nature of science) can only be the province of experts. The kind of "scientific objectivization" that Habermas is so anxious to preserve (and that he exemplifies, in his debate with Gadamer, in the person of the psychoanalyst) inevitably depends, insofar as it is scientific, on the temporally unconstrained pursuit of truth, which Husserl described as an "endless task" and which Habermas himself describes as necessarily free from the pressures of action and which, therefore, as Blumenberg points out, stands in "contradiction to the meager finitude of the life that the thinker-for-himself has disposition over." As Blumenberg says, one response to this contradiction is to delegate the function of objectivization and critique to a caste of experts, who can come closer to objectivity by virtue of their (as it were) "disembodied" identification with the pursuit of truth. But to do this precisely, as Blumenberg points out, is to abandon the Enlightenment's legitimation of thought "by the fact that everyone does it himself and for himself." "Any danger," he goes on to say, "would be worth confronting at this point to avoid having to pay that fatal price."[12]

What, then, is the alternative "accommodation" with our finitude that he has in mind? It is the acceptance of the bulk of our inherited mental and behavioral equipment—what Gadamer calls our "prejudices," but Blumenberg (following Arnold Gehlen) calls our "Institutions"—without explicit and specific rational justification. But not—and here is where Blumenberg differs from Gehlen and clarifies a subject on which I think Gadamer leaves his readers in some confusion—*not* in a state of immunity from criticism:[13]

> What the heading of 'Institutions' covers is, above all, a distribution of burdens of proof. Where an Institution exists, the question of its rational foundation is not, of itself, urgent, and the burden of proof lies on the person who objects to the arrangement the Institution carries with it.[14]

This is how the burden of establishing rational foundations is reduced to manageable proportions—without being eliminated, as in pure traditionalism. Blumenberg makes it clear throughout his work (beginning with the next page of *Work on Myth*, where he describes Thales of Miletus as successfully "reopening the proceedings" regarding this way to talk about the world as a whole) that the "burden of proof" of the "person who objects" can in fact be carried successfully, in the right circumstances. Reason, in that sense, can "prevail"—but, fortunately for us, our every move does not depend upon the occurrence of such an event.

Besides explaining why it is *practically* necessary for us to place a presumption[15] of validity on the side of tradition (so as to reduce the task of establishing rational foundations to humanly manageable proportions), Blumenberg also provides us with a general reason for thinking that the contents of our traditions—that is, our Institutions, from ordinary-language predicates to myths to manners—probably, in general, *deserve* such trust. They are, he says, the products of a process of selection that parallels, in the cultural realm, the selection that generates well-adapted species in nature—though in the cultural case what survives is precisely not individuals or populations of Homo sapiens but the well-adapted cultural *artefacts* that meet human needs. The example that Blumenberg uses is the development of myths, which he pictures as a "fine-textured and intensive testing of the reliable effectiveness of all the ingredients"[16] through the process of oral story-telling, in which the success, and thus the survival, of innovations depends entirely on the reception of those innovations by the immediate audience. It is easy to see how the innumerable acts, by innumerable individuals, of acceptance and rejection of cultural innovations of other kinds constitute a similar testing process that creates a reasonable presumption that the "product" that survives it meets human needs, even though no one may ever have consciously articulated—or even looked for—a *reason* for thinking that that should be true, in a particular case. The process can be, in that sense, just as "mechanical" as its biological analogue, *natural* selection.

Habermas, too, like many social theorists, wants to apply the concept of evolution to culture and society, but in his version (in his "Reconstruction of Historical Materialism") there is no real analogy to natural *selection*. Instead, Habermas conceives of evolution in terms of "learning" and consequently—as might have been expected—in a rather teleological manner.[17] Models of cultural evolution that combine (1) discontinuity with natural selection and (2) a close *analogy* to it, in the way that Blumenberg's model does, are rare and still not widely discussed, which I suspect is probably due (in part) to the difficulty of achieving a view of man that is as thoroughly nonanthropocentric and nonteleological as Blumenberg's is.[18]

Failing to find a cogent analogy between biological and cultural "evolution," Habermas (and Gadamer is no different, in this regard) also fails—throughout his work—to address in any direct or persuasive way the fundamental question between man's animal and cultural natures. In general, biology is notable by its absence from Habermas's thinking about man, preoccupied as that thinking is by man's special distinguishing characteristic and supposed goal: by reason, *Mündigkeit*, competence. For Blumenberg, on the other hand (who follows Gehlen, here), biology plays a crucial role in explaining what sets man apart from all living creatures, and it does so not (obviously) by erasing that division (in the manner of, say, Social Darwinism or sociobiology) but by presenting the *problem* to which human culture, or reason, is our unique solution. (So here, again, Blumenberg shifts our attention from a questionable *terminus ad quem* to a plausible *terminus a quo*.) We should not take it for granted, Blumenberg says, that a creature like man is able to exist at all:

> Man's deficiency in specific dispositions for reactive behavior vis-à-vis reality—that is, his poverty of instincts—is the starting point for the central anthropological question as to how this creature is able to exist in spite of his lack of fixed biological dispositions.

That is, man starts out with a major biological problem (initially, no doubt, a result of crucial ecological change by which the instincts of the creature that preceded man were rendered nonadaptive). Blumenberg goes on:

> The answer [to this "central anthropological question"] can be reduced to the formula: not by dealing with this reality directly. The human relation to reality is indirect, circumstantial, delayed, selective, and above all 'metaphorical.'"[19]

To confront reality directly—we can interpret, here—would be the terrifying experience of recognizing our biologically deficient state, our condition as (in Gehlen's term) *Mängelwesen* (deficient creatures). Seen in this light, culture—including "reason," as we know it—is the sum of the means we generate, over time, in order not to have to deal with reality in this way (the way we generate these means—our institutions, from predicates to myths to manners—being, of course, the process of cultural "selection" that I described earlier). If we look at culture independently of its biological matrix—not in terms of the problem it addresses but (perhaps) in terms of some supposed human telos—then it is easy to think of reason as an unusually gifted species's unusual means of *getting at* reality. But if, on the other hand, we take seriously the unique biological *problem* to which reason has been (part of) our solution, we can appreciate the possible rationality—in the sense of survival value—of cultural artefacts, such as myths, that connect us only indirectly, if at all, with reality, in that they have no evident rational justification that is specific to their case. Their "time-testedness" simply creates a (refutable) general presumption that they should be respected as meeting *some* kind of human need.

By lowering, in this way, the Habermasian standard for what can count as rational, so as to "accommodate" rationality to the constraints of our finite and biologically contingent condition, Blumenberg's "Darwinism of culture"[20] also clarifies and (for the first time) provides a rational basis for accepting, in general, the "authority" that Gadamer associates with "tradition," but which Gadamer is never able to distinguish clearly enough from the authority that derives from the provision of specific reasons in support of the particular item in question.[21] Just as Gadamer lacks Blumenberg's precise formulation of the relation between tradition and critique as a distribution of the burden of proof,[22] so he also lacks anything like this Blumenbergian account of the general grounds for the reliability of traditional Institutions, so that his traditionalism retains an element of dogmatism (or, alternatively, confusion) that is equal and opposite to and no more rational than Habermas's rationalist dogmatism.

To the complaint that I imagined Habermas making, then—that without a universal normative ideal of human competence, by which patterns of communication and (indeed) whole cultures can be objectively judged and found (to various degrees) wanting, our values and decisions will ultimately be arbitrary and irrational—to this I imagine Blumenberg responding that particular habitual modes of thought and action are, of course, open to criticism (by the lights that we have at a particular time, including whatever conceptions of universality and objectivity and of pluralism and tolerance we have at that time), but that since (as a result of our finitude) this sort of critical evaluation can be done only in a piecemeal fashion, it would be presumptuous of us to claim that the point that we moderns have arrived at in this process is closer to a comprehensive, universal ideal than any other stage in the process may be. For since all we ever deal with is a piece of it, we have no basis for assuming that the process, overall, objectively possesses the kind of unambiguous direction that is implied in concepts like 'competence,' *Mündigkeit,* and 'maturity,' so that a change brought about by piecemeal criticism will necessarily represent progress toward such a goal. Our making such a change—when we think that the critic's "burden of proof" has been met—does, by definition, imply that we judge this to represent *progress on the point in question.* But this "proof" cannot claim to be based on human nature and its relation to reality *in toto,* because we do not have a concept of human nature or its relation to reality *in toto* on which to base it. Rationalists like Habermas will reply that while we may at this moment lack such a concept, we should not despair but pursue one, since only by means of it can we be properly rational. The alternative, they think, is relativism, and relativism is an acceptance of ultimate irrationality. But this is what Blumenberg shows is not the case. To lack a concept of human nature or its relation to reality *in toto* is not to lack rationality all together or to be condemned to relying on what is merely an accidental historical inheritance. For that inheritance is not "accidental" in the sense of *arbitrary.* It is a product of selective process (the "Darwinism of culture") which we have some *reason* to think adapts it to our needs; and we are able, not to replace it *in toto,* but to criticize it rationally and revise it in a piecemeal manner. If this is a kind of "relativism," it certainly cannot be described as an acceptance of ultimate irrationality. It is simply a rational accomodation with the "meager finitude" of the lives that we have disposition over.

My suggestion, then, is that rather than betting everything on the possible establishment of first-order rational foundations (like Habermas), it may be more realistic, in view of our finitude and neediness, to rely on something like Blumenberg's combination of second-order rational Institutions and first-order rational criticisms of them.

This, then, is how Blumenberg threads his way between the horns of the rationalist/relativist dilemma. I would suggest that the means by which he does so—his "burden of proof" analysis, his (non–Social

Darwinist, nonsociobiological) Darwinism of culture and his interpretations of modernity, culture, and rationality in terms of their *termini a quibus,* instead of their supposed teleological *terminus ad quem*—are all sufficiently novel and robust, and their combination is certainly of sufficiently broad relevance and applicability that they should be examined and evaluated with care by anyone who is concerned with these issues.

13

History, Art, and Truth: Wellmer's Critique of Adorno

Lambert Zuidervaart

> Art's vocation is to unveil the *truth* in the form of sensuous artistic configuration, to set forth the reconciled opposition just mentioned, and so to have its end and aim in itself, in this very setting forth and unveiling. For other ends, like instruction, purification, bettering, financial gain, struggling for fame and honour, have nothing to do with the work of art as such, and do not determine its nature.
>
> G. W. F. Hegel, *Aesthetics: Lectures on Fine Art*

Hegel's view of the vocation of art suggests a close connection between the philosophy of history and the philosophy of art. This connection has remained deeply embedded in the tradition of German philosophy. German aesthetics implies questions of *Geschichtsphilosophie,* and vice-versa. Perhaps the connection is made most obvious by questions about rationality and truth in human history. Such questions figure prominently in the writings of Theodor W. Adorno, and they remain central for his successors. The reflections on history, art, and truth in Adorno's *Aesthetic Theory* crystallize conflicts about rationality that have been fundamental to German philosophy and indeed to modern societies.

Among the most interesting criticisms of Adorno's aesthetics in recent years are those of the German social philosopher Albrecht Wellmer.[1] In order to situate Wellmer's criticisms, let me briefly mention two directions in which Adorno's critique of rationality has been received. Some of Adorno's successors have retained the strongly negative cast of his critique of rationality but have surrendered his assumption that human beings need to achieve a rational reordering of what has been rationally disordered. Such followers lean towards political anarchism and cultural aestheticism. Their representatives in the academic world gravitate toward poststructuralism and deconstruction. For them, Nietzsche is more attractive than Kant.

Other of Adorno's successors take nearly the opposite tack. They retain the assumption about rational reordering but give up the negative cast of Adorno's critique of reason. Such followers lean toward social democratic politics and cultural moralism. Their representatives in the academic world include some of the more thoughtful critics of poststructuralism and deconstruction. For these critics, Kant is more attractive than Nietzsche. Common to both camps, however, is the tendency to find Hegel's totalizing approach to reason in history even more problematic than it was for Adorno.

Albrecht Wellmer is one of those who retain the assumption about rational reordering but give up the negative cast of Adorno's critique. Yet he remains receptive to the concerns of the other camp, perhaps more so than his close colleague Jürgen Habermas. Like Habermas, Wellmer has been reconstructing the central insights of Frankfurt School philosophy since the 1960s.[2] His reconstruction hinges on the Habermassian claim that Theodor W. Adorno's critique of rationality involves a "performative contradiction." Adorno attempts an ideology critique that questions the basis of all ideology critique.

According to Habermas, ideology critique normally tries to show that the theory being criticized conceals an inadmissible mixture of power and validity. In Horkheimer and Adorno's *Dialectic of Enlightenment,* however, "reason itself is suspected of the baneful confusion of power and validity claims, but still with the intent of enlightenment." The two authors try to show that the pervasive instrumentalizing of reason assimilates reason to power and destroys its critical force. This demonstration is paradoxical, for "it still has to make use of the critique that has been declared dead." Thus, a "performative contradiction" inheres in such a "totalizing critique," one that Adorno consistently tries to carry out in *Negative Dialectics* and *Aesthetic Theory.*[3]

On Wellmer's analysis, the fundamental constraint in Adorno's aesthetics is that it embodies a self-contradicting and totalizing critique of reason. Wellmer identifies three specific problems connected with this constraint. First, instrumental rationality is wrongly set in opposition to aesthetic rationality. Second, the work of art is overloaded as a model of reconciliation. Third, the notion of artistic truth becomes esoteric. To get around these problems, Wellmer employs a Habermassian model of differentiation and integration in rationality. He also replaces the notion of reconciliation with one of uncompelled communication, and he reconnects the concept of 'artistic truth' with validity in everyday speech.

Although the three problems are closely related, I shall discuss only the third.[4] First I shall summarize Wellmer's criticisms and his alternatives. Then I shall try to reclaim some of Adorno's approach to the theme of truth in art. This attempt will discuss two topics, namely the status of philosophical truth claims about art and the historiographic patterns implied by such claims. I focus on the theme of truth in art because a reconstructed concept of 'truth' is central to Wellmer's break with Adorno's critique of rationality. Wellmer's reconstructed concept is a postmodernist replacement for the Hegelian notion of a 'self-completing truth' that Adorno retains, despite his objections to Hegel's totalizing tendencies.[5]

Wellmer does not reject the concept of truth, but he does return it to the sphere of normal discourse. Following Habermas's consensus theory of truth,[6] Wellmer treats truth as one of the norms implied by any use of language for purposes of intersubjective communication. The result for Wellmer's aesthetics is that Adorno's notion of artistic *truth content* gives way to a notion of artistic *truth potential*. The latter notion is supposed to alleviate two problems in Adorno's approach to truth in art. It will be useful to review Wellmer's account of both problems before summarizing his alternative.

1. TRUTH CONTENT AND TRUTH POTENTIAL

The first problem has to do with the relationship between art and philosophy. The problem arises from the fact that Adorno's concept of artistic truth makes works of art depend on philosophical interpretation for disclosure of their truth content. Without philosophical interpretation, art works cannot really fulfill their cognitive functions. The problem is that Adorno "has to conceive of aesthetic knowledge as philosophical insight and the truth of art as philosophical truth."[7] Wellmer suggests two reasons why this is a problem: it privileges the presentational dimension of artistic truth above other dimensions, and it denigrates art's truth potential in ordinary aesthetic experience.

The second problem in Adorno's approach to artistic truth pertains to the relationship between art and history. Wellmer maintains that Adorno turns a utopian idea of reconciliation into "a central moment" of the truth content of the work of art. As a result, every attempt to unravel the truth content in a particular work of art becomes a single attempt to rescue the idea of reconciliation, which art as a whole is supposed to make knowable.[8] Wellmer does not clearly explain why this is a problem, but his reasoning seems to be that the actual function and import of a particular work get swallowed up in a utopian generalization that has little specific bearing on the historical situation for which a work's truth content is supposed to be important.

In describing these problems, Wellmer distinguishes between two meanings of artistic truth: aesthetic validity (*Stimmigkeit*; henceforth, $truth_1$) and presentational truth (*gegenständliche Wahrheit*, or $truth_2$).[9] According to Wellmer, Adorno holds that art can give us the $truth_2$ about reality only by virtue of the $truth_1$ of an artwork's aesthetic synthesis. At the same time, the aesthetic synthesis can be $true_1$ only if it allows social reality to come to appearance ($truth_2$). Because this reality is antagonistic, art can be $true_2$ only to the extent that it presents reality as unreconciled. Yet to present reality as unreconciled, artworks must achieve a "nonviolent aesthetic synthesis of the diffuse" whose validity places reality in the light of reconciliation. Such a synthesis produces the appearance of reconciliation, whereas reality remains unreconciled. Hence aesthetic synthesis can be $true_1$ only by

> turning against itself and calling its own principle into question—it must do this for the sake of truth which may not be had except by means of this principle . . . The modern work of art must, in one and the same movement, produce as well as negate aesthetic meaning, balance itself as it were on the razor's edge between affirmative semblance and illusionless anti-art.[10]

To circumvent both problems, Wellmer introduces a distinction between truth and truth potential. Truth can be ascribed to art, he says, but only in a metaphorical manner. Art does not literally contain or present truth. Nevertheless, a basis exists for the metaphorical ascription of truth to art, since artworks do have a truth potential. In denying a literal ascription of truth to art, Wellmer relies on Habermas's "language-pragmatic differentiation of the everyday concept of truth."[11] Wellmer distinguishes three dimensions in the everyday concept of truth: "apophantic," "endeetic," and moral-practical or normative truth. These terms denote dimensions of validity which all speakers have at their disposal. Other terms for the three dimensions are *truth* (*Wahrheit*), *truthfulness* (*Wahrhaftigkeit*), and *rightness* (*Richtigkeit*). Although Wellmer does not point this out, the use of truth to indicate the apophantic dimension may indicate that this dimension is the privileged one from which the endeetic and normative dimensions derive their meaning *as* dimensions in ordinary truth.

Be that as it may, Wellmer wishes to deny not only the literal ascription of apophantic truth but also the literal ascription of both endeetic truthfulness and normative rightness to the work of art. To explain why truth can be only metaphorically ascribed to art, he discusses the close connection between aesthetic validity (*Stimmigkeit*) and truth potential (*Wahrheitspotential*) in the work of art. He also examines the structure of aesthetic discourse about the work of art.[12]

2. AESTHETIC VALIDITY AND AESTHETIC DISCOURSE

By "aesthetic validity" Wellmer means a kind of fittingness internal to the work of art. It corresponds to the $truth_1$ of a work's aesthetic synthesis. Although Wellmer does not clearly say how the concept of aesthetic validity relates to the concept of 'validity' dimensions in ordinary discourse, it would seem to indicate a prelinguistic type of normativity. The truth potential of an art work, by comparison, would seem to indicate a prelinguistic type of apophantic truth claim. It corresponds to the artwork's presentational $truth_2$. To the extent that aesthetic validity and truth potential are prelinguistic, they can be normative and apophantic only in a metaphorical sense.

"Truth potential" refers to the potential of artworks for disclosing truth in ordinary experience rather than to their truth content as such. Indeed, Wellmer wishes to replace the notion of truth content with that of truth potential. The question for him is, not what makes an artwork true or false, but rather what makes it capable of carrying truth potential. His answer requires an explanation of the relationship between aesthetic validity and truth potential.

According to Wellmer, metaphors such as "disclosing" or "showing" reality capture the intuitive core of the traditional apophantic concept of artistic truth. The metaphors indicate that we can recognize (*erkennen*) what is being disclosed only if we are already familiar (*kennen*) with it as something that is undisclosed. At the same time, every detail is crucial in a traditional work of art: the reality being disclosed would be different if the work's sensuous configuration were changed. Thus there is an intimate connection between the disclosive power or truth potential of the work of art and the rightness or aesthetic validity of the work's construction.

Truth comes to be ascribed to art because of the way in which aesthetic discourse relates to aesthetic experience. Where there is controversy about what a work discloses (truth potential) and how well it makes the disclosure (aesthetic validity), the discourse points to aesthetic experience in a correcting and expanding manner. The aesthetic validity of the work must be perceived, and this perception involves both the work's being perceived as reality's self-disclosure and reality's being recognized as disclosing itself. Such aesthetic discourse simultaneously addresses both the aesthetic validity of the work and the "authenticity" of its "presentation." Furthermore, to discuss these matters, the participants must mobilize their own experience. This they must do in all three dimensions of truth, truthfulness, and normative rightness at once.

Because of the intimate connections between truth potential and aesthetic validity, on the one hand, and aesthetic discourse and aesthetic experience, on the other, it is easy to ascribe truth to art itself, even though a strictly literal usage would limit the term to discursive claims made about art:

> Neither truth *nor* truthfulness may be attributed *unmetaphorically* to the work of art . . . That truth and truthfulness—and even normative rightness—are instead *metaphorically* bound up with each other in the work of art may only be explained by the fact that the work of art, as a symbolic construct with an aesthetic validity claim, is at the same time the object of an *experience* in which the three dimensions of truth are linked *unmetaphorically*.[13]

Adorno's dialectic of artistic truth has given way to Wellmer's more differentiated account of how the work's aesthetic validity and truth potential function in aesthetic experience and aesthetic discourse. Adorno's allegedly emphatic and antirational concept of truth seems to have been tamed and rationalized. The philosophical disclosure of artistic truth content is no longer crucial. Utopian generalizations no longer threaten to swallow particular works of art. Everyday experience and ordinary discourse will suffice to uncover artistic truth potential.

The domestication of Adorno's concept of artistic truth is crucial for Wellmer's general project. But the price of domestication remains to be determined. On the one hand, the truth content of Adorno's *Aesthetic Theory* culminates in its conception of truth. Adorno's conception holds considerable promise for an age in which traditional ideas of truth no longer seem valid. *Aesthetic Theory* returns the question of truth to the center of philosophical aesthetics without reducing truth to a mere correspondence between propositions and facts, without simply existentializing truth into authentic decisions, and without boldy pragmatizing truth into the test of consequences. At the same time, Adorno shows how theoretical interpretations can honor cultural phenomena without isolating them from their social and historical settings. He emphasizes the importance of social consciousness for artistic truth. And he opens aesthetics itself to the test of exegetical fruitfulness rather than entrenching it behind a rigid methodology.[14]

On the other hand, Wellmer's criticisms indicate that Adorno's conception of truth is not completely satisfactory. Further reflection is needed on several topics. One is the concept of 'artistic truth' itself. Another is the status of philosophical discourse and philosophical claims about artistic truth. Still other topics include the historiographic patterns surrounding such claims, and the language in which Adorno couches his conception of truth. Let me restrict my discussion to the topics of philosophical discourse, philosophical truth claims, and the historiographic patterns surrounding such claims. My discussion will develop alternatives that partially derive from both authors.

3. PHILOSOPHICAL DISCOURSE AND AESTHETIC EXPERIENCE

Wellmer's concept of 'artistic truth potential' is supposed to deprivilege the presentational dimension of artistic truth and recognize art's cognitive functions in ordinary experience. In developing this concept, however, Wellmer not only ignores the question of how aesthetic experience relates to philosophical interpretation, but also counts all ascriptions of truth to art as metaphorical. In both cases, new questions arise as to the status of claims about artistic truth.

There is something odd about using the everyday concept of 'truth' to reconceptualize ascriptions of truth to art, for the application of truth to art seems like a peculiarly philosophical practice. If accurate, this impression would not mean that the ascription of truth to art is illegitimate, but it would suggest that the everyday concept of truth might not be the best source of information concerning the status of claims about artistic truth. What seems "metaphorical" from the perspective of ordinary language might not be metaphorical from the perspective of philosophy. In any case, the best starting point for understanding such claims would seem to be philosophical discourse, which always has something extraordinary about it, even among ordinary language philosophers.

To the extent that ascriptions of truth to art occur in philosophical discourse, the relationship of such discourse to aesthetic experience is crucial for understanding claims about artistic truth. There are two sides to this question. The first pertains to the way in which aesthetic experience informs philosophical truth claims. The second pertains to the way in which philosophical truth talk informs aesthetic experience.

1. Wellmer's discussion of truth potential helps one understand how aesthetic experience informs philosophical truth talk. Wellmer holds that controverted claims about a work's presentation of reality

must appeal to the participants' experience of its disclosive power (truth potential) and internal fittingness (aesthetic validity). This suggests that no amount of talking and writing will suffice to establish philosophical truth claims about art in the absence of looking and seeing or listening and hearing or reading and rereading the phenomena in question. An empirical basis is necessary for philosophical aesthetics, even though philosophy lacks the experimental and statistical methods of the natural and social sciences.

The pervasiveness of such a basis in Adorno's aesthetics helps account for the seriousness with which its truth claims must be taken. Adorno emphasizes the necessity of aesthetic experience for philosophical aesthetics, and his own aesthetics is saturated with an intense experience of modern art. In the context of traditional and contemporary philosophies of art, Adorno's emphasis and experience challenge the tendency of some philosophers to write about art without sufficient exposure to its subject matter. Even if truth were simply a correspondence between propositions and facts, insufficient exposure would threaten persistent falsehood in aesthetics. Accurate claims about art can hardly be made if it has not been experienced in such a way that the facts can be ascertained.

The necessity of aesthetic experience in philosophical aesthetics also indicates why analytic aesthetics has sometimes become no less dreary than the traditional approaches it was supposed to replace. Analytic aesthetics conceives of its task as a clarifying exercise in second-order discourse. The philosopher is supposed to sort out the concepts and claims contained in the aesthetic discourse of critics and audiences and, to a lesser extent, in the aesthetic discourse of scholars and educators in the arts. While the contributions of such an approach are undeniable, various limitations have become increasingly apparent over the years. Some of these limitations inhere in the way analytic aesthetics conceives its task.[15]

The analytic philosopher assumes that clarity and consistency are the primary criteria that aesthetic discourse should meet. Yet the experience that gives rise to aesthetic discourse is not of a sort that emphasizes clarity and consistency in the use of language. Consequently the philosophical search for clarity and consistency puts a demand on aesthetic discourse that the latter can hardly be expected to meet so long as it continues to render discussible the experience from which it arises. At the same time, proceeding at one remove from aesthetic discourse itself, the search tends to forget its obligation to submit philosophical claims about aesthetic discourse to the test of aesthetic experience. The result is all too often a philosophical discourse that is irrelevant for art critics, audiences, scholars, and educators, because it lacks any discernible references to art as experienced. The analytic philosopher who says that truth cannot properly be applied to art may thereby be ratifying the distance from art of an aesthetics that restricts itself to second-order discourse.

An emphasis on the necessity of aesthetic experience for philosophical aesthetics need not discount the importance of second-order discourse that can help shape aesthetic experience and the practices of art. A crucial criterion here is the ability to help tune the categories of aesthetic discourse to their peculiar subject matter without restricting their range to the subject matter itself. Adorno's discussion of "technique" is highly instructive in this regard. By conceiving technique to be simultaneously artistic and social, and by treating it in this manner, Adorno indicates how critics and scholars can concentrate on artistic phenomena without losing sight of their social implications. In fact, one of Adorno's major contributions has been to develop new categories that apply to contemporary artistic phenomena and that incorporate a keen social consciousness. These categories can help shape aesthetic experience.

2. Philosophical discourse on artistic truth can also inform aesthetic experience. This occurs in three ways. First, philosophical discussions of truth serve to highlight the peculiarly allusive references in even the least representational art. Philosophical attempts to judge a work's truth or falsity bring to mind what aesthetic experience and aesthetic discourse easily forget, namely that art discloses something about ourselves and our world, something that is hard to pin down but is nonetheless crucial.

Second, philosophical talk about artistic truth or falsity indicates the social and historical limits of aesthetic experience. It serves as a reminder that no matter how good the object, the experience, and the articulation of the experience, a question remains as to the point of it all. Where is it all headed, and is this direction desirable?

Third, philosophical discussions of truth point to the social and historical possibilities of aesthetic discourse. Such talk signals that the script is not finished and the performance is not over once an artistic phenomenon has been experienced and discussed. The phenomenon and the discourse will be absorbed into larger patterns and processes, where they will be more or less significant, more or less important.

By highlighting art's allusiveness, indicating the limits of aesthetic experience, and pointing to the possibilities of aesthetic discourse, philosophical talk about the truth of art reinserts aesthetic experience into the sociohistorical world from which it only seems to depart. Philosophical truth talk destroys the illusion of distance that clings to aesthetic experience and to first- and second-order discourses about art.

Thus, paradoxically, talk that itself seems so distant from everyday experience and ordinary language serves to bring these home.

4. PHILOSOPHICAL TRUTH CLAIMS

The ability of philosophical talk to inform aesthetic experience means, however, that philosophical ascriptions of truth to art cannot be considered as merely metaphorical. Perhaps some deconstructionists would be happy to say such ascriptions are no more metaphorical than any other use of language, since all language usage is metaphorical and lacks objective reference. But this would amount to throwing out the baby with the bathwater. Instead, the suggestion that philosophical ascriptions of truth are not merely metaphorical should be understood as making three points. First, philosophical truth claims about art are no more metaphorical than some other philosophical truth claims. Second, philosophical truth claims about art make meaningful reference to the import of art and aesthetic experience in the modern world. Third, philosophical truth claims about art provide part of the basis for a philosophical theory of truth.

The first point can be illustrated by reference to philosophical claims about the truth of propositions in science. At one level, such claims are fairly straightforward. The philosopher simply puts forward the claim *P* that scientific claim *S* is true. At another level, however, a philosophical claim about the truth of a scientific claim is less straightforward, for the philosophical claim *P* might itself be true in a sense that is different from the way in which the scientific claim *S* is true. At this level the "truth" of philosophical claim *P* calls for a philosophical theory as to the criterion of truth. In elucidating whether claim *P* is true in the same sense as claim *S*, the philosopher must put forward additional claims (P_n) that might be true, but perhaps not in the same sense as either *P* or *S*. If by "metaphorical" one means that a claim does not apply in a straightforward sense, then, compared with scientific claims, philosophical claims P_n about the truth of philosophical claims relative to scientific claims could well be metaphorical. This need not mean, however, that such philosophical claims P_n must be untrue. It would simply mean that, being highly mediated, they might not be true in exactly the same sense that scientific claims are true. To say that philosophical claims P_n can be true only if they are true in the same sense as scientific claims would be to put forward another philosophical claim, one that might itself violate the strict sense of scientific "truth."

Of course there is an important difference between the metaphorical character of philosophical truth claims about scientific claims and the metaphorical character of philosophical truth claims about works of art. The philosopher who ascribes truth to a work of art is not ascribing to it propositions, claims, or other discursive entities. It would be a mistake, however, to conclude from this fact either that the work of art and a philosophical truth claim about it cannot both be true or that the truth of the work of art and the truth of the philosophical truth claim must both be *merely* metaphorical. Rather, the philosophical truth claim cannot be true in exactly the same sense as the work of art is true, and in each case the truth is derivative from a unifying experience and concept of truth. Both the diversity and the derivative status of such meanings of truth allow philosophical truth claims to refer meaningfully to the import of art and aesthetic experience in the modern world. If there were no diversity, there could be no reference, and if there were no derivation from a unifying experience and concept of truth, the reference could not be meaningful.

Meaningful references provide a second reason for saying that philosophical ascriptions of truth to art are not merely metaphorical. Truth talk about art is not simply the figment of an Hegelian imagination, no more than works of art are merely physical, perceptual, and artifactual objects. Works of art in the modern world are also cultural and sociohistorical objects whose production and reception unavoidably involve prelinguistic stances toward truth and falsehood. These stances do not have to be spelled out in sentences and propositions in order to be stances on the truth or falsehood of some cultural practice, social pattern, or historical tendency. They can take shape in works of art, not as a "message" or "idea" somehow separate from these works, but as that which, in the work, the work is all about. Philosophical truth talk does not simply impose truth claims on the work or reconstruct the work in philosophy's image. Rather, to use Adorno's language, philosophical truth talk extrapolates from the work that which, in the work, the work is all about. What gets extrapolated exists independently of its extrapolation, but not in separation from the work from which it is extrapolated.

Philosophical claims concerning the relationship of a philosophical truth claim to the truth content of a particular work have a status similar to philosophical claims P_n concerning the truth of a philosophical claim *P* about the truth of a scientific proposition *S*. In the end, such high-level claims call for a philosophical theory of truth. What philosophers have often failed to consider, however, is the extent to which philosophical truth claims about art provide part of the basis for such a theory.

By making this connection explicit, Adorno provides us with a third and final reason for saying that philosophical ascriptions of truth to art are not merely metaphorical. They are not merely metaphorical because what philosophers take truth to mean is informed in part by the philosophical truth claims they make about art.

Consider, for example, the philosopher who not only denies that a particular work of art displays truth content but also denies that truth can be meaningfully ascribed to any work of art. Usually the latter denial will commit one to a theory of truth according to which only sentences, propositions, and other discursive entities can properly be called "true." An argument for such a theory would consult not works of art but rather the very discursive entities already declared prime candidates for truth or falsehood. If one then pointed out that there exists a type of discourse, namely, philosophical discourse, in which truth is regularly ascribed to art, the reply would probably be that such ascriptions are surely metaphorical or imprecise.

Consider, by contrast, the philosopher who not only makes truth claims about particular works, but also holds that in general such claims are meaningful. Here too the philosopher is usually making a commitment to a philosophical theory of truth, but to a theory in which things other than discursive entities can properly be called "true." Such a theory allows one to consider philosophical ascriptions of truth to art as more than merely metaphorical.

To argue against considering philosophical truth claims merely metaphorical does not establish that art itself is literally true or false. The argument as presented pertains to philosophical ascriptions of truth to art. It does not give an account of the truth of art as such.[16] No more has been attempted than a meta-philosophical clearing operation. Yet the argument does suggest a promising line for future investigation. It may be worth one's while to examine the extent to which philosophical theories of truth are themselves informed by the absence or presence of reflections on what some philosophers call "artistic truth." Whether one calls it truth content, truth potential, or something else, the nondiscursive but experience- and world-disclosive capacities of art seem relevant for what philosophers try to capture when they put forward a theory of truth. What this relevance comes to, however, is far from clear, as is the content of philosophical claims that ascribe or deny truth to art. Because of the close connection between philosophical truth claims about art and philosophical theories of truth, it becomes extremely difficult to adjudicate the conflict between philosophers who do and philosophers who do not think that such claims are merely metaphorical.

5. PATTERNS OF HISTORIOGRAPHY

The difficulty of adjudication becomes compounded when one takes Adorno's position that the truth of art is historical. Not only does this position conflict with some traditional notions of truth in Western philosophy and religion, but it also commits one to making comprehensive claims about history of a sort that contemporary historians are loath to make. Faced with traditional notions of truth as eternal, one must give a plausible case for the legitimacy of making philosophical claims about the historical truth of cultural phenomena. Faced with contemporary skepticism, one must indicate the possible fruitfulness of making such claims. Actually, the case for legitimacy and the indication of fruitfulness are closely linked. Current conditions militate against making philosophical claims about historical truth. Both the legitimacy and fruitfulness of such claims depend in part on their providing a way to maintain critical consciousness within the postmodern culture of consumer capitalism.

Adorno's own historico-philosophical evaluations of modern art provide influential examples of the sorts of claims that are needed. At the same time, his concept of an artistic "context of problems" holds considerable promise as a category to guide philosophical claims about the historical truth of cultural phenomena. This category helps one highlight artistic contributions without foreclosing on future possibilities. The category also helps one construct lines of continuity and discontinuity without imposing an empty unity on the historical process.

To locate cultural phenomena in a "context of problems" is to avoid both the narrowness of technical historiographies and the imprecision of global philosophies of history. To evaluate the contributions of cultural phenomena within their context of problems is to avoid both the positivism of merely descriptive accounts and the idealism of strongly prescriptive accounts. To argue for the legitimacy of such evaluations is to take issue with both the historical relativism of poststructuralism and the historical dogmatism of orthodox Marxism. In all these respects Adorno's approach has much to offer.

His approach becomes problematic, however, insofar as it fails to give a systematic account of its own construction of specific contexts of problems. Despite his emphasis on import and technique, for example, Adorno does not provide the periodizations and classifications warranted by historical patterns in import and technique. Instead, he tends to give us unrepeatable, exemplary treatments of preselected works. This tendency makes his constructions seem arbitrary, even though they rely on a hidden set of historiographic patterns. What is needed, then, is a more explicit presentation of the historiographic patterns within which cultural phenomena are being evaluated.

Without presenting such patterns, which it would make little sense to do apart from an actual historiographic account, one can nevertheless mention the sorts of patterns that need to be presented. These can be labeled synchronic, diachronic, and "perchronic" patterns.[17] Synchronic patterns pertain to problems widely shared by practitioners at a certain time. Diachronic patterns pertain to changes in these problems and their solutions from one generation or era to the next. Perchronic patterns pertain to relatively long lived traditions that inform a cultural practice and that intersect both synchronic and diachronic patterns.

To give a precise and comprehensive historical account of cultural phenomena would thus require the construction of a three-dimensional context of problems. The string quartets of Béla Bartók, for example, would have to be located with respect to twentieth-century challenges of composition and performance. They would also have to be inspected as giving new solutions to older problems in this genre as well as providing new problems for subsequent practitioners. And they would have to be situated in a tradition of purely instrumental music going back several centuries. All three dimensions would have to be explored if one wanted to give a defensible evaluation of the historical truth of Bartók's string quartets.

If one wanted to avoid the narrowness of technical historiographies, however, one would also have to read behind the lines, as it were, of the patterns mentioned. Adorno's reading treats the work of art as a sociohistorical "monad." This category suggests that one must go beyond strictly literary or musical or artistic patterns in order to make sense of literary history or music history or art history. As is clear from Adorno's own interpretations, to go beyond these patterns one must have a larger picture of the historical process. Despite the problems inherent in a global philosophy of history, something like this is needed for any historiography of the arts that wishes to exceed the writing of technical monographs. A similar point could easily be made about the history of philosophy in relationship to other histories.

In fact, Adorno's reflections on the history of philosophy can shed an indirect light on art historiography. Within the history of philosophy, he asserts, there appears something of the movement of history as a whole.[18] Adorno's own studies of Kierkegaard, Husserl, and Hegel attempt to disclose something of this larger historical movement. Most important in the present context is Adorno's assertion, not his attempts at carrying it out.

Adorno's claim about the history of philosophy helps illuminate what has been described as "reading behind the lines" of strictly artistic patterns. To the extent that the arts have become integrated into an institution of art in Western society, the history of art can be said to have acquired its own integrity. This integrity should not be simply equated with either professionalization or specialization. If the history of art does have its own integrity, then this can be thought to provide impetus not only to the historical unfolding of art but also to historiographic attempts to grasp this unfolding. One need not generalize speciously from more technical historiographies in order to write a general historiography of the arts, nor need one impose inappropriate theorems of philosophical historiography. The history of art is neither a convenient fiction nor an ideological imposition. It is an actual process that calls for a general historiography of the arts, one that reads across the lines of strictly literary, musical, and other patterns.

Furthermore, the history of art need not be studied as if it were separate from the histories of other phenomena, whether these be political, economic, philosophical, or religious. One can emphasize how internal to the history of art the entire movement of history is, and one can expect that comprehending art's history will require some grasp of the entire movement of history internal to it. As Adorno's own writings demonstrate, one of the better ways to achieve this grasp is by way of an immanent but critical analysis of artistic phenomena. At the same time, Adorno's assertion about the history of philosophy suggests that, no matter how comprehensive, one's historiographic account will not suffice for comprehending the entire movement of history. Both the history of art and history as a whole continually elude our grasp and reorient our historiography.

None of this means, however, that philosophical claims about the historical truth of cultural phenomena are doomed to failure. Instead, such claims are crucial to any historiography of art that wishes to respect both the integrity of art history and its connection with history as a whole. Philosophical truth claims are the most comprehensive historiographic judgments that one can make about artistic phenomena. Such claims bring together one's evaluation of the phenomena in a context of problems and one's understanding of the historiographic patterns that inform this evaluation. To say of a work of art that it is true is to make a discussible judgment concerning its contributions in a certain time and tradition as well as over the years. To say this is also to make explicit how one thinks the work of art stands in the entire movement of history. If one acknowledges that even this claim is caught up in history, and if one does not pretend that a truth claim is itself the truth, then the claim can be legitimate and fruitful.

Of course, such a claim will seem illegitimate both to those who think truth is eternal and to those who consider it unknowable. Compared with traditional absolutism and contemporary skepticism, however, there is a double advantage to the practice of making philosophical truth claims as comprehensive historiographic judgments. On the one hand, this practice does not try to elevate critical consciousness above current conditions. On the other hand, critical consciousness is not surrendered to the push and pull of contemporary culture. The legitimacy and fruitfulness of making historico-philosophical truth claims about art are linked to the need to maintain critical consciousness within a culture that makes all truth claims seem presumptuous or irrelevant. It is in providing means to resist the glitzy culture of consumer capitalism that Adorno's challenge and legacy lie.

Part 5

Narrative Fictions: Theaters of Danger

The question of narrative organization, as a chronological and causally structured sequence of events, haunts since Aristotle the definition of *mythos* as the essence of the dramatic genre. *Mythos* is defined by Aristotle as the "representation of action" and plot is the defining trait of tragedy as a genre. The structural principles for the organization of narrative thus appear to coincide with dramatic principles. Does the drama of narrative imply through *mythos* its convergence with theatricality? Although sharing the capacity for fictionalizing the self, by representing its participation and experience of the world, are we to believe that narrative is nothing more than a form of dramatization? More importantly, if narrative is not dramatic in the theatrical sense, where does its "drama" lie?

These are the questions that Dana Rudelic raises in the attempt to ascertain the status of narrative for both narratology and psychoanalytic theory. Her project is to dissociate narrative from its identification with drama, since such an analogy reduces narrative to the logic and chronology of the Aristotelian *logos* and *mythos*. Moreover, this account mistakes the birth of narrative with the foundation of the symbolic and oedipal order in tragedy and thereby misrepresents it as a tragic fiction of identity. Against this definition, Rudelic highlights the capacities of narrative to integrate within itself the inexplicable or the irrational (*alogon*). Whether this other is poetic or illogical (impossible), it marks the permeability of narrative by other discursive modes or genres, which according to Rudelic defines narrative as a "transmodal" space. Thus narrative tells a double story: its coming into being as a specific literary genre corresponds to an affirmation of its dramatic character (a "fiction of identity") at the same time that its transmodelizing features interrupt and recode the identity of fictional narrative. By restaging the unity and function of narration, Rudelic inscribes within the discourse of narration the possibility of a psychoanalytic cure.

Carol L. Bernstein examines the ethical prescription of narrative by locating it, not in the didactic aspects of narrative, but in its omissions or ellipses. Challenging the moral imagination of narrative, she inscribes moral insight into the aesthetic and rhetorical complexities of narrative. She describes the force of narrative in terms of the secondary aspects of narration, that is, in the plurality of readings that it engenders. Ellipsis disrupts the *mythos* of narration by inscribing within it a metaphorical gamble, thus allowing the reader to "hedge one's bets." This is why, according to Bernstein, narrative may be most ethical when it is most suspect and ethics most persuasive when its metaphorical character is deliberately staged.

David Halliburton's essay invokes the questions regarding the definition of narrative by exploring the didactic potential of drama. He examines Brecht's social and political mandate, manifest in his attempts to "dialecticize" theatre through an appeal to experience, one that redefines its dramatic character through an inclusion of narrative, musical, and visual documentation and theoretical concerns. As Halliburton points out, Brecht's movement from an epic theater to the *Lehrstuck*, and later to a "dialectical theater," represents his effort to think of experience in relation to dialectics. But Brecht's notion of experience involves an experimental attitude towards it, leading to an "alteration in the demonstrated experience, such that an alienation effect is achieved." Adopted from discussions of narrative, this alienation effect disrupts the unicity of experience, fracturing and reframing the meaning of theater as a "duration within the world." While equating Brechtian theater with the ethnic theatre of ritual, Halliburton exposes the dangers of dialectical sublation as it confronts its subsumptive potential. Unlike Artaud's theatre of cruelty, Brecht subordinates his theater to ideology, thereby both inaugurating and also endangering his theater of danger.

14

Tragic Fiction of Identity and the Narrative Self

Dana Rudelic

Contemporary narratology seems to agree with the psychoanalytical theory on the fact that the narration of a story presupposes a capacity of fictionalization, of representation of the self in the exterior world perceived through teleological relationships of causal and chronological ordering and governed by proairetic and hermeneutic codes. Critics as different in their approaches as Gerald Prince, Peter Brooks, or Gérard Genette, in their definitions of narrative as a chronologically and causally structured sequence of events, all partake in what may be defined as an Aristotelian heritage of the structuralist model of narrative, namely, an identification of narrative organization with the structure of mythos, considered by Aristotle as the "soul of tragedy" and as the essence of the dramatic modality itself.[1]

Julia Kristeva illustrates well this point of view when, from a standpoint of both poetician and psychoanalytic theorist, she affirms with M. de M'Uzan that "the first narrative, first true past of the individual is elaborated at the moment of Oedipus, that is, at the moment when all earlier stages are reassessed, recovered in a frame of desire from now on constantly mediatized by the problematic of castration."[2] If we admit as an evidence what these different views of narrative all seem to imply, namely, that narrative may display dramatic traits and signal a capacity of the subject to structure the discourse chronologically and causally, as well as a capacity of fictionalization and dramatic representation of oneself in the exterior world, are we to conclude that narrative can be reduced to that sole instance of discursive practice, and consequently should we identify the moment of narrative articulation with the installment of these very capacities, namely, with the advent of the symbolic order and of the Oedipus complex?

My intent is to show, first, that this point of articulation identified by psychoanalytical theory as properly narrative rather determines the articulation of dramatic modalities of discourse: characterized by the oedipal emplacement, by the installment through the family triangle of characters as figures of the Other, the symbolic is first the Law around which is played "an original drama," the prototype of which is to be found in tragedy. Second, I shall argue that such an identification of narrative with a properly dramatic and symbolic functioning reduces narrative to the logic and chronology of Aristotelian *logos* and *mythos* and frames a complex enunciative position of "narrative self" into the family triangle of "unification of the subject in the oedipal relation through desire and castration thereby articulated."[3] Finally, I shall maintain that such a narratological and psychoanalytical staging of narrative origin in a parricidal drama "mistakes" narrative for a drama and misrepresents it as a "tragic fiction of identity."

I shall begin by examining the question of dramatic modality as properly symbolic and oedipal. According to the Freud of *Totem and Taboo,* the tragedy of ancient Greece originates as a repetition of the totemic ritual of the murder of the primitive father. Claude Lévi-Strauss sees the equivalent of the *Vatertottung* as a constitutional event of social order, at the level of the history of the subject in the appearance of language. Indeed, as Lacan says, it is "in the name of the father that we must recognize the support of the symbolic function which, from the dawn of history, has identified his person with the figure of the Law."[4] If we turn to the dramatic genre itself, certain of its characteristics stand out. First, the importance of the technical vocabulary of Law and the centrality of the notion of the sovereign authority and its "lawful interpretations" in ancient Greek tragedy have been underlined by Vernant and Vidal-Nacquet;[5] similarly, the importance of the god-king-father figure in French classical tragedy has been sufficiently dealt with for us not to linger on it. But, more important, as Vernant and Vidal-Nacquet argue, in the culture of ancient Greece, tragedy also opens another space, a space of the imaginary, felt and understood as human artifact. The consciousness of fiction is then, as they put it, "constitutive of dramatic spectacle; it appears simultaneously as its condition and its product."[6] From these preliminary remarks, my argument appears already: through its own textual body, tragedy "symbolizes" or, rather, stages as fictional this double origin, represents the stake of its own modality: the symbolic law of father, god, and king that founds it.

If we pursue Freud's and Lévi-Strauss's parallel of the history of social order and the history of the subject, we may wonder at what moment of his development the subject acquires this capacity of (auto)representation and fictionalization. As Jacques Lacan specifies, before entering the series of so-called secondary identifications (Oedipus) and before being objectified in a "dialectic of identification with the other" with the jubilation of the specular image, the infant while still in its dependent, nonunified phase, rushes into a primordial form that Lacan calls the "Ideal-I" (*je-idéal*). This identification with the mirror image is already and yet is not quite an identification with the other. The specificity of this form resides in the fact that it "situates the instance of ego, before its social determination, in *a fictional line*, forever irreducible for the individual, or rather, that will only asymptotically coincide with the future becoming of the subject, whatever may be the success of dialectical syntheses that should resolve for the I the disaccord with its own reality."[7] This first identification already structures a symbolic mold for the ego. It is already this image in the mirror, the illusion of dramatic identity of the self as the other, that constitutes the space of ego as fiction: a fiction of *unity* (since, contrary to the unified visual perception of body as a whole, an infant from within still experiences his or her body as a sum of predominantly disaggregated motor functions): a fiction of *identity*, since, even before being itself, that is, the other, the ego is already constituted as fictional. Its fictionality does not derive from a mask superimposed onto a preexisting identity; fiction already belongs to this "first" identity and renders it possible.

But, according to Jacques Lacan, the identity of the "Ideal-I" which inscribes the subject in a fictional line, as such remains forever separated from the subject.[8] First instored at the moment of the "mirror stage" (six to eighteen months), this identity will never belong to the subject (since it is fictional), and the subject's efforts to coincide with it through social identifications or through sublimated literary representations will remain eternally vain. Finally, this specular image is the secret cause animating all future totalizing representations and roles of the subject in tragic quest of an unthinkable "absolute subject": the phantasy of wholeness, the mirage of self-sufficiency and the illusion of autonomy are all but disguises of an ego staging its tragic quest through imaginary adventures. Thus the dramatic mode of the plotting (*mythos*) and of fictional representation (*mimēsis*) underlying all these future spectacles allows the original, suppressed tragic image that founds the identity of ego to appear disguised as a story of an-"other," thus perpetually relived in a substitutional, representative form without ever having to be named directly.

Consequently, by its visual, representative nature, with its logic of seeing and displaying, the dramatic modality itself could be seen as already inscribed in the first identification of the "mirror stage," the first tragic spectacle of fictional identity, the moment at which appear characters as figures of the other, when the ego is first detached from the object and launched in the series of secondary, oedipal identifications that will come to constitute its identity. Drama thus becomes one of the objectifying, enunciative instances through which the subject gains access to the symbolic logos and that progressively constructs the identity of his ego.

Recent research in biopsychology of children seems to confirm this hypothesis. As a mode of enunciation, characterized by a dialogical structure and by its fictional nature, in the process of language acquisition, the dramatic modality clearly detaches itself from other discursive and enunciative practices. Among a number of different communication skills, the ability to role-play, to "play as if," as well as the first real dialogue (as a series of questions and responses on the same subject), signal the capacity to project oneself in a nonimmediate situation, as well as a capacity to decenter oneself and to take into account the point of view of the other. Both of these dramatically colored modal specificities are acquired during the fourth year of life (the end of Oedipus). Immediately before that age, and following the "semiotic" moment, at the age of three to four, children are already able to produce discourse without it being strictly speaking either dialogical or fictional. Rather, as they speak, children "narrativize," in a sort of a free association, in a play of free signifiers that are not yet attached to a code of fixed signifieds they will ultimately come to share.[9]

As these experiments show, the advent of the symbolic should not be taken for an instant change. Rather, as Julia Kristeva specifies, there is a moment in this transitional phase between the semiotic and the symbolic, during which the two stages of the development of the subject overlap or, more exactly, as she puts it, where the symbolic includes a part of the semiotic. It is in this "in-between space," where the semiotic is not yet entirely abandoned and where the symbolic is not completely mastered, that we shall look for the moment of narrative articulation, where outside the oedipal scheme already scintillates a narrative positioning proper.

How does psychoanalytic theory describe this moment? It is a state where the ego is already formed but not yet the exterior object, rather a non-object that is, as Kristeva suggests, "the ego of the subject himself, not yet entirely constituted."[10] The nonformation of the object from the outside as such renders the identity of the ego unstable since its identity cannot be posed without being differentiated from the other, its object. At this stage the ego is fragile, undefined, and, just like its nonobject, submitted to the spatial ambivalence as well as to the ambivalence of perception of pleasure and pain. In short, this moment corresponds to what Freud's topology names "primary narcissism," the zone "of impurity" that does not know its specific frontiers and, as Freud puts it in *Totem and Taboo,* is constituted by a play of projections of the exterior toward the interior and vice-versa.

The importance of this moment for artistic practice has been sufficiently emphasized. As Sarah Kofman summarizes it, the narcissistic structure appears as the key for artistic activity, and it characterizes the psyche both of the artist and of the art amateur.[11] Similarly, Winnicott studies creativity and play in relation to this period, and Melanie Klein, while negating the "narcissistic stage" proper, makes of the various "narcissistic states" the object of her research. Finally, both Jacques Lacan and Françoise Dolto differently underscore the fact that primary narcissism precedes and is to be distinguished from the "mirror stage" as a period during which one may not yet speak of unity of the subject but rather of degrees of coherence.

In this difficulty of differentiating the other from the same, while faced with what is already posed in its "haecceity,"[12] I detect the main narrative device: the narrative capacity to integrate in itself what it senses as most alien to it, that heterogeneous, irrational "other" (*alogon*)[13] that it engenders and that it nevertheless senses as the "intrusion" of the other as "not yet narrativized" (the poetic) or "the already symbolized" (dramatic) or as Jacques Derrida puts it, narrative as "the invention of the other in the same."[14] Such an approach to narrative accounts for its fundamental instability and throws a new light on repeated efforts of critics to explain as properly narrative also the moments where narrative "seems to depart from its own nature," as one critic puts it, and on the specificity of the history of the novel as a genre that continuously transgresses the frontiers of other literary modes and genres.[15]

This narrative capacity to integrate the other, above the autoerotic annulment, and without the symbolic interdictions and exclusions, makes narrative build its own identity on the alterity of the other as that which it senses as most proper to it (*alogon*).[16] This impossibility of narrative definition means that one should look for narrative identity paradoxically where narrative is not.[17] This narrative unnameable, I would like to suggest, revives a particularity of primary narcissism, folds around an undecidable borderline with the other mode, other genre, an easily overstepped limit both "through pleasure and pain."[18] Transposed in terms of narrative language, this means that narrativity comes into being already within the permeability of modal frontiers, within a "transmodal" space shared by the semiotic and the symbolic at the moment of the narcissistic nondefinition of the subject/object separation.

Psychoanalytic practice, with discourse as its sole medium, describes this unsettled, fluid model as operating several levels. On the one hand, a dramatized model of narrative, the basis of which resides in the family protagonists, is elaborated in the neurosis of transference (hysterical and obsessional). A hysterical subject thus suffers from reminiscences representing his experience in "animated images"[19] and visualizes his experiences to the point of living scenic fictions and of finding the equivalent of acting in language. On the other hand, insofar as it moves away from this dramatic model, the narrative discourse is engaged in a search for the unconscious foundation of neurosis. Thus, the "subject in process" lives an experience that the schizophrenic pushes to the extreme and where "this process ruptures the totality of a visionalized object and invests its fragments (colors, lines, form), themselves linked to the sounds, words, and signification that are readjusted to new combinations."[20] Finally, in this scheme, while oscillating between these two poles and underlying the two positions, the narrative self abides neither the symbolic law of a tragic, dramatic Oedipus nor the one of the predominantly poetic, semiotic "anti-Oedipus." In constant displacement, it reminds us of that "trans-Oedipus" of which Kristeva speaks in relation to the texts of Georges Bataille and who, in constant rebellion against generic fixation, transcends all permanent modal stasis.

The narrative self, though not entirely exclusive of the "dramatic identity" of the ego as capable of staging its fictions, is nevertheless a space of subjectivity that can be characterized as a dialogical self, as a "subject in process," the empirical (or dramatic) subject intertextualized. The "narrative self" as such is the space of "nonego," a "centric" space as Ann Banfield has argued,[21] a space that is neither the one of pure objectivity (of the predominantly poetic *chora*) nor the symbolic space of pure subjectivity as forever separated from the object (the space of representation as a tragic and dramatic illusion of ego). Rather, it is the "in-between" space of subjectivity reduced to the subject as "exclusion internal to its object" (Lacan), a space that can be recorded only through narrative language.

This "narrative self" underlines the authorial discourse, whether of a novel or of an autobiography, and while always transcending the representational limits of fictionality, it undermines the dramatically fictional mythos and inscribes the narrative discourse in the social, historical, and bodily reality of the subject. It is this same mechanism that enables the analysand to utter his discourse, as "empty" (Lacan) as it may seem, and allows it to be heard. It is only as such that narrative may be considered as the medium of the psychoanalytic situation that finds in it, as Kristeva suggests "the most archaic form of discursive elaboration of the subject's experience."[22]

Consequently, if indeed narrative corresponded to a discursive modality regulated solely by the unification of the subject in an oedipal relation of desire and castration thereby articulated, as psychoanalytical theory suggests, or to a chronological and causal sequence of represented actions and events, as narratology generally holds, psychoanalytical practice would find very little interest in it. The psychoanalytical text itself would be but one of the many stories, epics, or dramas that the subject of theory stages compulsively, unable to exit from their fictional frame, helpless in front of their overwhelming determination. As a parallel text, woven in the margins or, as Freud would probably put it, in the underground of these stories of identity, of the Aristotelian *mythos* and *logos*, narrative rather functions as a transmodal dialectic, setting in motion the modal identities, simultaneously sensed by them as a series of nonsystemic, disruptive interventions that constitute a menace to their unity and identity.

Finally, while we continue to hear and read in narrative only the dramatic fictions of our own imaginary, interminable adventure-stories that stage our own ego as an immortal hero in search of a perfect correspondence with the archaic image of "the mirror parade," our own perception of narrative will remain but a "tragic fiction of identity." Whereas the specificity of the analytic situation is precisely to push gradually the narrative discourse out of its "emptiness," to render it therapeutic by restoring it to the multiple range of its modalities, similarly, one of the main tasks of literary critics should be to render their floating attention available to these contradictory aspects of the narrative text: its apparently coherent and regulated modalities assembled in a "dramatic story," in a "fiction of identity," as well as its transmodalizing features permanently decoding, recoding the subject through discourse, thereby generating a new enunciative position of the "narrative self."

15

Ethical Ellipsis in Narrative

Carol L. Bernstein

What reason would one have to be skeptical about the place of ethics in narrative? To question it would seem to question the humanistic nature of literary tradition, where narrative seems so preeminent an ethical vehicle. The ethical is so frequently intertwined with our conceptions of referentiality that the mimetic function of language itself might be at stake together with the ethical. Even the contemporary critical privileging of allegory, foregrounded in the writing of Paul de Man, which would seem to relegate the "spiritual" to a realm sharply distinct from the domain of concrete description, confers upon narrative sharply defined ethical meanings: here are the sites in which man's "authentically temporal destiny" is unfolded.[1] Nevertheless, there are grounds for skepticism. If we distinguish among types of narrative, then the domain of the story is moral, as Walter Benjamin points out, while the novel, the exemplary form of modern narrative, quests for the "meaning of life."[2] The storyteller, who leaves his own traces upon the story, is part of a vanished community toward which the novelist can at best gesture; an ironic form that bespeaks its own isolation, the novel is reduced to ethical impotence. If the novel is—and here Benjamin quotes Lukács—the "form of transcendental homelessness," then the separation of life and meaning challenges the certainty of the allegorist. Insofar as the ethical entails direct routes to meaning, pitting "moral" against "aesthetic" values, this kind of moral shorthand seems to blank out the free play of language that is so crucial to the literary enterprise. One chapter in aesthetic history, exemplified in Nietzsche's *The Birth of Tragedy*, aligns the aesthetic with a dynamic "life" against the stifling weight of morality. "An ethical sympathy in an artist is an unpardonable mannerism of style," Oscar Wilde remarks, verging upon oxymoron.[3] Finally, the intervention of psychological concerns in narratives tends if not to preempt at least to defer ethical questions while psychology conducts its interior scrutiny. Intention and affect, banished with the advent of New Criticism, return as the objects rather than as the criteria of critical scrutiny. In the pressing contexts of history, psychology, and language, ethical questions are subjected to the operations of irony and to the error, division, and loss of control that accompany it in narrative. From a narrative point of view, the most interesting ethical situations are often the most ambiguous. To act with honor, Vernon Whitford suggests at one point in Meredith's *The Egoist,* is to play the fool.[4] It is when ethical aphorisms threaten to become narrative aporias that novels come into their own.

Some of the most powerful representations of the relation between narrative and ethics rely upon rhetorical arguments. The combination of the moral imagination and the creative imagination, attention and insight, Martha Nussbaum writes, makes the novel the "paradigm" of moral art.[5] Both figurative language and the figurality of structure serve the cause of moral clarity, whose proper vision must transcend the immediate and the sensory. Although seeing clearly is tantamount to seeing morally, that latter position depends upon an imagination that can be manifest only in writing that is both concrete and metaphoric. The metaphoric and the literal turn out to be on comfortable terms with each other, insofar as metaphor, ambassador extraordinary from the court of imagination, presents truth with its rich array of rhetorical forms. From a Jamesian perspective, the degree of aesthetic difficulty or complexity is also the measure of moral insight. Not only is the narrator a purveyor of truth, but his or her rhetorical figures, having traversed the route of personification into fully formed characters, enact a drama of moral choice. If moral acts are not always fully sacrificial—as they are in Nussbaum's discussion—then they are at least renunciatory: the figure for moral choice would be metaphor, or substitution, rather than metonymy, with its "and then . . . and then," or its catalogues of privileged objects and actions. In such scenarios, nevertheless, the renunciations demanded by choice are covered by the richness and ambiguity of figurative language. Figuration acts in a compensatory manner, veiling the loss entailed by substituting the ethical "either/or" for the "both/and" of desire, if not of indecision. The role of metaphor in ethical situations is then deeply ambiguous, insofar as it acts both to articulate truth, to get beyond the veil, and to substitute its own fullness for an underlying lack. (Poetry, Shelley observes, "spreads its own figured curtain or withdraws life's dark veil from before the scene of things," as if to confirm this double, even duplicitous role.[6]) Yet to the extent that these arguments make ethical choice not only an explicit component of narrative, but also analogous to or even identical with aesthetic shape, they raise specters of narrative aporias. Metaphor, Derrida remarks, is elliptical, counting "with a determined absence."[7] In this context, it seems fruitful to inquire into figures of absence or not-naming or reduction or ellipsis, and into figures of plenitude, or of saying too much, represented here by certain forms of repetition. The strategies of ellipsis and repetition in narrative evoke a moral ambiguity that is not easily resolved.

Here are three narratives:

1. Tancred "unwittingly kills his beloved Clorinda in a duel while she is disguised in the armor of an enemy knight. After her burial he makes his way into a strange magic forest which strikes the Crusaders' army with terror. He slashes with his sword at a tall tree; but blood streams from the cut and the voice of Clorinda, whose soul is imprisoned in the tree, is heard complaining that he has wounded his beloved once again."[8]

2. A handsome English couple, theatrical in appearance and "moving like creatures who were fulfilling a supernatural destiny," go for a sail off the coast of Genoa. The young wife, who hates her husband and who has been forced to go on the boat, is "afraid" not of outward dangers but of her own wishes.[9] She kills him in her thoughts. When the wife is next seen, her husband has drowned and she, having jumped in after him, has been retrieved from the water. Sailors tell of an accident. Recounting the episode, the wife says that her husband was struck while turning the sail, that she saw him sink, that he called for the rope as the boat moved away but that she held it in her hands. She is convinced that her inaction was the externalization of her evil longings: "I only know that I saw my wish outside of me."[10] A listener tells her that since her husband could swim, he must have been "seized with cramp," and that she could not have saved him.

3. It is discovered that a much-admired literary figure has written anti-Semitic newspaper articles during the Second World War. A friend and colleague writes of the war "that this man must have lived and endured in himself. He was this war. And for almost a half century, this order was a war because it could not remain a merely private torment. It has to have marked his public gestures, his teaching and writing."[11] Although the shape of this torment is unknown, it has to have left or to have imposed signs on his life.

These narratives will be more or less familiar to readers. The first is an account of Tasso's epic, *Gerusalemme liberata*, which Freud proffers as an example of repetition where the subject appears to be passive and without influence, where he appears to be "pursued by a malignant fate" but where, from a psychoanalytic perspective, he may be assumed to have in some way "arranged" his own fate (with the help of "early infantile influences"). Such a scenario is even more impressive to Freud than those in which the subject discernibly takes part in his or her own fate. Rhetorically, it plays a strategic role in *Beyond the Pleasure Principle* because it is so placed as to be the crucial passage confirming the "compulsion to repeat." Compulsion is at work when it is least apparent: the very events that seem to depend upon chance or accident are those that attest to the individual's coherence and psychic trajectory. It is the rhetoric of suppressed paradox, the denial of what would seem to deny the compulsion to repeat, that is decisive. At this point, my commentary must branch. In the first line of argument, the attribution of such behavior to the individual himself places him morally at risk insofar as he is "responsible" for what he does. Tancred's failure to perceive Clorinda in the tree, as in the armor, amounts to a visual ellipse that no moral summing-up can countenance. Construed after repeated action, desire appears as its aftereffect, as disguised a figure as Tancred's beloved. ("Compulsion" is, nevertheless, ambiguous because it implies that the subject is not entirely free to determine his behavior even if it comes from within: "he is compelled" is a passive construction.) In the second line of argument, Freud's brief account of the narrative foregrounds its "moving poetic picture" but does not address any ethical issue. What matters is the fatal or fateful repetition that does not seem to depend upon any identifiable character trait but that nevertheless leads Freud to posit, with what seems to be a leap in reasoning, the compulsion to repeat. The representation of a narrative, the narrating, exists in tension with the prior text. Repetition, the tension between chance and compulsion, inhabits the action, the telling, and the theory: the narrative's claims to coherence rest upon ellipsis. Can one speak of a *failure* of perception? Masking and illusion are precisely the tropes that represent such a clouded vision. But even when Freud assumes authority in the final telling, he shuns moral pronouncement. It is as if the figure for theoretical progression in this text were the tossing of the child's wooden reel in the *fort-da* of the prior chapter: thought proceeds by going beyond itself and it will only later be "wound up," as it were.

The second narrative, part of the denouement of George Eliot's *Daniel Deronda*, allows its subject to tell her story of the drowning as part of a tryptich, a moral *fort-da*: sailors recount it as an accident; Gwendolen Harleth tells it as a story for which she feels responsibility for her evil wishes and assumes that they can affect the course of external events: those events are the evil wishes turning to confront her. Her delayed jump into the sea is as much a leap away from herself and her "crime" as it is an attempt to save her husband. Wish and fear exist in a metonymic relation, one to the other, and appear in narrative in the shape of repetition. Whether implied or explicit, the double or triple narrative plays out the compulsion to repeat (here somewhat distanced as a property of the "narrating" itself); the enigmatic nature of "fate" as that which seems to be now what "happens," now what one actively desires; and the ambiguous moral position projected by the narrator and the principal players in this drama.

The third narrative is, of course, recognizable as the story of Paul de Man's wartime journalism, recounted by Jacques Derrida in "Paul de Man's War." Like the other two, it is a multiple narrative, to be read first as the story of de Man's literary career, second as the account of the response of the academic and journalistic communities to that career, and third as Derrida's account of de Man's interior life. More specifically, that third account emerges as hypothetical, framed in the conditional mode of "must have" and "could not" and related to the narratives of Freud and Eliot by its insistence that the interior life must be betrayed in "signs." If Freud posits that the poetic or the psychological subsumes the ethical, and Eliot, that the practical determines the ethical, then Derrida faces a different paradox, that of the responsibilities of friendship, which will be determined by a narrative that may not be knowable. What secret shape can de Man's narrative have? Whose is the responsibility to reconstruct, to represent, that story? To represent it in an exculpatory way? And will that secret shape make the highest sign of friendship, that forgiveness that is possible only in the face of the direst, most antipathetic circumstances, the proper response? The responsibilities of friendship arise in the face of the unknowable. There is an uncanny echo here of Derrida's comment on metaphor's oblique relation to truth: "As the moment of the detour in which the truth might still be lost, metaphor indeed belongs to *mimesis,* to the fold of *physis,* to the moment when nature, itself veiling itself, has not yet refound itself in its proper nudity, in the act of its propriety."[12] If, like friendship, metaphor is "proper to man,"[13] it depends upon a certain hiddenness and deferral of truth. Like metaphor, then, friendship is a risky business whose proper nature, whose very propriety, emerges in that marginal space in which truth can be lost. The proper narrative of friendship derives its sustenance from the detours in which the obligation to repeat or to speculate metaphorically defers the false closure in which metaphor would ultimately be discarded. The transfer of narrative responsibility to Derrida ensures the continuity of a friendship in which memory and speculation are on cordial terms with each other.

Narrative makes its own demands. I am "impelled" to address aesthetics, Freud writes at the beginning of "The Uncanny," echoing without naming as a prior text the narrator's compulsion to tell the story of Nathanael in "The Sandman."[14] In part through repetition, the psychoanalyst will attempt to delineate a structure of feeling. Both Freud and Hoffmann are impelled to relate the domestic to the uncanny in texts that call to account the aesthetic or the psychoanalytic. If narrative is inherently duplicitous, if it is compelled to play out its own compulsion to repeat and if narratives are often predicated upon hidden, reversed, or deferred moral directives, what partnership can we discern between ethics and narrative? Let us look at one other narrative. In the opening scene of Hitchcock's *Vertigo*, a police officer follows a policeman who is chasing a criminal across the rooftops of San Francisco. The officer slips and hangs several stories above the street, over an abyss; the policeman tries to help him and falls to his death. The officer suffers afterwards from vertigo, although psychiatrists tell him it wasn't his fault. Subsequently, he finds himself twice in a high place where a death is staged, and although neither death is technically his fault, the repetition leaves ground for suspicion about some form of complicity. Thus the repetition compulsion, situated indeterminately somewhere between the pleasure principle and the death instinct, between external fate or chance and internal drives or subjective coherence, leads us both to suspend the ethical and, by its formative role in narrative, to suspect hidden ethical issues.

If we are to take these narratives seriously, then Tancred's sword, which ostensibly slays either his male enemy or nature, represents his murderous impulses toward (the soul of) his beloved Clorinda. Although the first deaths belong to an externally related series, the second ones signify—or betray—Tancred's own aggressions. It is not aggression itself that is hidden but rather the object of the aggression. Although the continuity of the self is to be predicated upon aggression rather than eros, the ambivalence to the beloved is crucial. Indeed, Freud's accounts of repetition include anger, betrayal, upset and replacement, and fatality: narrative, inseparable from repetition, constructs a self that is by its nature subject to an ethical accounting.

How, then, can the self that is subject to a closed system that precludes choice participate in a scenario concerning choice? One answer would be that under such circumstances, the choice lies not in the actor, in the first narrative, but in the reader or interpreter, in the second narrative. Freud, as the reader of Tasso, makes an interpretive choice, although he too implies that he is compelled by the evidence. But the evidence is enigmatic, and we should note here the ellipsis that characterizes an epic poem as a psychological fable without explicitly explaining why passive repetition is the most compelling evidence for a mental "compulsion to repeat." "There is nothing that commends a story to memory more effectively than that chaste compactness which precludes psychological analysis," Benjamin writes.[15] Here power accrues to narrative by dint of the suppression of its compelling force. Narrative covers an explanatory gap: "Enough is left unexplained," Freud writes of traumatic dreams, to justify the hypothesis. Dreams and long poems, as well as Freud's own text, participate in this elliptical argument. Meaning, Benjamin notes, comes to the writer at the moment of death; dearth-in-meaning, Harold Bloom suggests, characterizes the strong poem. [16]

Derrida's account of de Man's career is similarly written over a biographical ellipsis or abyss where the conditional mode corresponds to the hypothetical. But while the biographical omissions are directed to de Man's position as the actor, Derrida's narrative poses the issues of responsibility to contemporary narrators. Derrida writes, "If it is now a matter of responding and of taking responsibilities, then we do so necessarily, as always, in situations we neither choose nor control, by responding to unforeseeable appeals, that is, to appeals from/of the other that are addressed to us even before we decide on them." Derrida identifies the future as the unforeseeable, thus naming "in effect a future that it was absolutely impossible for me to see coming."[17] The unknown future of an unknown past constructs his narrative: to be open to narrative, then, is to be open to uncertainty, and to what comes to one without the possibility of choice. The narrative of a war must proceed on the basis of a hidden temporality.

"Permit me an ellipsis here since I do not have much more time or space," Derrida writes near the end of his long essay. The ellipsis takes the form of an aphorism about the undeniability of responsibility: *"there is some* [responsibility], *one cannot deny it, one cannot/can only deny it [on ne peut (que) la dénier] precisely because it is impossible."*[18] As de Man's friend and the narrator of a period of de Man's life, he "is left to meditate, endlessly," on the reasons for de Man's silence: here, too, repetition assumes a quasi-passive form in order to address the ethical issues that have emerged from a biographical ellipsis. Derrida's own ellipsis, however, is the figure that enables the acceptance of an impossible responsibility: where de Man was silent, he must read "the traces of [de Man's] suffering" in the texts that are a "wound" for him.[19]

In *Daniel Deronda,* the privileged insight of the novelist allows us to know the thoughts even better than the deed. Gwendolen's action is her inaction: her failure to throw the saving rope. Her remorse is directed to her evil wishes, as if they had been the effective causes of the drowning: and her remorse is what convinces Daniel of her "recoverable nature." Daniel's own position, then, is divided: he is willing to let Gwendolen off the hook, practically speaking, by constructing a hypothetical narrative: but he is equally willing to hold her to account—in reverse, as it were, by excusing her evil wishes because she is remorseful about them. In dreams, Freud writes, we do what we cannot do in actuality: our wishes save us. Gwendolen's deep wound is that wishes have not saved her: wishing or dreaming has cast no *cordon sanitaire* around Gwendolen's thoughts.

The chapter leading up to the drowning opens with the relation of a similar episode in Dante's *Purgatory.* Gwendolen is all too open to figure, to "her own wishes, which were taking shapes possible and impossible, like a cloud of demon-faces."[20] Some time after the event, Gwendolen still feels as though she had been lured to take part in some "Satanic masquerade,"[21] and she wonders whether she has become one of the evil spirits. Eliot's repetition of the figure keeps open that self-wounding, that moral confusion of wish, deed, and remorse.

Ellipsis therefore seems to be a way of hedging one's bets but, nevertheless, a metaphorical gamble in narrative: it plays the game of hypothesis or of proffering figures for what is inevitably absent. Yet in each one of the narratives examined here, whether poem, novel, or history, there is an element of the uncanny: like the return of the repressed, what one does not know returns as a wound that one suffers or inflicts, and the wounding is repeated without that knowledge. Repetition is here in collusion with ellipsis.

We are left, finally, with the paradox that narrative may be at its most ethical when it is at its most suspect, when it risks error and obfuscation and courts the hypothetical, and when it allows indeterminacy to determine its shape. For moral decision may be more metaphorical than we thought, a term whose proper domain may be represented in narrative, but whose boundaries are forever elusive.

16

Dialectics of Experience: Brecht and the Theater of Danger

David Halliburton

From at least as early as the Socratic dialogues until as late as Brecht's attempt to "dialecticize" theatre, dialectic and experience have shown a profound interconnectedness. But for all the showing there has not been much seeing. Brecht is an exception. Brecht saw and proceeded to forge, first in epic theater and then in the *Lehrstück*, an experimental crucible in which the interconnectedness could be explored. In doing so, he rivaled Hofmannsthal in drawing on tradition, Artaud in innovating, and Wagner in synthesizing. Theater had never seen quite the interplay of narrative, song, instrumental music, visual documentation and theory-in-practice that Brecht provided; and it would never be the same again. Late in life, the playwright focused anew on the challenges he had taken up in the *Lehrstück* to create a rigorous dialectics of experience for the stage. This being an enterprise for which neither the name of epic theater nor of *Lehrstück* seemed apt, he substituted the working title of "dialectical theater." From first to last, Brecht kept his attention trained at all times on everyday experience. As my title indicates, the present discussion concentrates on experience in relation to dialectic, with particular concern for a dialectical problem that leads the playwright *beyond* a theater of cruelty, as it were, and toward a theater of danger, in which his approach risks dissolution at the very height of its success.

EXPERIENCE, EXPERIMENT, AND THEATER

In a 1926 interview Brecht already underscores the connection between dialectical process and everyday experience: "I may confine my plays to raw material, but I show only what is typical . . . Even when a character behaves by contradictions that's only because nobody can be identically the same at two unidentical moments."[1] To be effective in the theater, such contradictions, which are otherwise so easily passed over in "ordinary" life, must be shown or demonstrated; hence the famous alienation-effect foregrounded by Russian formalists in their discussions of narrative techniques and retooled by Brecht for the theater; hence too the distillation of demonstration into "the general gest of showing, which always underlies that which is being shown, when the audience is musically addressed by means of songs."[2]

Seeing himself as some sort of a scientist, Brecht was willing in principle to operate experimentally on any and every experiential phenomenon, "experimental" meaning in this case analytical, the not surprising consequence of which is that narrative breaks down into the episodic, the serial, and the gestic (which is not to say any of these is *solely* a feature of narrative). In dramatic terms, the trick is to throw into relief the ways in which the story gets from one episode to another—to point out unmistakably where its knots are tied. In 1931 Brecht takes recourse to Hegel's famous nodal points (*Knotenpunkte*): "We made a short film of the performance, concentrating on the principal nodal points of the action and cutting it so as to bring out the gests in a very abbreviated way . . . ."[3] In ideal dialectical terms, *such a juncture enables the negation, part or whole, of what has preceded, such that, being itself no less liable to negation, a subsequent state can realize in its own sublated terms whatever is for its purposes worthy of being preserved from the stages preceding.* Less technically: in a liminal juncture too much seems to happen, and everything that happens seems to happen at once, yet something is all the while undergoing a processual conflation of continuity with transformation. In epic theater and the *Lehrstück,* as presumably in the later form of dialectical theater as well, something hitherto unnoticed suddenly looms up at the audience, alienating its sense of normality, simultaneously demonstrating to its members that they are having an experience, that the experience is of something they have not experienced previously in just this way, and imposing the imperative of having somehow to deal with it. This crucial process, with its inherent dangers, will be considered more fully when the discussion turns to the relation of sublation to subsumption and the significance of both for the theater of danger.

Brecht's experiments with experience amount to a modernization of Francis Bacon's preoccupations in *Novum Organum*; hence the title of the program statement of 1948 "A Short Organum for the Theatre." For a repertoire of experimental materials, so to speak, the playwright need only show everyday life in its most typical and mundane modes.

While conventional critics took Brecht to task for doing just this, one should bear in mind that *mundane* emerges in the Renaissance (1475) to express precisely the world of everyday things that is the shared environment of everyone:

> A simple way of alienating something is that normally applied to customs and moral principles. A visit, the treatment of an enemy, a lovers' meeting, agreements about politics of business, can be portrayed as if they were simply illustrations of general principles valid for the place in question. Shown thus, the particular and unrepeatable incident acquires a disconcerting look, because it appears as something general, something that has become a principle. As soon as we ask whether in fact it should have become such, or what about it should have done so, we are alienating the incident.[4]

It should be noted, first, that alienation here involves what are basically narrative *gests*. Portraying a visit or a lovers' meeting requires the telling or retelling of *what* visit or meeting. At the same time, the cash value of that process, as William James would say, is what it boils down to, its ultimate purport or principle. This is precisely the process Kenneth Burke calls temporizing essence, by which the merely conative is represented as factual, "what ought to be" become "this is what happened." During the last century, with its historicist inclinations, "the spontaneous thing to do always was to treat questions of *essence*, or *logical* priority, in terms of *temporal* priority. Thus the historicist style of expression led [Poe] into a quasi-temporal or quasi-narrative way of stating a relation between poetry and poetic principles, though this relation actually is not temporal at all."[5]

To alienate the incident is to make it stand out from the rest of the story in a liminal juncture that by definition cannot last. A crisis is created and the audience abused, by conventional standards, because it is being denied the experience it thought it was having and is cruelly being forced not merely to find but to create another experience in its place. Such incessant destruction and re-creation—such negation and negation of negation, to borrow the language of dialectic—is crucial to creating the chaotic effects for which Brecht has often been both praised and criticized. But if this is chaos, it is a case uncomfortably like the murk and jumble of everyday life on which it draws.

An earlier discussion, probably dating to ten years earlier, bears even more eloquent witness to the infinitude of experience. The discussion can serve indeed as a reminder of Dewey's suggestion that an experience can generate any number of theories. The experience in question involves a common street scene in which an eyewitness to a traffic accident demonstrates to bystanders how the accident came about. The demonstrator in this situation performs actions but is not an actor in the orthodox acceptation, which holds that action derives from character: the actor acts as he does because he identifies with an antecedent, author-created character whose binding nature is such that he cannot do otherwise. By contrast with this mimetic posture, the street demonstrator has no such antecedent character with which to identify. How can he know, for example, the kind of person the driver of the vehicle may be? The demonstrator knows only what he can demonstrate, and that is the action that he experienced. The issue here is not alienation in the previous sense but a closely related phenomenon, which is the manner in which the audience's experience is shaped by the ordinary experience (the accident) mediated by the demonstrator. For such a role no Stanislavsky graduates need apply, the demonstrator having too little experience of the persons involved in the accident to identify with them as Stanislavkian actors identify with *dramatis personae*. The demonstrator communicates no more and no less than what he experienced, and what he experienced were precisely actions. To approach the matter from a different angle, the demonstrator must differentiate between his performance as communicator of actions and the subject giving rise to that performance:

> One essential element of the street scene lies in the natural attitude adopted by the demonstrator, which is two-fold; he is always taking two situations into account. He behaves naturally as a demonstrator, and he lets the subject of the demonstration behave naturally too. He never forgets, nor does he allow it to be forgotten, that he is not the subject but the demonstrator. That is to say, what the audience sees is not a fusion between demonstrator and subject, nor some third, independent uncontradictory entity with isolated features of (a) demonstrator and (b) subject, such as the orthodox theatre puts before us in its productions. The feelings and opinions of demonstrator and demonstrated are not merged into one.[6]

This is to say that in the epic theatre, the basic rendering of experience, of which the street scene is an epitome, is effectively allegorical. Whereas the Stanislavskian program is inherently symbolic, calling for identification between actor and character, epic theatre demands that the *dramatis personae* and their impersonators retain their separate identities. Charles Laughton as Galileo never ceases to be Charles Laughton; rather than bring Galileo to life, the actor brings life, his own and that of his society, to Galileo. Equipped with "his own opinions and sensations," rooted as these are in shared social existence, the actor is a lens through which that existence can shine on, in, and through the character in question.[7] In the process the character, the actor, and the audience's own meta-experience of the two-way experience thus allegorized come under interrogation. At all times the otherness and artificiality of the relation between actor and character, like the relation between demonstrator and subject in the street scene, remains in view in much the same way as Brecht's visual documentations (signs announcing songs, screen projections, and the like) remain in view. Given the assertive artificiality of these processes, and, given the visual nature of epic theater's documentary props, one discerns a more than accidental affinity between the latter and the emblems in emblem books and other types of traditional figurations whose correspondence with the indicated other (virtue, vice, holiness, sin) does not require that the figuration yield up its own identity.

The experience of the audience, on which this entire enterprise turns, is just as interpretive in its own way as the experience of the actor: through the actor's interpretive experience the audience experiences interpretively. If the alienation effects and the gests and instrumental music and costumes and songs and visual documentations are successful; if, that is, the members of the audience are forced to see themselves *mutatis mutandis* as Laughtons too, not to mention Galileos, then their interpretive experience is an enabling one on the basis of which they cannot only better comprehend the world but begin to change it.

The world is not "outside" the theater, as more orthodox theories of theater would have it; you do not check your experience at the door before entering the auditorium, there to receive sedation in the dark—though that is precisely the state of the audience, according to Brecht, when "advanced music" is performed.[8] A theatrical phase of experience is, notwithstanding the discontinuities it may embrace, ultimately continuous with other phases of experience: phase because theater is a duration within the world, so that, whereas one cannot say either that the world is outside the theater or that the theater is outside the world, one can say of such and such an experience that it transpired, for example, "after" the theater. This means, not that the particular theatergoer's life began immediately thereafter, but that the duration went on, reaching back out into the street and its scenes.

The street scene, then, is where the spectator returns because the street experiences occur before, during, and after the theater experience. This is partly a statement about lived time. When you go to the theater you bring with you, in you, of you, what you have experienced before going; during the time in which the scenes of the play take place, scenes of the street take place too. But when you make your way again to the street, the experiences you undergo are "after-theater" only in the sense described above: you do not necessarily cease to experience the theater merely because you leave the auditorium, any more than you necessarily cease to experience what you have been reading when you lay down your book. When you go home the theatrical duration endures, ringing in your memory and tingling in your nerves. The statement also points to the street scene as a source of patterns, or, as Brecht at that time would have preferred to say, of models. The power of such a scene is forcefully put: "The street scene determines what kind of experience is to be prepared for the spectator."[9]

Back on that street we find our demonstrator coming under interrogation: "One of the spectators might say: 'But if the victim stepped off the kerb with his right foot, as you showed him doing . . . ' The demonstrator might interrupt, saying: 'I showed him stepping off with his left foot.'"[10] The experimental attitude toward experience so typical of Brecht is here made the clearer by the use of the conditional tense. In the experimental attitude the playwright shows that the dialectic rhythm of epic theater narrative operates in the street as it operates in the theater, the difference being that in the present instance we hear the playwright thinking aloud, as it were. He shows as well that the agonistic tempo runs faster and is more reciprocally polarized than in early dialectic; for no sooner has the demonstrator been interrogated, which is to say interrupted, than he interrupts in turn: in a moment the contradiction finds itself contradicted. The experimental focus becomes an alteration in the demonstrated experience, such that an alienation-effect is achieved. To accomplish this, however, a turn of the screw is required, namely an intensification of attention to detail together with a radical deceleration of tempo: "By arguing which foot he really stepped off with in his demonstration, and, even more, how the victim himself acted, the demonstration can be so transformed that the A-effect occurs. The demonstrator achieves it by paying exact attention this time to his movements, executing them carefully, probably in slow motion; in this way he alienates the little sub-incident, emphasizes its importance, makes it worthy of notice."[11]

Comprehending the scenic unit requires the breaking down of its seemingly unitary presentation into the units of which it is constituted in turn. The process, which typically discloses tensions and contradictions not previously perceived, proceeds if necessary down to the microlevel, of, for example, the individual gest. In preparing with Laughton for the Los Angeles production of *Galileo*, "our first concern throughout was for the smallest fragments, for sentences, even for exclamations—each treated separately, each needing to be given the simplest, freshly fitted form, giving so much away, hiding so much or leaving it open."[12] That the process aims finally at synthesis, at recomposing what such "scientific" analysis has decomposed, is indicated in the title of the essay in question: "Building up a Part: Laughton's Galileo."[13]

In the street scene the largest constituent unit of experience, the scene itself, is divided into the critical incident, then divided again, as indicated in the discussion above, into the subincident. But however scientific Brecht wants his experiments to sound, the scientific approach is itself seen to be instrumental, a mediator between the scientific community and the larger community, whose experience remains the ultimate point of reference of specifically theatrical art. In elucidating the role of the letter, as the discussion of the street scene does, Brecht first indicates the debt of the street corner to the theater proper, then contradicts that thesis, then turns it into its reciprocal polar position: "And so the epic theater's alienation effect proves to have its uses for the demonstrator too; in other words it is also to be found in this small everday scene of a natural street-corner theater, which has little to do with art. The direct changeover from representation to commentary that is so characteristic of the epic theater is still more easily recognized as one element of any street demonstration.[14] What is here called "commentary" is called "discussion" in a *Lehrstück* such as *The Measure Taken.* Each is like a knot in the series of episodes forming a narrative, a nodal point whose energies require redirection into further episodes, new nodal points. In principle, the energies can lead practically anywhere; I will consider below the dangers inherent in an experiential process so open ended.

This discussion has itself reached a juncture sufficiently liminal to suggest the value of the following, preliminary summing-up: Brecht's theatrical practice, whether in the epic theater or what I am calling the "theater of danger," is dialectical because of the way in which it is narrative, narrative because of the way in which it is dialectical, and experiential because of the way in which it is narrative and dialectical. Given what has been said here concerning the temporizing of essence, it should be recognized that the *because* is in fact a free syncategorem that could be repositioned anywhere in the clausal series, the ultimate effect of which would still be to indicate, accurately enough, that dialectic, narrative, and experience are precisely cofoundational.[15] The reader is thereby made "safe" for the essentializing in Brecht's observation that: "everything hangs on the "story" . . . The "story" is the theater's great operation, the complete fitting together of all the gestic incidents, embracing the communications and impulses that must now go to make up the audience's entertainment.[16] Theatrical experience nonetheless remains the element, as Henry James would say, in which the story comes to the fore: epic theater is epic *theater,* corporally enacted in some concrete here and now.

Precisely how this enactment proceeds is one of the least understood of experiential and, more particularly, aesthetic phenomena. Nor has anyone made entirely clear what concretely happens in the alienation-effect. We do know, of course, that in Brecht, as in Hegel and Marx, alienation so thematizes as to conduce to consciousness, the sine qua non of subsequent action with respect to whatever is envisaged as the object of such consciousness. On this whole question, and on the relation of consciousness to drama, John Dewey's *Experience and Nature* proves surprisingly helpful. "Every case of consciousness is dramatic," he states aphoristically; "drama is an enhancement of the conditions of consciousness."[17] Although the ensuing elucidation is more complex than first appears, it will be possible here to tease out certain leading ideas, the first of which is that language in drama illuminates in a way unknown to immediate consciousness: we have the experience of sweet or red without the explicit mediation of words, because of whose absence the having is neither communicated nor known. "But words, as means of directing action, may evoke a situation in which the thing in question is had in some particularly illuminating way. It seems to me that anyone who installs himself in the midst of the unfolding of drama *has* the experience of consciousness in just this sort of way; in a way which enables him to give significance to descriptive and analytic terms otherwise meaningless. There must be a story, some whole, an integrated series of episodes. This connected whole is mind, as it extends beyond a particular process of consciousness and conditions it."[18]

"There must be a story" epigrammatically announces what will come to be called a "master narrative," the precise nature of which is not, unfortunately, a point on which the philosopher is especially lucid. What he suggests, however, is again a sense of element, of a condition of possibility and of that possibility realized as medium, ambiance; in which case what Dewey calls "mind," associated by him implicitly with meaning, perception, significance, knowledge, and communication, is that concrete continuum in which *any* experience is experienced. Such is the case despite the fact that no thematization can make the elemental (functioning something like a "background") directly accessible as a whole any more than the "elemental presence of the earth" can be made accessible as a whole: "The earth as a theoretical object is a globe, a planet. But the earth is also constantly present in the background of our sensorial experience, as the original reservoir of solidity and repose, upon which landscapes are at rest. Lacking profiles, its contours being impossible to encompass with our gaze, unexplored, it is not susceptible of becoming an object of perception."[19] Such elemental presence functions as a tacitly acknowledged continuum much in the manner of

Dewey's "mind," which, precisely because of its continuous nature, persists in being despite the fact that it is never directly present in its extension and entirety. Dewey thus speaks of "the operative presence of a continuum of meanings, emotional and intellectual," that are constitutive of an experience of a play; a continuum that, like earthliness, or more especially like the light of day, affords such "suffusive presence in what is now said and done" that "the purport of past affairs is present in the momentary cross-sectional idea in a way which is more intimate, direct and pervasive than the way of recall."[20] If there must be a story, some continuous experiential "whole," this signifies, not some totality gliding in the ether, to be materialized on command, but concrete connectedness; for, like the mind, the story or whole is an integrated series of events (the specifics differing with the work in question) occurring right here and now in this place.

All drama consists in an integrated series of episodes but may be distinguished according to the degree of tension and, thus, of potential contradiction in a dialectical sense, between the integration and the seriality. For emphasis upon the former, one can look to the classical drama in seventeenth-century France; and if these practices don't always match up with received ideas (on the unities, for example), at least the theory tries to. For emphasis upon the latter one can look to the modern dramatic tradition, which, at least since Buchner, has used to advantage fragments, abrupt transitions, extreme brevity, change of pace, and violent contrast. Unless or until the audience gets used to such practices, the effect is disturbance and disruption; yet even disturbance and disruption are educational insofar as they redirect attention to the "madeness", arbitrariness, and contradictoriness of what transpires on the stage. They point out to the spectators that the thoughts and feelings they are having are those not merely of theatrical, but of consciously theatrical experience. For playwright and philosopher alike, redirection is of the essence, consciousness being "that phase of a system of meanings which at a given time is undergoing redirection, transitive transformation."[21]

To speak of phases of meaning that undergo redirection and transformation is to speak of an educational process. But if the terms are Deweyan, the thinking is no less Brechtian, the creator of the *Lehrstück* being as concerned over *Bildung* within and without the theater as Dewey is concerned about it within and without the classroom. The medium or, again, the element in which education takes place, insofar as the dramatist is concerned, is to a large degree the theatrical experience itself.

From at least as early as the Renaissance, theater has drawn attention to itself by presenting on its site a simulacrum of the relation between the piece being performed and the audience experiencing that performance. This meta-relation we call "a play within a play" is more the exception than the rule; the exceptions compose a memorable repertoire extending from Hamlet as playwright, director, and stage manager to the dispersed Pirandellan ensemble that wants to know in what, if any, play its members exist. As radical as these moments are, in their own way, they still derive from an experiential paradigm that is inalterably specular. The members of the audience are invited not into the stage world but, as it were, toward it. They may see and hear people like themselves on stage and before the lights, but they are still seeing and hearing "transcendentally," as members of an essentially passive audience. The long-superseded practice of seating privileged spectators on the stage, a practice that remained popular late into the eighteenth century, is only a qualified exception to the rule. On the one hand, the spectators occupy positions in view of the audience; on the other hand, they do not figure among the *dramatis personae*. True, whatever they do while on stage belongs in some sort to the audience's experience as a whole, but only as experience of a *spectacle*. The orbit of Sartrean gazes is complex and instantaneous. As the audience in the hall watches the audience on stage as well as the acting company, the members of the audience on stage watch the members of the acting company, and probably the audience in the hall as well, to that extent giving that audience a taste of that being-looked-at that is central both to the stage audience and to the acting company. Peter Shaffer's revival of on-stage position of spectators underscores the obsolescence of the former practice. For his part, Brecht threw it into relief—alienated it from its "second nature"—by shifting the musicians from the pit onto the stage, where they could be watched and watch their watchers watching them while watching themselves being watched.

The situation is very different in the *Lehrstück*, or "didactic cantata," where experience is designed to be more immanent, participatory, direct, and concrete.[22] Resisting specularity by dispensing altogether with an audience, dispensing therefore with an assumed point of transcendental point of reference, the *Lehrstück* is acted by performers for one another; the professional acting company is replaced by a worker's council, a student group, or some other type of "grassroots" cultural organization.

This is a crucial point. How well a political agenda will be carried out depends in no small measure on the manner in which people are brought together and on the unit and level selected in that process of collectivization. In practice, a rough correlation obtains between unit and level, the former tending to be smaller as the level is lower, and vice versa. The minimal unit of collectivization must be modest enough in size and low enough in level to permit broad participation and dialogue together with an effective procedure for communicating and for making decisions. Otherwise the organization faces the danger of dissolving into a Sartrean seriality, or dispersion along an axis at once arbitrary and random, as in the queueing of prospective passengers at a bus stop: arbitrary because they have to line up in a certain way and random because it is a matter of chance who happens to be lining for a certain bus at a certain place and a certain time. Such dissolution threatens from the moment when theory, with its cool abstractions, enters the stage of practice, where temperatures run high. *Pace* Brecht, Lukács engages the problem in a statement that has the additional interest of illustrating the previously noted connection between storytelling or "temporizing" and the principle of "essence" thus conveyed. Lukács's statement first presents a present-tense narrative in which: "on the level of pure theory . . . antagonisms are only expressed in the form of discussions which can be contained within the framework of one and the same organization without disrupting it."[23] There then comes a liminal juncture, a sort of dramatic nodal point, in which hidden contradictions spring forth: "But no sooner are these same questions given organizational form than they turn out to be sharply opposed and even incompatible." Whereupon the principle to be drawn from this condensed story line finds expression in deontological terms: Every "theoretical" tendency or clash of views must immediately develop an organizational arm if it is to rise above the level of pure theory or abstract opinion, that is to say, if it really intends to point the way to its own fulfillment in practice."[24]

Which is just what any politically oriented group aspires to do. When the group in question is revolutionary, the issue of unit and level can be cruelly decisive, which is why strong answers to the question were heard too little or too late. Thomas Jefferson suggested that governance on a local level should be reposed in "small republics" or wards with broad responsibilities and rights, including the right to elect representatives. Organizations of just this type became a recurring feature of subsequent revolutionary periods, from the Paris Commune of 1870 to the councils or *soviets* set up in Russia in 1905 and again in 1917. In the next two years, German workers, soldiers, and peasants organized councils of their own; as it happens, Brecht was in Munich in the winter of 1919 when these councils staged a demonstration at the Deutsches Theater. Characterized by spontaneity of formation and by full participation, the councils could look utopian to observers who knew only too well that their relative want of partisanship represented an imminent danger to any and all other organizations, which were united precisely by party interests.[25]

It is within the context of these participatory, small-scale groups that *Lehrstück* performers dialectically negate the conventional audience, which is however sublated in that the audience function is *aufgehoben* (canceled), but in a measure preserved and elevated in the ensemble, whose members are less members of an audience for being at the same time performers. Educational convention is negated to the extent that responsibility for learning is assimilated by the empowering group whose members are at once those being educated and the educators. This amounts to a fuller negation, evidently, than is accomplished by Artaud, who endeavors to move the audience closer toward immanence in the sense of unmediated participation in the action being staged, but without negating the existence of the audience in order to sublate it in the Brechtian way. Artaud moves in a similar direction, nonetheless; and if he is sufficiently dialectical, and Hegelian, to speak of Tibet and Mexico as the "nodal points of the world culture," he also sees himself, with Brecht, in a revolutionary capacity, as illustrated by his design for an anti-imperial spectacle called *The Conquest of Mexico*.[26]

In any case, my description of the *Lehrstück* clearly has a "pure" model in view, not the mixed and volatile piece of fateful discourse that the Brechtian didactic cantata tends to be. It is pure because it takes dialectical sublation at face value, whereas the latter, whether as abstract concept or concrete process, is as problematic as it is provocative. Merely to list the authorities who have come to such a conclusion would take far more space than the format of this discussion allows. Here it must suffice to suggest the extent to which dialectical sublation, in the concrete case of the *Lehrstück*, is problematized by the possibility of an inherent contradiction between sublative and subsumptive process.

SUBLATION/SUBSUMPTION

While in English logic, to sublate is to deny, to perform the reverse of positioning, Hegel had already hypostatized both a denying *and* a preserving. In J. H. Sterling's wording, "A thing is sublated, resolved, only so far as it has gone into unity with its opposite."[27] A much more venerable term, *subsume* means to bring something, such as a statement, under something else that is more inclusive or somehow stronger, a definition modified by Coleridge, Hegel's contemporary, to cover the process by which an idea, principle, term, and the like, is brought under a rule or is included in something larger or higher.[28] In its nominal form emphasis falls less on the notion of including than on the notion of being brought under, except in the case of Scottish law, where a subsumption is a narrative of an alleged crime, that is, something brought under an action (such as libel) in support of that action.[29] In the preceding century supportive use of "story" to state pertinent facts is already the first sense of narrative as noun. For present purposes, then *subsumption* signifies *a hierarchical relation of supportive subordination inclusive of factual representation in a narrative mode.*

To lend more concreteness to the discussion, *The Measures Taken* (*Die Massnahme*) will serve as our example when questions require a degree of textual specification greater than the degree required in generic contexts. In this instructional play the cadre of agitators, switching roles, become the Young Comrade, two Coolies, the Trader, and other characters, in order to justify themselves in the eyes of the Control Chorus for having exterminated Young Comrade. In their narratives the latter is shown committing a series of major strategic errors, which are equally errors of political judgment, as a consequence of which the revolutionary mission is aborted and the lives of the cadre jeopardized. In one of several "discussions," which tend to interrupt the narrated action for a give-and-take between the cadre and the chorus, the Young Comrade arrives at the state of *Einverständnis* (knowing acceptance), which enables him to submit to death in the knowledge that in the long run the Communist Party has been correctly served.

Einverständnis is essential to *Aufhebung*. For if it is one thing to be negated in the ultimate way (i.e., killed), it is another, "higher" thing to negate that negation in turn, so as to continue enabling the revolutionary cause. A conscious act, acceptance is (to abbreviate Dewey's formulation) a re-directive transformation, such that the revolutionary spirit can rise to a higher state, not despite the sacrifice of the individual, but because of it. Hegel himself speaks of the phenomenology of *Geist* as the Golgotha of the Spirit—its "dialectical-speculative crucifixion," in Heidegger's phrase.[30]

At the same time, every feature of this process that can be embraced as sublation conduces as well to subsumption. The process is hierarchical through and through, the organization of power conforming, in fact, to the conventional model of the pyramid, with the performing group, whether of workers, peasants, students, or soldiers, constituting the broad base. The next level is occupied by—to borrow from a 1943 presentation by Mao—the party's "own excellent cadres endowed with rich personal experience," the latter being in fact the organizations the chairman was then addressing.[31] At the apex of the pyramid we find, of course, the party. But just what and who are the party, the Young Comrade wants to know, to which the three other Agitators reply:

We are the Party
You and I and you all—all of us.
The Party is in that suit you are wearing, Comrade,
And is thinking in that head of yours.[32]

Contradiction: if it really is incarnated in the Young Comrade, the party, being self-identical, cannot negate itself as it would if the Young Comrade should split with it. The very fact that the latter has a choice to make enables the attempt at negation initiated by the other Agitators: if they convinced him of their thesis, and if he accordingly subordinates his private feelings to party interests, the state of contradiction will be resolved. Thus their appeal: "We may be wrong and you may be right. / Therefore do not cut yourself off from us!"[33]

To make a choice correct for the party, the Young Comrade need only allow "The Teachings of the Classics," which is the title of scene 1: "We bring you nothing. But over the frontier to Mukden we bring the Chinese workers the teachings of the classics and the propagandists, the ABCs of Communism: to the ignorant, instruction about their condition; to the oppressed, class consciousness; and to the class conscious, the experience of revolution."[34] The narratives and songs that follow make these abstractions more concrete. In scene 3, for example, the Agitators instruct the Young Comrade to tell the coolies about wooden-soled shoes to keep them from slipping as they tow barges. He is to operate, in other words, at level one, which consists of instructing the ignorant about their condition, a point on which the Agitators are quite explicit.[35] But the Young Comrade attempts in effect to operate on the third level; being already class conscious, he is ready for the experience of revolution—but the revolution is not ready for him. When he gives in to pity, interfering with the overseer's way of towing the barges and challenging the overseer directly, he gets himself and the other cadre members debarred for a week from the central city, where they need to work.

Again, when we hear the Four Agitators say, "Daily we fought those old associates: Oppression and Despair," we are getting a narrative distillation of a virtual infinitude of social, political, and economic experiences.[36] Brecht is equally at pains to draw upon specifics of historical circumstances: "Then we heard there was conflict between the merchants and the British, who ruled the city, on account of tariffs. In order to exploit this rulers' quarrel for the benefit of the ruled, we sent the young comrade with a letter to the richest of the merchants. It said: "Arm the coolies!'"[37] Too many commentators have labored under the illusion that this and other references to Chinese situations are decorative touches for exotic flavor or coded allusions to German or Russian developments. While the latter may be partially the case, it is clear from preponderant evidence that Brecht was drawing on experiences recorded in China in the five years preceding his composition of the play.[38] The conflict cited by the Agitators was a documented datum in China exploited in the 1920s by British and other foreign capitalist interests. During this period the Chinese Communist Party, dependent on a Comintern controlled from 1924 by Stalin, saw no alternative to forging a front with, or even subordinating itself to, the Kuomintang, the party of the "rulers," in the language of the Agitators, since that party also sought the removal of foreign presences together with the existing Peking movement.

When Brecht has the other comrades tell their youngest member to do all he can to facilitate the arming of the coolies by the rulers, they are doing just the sort of thing that their historical counterparts actually did in order to achieve identical goals. Their action, that is to say, is at once typical and concrete. Brecht makes the rice trader with whom the Young Comrade has to negotiate the richest of all the merchants and one, moreover, who is aggressively corrupt and inhumane, as evidenced by the parody of Hobbesian self-interest and commodification in "The Song of Merchandiser":

> What is a man actually?
> Do I know what a man is?
> God knows what a man is!
> I don't know what a man is
> I only know his price.[39]

In thus stylizing the moral stance of the merchant and in maximizing his corruption and cruelty, Brecht is using poetic license to give to an historically concrete state of affairs its narrative-dramatic-musical correlative. In thus recording in epic theater what has already been recorded in public documents, he is also giving a kind of generic status to what I have called the "problem of cruel decisions." In the present instance and on a collective level this comes down, as noted above, to deciding to ally with a hated rival against an even more hated mutual enemy; individually, this comes down to deciding that it is strategically correct to ingratiate oneself within the very embodiment of Kuomintang corruption, since that is the only way to achieve the goal of arming the coolies against the British. In the event, a decision this painful translates into the equally cruel problem of executing the apposite plan of action. To assure the revolution that is the goal of the party one must sacrifice one's own feelings, even one's life.

This play, which raises so many issues, including the nature of the Party, does not raise the issue of the author's role. Explicitly at least. Implicitly, it is of course everywhere insofar as everything comes from

Brecht. But if he is to this extent immanent he is equally "outside" the narrative-dramatic-dialectical dynamic, as the transcendental authority who has already made the necessary decisions and executed the requisite actions. Given this, and given the preeminent role of the party, one must reckon with that other cruel fact that is the concordance between that role and the policy line of the Comintern under Stalin. The nexus has made East German critics particularly nervous: As an important communist artist, Brecht offers a special problem for these critics. His revolutionary commitment must be maintained, but not in any way that might prove awkward in the present. They do not want to speak of Brecht in connection with Stalin—the individual most prominently responsible for Brecht's specific experience of living revolutionary tradition.[40]

Not the least of the playwright's cruel decisions is the destiny he determines for the Young Comrade. In apparent contradictions, the final message of the piece declares that changing the world requires, among other things, "COMPRESSION OF THE SINGLE MAN AND OF THE WHOLE."[41]

On the former question, the role of the individual, Sartre's discussion of "The Constituted Dialectic" is suggestive. In particular, Sartre scrutinizes the function of just such an "organiser-agitator" as the Young Comrade: "He is a medium and he knows it; and if he acts . . . it is through the group, and in secret. But since the orders of the people issue from his mouth, since the reorganisation has to be carried out through his individual *praxis*, and since his exhortations and gestures indicate the common objective, we have to conclude that popular *praxis* is essentially capable of being created, understood and organised *by an individual*."[42] Given the dialectical nature of our subject, it seems only fitting that as a gloss on Brecht this statement can be read in contradictory ways. In the first place, it evidently departs from the Brechtian position, which loads the group with all the crucial actions and ultimate responsibilities. Moreover, in *The Measures Taken* the performers experience three enacted stories in which a critically positioned individual not only fails to forward the revolutionary cause but also endangers the mission and the lives of his comrades and himself. If this way of putting the matter does not convince, there can be no doubt that the playwright disagrees absolutely with Sartre when he goes on to specify in the same passage "that the group can define its common action *only* through the mediation of the individual designation" (emphasis added).

But in the second place, the statement agrees with the playwright's conception of the individual organizer-agitator. On the grounds of *principium individuationis*, any plurality minimally consists in the individual members constitutive thereof. More concretely, the practice of the revolutionary group, such as the one Brecht presents, presupposes that each member qua individual accedes to the interests of all together. That the individual in question fails to perform his assigned task is not decisive. What is decisive is that he agrees with the destiny determined for him in the interests of the group, even if this means his liquidation.

Sartre has been employed here merely to throw into relief what is already given in *The Measures Taken*: either the single man is *not* taken sufficiently into account, the proof being that he is sacrificed for the good of the party; or the single man *is* taken sufficiently into account, the proof being that he sacrificed himself, in effect, for the good of the party. In both cases, it is the same sublation through *Einverständnis*, which is to say the same subsumption, for the movement that cancels the limitations of the individual to recover his gest on the level of transcendence is the very same movement that renders the individual subordinate to that very level.

The polarity between sublation and subsumption, which can be translated into, respectively, revolutionary transcendence or revolutionary failure, is a correlate of the political space separating a wry and restless man of letters from an authority whose rule dictates strict adherence to transcendentally propounded doctrine.

But Brecht "builded" better than he knew. Or to paraphrase an apothegm of Faulkner's: his art believes before his ideology remembers. His art believes that educative purposes are legitimately served in a dramatic mode of radical experiential immediacy, an immediacy otherwise reserved for ethnic rituals. Although a similar claim can be made for the undertakings of Artaud's "Theater of Cruelty" as well, its innovations and revivalisms largely remained visionary and theoretical. In its casting, the *Lehrstück* is democratic, providing every performer with the opportunity of assuming every role and telling every story. But there is no telling where such may lead. If we are to take the playwright at his word, his commitment to "the new social scientific method then known as dialectical materialism," which he announced in 1948, means that everyone is free to change: "There is a great deal to man, we say; so a great deal can be made out of him. He does not have to stay the way he is now, nor does he have to be seen only as he is now, but also as he might become."[43] In 1933 Brecht was already calling for a less determinate, more open-ended aesthetic in order to enable more dynamic experiences: "The new school of playwriting most systematically see to it so that its form includes 'experiment'. It must be free to see connections on every side; it needs equilibrium and has a tension which governs its component parts and 'loads' them against one another.[44]

Such a concept conjures up a theater that is a danger to itself in that it implants in its very mode of aesthetic organization a principle of fateful contradiction. There may be no way, ultimately, of controlling the loading of part against part; anyway, equilibrium is as much a dynamic as a static phenomenon, and the matrix of action in which the performers of the *Lehrstück* engage themselves is a *moving* matrix. I mean that through the changing of roles, through immersion in the contradictory experiences embodied and in their resolution, the performer undertakes what Brecht calls "self-production."[45] But each new role teaches what it is like to be made over, to make *oneself* over, in a process of re-directive transformation, which by definition cannot achieve perfect closure. A recognition or at least a glimpse of this prospect may be part of the explanation for the tentativeness Brecht discloses as he feels his way, in the last year of his life, toward a more genuinely dialectical theater. He cannot have been unaware, at the same time, of the contradictions implicit in a creative praxis energized by a dedication to freedom but shadowed by the *Einverständnis* required by the interests of the party. To be thus aware is to recognize, if only imperfectly, that the true cruelty and the true danger are at the heart of the creative enterprise as conceived. For the sake of sublation it vows to remember ideology at the expense of forgetting art, at the possible expense, indeed, of sacrificing itself.

The creation of a drama on dialectical premises challenges the dramatist to believe his art before he remembers his ideology. Which is not to say that the *Lehrstück* in general or *The Measures Taken* in particular have met the challenge with complete success. The latter, for example, is hardly open ended. The stories being told eventually come to an end, with the Control Chorus sounding choral indeed, even hymnal. But this is fundamentally experimental theater, a theater aiming at new powerful experiences in new powerful ways, which has its most revealing moments when its tensions, its loadings and counter-loadings, are most dialectically intense and are thus, at least potentially, at their most contradictory and hence revolutionary stage. Such a moment occurs in the final scene when the Agitators narrate their last experiences:

> The time was short, we found no way out
> As one animal will help another, we too
> Wished to help him
> Who had fought with us for our cause.
> With our pursuers on our heels
> For five minutes
> We pondered the possibility,
> Think of it again now

You think of it.
Pause.[46]

The specification of five minutes is an important one because it is concrete detail. It is a constraint not of their choosing that is absolutely crucial in what they *are* free to choose. Their position resembles that of the ship's officer who, after his vessel is sunk and the lifeboat is in danger of sinking as well, must decide which occupants to sacrifice to the waves in order to save the others. This is education at white heat: the Agitators are teaching the Chorus to feel what it was like to face an irreversible, all-or-nothing, hurried choice; and at the same time, like all good Marxists, they want to raise the consciousness of the Chorus, to make its members know what it was like. Only in this way can their otherwise criminal act be canceled and through sublation preserved in its positive intent. But when sublation comes, can subsumption be far behind?

The Agitators' story concludes with their killing of the Young Comrade and their justification for doing so:

> It is not granted to us, we said,
> Not to kill.
> At one with the will to change the world that will
> not be denied
> We formulated
> The measures to be taken.[47]

Like their counterparts in the French Revolution (extrapolating from Hegel's account), the Agitators experience a chiliastic convergence of the sempiternal absolute coming into time, concretized in the self-realization of its now-worldly spirit. A theater that would "dialecticize" experience through alienation-effects in order to change the world is truly endangered when it subordinates itself to something so faceless as will. Which is not to tell Brecht anything he didn't know. Early in the play the Agitators blot out their faces so as to assume Chinese disguises: sublation requires such sacrifices. By a similar process the face of Stalin and Stalinism, the incarnation of the party, not to mention cruelty, at the time Brecht was writing his education plays, is blotted out too.

In all its liminality, dialectical sublation, as it comes down from Hegelianism to Marxism, confronts the chronic danger of becoming subordinate to its subsumptive potentiality. When a Stalin is in power, the danger is the more acute, not least when his face is blotted out by the mask of will. Hannah Arendt states the danger concisely: "Left to itself, man's Will 'would rather will Nothingness than not will,' as Nietzsche remarked . . . in other words, the famous power of negation inherent in the Will and conceived as the motor of History (not only in Marx but, by implication, already in Hegel) is an annihilating force that could just as well result in a process of permanent annihilation as of Infinite Progress."[48] If it is the case that Brecht's ideology remembers before his art believes, then the theater of danger leads toward annihilation. If it is the case that his art believes before his ideology remembers, then the same theater leads toward progress. Brecht's struggle to go beyond epic theater, to do something unattempted yet in prose or rhyme by rendering experience productively dialectical, points to the possibility that he saw the danger.

Hölderlin already sees experience in dialectical terms:

> Where danger is, grows
> The saving power also.[49]

Working from much the same assumptions, Hegel, Hölderlin's friend, did find, by his own measure, the saving power. Marx, as Hegel's heir, and with the same qualification, found it too. Whether Brecht did as well remains a question. Brecht being gone, his fate lies, as always, in the hands of posterity. Which is not to say that as members of his audience we must play Control Chorus to his Agitator. It is to say that we have an opportunity to leave off deferring, an opportunity to "think about it *now*." The playwright should be credited, in my view, with courageously countering the political right at a time when many of his compatriots had yet to learn how dangerous it would be, in the long term, to do anything else. In response to the Wagnerian quest for a *Gesamtkunstwerk*, Brecht drew upon "high" culture and popular culture, on narrative, song, instrumental music, and visual documentation, to create a condition of possibility for transformative educational experience. He accomplished all this, however, at a heavy price. For all its experimentation with experience, the didactic cantata, instructional play, school opera or *Lehrstück*—call it what you will—remains dangerously subordinated to what was most problematic in the playwright's political commitment. And in doing so it is not merely endangered but endangering.

The best face that can be put on what is otherwise blotted out runs something like this: to the degree that the *Lehrstück* mediates a genuine historical sublation it is its own reason for being and for ceasing to be.

Part 6

Beyond Dialectics: At the Limits of Formalization

The last two essays in this volume touch upon issues at the limits of dialectics: they deal with notational and formal paradoxes that break down temporal and discursive logic of traditional philosophical discourse. The concerns of these two essays seem at first sight unrelated. Charles Shepherdson's essay examines the status of psychoanalysis as a discourse of knowledge through a detailed reading of Jacques Lacan's "Discours de Rome" (1953). It explores the link between the symbolic order and the formalization of the analytic enterprise. Joseph Arsenault's and Tony Brinkley's essay problematizes the question of historical evidence, insofar as it challenges the linguistic and logical limits of historical discourse. At issue is an encounter between Wittgenstein's and Lyotard's conceptions of the "Liar's paradox" as symptomatic of the limits of formalization. In both of these essays, questions about personal memory and the reality of history weigh heavily, though the burden and urgency of these questions is expressed in different ways. If for Shepherdson "fate" is at issue in a psychoanalytic sense, that is, as a particular kind of personal history inscribed in a symbolic order, for Arsenault and Brinkley, the fate of historical evidence is at stake, insofar as it challenges the logic of historical discourse.

According to Shepherdson, Lacan uses the terms of *fate* and *repetition* not so much to raise the question of history as to inquire into the status of psychoanalysis as a science, since psychoanalysis is in its own way an inquiry into the past. However, psychoanalysis does not seek to reconstruct the subject's actual history. The hysterical revelation of the past is different from a historical account, since, as Lacan explains, it "presents us with the birth of truth in speech, and thereby brings us up against the reality of what is neither true nor false." The status of history in the context of hysteria is particular: this is a history that can be rewritten and has no formal existence in and of itself, since "the inscription of the past is its only reality." Arsenault and Brinkley are less interested in the disciplinary questions defining history than in methodological questions raised by historical testimony, particularly in cases when witnesses are reluctant to speak. They begin with Wittgenstein's "case of the Liar" in order to demonstrate along with Gödel the logical impasse generated by this formulation. The paradox of the Liar signals an "inability to express, the restrictive character of the formal idiom that precludes the formalization of particular properties." This instance, which documents the difference between formalization and what is formalized, is juxtaposed with Lyotard's discussion of the revisionist arguments of the Holocaust. Arsenault and Brinkley demonstrate the limits of historical evidence, as long as it is conceived according to logical idioms (of inclusion or negation) that restrict its indexical character. Thus the question of the meaning of the historical relies, like the paradox, not on "cognitive content but on pointing out," that is, in its indexical function. An index points; it asserts nothing, implies nothing (Peirce), and thus, as the authors note, it cannot lie. By considering the indexical character of history, its "pointed" or "pointing" nature, Arsenault and Brinkley relocate its reality within a deictical order, no longer restricted by formalization. Shepherdson observes that the difference between psychoanalysis and psychology is defined in regard to our conception of history. He observes that in psychotherapy one learns to change, adapt to and accept the past, according to cognitive models that can be conceived without a specific understanding of the role of the unconscious. While recognizing the inevitability of determination by the symbolic order, Shepherdson attempts to disengage it from cognitive models. Hence his effort to distinguish the symbolic from its analogies to structural linguistics (Saussure) and structural anthropology (Lévi-Strauss). This attempt to reify the referential scope of the symbolic order, by resisting its immediate reduction to sociohistorical context, is intended to expand the horizon of psychoanalysis. It is Shepherdson's answer to the purely psychological orientation of most forms of therapy. By submitting itself to speech, to the discursive specificity of the subject, Lacanian psychoanalysis opens the way for an inquiry into the hysterical constitution of the subject as the symptom of a symbolic order for which there is no cure—that of history. It is not by accident that Arsenault and Brinkley keep on returning to a statement that captures the trauma of history, as witness and proof of its own nonexistence: "This world is not this world." This statement of nonidentity, or rather, nonbeing, at the very moment that one attempts to situate oneself within and designate the world, captures the impossible congruence of indexicality and reference, a struggle between psychoanalysis and history.

17

At the Limits of Formalization

Joseph Arsenault and Tony Brinkley

> However this war may end, we have won the war against you; none of you will be left to bear witness, but even if someone were to survive, the world would not believe him. There will perhaps be suspicions, discussions, research by historians, but there will be no certainties, because we will destroy the evidence together with you . . . We will be the ones to dictate the history of the Lagers.
>
> SS guards to Jewish prisoners

> You are informed that human beings endowed with language were placed in a situation such that none of them are now able to tell about it. Most of them disappeared back then; those who survived rarely speak about it. When they do speak about it, their testimony only bears upon a minute part of this situation. How can you know that the situation itself existed?
>
> Jean-François Lyotard

1. IMPLICATION

"Think of the case of the Liar," Wittgenstein suggested. "It is very queer that this should have puzzled anyone—much more extraordinary than you might think: that this should be the thing to worry human beings."[1] The remark, from a lecture at Cambridge in 1939, is one of a series of comments on the subject. From 1937: "Is there harm in the contradiction that arises when someone says: 'I am lying.—So I am not lying.—So I am lying.—etc.'? I mean does it make our language less usable?"[2] And, again from the 1939 lecture: "The thing works like this: if a man says 'I am lying,' we say that it follows that he is not lying, from which it follows that he is lying and so on. Well, so what? . . . What does it mean to say that one proposition follows from another?"[3] What does it mean to imply? When I say that I am lying, why would I mean to imply anything at all? "Something surprising, a paradox, is only a paradox in a particular, as it were, defective surrounding. One needs to complete this surrounding in such a way that what looked like a paradox no longer seems one."[4]

2. CONTRADICTION

If I say that I am lying, this implies that I am telling the truth. Given a particular logical idiom in which the *false* is opposed to the *true*, *yes* to *no*, *x* to *not-x*, in other words the Law of Contradiction, we discover—at least in the case of the Liar—that if *true* then *false*, if *yes* then *no*, if *x* then *not-x*. We could say that the Liar is an interpretation of the statement "I am lying." Then we "run up against the limits of language . . . the running up against *points to something*."[5]

3. FORMALIZATION

We can define a formalization as an interpretive idiom that is governed by two logical operators: implication (a proof relation: *if x, then y*) and exclusion (though you must include *x* or *not-x*, you cannot include both). In a formalization, any existential relation will be represented as an implication. Inclusion will be determined by the rule of exclusion. A proof is an implication that does not lead to contradiction. We assume that what is provable is also true, that an implication that leads to a contradiction is false. A paradox is an implication that leads to a contradiction but does not seem to be false.

4. THE INDEXICAL

But what can you *do* with a paradox? "Isn't this just a useless game?"[6] These questions presuppose that the paradox is a proposition *to be implied* and *used to imply*, and what confuses us is that any use of the paradox confounds the rules of such an application. Suppose, however, that we consider the paradox as a form of statement that *is not implied* and *does not imply* in the way cognitive implication works, but that one draws conclusions from paradox as one does from deictics or descriptions: one concludes things about the *situation* it establishes or places us in. The formal irresolvability of paradox on the basis of cognitive content suggests the consideration of paradox as indexical—in Peirce's sense—where meaningfulness does not depend on cognitive content but on pointing out ("a pointing finger being the type" of the indexical). An "index asserts nothing," and thus does not imply. "It only says, 'There!' It takes hold of our eyes, as it were."[7] We note in passing that an index—unlike a proposition—cannot be said to lie.

5. IN THIS CASE THERE IS HARM

Another version of the Liar, an extreme case: "[Someone] complains that he has been fooled about the existence of gas chambers, fooled, that is, about the Final Solution. His argument is: in order for a place to be identified as a gas chamber, the only eyewitness I will accept would be a victim of this gas chamber; now, according to my opponent, there is no victim that is not dead; otherwise, this gas chamber would not be what he or she claimed it to be. There is, therefore, no gas chamber."[8] When the victim testifies, we reduce what is said to a paradox like that of the Liar. Either you are a victim or you are not (*x* or not-*x*), but if you are a victim as you say, then you are not (if *x*, then not-*x*). Since the victim in these circumstances would be unable to speak of these circumstances.

6. A RESTRICTED IDIOM

Consider a situation in which we are entitled to only three words: *x*, *or*, and *not*. I say: "*x* or . . . " Then I pause. Then I say, "or not not-*x*." Given the same three words, someone interprets "not not-*x*" as "*x*." In another idiom, however, what I might have said was "*y*."

7. THE DIFFEREND

"A case of conflict," Lyotard writes, in which a wrong results because "the rules of the genre by which one judges are not those of the judged genre or genres of discourse."[9] I wish to indicate the existence of a wrong, but I find myself in a situation where I am told that the wrong can only exist subject to implication and exclusion, that judgment is formal, though I may not have anything formal to say. Given a formal power that concerns itself with proof, what I say may "remain unactualized."[10] "Human beings endowed with language" but "placed in a situation such that none of them is now able to tell about it."[11] "Reality is not what is 'given' . . . it is a state of the referent" as determined by the protocols of an idiom; it is specific to that idiom.[12] Someone wishes to phrase a reality that the genre by which one judges precludes. Someone "is divested of the means to argue and becomes for that reason a victim."[13]

8. "IT'S ALL LIES"

Wittgenstein imagines someone who "comes to people and says: 'I always lie.' They answer: 'Well, in that case we can trust you!'—But could *he* mean what he said? . . . — 'I always lie!'—Well, and what about *that*?—'It was a lie too!'—But in that case you don't always lie!—'No, it's all lies!' "[14] What does this story indicate? "He doesn't mean the same things that we do by 'true' and by 'lying.' "[15] Or he is trying to point something out that we are unable to hear. As we listen, what we hear is the formal equivalent of what he is trying to tell us. Though we do not understand, he still has an effect. At some point we will imagine that what we heard was a paradox; this indexes his resistance to our idiom.

9. THE DEICTIC

"One might ask, 'How on earth did this happen? . . . ' You want to know why a contradiction comes with 'I am lying' and not with 'I am eating.' In the first place it doesn't happen in our ordinary use of 'I'm lying.' "[16] The Liar (a paradox) requires an initial interpretation: "I am lying" is replaced by "If I am lying." It is as if I were to say, "This," and you were to interpret the deictic as "If this." An indication turns into the antecedent of an implication, from which a consequent necessarily follows: *if . . . then*. You assume that the meaningfulness of what I say demands that it be made implicative. I was just trying to point. "What is 'learning a rule'?—*This*. What is 'making a mistake in applying it'?—*This*."[17]

10. THE CAVE OF FORMS

Wittgenstein offers this analogy for the effects of a formalization: you are asked to project figures of various shapes onto a screen; images on the screen will "formalize" the projected shapes. You decide on a method of projection such that—regardless of the shapes of the figures—the representations on the screen will "all be circles."[18] This method of projection, which obscures distinctions and creates an illusion of uniformity, also blocks a strategy of interpretation that would infer the shape of a figure from the circle that represents it. Someone might look at the screen and assert, "There are only circles."[19] He or she might create a logic of circumferences as a logos of realities. However, "the mere fact that a figure . . . is represented as a circle . . . by itself tells us nothing . . . That an image . . . is a circle is just the established norm of our mapping."[20]

Wittgenstein's analogy recalls Plato's cave, men "fettered from childhood" who see nothing "except the shadows cast from the fire on the wall . . . in front of them." They "deem reality to be nothing else than the shadows."[21] Plato's cave characterizes a world of appearances, but to generate a formalization is to produce such a world as well.

Picture prisoners in a cave of forms. What will constitute knowledge in this case is not a vision of the forms—they turn out to be shadows on the wall. What will constitute knowledge is an understanding of the production of the formal notation, the production in a restricted idiom of a particular kind of appearance. We represent a variety of shapes as a variety of circles. This is analogous to the decision to represent a variety of existential relations as implications. An alternative might consist in precise description, how "different figures . . . are mapped . . . by different methods of projection." If I wish "to construe circles . . . as representations . . . I shall have to give the method of projection for each circle."[24] So also for each implicative relation. Each paradox. Each substitution. Exclusion. Indications of projection and distortion.

11. NEGATION

One attempt at reading the Liar goes as follows: working from implication it interprets the contradiction as a moment of negation, what might be termed "sublation," a canceling that subsumes. Dialectic. "The passage from *x* to not-*x* and the passage from not-*x* to *x* will be expressed together by a third term (or phrase) *y: If x, then not-x, then y;* and *If not-x, then x, then y.*"[23] This eliminates contradiction by introducing temporality. In interpreting the implicative relation, it takes "then" as a deictic that marks the passage of time: *if it is true, then later it is not,* and *if it is not true, then later it will be.* The temporality in this case is the time of the interpreter, of the movement of interpretation from the antecedent to the consequent. As if thought were essentially an interpretive response to paradox. Dialectic will impose this movement on every existential relation. The Liar as "the linchpin of Hegelian dialectical logic."[24]

12. DIALECTIC

Whereas a formal idiom represents existential relations as instances of implication, dialectic represents the existential as particular instances of paradox. We could respond to dialectic as Wittgenstein responds to the Liar: "It is of interest because it has tormented people, and because this shows how tormenting questions can grow out of language."[27] In the case of the Liar, the torment (or fascination) seems to lie in this: that logical operators have been invoked for a case where they do not apply. Dialectic could be regarded as a formalization of the instance in which logical operators have been invoked for a case where they do not apply. In terms of the formal system, the instance is expressed as a paradox that dialectic then adopts as a universal logical operator. There is something curious about this procedure. Why is the effect of a restricted idiom more compelling than a description of the restrictions that produced this effect?

13. EVERY SENTENCE IN THIS SECTION IS ———

Think of the Liar, of the particular logical operator that dialectic adopts as its own. Russell attributed the Liar to the effects of self-reference and generalization: "The paradox rests on the faculty of a phrase to take itself as its referent. . . [A] proposition. . . that refers to a totality of propositions. . . cannot be part of that totality."[26] Self-referential statements are not inherently paradoxical, however. For example, we can formalize the statement, "every sentence in section 19 of this paper is in English," without producing a paradox. Why is this not the case for a sentence in the same section which says of section 19 that "the last sentence in section 19 of this paper is false"?

14. THE LIMITS OF FORMALIZATION

Consider a different interpretation of the Liar (we are quoting from a 1934 lecture of Gödel's on undecidability): "The solution, . . . that the proposition cannot say something about itself, is too drastic." It is possible "to construct propositions which make statements about themselves, . . . a proposition [within a formalization] which says of itself that it has this property." However, "this construction can only be carried out if the property . . . can be expressed in the [formal] system." With regard to the Liar, "the solution . . . lies in the fact that the latter is not possible for every property."[27]

For Gödel, what the Liar signals is an inability to express, the restrictive character of the formal idiom that precludes the formalization of particular properties. This conclusion can be demonstrated formally, but it does not provide a formal solution (it takes outside evidence into account, unformalizable properties). Gödel argues on the basis of indexicality—inasmuch as the Liar both is and is not a formal expression.

15. THE LIAR

With regard to the Liar, it is possible to discuss the restrictive character of a formal idiom in more detail, to mark quite specifically what the projection leaves unexpressed. "Truth" is formalized as "provability," that is, within the formal idiom, assertions of truth and falsehood are projected as implications that are subject to contradiction. To say that a statement is false means that it is implied with contradiction. This leads to a curious result: suppose that the last sentence in section 19 said that "the last sentence in section 19 of this paper is false," that is, that it "is *implied with contradiction*." This would turn out to be true. Both true and disproven. The Liar marks the difference between formal implication (which in this case leads to a contradiction) and a truth that cannot be formalized but that points itself out. Gödel suggests that the Liar implies that the number of true statements exceeds the number of provable statements.[28] We might also regard it as evidence that not all evidence can be implied, that there will always be indications that are not subject to implication and exclusion.

16. THE INDEXICAL

When we work in terms of a formal idiom, what is excluded from our thoughts? What can we *not* think about? Michael Dummett notes that from the perspective of a formalization, indexicality is an "inconvenience" or "imperfection," to be "eliminated from a purified logical notation, as having the gross disadvantage that the thought expressed is not fully determined by the words or symbols used."[29] This might also serve as a description of the disadvantage that the Liar involves; it points (as Gödel recognized) to the incompleteness of the idiom. What it could also be said to demonstrate is that the "imperfection" of indexicality can never be completely eliminated.[30]

17. INTERPRETATION

The Liar offers a formal interpretation of the statement, "I am lying." Dialectic provides an interpretation of the paradox which results. As Peirce suggests, interpretation involves substitution: one sign for another, "an equivalent sign . . . the interpretant of the first."[31] Peirce distinguishes between a semantics that depends on interpretation and a semantics that does not. A sign that "signifies what it does by virtue of its being understood to have that signification . . . would lose the character which renders it a sign if there were no interpretant" in response, but indexes do not depend on interpretation for their significance. Something "with a shot in it is a sign of a shot . . . whether anybody has the sense to attribute it to a shot or not."[32] Evidence requires a semantics of its own, because evidence, which is indexical, is not constituted by interpretation.

18.

We shall name the paradox presented in section 6 "The Gas Chamber." It produces a differend, but only so long as you ignore what it indicates. You construct an idiom that excludes the possibility that a victim can bear witness. As a formal equivalent of gas chambers and crematoria—engineered to produce the nonexistence of their victims—the Gas Chamber has been engineered to produce the nonexistence of evidence. Even when victims have disappeared, evidence has not: the testimony of survivors, ruins of the gas chambers, earth mixed with ashes and bone fragments. Documents. It turns out that nonexistence is too difficult to produce. So now against the evidence, you offer a paradox, as if this were not evidence against you. What we discover is that evidence has the character of dreams: Freud found that the interpretation of a dream could be regarded as more dream. The interpretation of evidence—including the denial of evidence—is more evidence. Evidence turns the Gas Chamber into evidence against those who employ it.

When we hear the Gas Chamber, it is hard not to respond to the unsoundness—as well as the obscenity—of the argument, to the actuality of the gas chambers that has forced those who wish to deny them into such an argument. The paradox indicates an idiom that will not conform to evidence; it indicates the actuality to which the idiom will not conform. Evidence creates a dilemma that the Gas Chamber mirrors. If you do not silence the evidence, you will be required to live with its existential burden, but the silencing of evidence can always testify against you. If nothing else, the silencing is not silent and is unable to keep silent. The Gas Chamber speaks of its victims.

19. THE TRACE

"Referring to the object that it denotes by virtue of being really effected by that object," an index is an existential sign. While it participates in its referent, this is in the sense not of self-reference but of an existential connection that is not subject to the restrictions of an interpretive idiom. To emphasize the phrases of an idiom and the dependence of reference on these phrases is to ignore the participation of phrases in an interplay of material reference. Euphemisms between bureaucrats, for example, were also "a form of action"[33]: "there were also certain groups that Himmler put down for 'priority accommodation.' "[34]

One might say of evidence what Levinas says of the trace, that "it can be taken for a sign," but it "is not a sign like any other": "it is exceptional with respect to other signs in that it signifies outside of every intention of signaling."[35] Outside of every idiom. "Its original signifyingness is sketched out in, for example, the fingerprints left behind by someone who wanted to wipe away his traces and commit a perfect crime."[36] Phrases that are like fingerprints: "The head of the Vilna Gestapo told us, 'There are ninety thousand people lying there, and absolutely no trace must be left of them.' "[37] Words that are traces. "He who left traces in wiping out his traces did not mean to say or do anything by the traces he left behind."[38] What he failed to take into account, however, was his otherness with respect to his intentions, the otherness of his phrases with respect to the intended referent. "Every sign is a trace" because "in addition to what the sign signifies, it is the past of him who delivered the sign."[39] An entanglement. "Living means leaving traces."[40]

20. HISTORY

Nietzsche argues that there are "only interpretations," not "facts," and that each interpretation involves a will to power.[41] This confuses the readability of evidence with the interpretation of evidence. It could eliminate the constraints of history were it not also the past.

On what is the Gas Chamber based? Perhaps "the locations of the extermination processes have assumed aspects difficult to define and situate in time," but "uncertainties are both habitual and traditional in building an historic reality."[42] "Like the man in Plato's cave," the historian "sees only the reflection and shadows."[43] He is restricted to "forms of inexactitudes."[44]

In the case of the Gas Chamber, uncertainties—intensified by Nazi falsifications—become "pretexts for casting doubt."[45] This is not to entertain the interpretive uncertainties that evidence poses for the historian, however. "This is nothing more than a stubborn refusal."[46] It proposes an argument that "goes against all evidence."[47] The "argument is very simple: any evidence of massive extermination of the Jews in the gas chambers is unacceptable."[48] The Gas Chamber deals with evidence as if it were an act of will. The "approach can be summed up as follows: 'There cannot exist what must not exist.' "[49] For example: if the gas chambers do not exist, then "concerning the 'gas chambers,' there is nothing . . . The nonexistence of 'gas chambers' should be regarded as welcome news; to hide this news from the world would be an injustice."[50] Faurisson's conclusions include: "The Hitler 'gas chambers' never existed . . . The 'genocide' (or 'attempted genocide') of the Jews never took place . . . The alleged 'gas chambers' and the alleged 'genocide' are one and the same lie . . . The participants in the lie know its days are numbered. They distort the purpose of the Revisionist research. They label as 'resurgance of Nazism' or as 'falsification of history' what is only a thoughtful and justified concern for historical truth."[51]

21. EVIDENCE

Before there is admissible evidence, there is evidence. There is readability before interpretation. Idioms respond to a readability that is never completely available but is often sufficiently available to be read. Evidence obliges us to read it. To ignore it is indicative of an exclusion or repression, and that too is readable because that too is indexed. Unlike interpretation, evidence is not an act of will. "There exists 'not yet conscious knowledge' of *what has been* that has a claim to the structure of awakening."[52]

The Gas Chamber can produce the differend, but only so long as its idiom seems self-contained. You regard reference as defined by the idiom; you turn the victim's testimony into a lie. But the victim who bears witness does not testify on the basis of this idiom. She offers the legibility of evidence.

22. OBLIGATION

Lyotard follows Aristotle and Kant in marking "the heterogeneity between ethical phrase[s] and cognitive phrase[s]."[53] Despite the temptation to infer ethics from knowledge—what you ought to do from what you know to be the case—there is no proof for a moral law. Or, as Wittgenstein suggests, ethics "has nothing to do with facts"[54] because "the ethical is not a state of affairs."[55] "Even when I am describing a murderer," even "in the complete description," an "ethical proposition never occurs."[56] On the other hand, under particular circumstances, ethics may require of us as accurate a description as possible; the cognitive phrase (whatever its inadequacy as interpretation) becomes a response to a moral imperative—in the case of Auschwitz, for example, and in response to the evidence. At least in this case, one might say of the evidence what Levinas says of another's face, that it addresses me—as a visitation from an other that returns to an other, that it "*summons me,* questions me, stirs me, provokes my response or my responsibility."[57] The readability of evidence requires you to receive the "voice that speaks to you," "the obligation with respect to the one who is speaking."[58]

23.

"So I went into the gas chamber," Filip Müller recalls. I was "resolved to die."[59] Several women came up to him, there in the gas chamber. One, whose name was Yana, said, "It helps no one . . . you have to return. You must be a witness." She and the others pushed Müller from the gas chamber.[60]

This will not be interpreted as evidence, given: (1) the definition of the victim that the Gas Chamber requires; (2) the paradox of the Liar this definition allows me to construct. At the same time, if the paradox "disproves" Müller's testimony, if it dismisses the woman in the gas chamber, what is ruled inadmissible is nonetheless indicative. We might follow Lyotard and say that the paradox indexes the differend that "is signaled by the inability to prove," "the unstable state and instant of language wherein something which must be able to be put into phrases cannot be."[61] In this case, however, something which has been phrased is simply prohibited, repressed. The phrase is inexpressible, but only within the context of a particularly obscene formalization. The Gas Chamber is the mark of the repressed phrase in the obscene formalization that represses it.

"It is hard to read *Le Différend* without linking and historicizing the relations."[62] To conceive of the differend in this case is to accept a reality as the Gas Chamber has produced it, to work from this deprivation. "They will believe us, who will deny everything . . . We will be the ones to dictate the history of the Lagers."[63] Getting past the Gas Chamber and the differend it produces may not require a new idiom, however, "new rules for forming and linking phrases," "idioms which do not yet exist."[64] It requires that we adopt the position of evidence—nothing more nor less, nothing other than learning to read what is evidenced—including by the Gas Chamber, for example. The process of reconstituting a loss, whether a loss of expressive power or of a life, requires that evidence be seen in the widest scope of intent and meaning, and that anything less—since it distinguishes between admissible and inadmissible—be recognized as additional evidence.

24. THE DEICTIC

Peirce decribes the indexical as a "deictic gesture." It is curious to watch the ways in which the force of such gestures can be restricted.

In Kant, for example, where "the question of the *There is* . . . is quickly forgotten for the question of what there is,"[65] that is, for interpretation. Or, in Hegel, where the deictic is interpreted as a negation of individual referents: I point at an object and say "This"! I turn in a semicircle and say "This!" once more. I negate the particularity of each referent by subsuming it into the uniform sense of a concept: 'This.'[66] This restricts us to the shadows on the wall. "Negation is a way of taking into account what is repressed . . . though not, of course, an acceptance of what is repressed."[67]

25.

"Deictics are designators of reality," Lyotard writes. "They designate . . . a given," but only as presented "with the universe of the phrase . . . It [the given] appears and disappears with this universe."[68] Survival dependent on the designation of an idiom. The Obscenity of the Gas Chamber requires this implication where the loss of a phrase is the equivalent of a death.

The Gas Chamber requires a particular context: "that the facts, the testimonies which bore the traces of *here's* and *now's*, the documents which indicated the sense or senses of the facts, and the names, finally the possibility of various kinds of phrases whose conjunction makes reality, all this has been destroyed as much as possible."[69] Given this context, perhaps one can argue that nothing with any certainty can be indexed. "The indetermination of meanings left in abeyance, the extermination of what would allow them to be determined, the shadow of negation hollowing out reality to the point of making it dissipate, in a word, the wrong done to victims that condemns them to silence . . . ."[70] Consider a different context, far closer to the case—in which the evidence is overwhelming. It is evidence that motivates the requirement that the definition of a victim be sufficiently restrictive in order to generate paradox. It is *because* of evidence that a misreading of the deictic would be required. It is also because of the evidence that misreadings of the deictic become untenable. In other circumstances, the question of the *There is* may be quickly forgotten, but not in this circumstance. "An old—a very old—woman turned her arm over, disclosing the bluish tattoo, and said simply: 'I was there.' "[71]

26. NARRATIVE

You can listen to an idiom for what it says or what it does not say. You can also listen to its response, to what it repeats. Yaffa Eliach says that if you listen very carefully to a story, you can also hear the story it repeats.[72] Traces survive in the retelling, phrases that have been formalized recur in the formalization. Someone proposes a narrative in which "documents clearly show that the German 'final solution' policy was one of emigration and deportation, not extermination."[73] This narrative has a history. Rupert Brandt, personal assistant to Himmler, writes to Richard Korherr, SS statistician, concerning the revision of a report in which one euphemism for the Final Solution will be substituted for another: "He [Himmler] wishes that in no place should one speak of a 'special treatment of the Jews' (*Sonderbehandlung der Juden*) . . . The formulation should therefore be as follows: ' . . . they passed through the camps' (*Es wurden durchgeschleust durch die Lager*)."[74]

27. "THIS WORLD IS NOT THIS WORLD"

We will take this out of its narrative context; we will say that it is paradoxical. This world (x) is not this world (not-x). "This" refers to the same linguistic moment in each instance. "This" negates realities in each case. "World" is hardly relevant to the reading. If this, then not-this, and so forth.

And as a fragment of a story: "We were completing a long interview, during which he told me many things . . . He looked about the comfortable room in his house with its beautiful view . . . sighed deeply, and said, 'This world is not this world.' "[75] And as a less fragmented story: "an Israeli dentist who had spent three years in that camp . . . details of SS dentists' supervision . . . in his house with its beautiful view of Haifa," where he "sighed deeply, and said, 'This world is not this world.' "[76]

The same phrase repeats: "this world . . . this world." Each is indicative of a situation, one points to the world with gas chambers, the other without. We are unable to decide which: this world without gas chambers is not this world with gas chambers; this world with gas chambers is not this world without gas chambers. And in each case, the same world. Haifa. Auschwitz.

Rather than choose between these readings, to feel their burden—of the events that produced the phrase. "When we listen / we hear something taking place / in the past."[77] So long as interpretation responds to paradox (whether as formalization or its dialectic sublation), the response will be restricted to a play of negation and self-reference: "this world" refers to "this world." When the phrase is taken indexically, it indicates a narrative whose interpretation is constrained not by logic but by history. It might be connected with this story, from outside the Lager: "a dream within a dream . . . with my family . . . the green countryside . . . a deep and subtle anguish": "everything collapses and disintegrates around me, the scenery, the walls, the people, while the anguish becomes more intense and more precise. Now everything has changed to chaos; I am alone in the center of a gray and turbid nothing, and now, I know what this means . . . I am in the Lager once more, and nothing is true outside the Lager."[78] "This world is not this world."

28.

From outside the Lager, Primo Levi has this memory of Auschwitz: "The operation was slightly painful and extraordinarily rapid: they placed us all in a row, and one by one, according to the alphabetical order of our names, we filed past a skillful official, armed with a sort of pointed tool with a very short needle . . . For many days, while the habits of freedom still led me to look for the time on my wristwatch, my new name ironically appeared instead, its number tattooed in bluish characters under the skin."[79] For a name, a number and also for a sense of time. A formal operation and a fragment of a story. For the purposes of this formalization, the particular numerical notation is not significant. Any convention of notation might have been adopted. The number implies that its bearer will no longer exist. If you wear this number, then you won't.

You could stipulate that no one wearing such a number could bear witness, that those who were in this situation are unable to testify about it. Evidence could be forbidden. The formalization of the witness as the Liar. "A proposition . . . that refers to a totality of propositions . . . cannot be part of that totality." What then does the number become? We will say that the number is not evidence. Does this mean that the number is not evidence? "At a distance of forty years, my tattoo has become a part of my body. I don't glory in it, but I am not ashamed of it either . . . I don't have it erased . . . Why should I? There are not many of us in the world to bear this witness."[80]

18

On Fate: Psychoanalysis and the Desire to Know

Charles Shepherdson

> All men by nature desire to know.
>
> Aristotle, *Metaphysics*

> The level which a science has reached is determined by how far it is capable of a crisis in its basic concepts.
>
> Heidegger, *Being and Time*

> The attempt to submit chance to thought implies in the first place an interest in the *experience* of that which happens unexpectedly. (emphasis added)
>
> Derrida, "Mes Chances"

1. INTRODUCTION: *UMSCHLAG, METABOLE*

This paper has its point of departure in some remarks Heidegger makes in *Being and Time* about Dasein's historicality. In division 2, chapter five, he says that the science of history that objectifies its field by conceiving of the being of the past as something present at hand, as "a present that has been," thereby *forgets* the primordial historicality of Dasein, which in fact makes history possible in the first place. In this way, the very movement whereby history seeks to *know* the past in a rigorous fashion turns out to be a betrayal that obliterates the question of what it means to be at all *capable* of having (and *destined* to have) a past. Now Lacan makes a similar claim about those conceptions of psychoanalysis that seek to guarantee their scientific status by introducing a technique (this includes both medical and psychological techniques—psychoanalysis understood either as "natural" or as "human" science) that would provide the field of analysis with a proper degree of objectivity: such efforts conceive *the being of the subject* as something present at hand, essentially like a thing, thereby refusing the most fundamental features of the Freudian discovery in the very movement by which they pretend to make Freud scientific.[1] Lacan opens the "Rome Discourse" by pointing to precisely this betrayal of the unconscious: "Such awe seizes man when he unveils the lineament of his power that he turns away from it in the very action employed to lay its features bare."[2] As Heidegger points out in regard to the discipline of history, for Lacan too, what is most fundamentally betrayed is the relation between the object of investigation and the original temporalization that constitutes it. This is why Lacan claims, in "The Agency of the Letter," that "by his discovery, Freud brought within the circle of science the boundary between the object and being that seemed to mark its outer limit."[3] The very objectification that characterizes a certain conception of science (including medicine and psychology, as we shall see) is thus a betrayal of Freud's way: "Any technique that bases its claim on the mere psychological categorization of its object is not following this path."[4]

To this first problem, concerning the object or field of inquiry, a second, still more difficult, must be added. For it is clear that Heidegger's inquiry into the relation between being and time not only alters *the regional discipline* of history (the object of knowledge), but also recoils upon Heidegger's own thinking and thereby disrupts the project of *phenomenology itself,* understood according to the Husserlian ideal as rigorous science. In this way, the investigation undertaken at the beginning of *Being and Time,* which is intended to radicalize phenomenology *als strenge Wissenschaft,* turns out to produce its own overturning. In the following years, Heidegger's efforts were more and more directed towards exploring what happens to philosophy itself in this movement of dislocation. In his lecture course of 1928 on Leibniz, *The Metaphysical Foundations of Logic,* for example, Heidegger writes: "Precisely the radicalization of fundamental ontology brings about the above-mentioned overturning of ontology out of its very self."[6] This provides a first indication of our thesis: *Umschlag, metabole.*

Heidegger also claims, in a manner that brings him telepathically close to Lacan, that only with this overturning of fundamental ontology as "rigorous science" can the ethical relation be thought: "Here the question of an ethics may properly be raised for the first time."[6] Similarly, in his lecture course of 1964, Lacan writes that "the status of the unconscious, which is so fragile on the ontic plane, is ethical."[7] The question for us is therefore not simply what psychoanalysis understands to be its *object of inquiry*, in contrast to both psychology and medicine, but also what happens to *psychoanalysis itself* as a kind of knowing, as it conceptualizes this object. This is what it means to take up the question of fate in psychoanalysis.

It is perhaps worth recalling at the outset that Lacan does not ask whether psychoanalysis is a science—a question that would take scientific knowledge for granted as an ideal to which disciplines like psychoanalysis might aspire or that they might fail to attain. Rather, his question is: "What would be a science such that it could include psychoanalysis?" This question, posed somewhat obliquely in the "Rome Discourse," assumes a central place at the very outset of his 1964 seminar. There he suggests that the entire basis of the Freudian discovery, and with it the very possibility of psychoanalysis, is consigned to oblivion by the effort to put the Freudian field within the same *arena of truth* that characterizes medicine and psychology.[8] Instead, he situates analysis, which in its institutional life shows every sign of being organized like a church (the text is "Excommunication"), according to the usual antithesis, between science and religion.[9] But it is not so much a question of deciding how to place psychoanalysis in one of these two camps as it is of seeing what displacement they themselves undergo, in the light of psychoanalysis: Psychoanalysis, whether or not it is worthy of being included [the tone here should make his position clear enough] in one of these two registers, may even enlighten us as to what we should understand by science, and even by religion."[10] Now one knows something about the psychoanalytic perspective on religion from Freud's so-called anthropological writings; but with the stress so many interpreters have placed upon Freud's medical and biological orientation, it is not clear what Lacan's position with respect to the question of science would be, though it is vaguely said that his emphasis falls on language rather than on biology. One might even be tempted to believe, on this basis, that his position on the scientificity of analysis is that of a "linguistic structuralism," one that might lead to a certain formalization, as Husserl's interest in mathematics was initially directed towards an effort at formalization in the regions of psychology and history. We know, however, that this effort at formalization eventually issued, as phenomenology developed, in a radicalization of history that *had effects on mathematics itself*.[11]

Without going into this problem in any detail, let us simply underscore two elementary points. First, the question of science cannot be posed without giving attention to history: "What specifies science is having an object," Lacan says. But we must be very prudent, because this object changes, and in a very strange way, as a science develops . . . it is possible that these remarks will force us into an at least tactical retreat, and into starting again from the idea of praxis.[12] Thus, whatever might be Lacan's debt to structural linguistics, the question of science will entail a consideration of history and a conception of praxis. The second point is that the question of science will lead him to something that is normally excluded from science, that is, excluded, indeed, in order to establish the very possibility of scientific objectivity—namely, desire. Here, Lacan refers us to a remark by Diderot regarding the curious discipline (is it a science?) of alchemy, "namely, that the purity of soul of the operator was, as such, an essential element in the matter." It is precisely the question of science, then, that leads Lacan to ask "What is the desire of the analyst?" "Can this question," he adds, "be left outside the limits of our field, as it is in effect in the sciences?"[13]

In the same section of *Being and Time* (division 2, chapter 5), Heidegger develops his claim about history by introducing two terms, *fate* and *repetition*. He writes, for example: "Once one has grasped the finitude of one's existence, it snatches one back from the endless multiplicity of possibilities which offer themselves as closest to one . . . and brings Dasein into the simplicity of its fate. This is how we designate Dasein's primordial historizing."[14] "Dasein's primordial historizing" is therefore not so much a subjective *freedom of choice*, open to an "endless multiplicity of possibilities" as, paradoxically, something closer to "fate." Freud says something similar when he describes a great variety of persons—those who strangely find that (as chance would have it) all their closest friends abandon them in anger, or that every professional advancement must be declined because (by chance) it would interfere with some unwanted but unavoidable commitment recently foisted upon them—persons who, Freud says, appear to be pursued by a malignant destiny, one that appears quite by chance, but that has all the character of fate (this is Freud's word).[15] Elsewhere Heidegger writes: "We characterize *repetition* as a mode of that resoluteness which hands itself down—the mode by which Dasein exists explicitly as fate."[16] Thus, with equal peculiarity, Heidegger uses the unexpected word *repetition* to designate, not sameness (for what repeats is not the "identical"), but rather Dasein's capacity to hand itself down to itself in a manner that *gives rise to history*, rather than to the lawful sequences that characterize the "determined" world, the material universe that is subject to the inevitable chain of causes and effects. "It is strange," Lacan remarks, by way of criticising current positivistic and quantitative conceptions of psychoanalysis along the lines of scientific law, "that materialist thought *forgets* this recourse to the heterogeneous" that was its original inspiration, a forgetting that amounts to a "degradation of true science" that now results "in the positivist reversal that makes the human sciences" into an enterprise that classifies them as nothing more than "the crowning glory of the natural sciences."[17]

The discussion is extremely complex, but it is clear that, for Heidegger, "fate" does not imply *determinism* any more than "repetition" implies sameness. Rather, the analysis of fate and repetition would open upon Dasein's primordial historizing, that original possibility of temporalization, which the science of history forgets but which, in fact, makes something like history possible (and inevitable) in the first place. By turning to this forgotten temporalization, Heidegger's analysis does not so much secure the scientific ground of history as subvert, on behalf of history, the conception of knowing to which history had laid claim—discovering in the process a certain movement in phenomenology as well. And when Lacan takes up a version of these two terms, *fate* and *repetition,* as he does in many places, but perhaps most obviously (1) in his treatment of *tuche* in *Seminar XI,* and (2) near the end of the "Rome Discourse," it will be in order to raise the question not so much of the science of history as rather of psychoanalysis as a science—psychoanalysis being, in its own way, an inquiry into the past. To anticipate, we might say that the *inevitability of determination* by the symbolic order has as little to do with the usual concept of *'determinism,'* as the notion of *repetition* in his understanding of the death drive has to do with *sameness.*

In short, just as, for Heidegger, the understanding of Dasein's mode of being will transform not only our conception of various regional sciences such as history, but also our understanding of philosophy itself, so, too, Lacan's return to Freud will distinguish sharply between the object of psychoanalysis (this is nothing other than the problem of the "subject") and the object of the sciences of medicine and psychology, and in the process he will encounter the question of what happens to psychoanalysis itself as a kind of knowing, and thus what it would mean to speak of psychoanalysis as a science. It will not be possible to develop these initial remarks fully, in so short a time; but it will be possible to raise the question of science by considering the place of fate in psychoanalysis.

2. A TEMPTATION: S/I ?

> Being is prior neither ontically nor logically, but prior in a primordial sense that precedes both . . . But

> this is the problem. It is precisely the problem of how being is "earlier," how it, qua being, originally relates to time . . . And as long as this problem is not posed or only relatively solved, even the use of the term "a priori" remains unjustified and unwarranted, as does the talk of "a posteriori" and the distinction in general.
>
> Heidegger, *The Metaphysical Foundations of Logic*

It would be tempting to regard psychoanalysis as one more form of transcendental philosophy, in which the unconscious would serve as a formal basis upon which the field of consciousness could be determined. Mechanisms of repression, economic and topographical models, systems of representation, transcription, translation, distortion—a whole series of apparently Freudian concepts could easily be summoned up to serve in establishing a systematic or scientific model for the new domain called the "unconscious." Thus, the claim that Freud disrupted the primacy of knowing and displaced transcendental philosophy would in no way alter the fact that the unconscious appears to have become a field of research with quite highly determined structures, mechanisms, and regularities. One could easily pretend to find in Lacan a whole series of remarks suggesting that the unconscious plays the role of an a priori foundation, in the sense that it would designate the limits and formal structure of the field within which consciousness would come to operate. This temptation could be followed at three different levels—(1) for acts of speech, (2) for the relation of the subject to the symbolic order, and (3) for the conception of personal history. These three levels correspond to the three principal divisions of the "Rome Discourse"—the first of which, according to the titles of these sections, is concerned with "empty and full speech in the subject," the second, with the "symbol and language as structure and limit of the field," and the third, with temporality.

"Speech in the Subject": Saussure and the Law

In the first case, it would seem to be a matter of speech and language: the unconscious is governed by laws, according to Lacan, that are like the laws of language and that precede and determine in advance any particular act of speech. Consequently, the "particular effects" that any individual may experience would appear to be based upon a prior organization: "the particular effects of this element of language," he writes, "are bound up with the existence of this ensemble, *anterior to any possible link with any particular experience of the subject.*"[18] Thus, in keeping with Saussure's distinction between *langue* and *parole,* we would seem to be concerned here with differentiating individual acts of speech from that systemic totality of signifiers that serves—one can now use the philosophical term—as their "condition of possibility."[19] In "The Agency of the Letter" Lacan writes: "language is not to be confused with the various psychical and somatic functions that serve it in the speaking subject—primarily because *language and its structure exist prior.*"[20] In the relation of speech and language, therefore, the hierarchy and order of priority would appear to be unmistakable. This would be the first form of our temptation, written S/I, according to which the laws of the "symbol" are primordial and constitutive for every individual, personal, "imaginary" act of speech.

But is this in fact what the concepts of the 'symbolic' and the 'imaginary' mean? Are they in fact to be understood according to the model of Saussure's distinction between *langue* and *parole,* or by analogy with the distinction between an a priori set of structural conditions and an a posteriori act of speech—as two orders that stand in this relation of priority (temporal? logical? ontic? psychological?) to one another? What would such "priority" even mean, and how does Freud's understanding of a whole series of temporal concepts—memory, retroaction, psychic causality, repetition, history, and other fundamental psychoanalytic terms—stand in relation to these notions of "priority" and "structural conditions of possibility," which are almost universally used to understand Lacan's writings? How is it that the basic concepts of metaphysics are still consistently employed to read texts which are directed toward their dissolution?

In spite of this elementary problem concerning time (the "before" and "after"), and the problem of what "constitution" might mean in this context, it is quite common to hear that Lacan's so-called linguistic reinterpretation of Freud asserts that "the unconscious is structured like a language," and that one can understand this to mean his work repeats something like Saussure's discovery that the laws of this "unconscious language" operate independently of the speaker's intentions, in the sense that one must bracket out the level of the "signified" (consciousness), in order to attain the level of legality that is proper to the "signifier" (the unconscious) in its autonomy. To some extent, this analogy, by which the speaker's intentions are distinguished from what is manifested in the discourse, has its appropriateness, and, yet, even as his readers are guided by this link with Saussure, they know that Lacan's task is not at all that of linguistics—let me stress, of linguistic science—since psychoanalysis is concerned with the unconscious of the subject, which is not at all identical with a generalized and "objectifiable" domain of inquiry such as that which concerns structural linguistics.[21]

It is in fact precisely its conception of the object that distinguishes psychoanalysis from other sciences that claim objectivity by leaving out of consideration "the desire of the operator."[22] This is why Lacan writes, in the "Rome Discourse:" "It is in the abstract objectification of our experience on fictitious . . . principles of the experimental method, that we find the effect of prejudices that must be swept from our field if we wish to cultivate it according to its authentic structure."[23] Lacan's refusal of the "objectification" of the psychoanalytic "experience" and his insistence that Freud's discovery is of a different order than that which is formalizable according to the model of the "experiment" (see the discussion of Jules Masserman[24]), is thus ultimately linked to his conception of the very domain or field of psychoanalysis, its "object" of knowledge and, indeed, the "object" or purpose of this knowledge. This is not to say, of course, that in avoiding the "objectification of our experience," Lacan would return us to a "subjectivism" in which the analyst would simply be guided by the subjective feeling of the client—a "therapeutic" orientation from which Lacan takes his distance, both in his remarks on affect, and in his criticism of those who focus on the "here and now" of the analytic situation, believing that the client's feelings and emotional responses (the client's "subjectivity") will compose the principle means of access to the past, insofar as this "immediate experience" of the analytic situation is thought to reanimate the subject's history. The conception of the subject's history, and of the means of access to it, does not lie simply at the level of this "subjective" experience. Lacan writes: "Nothing could be more misleading for the analyst than to seek to guide himself by some supposed 'contact' with the reality of the subject. This cream puff of intuitionist and even phenomenological psychology has become extended in contemporary usage.[25] But this is to disregard "the intersubjective continuity of the discourse in which the history of the subject is constituted,"[26] that is to say, the symbolic network without which no subject's history is conceivable. Psychoanalytic anamnesis, then, is "not a matter of reality but of truth" (my emphasis): "Freud is not concerned with biological memory, nor with its intuitionist mystification, but with rememoration, which is to say, history."[27] So it is not simply in the here and now that one finds a repetition of the past (repetition does not have this meaning for Lacan).[28] Rather, Lacan focuses on the discrepant relation linking what is said in the immediate moment to that material in the discourse, that symbolic debris, that does not belong with what is said and even "interferes with the communication," and this discrepancy is manifested through the imaginary, "personal" and "subjective" relation between the analyst and the client: "The only object that is within the analyst's reach is the imaginary relation that links him to the subject's ego." The analyst cannot, and should not, disregard this relation but should "use it to regulate the yield of his ears . . . in order not to hear [as the gospels say], in other words, to pick up what is to be heard."[29] This gives us one aspect of Lacan's definition of the unconscious as "that part of the concrete discourse, insofar as it is transindividual, that is not at the disposal of the subject in establishing the continuity of his concrete discourse."[30]

One can see that Lacan's position on science will also entail a reconsideration of what history itself is and how the analytic mode of access to the past must be conceived. For the moment, however, let us simply remark that, if Freud's discovery does not belong with the natural sciences, its difference from humanistic psychotherapy should be clear. The concept of the symbolic order is precisely what modifies this "subjective" version of the psychoanalytic discovery, which is still so often found behind most repudiations of "objective science."

Since it is a matter of the subject's history—a history that is manifested, not entirely through the "evidence" of stories, legends, memories, and mythological reconstructions of the subject (conscious history), but also through symbolic debris (the *lapsus,* the mistake), which displays a logic that is nonsense from the point of view of the subject's consciousness of the past—one can see that Lacan's refusal of the "objectification" proper to experimental sciences ("natural sciences"), will be linked, not to a "subjectivism," but to a conception of the subject's symbolic destiny, a conception that has a fundamental bearing on his understanding of history as well. What in fact is the "being" of the past? This brings us back to the topic of fate with which we began: for if it is not a "natural science," neither is analysis a "human science" in the mode of the *Geisteswissenschaften,* the so-called sciences of history. In fact the analyst, Lacan insists, "does not have to know whether the subject has remembered anything whatever from the past."[31] Lacan also insists that it is never a question of reconstructing the subject's actual history, in order to know whether the subject is lying or is misled about the truth. "The ambiguity of the hysterical revelation of the past," he writes (we are still in the first section of the text), "is due not so much to the vacillation of its content between the imaginary and the real, for it is situated in both." Rather, this revelation of the past, unlike the historian's, "presents us with the birth of truth in speech, and thereby brings us up against the reality of what is neither true nor false. That is the most disquieting aspect of the problem."[32] Lacan will stress here the difference "which separates authentic historical research from the so-called laws of history." This distinction is what separates the generalization (the "so-called laws") according to which "every age finds its own philosopher" to express "the values then prevailing," from what Lacan calls "research into the particular events of a subject's history."[33] What does it mean to speak of a "particular event" here? Is particularity not precisely what defines the historian's "object of knowledge"? Lacan adds: "to say of psychoanalysis or of history that, considered as sciences, they are both sciences of the particular, does not mean that the facts they deal with are purely accidental . . . or that their ultimate value is reducible to the brute aspect of the trauma." That is, to the "event" understood as a factum, something that "happens" and then is over and done. Instead, the "event," psychoanalytically speaking, is to be understood in a way that takes account of the fact that "many restructurings of the event take place, as [Freud] puts it, *nachträglich*, at a later date"—which "prompts me to make a distinction between what might be called the primary and secondary functions of historization."[34] This distinction separates the "fact," which "occurs," from its "historization," its inscription within the psychic economy of the subject. The latter is a history that can be rewritten, and the former, strictly speaking, does not exist, since the inscription of the past, in one register or another, is its only reality. Thus, in various ways, Lacan distinguishes the psychoanalytic conception of history from the historian's, precisely in his effort to rethink the science of psychoanalysis by contrasting it with both natural and humanistic sciences. Lacan will return to precisely this point at the conclusion of the entire text: the "subject," he says, can only be "understood as meaning the subject defined by his historicity." And the analyst is concerned with what is "at every instant present in what this history possesses as achieved," namely, "the past in its real form, that is to say, not the physical past whose existence is abolished, nor the epic past as it has been perfected in the work of memory [i. e., the ego's past, the conscious past] . . . but the past which reveals itself reversed in repetition."[35] Let me not develop the complex account of history here, but only note the following point, which returns us to the question of Lacan's relation to the science of linguistics: if Saussure's effort was to establish linguistics in its independence from speech, thereby freeing the science from contamination by subjectivity, isolating the linguistic realm in its autonomy and demonstrating the laws governing the object itself, Lacan, by contrast, does not aim at a science of the symbol in its autonomy (for this is not the object of psychoanalysis) but approaches the subject of the unconscious, which is produced by an exceptional relation between the imaginary and the symbolic.

This relation cannot be said to correspond to a structure in which the imaginary would be derivative and secondary to the symbolic, in such a way that the psychoanalyst would seek to bracket the imaginary in order to reveal the symbolic in its autonomy. Psychoanalysis is simply not a science of the symbol in this sense. And Lacan does not say that the unconscious is language, even if it is manifested in accordance with the laws that govern the symbol. Such a reading would amount to nothing less than an obliteration of the notion of the subject of the unconscious. The very title of the first section of the text indicates clearly that its focus is not in fact "speech and language" (*parole* and *langue*) at all, but rather "speech *in the subject*." It must therefore be a question of thinking the relation S/I in another manner than that which is suggested by this analogy with Saussure and the science of linguistics.

"The Structure and Limit of the Field": Lévi-Strauss and the Law

In the second section of the text, "Symbol and Language," it is a matter of subject and structure—not speech and its linguistic conditions, but the subject and the cultural order: the realization of the subject would seem to be conceived, according to Lacan, only against the background of a symbolic order that, in relation to all imaginary or individual constructions, is primary, fundamental, and determining. This would be the second version of our temptation, written S/I, by which the "individual" would be constituted by the symbolic order: "The marriage tie," Lacan writes, "is governed by an order of preference whose law . . . is, like language, imperative for the group . . . but unconscious in its structure [and] it is perhaps only our unconsciousness of [this] permanence that allows us to believe in the freedom of choice.[36] We would seem to be concerned, then, with a relation of grounding and, one might even say, "causality," according to which the subject is formed in accordance with the exigencies of the sociohistorical context. Let us consider this parallel between the concept of the symbolic and the historical context.[37] A reading based on the "permanence" of the law would lead (and has led) to a discussion as to whether Lacan is enforcing the law or describing it, that is to say, whether his theory is "revolutionary" or "patriarchal," whether it seeks to change the symbolic order or to promote its sinister inevitability, on behalf of the current state of culture. The problem with this reading is that what is presupposed by such a discussion is a point concerning history and, in particular, the notion that the symbolic order can be identified with a specific *historical* arrangement.[38]

Thus if Lacan is thought to claim inevitability for this arrangement, he is said to make "universal" what is in fact "culturally specific" (for instance, patriarchy).[39] A similar problem is raised in regard to the work of some French feminist writers, in particular Kristeva and Irigaray, about whom it is asked whether their use of the term *woman* commits them to an "ahistorical" argument or whether they acknowledge historical specificity. In this way one can try to manufacture a debate between "essentialist" and "anti-essentialist" (historical) thinkers. What must be considered, however, is that these guiding concepts themselves—the 'universal' (which is not culturally specific) and the 'historical' (which is)—are part of what is at issue in Lacan's thought, not only (1) because the conception of history that is used in this debate between "essentialist" and "anti-essentialist" thinkers is one of the terms under revision, both by that work that raises the question of "woman" and by the psychoanalytic elaboration of the symbolic, but also (2) because sexual difference, as Lacan conceptualizes it, can be grasped *neither* as a distinction between two "ahistorical universals" (a natural or biological difference between the sexes) *nor* as a distinction that is simply historical (in the sense in which it is sometimes argued that sexual difference is a *cultural* production, entirely attributable to the linguistic and historical particularity of a given society). With the conception of the imaginary and the symbolic, then, Lacan is in fact suggesting the shortcomings of a discussion of sexuality that is bound by the opposition between biologism and culturalism, or historicism and essentialism.[40] It is in this context that we must consider more carefully the topic of the second section of the "Rome Discourse," namely, the symbolic order and, in particular, its relation to the category of history, which is in fact a central theme of this section.[41]

Freedom and Determinism

Let us also note that one might claim to find, in the passage cited above, which contrasts the "permanence" of the symbolic with the naive belief in "freedom of choice," not only an opposition between the a priori laws of the symbolic and the a posteriori decisions (e.g., marriage) on the part of a subject, but also a second familiar dualism, namely, free will and determinism. Such a reading also entails a presupposition regarding history, which is brought into question by Lacan's work. The debate between free will and determinism would suggest that Lacan is dealing, through the "imaginary," with the familiar notion of the individual or person (free or determined) and, through the "symbolic," with the usual concept of cultural or historical conditions, which might be said to "determine" the formation of the individual.[42] A reading oriented by these terms would obviously have consequences for our understanding of Lacan's position regarding history as well. For one might then expect to find Lacan forcing a choice between "cultural determinism" (the law of the signifier is commonly thought to entail this conclusion) and "individual freedom" (which analysis is commonly thought to elaborate under some such goal as "liberating desire"); or else one might take Lacan to be formulating some version of a synthesis, a dialectical position according to which "freedom means determinism," this being one of the most common understandings of the concept of castration, namely, that one only acquires subjective "freedom" through the law, since outside of culture, in the "absolute freedom" of the uncastrated or lawless subject-without-culture, there is only psychosis.

This is not entirely mistaken, but such a (vaguely Hegelian) formulation that orients our reading by means of the categories of the individual and the social group or state in no way requires us to arrive at the idea of the unconscious, and it allows us to understand the law as identical with the notion of "socio-historical conditions of existence"—a notion that animates contemporary cultural studies and underlies what is called "new historicism" but that in no way brings us into a specifically psychoanalytic arena.[43] In this way, the question remains entirely obscure as to what is at all specifically psychoanalytic about these too-quickly familiar terms, the *imaginary* and the *symbolic.* As in the previous section, it is a question of what is to be understood by the relation between these terms. For this relation is not simply analogous to the relation of grounding or constitution that one might be tempted to see (in the first section) in the distinction between *langue* and *parole,* or (in the present section) between the individual and the historical context.[44] "Nowhere does the distinction I make between the *individual* and the *subject* make itself felt more strongly," Lacan writes in the section.[45] Like many conceptually radical notions, these terms, the *imaginary* and the *symbolic,* are immediately identified with the very structures they were elaborated to contest. Such, as we have said, is the case within the psychoanalytic community as well, in which Freud's thought was immediately translated into the most familiar and least disrupting equivalence that could be found for it; and this is precisely the point behind the opening sentence of Lacan's introduction to the "Rome Discourse": "Such awe seizes man when he unveils the lineament of his power, that he turns away from it in the very act employed to lay its features bare. So it has been with psychoanalysis."[46]

Being in the Hands of the Machine

Let us therefore consider Lacan's distinction between the symbolic order and the socio-historical context that is so often used as its equivalent. At this point we are in a position to see that a more accurate analogy (if one is required) for the symbolic order than the socio-historical context would in fact be the order of the machine, *techne,* the line dividing nature and culture, separating the human from the animal and generating the debilitating, perverse, anonymous (unnatural *and* inhuman) machinery of neurosis that is concomitant with the dubious glory of human culture and our historical dispersion into difference.[47] The symbolic is thus closer to that constitutive fact of being-used-by-tools, being in the hands of the machine, and above all the implementation of the writing machine, to which Lacan sometimes directs our attention by references to tattoos, which inscribe the human tribe (*trieb*) against the grain of nature, compelling us into the trauma of history as a result.[48]

This second level of our discussion, therefore, is decisive in its consequences for our understanding of history. In this section of the "Rome Discourse," it is a question, not of speech and language (as we are mistakenly tempted to interpret the first section), but of the subject and culture—and one might take this to mean it is a question of the relation between the subject and the historical context, a relation, moreover, in which the symbolic would appear to be "constitutive" of the subject. This is the "argument from construction" governing "new" historicism. But what proves to be most striking is that the notion of the symbolic has a bearing not just on the "formation of the subject," but on the concept of history as well. Let us return to our quotation, according to which "the marriage tie is governed by an order of preference whose law is, like language, imperative."[49] The symbolic order, he adds, is determining not only for "individual experience" but also for the collectivity—that historically specific organization that is often wrongly identified with the symbolic order. Thus, when Lacan distinguishes between the order of history and the order of the symbolic law, he is led to speak, not of the dyad of "nature and culture"—a pair of concepts that is usually taken to imply a contrast between nature and history—but rather of "nature, society, and culture,"[50] the last two terms being those that insist upon a distinction between the dimension of history ("society") and the symbolic order ("culture").[51]

It is therefore clear that the relation between the imaginary and the symbolic would not be properly grasped by analogy with the usual process of situating the individual within a cultural context, or by referring the "person" to the specific norms of the "community": "reference to the experience of the community settles nothing," Lacan writes in "The Agency of the Letter." "For this experience assumes its essential dimension [the symbolic] long *before the drama of history is inscribed in it*"—its essential dimension being that which "lays down the elementary structures of culture."[52] In the "Rome Discourse," the same point is stressed: "No one is supposed to be ignorant of the law . . . No man is actually ignorant of it, since the law of man has been the law of language since the first words of recognition presided over the first gifts . . . uniting the islets of the community with the bonds of symbolic commerce."[53] And if one is tempted to mistake this remark about the "bonds" of the "community" for an assertion about a "social contract" theory by which *already given subjects enter* (consciously, through contractual law) into a community, Lacan immediately adds: "Is it with these gifts or with the passwords that give them their salutary nonsense that language, with the law, *begins*?" Does the subjective institution of the gift, that is, the conception of a "pact" as a human "invention," like the invention of particular laws, correspond to what Lacan speaks of as "symbolic law"? The answer is no, "For these gifts are *already* symbols" (emphasis added). Once again, a line is drawn between, on the one hand, the "social," the "historical fact," the constituted law, and, on the other hand, the "cultural" law that is already there, which is constitutive and which is not an "instituted" and human law, given in history but, on the contrary, an "inhuman" law that gives history and is thus, as the theological formula puts it, in reference to the divine, the law that dates "from the beginning." At this point, with the "already," of a certain inhuman "contract"—though his words are "gift" and "debt"—Lacan turns to the Oedipal conflict, the details of which are beyond our present topic.[54] Here, let us only note that even the effort to situate individual experience within the context of a collective history must in turn be referred back to a more fundamental symbolic order that thereby assumes, like the gods, the peculiar position of having been there *in the beginning, before time was* (we will return to these phrases).

The Law of History

This distinction between the socio-historical context and the symbolic order having been made, however, we must return to the question of science, for this is precisely where the temptation of a transcendental reading is strongest. Following Lévi-Strauss, Lacan might seem to make the radical move from what is usually understood as cultural anthropology (a "historical" discipline) to a rigorously structural anthropology (a science of man), whereby he would seem to shift from a consideration of what makes a society historically specific to a consideration of the fundamental order of culture as such. And in fact, Lacan is concerned not so much with the historical specificity of a given culture as with the question of the division between nature and culture (assumptions about this division being decisive for one's conception of subjectivity, as the discussion of freedom [Spirit] and determinism [Nature] suggests). It is this division, structuring the human against the grain of nature, that is understood as the law and that every subject must encounter (this is the "imperative")—which in fact, to be more precise, has presided like fate over the birth of every subject, so that one cannot properly speak of a "subject" who is given and who might then subsequently come to "encounter" the symbolic.

Heidegger's analysis of Dasein has a similar point of departure: with the analysis of "being-in-the-world," one cannot properly speak of an autonomous subject who might subsequently enter into the world and the relation to the other. Derrida writes of this as precisely the point at which Husserl's analysis of the ego—which depends on the phenomenological reduction in order to isolate its proper object of analysis—begins to falter: "Between consciousness and the 'world,' the rupture, even in the subtle form of the reduction, is perhaps not possible. It is in a certain 'unheard' sense, then, that speech is in the world."[55] In fact, this illusion of a monadic subject, which obviously persists and must be accounted for, is not given at the start but contructed "after the fact," as a sort of "a posteriori origin." The illusion of an originally monadic subject is not at the origin but it is a later construction that acquires the mythical status of "having always been there before"—a retroactive mode of temporality. Now this is precisely the problem of the genesis of the ego in Freud. As Laplanche puts it: the ego is indeed an object, but a kind of relay object, capable of passing itself off, in a more or less deceptive and usurpatory manner, as a desiring and wishing subject.[56] The ego, one might say, is this figure, the part that takes over (indeed "represents") the whole.[57]

Once again, it is a question of time: for to assert the subject as existing "prior" to its encounter with the symbolic is to miss the claim that the symbolic has the character of being always already there, while the ego, for its part, is not an original phenomenon but a later formation (Lacan calls it a "precipitate") that claims to have been an origin. The symbolic is thus attended by a conception of time according to which one can no longer speak of a subject as "first" existing and then (developmentally) encountering, or *learning to adapt* (consciously) to the symbolic, or working to change it (though this notion is found in the misreading of Freud according to which the ego adapts to reality, as an organism adapts to its environment). Such a linear, developmental conception of time, however abstract and remote it may seem to be from the question of history, in fact guides our thinking about both personal and historical change (because it informs our understanding of what the "person" and "history" are in the first place), and it is a conception of time that Freud's work obliged him to abandon.

In short, the law dividing nature and culture is not the law of a particular historical group (the socio-historical context), a law produced *in history*, but rather the law *of history*, the law that in the first place compels us into history (makes us *capable*, in Heidegger's phrase, of being-historical, of remembering and forgetting), dislocating the human animal, forcing a rupture with the cycle of nature, driving desire into the destructive and perverse machinations of what we used to proudly call "humanity."[58] Follow Lacan's denunciations of those analysts who appeal to "instinct," or to naturalistic explanations of human development, for their understanding of what the subject's history means, and this law will be found behind his objections: "seeing it [the anal stage] as a mere stage in some instinctual maturation leads even the best minds straight off the track . . . why not look for the image of the ego in the shrimp?"[59] The point is not simply that instead of natural sexuality and organic development, the human being is determined by socio-historical conditions, but rather that every "subject" *must* have a history, that subjects are not only *capable* of having a history, but also *destined* to have one, even, and perhaps especially, in the mode of "not-having" (and, if this were not the case, there would not be an issue as to *whose* history is publically written and valorized, and whose history is unwritten—for, as we know today, the unacknowledged or "repressed" history is never lacking "in fact" but only in its not having been acknowledged. There is no such thing as a subject who has no history—whence the stupidity of the remark still occasionally heard, that, for instance, "if 'they' had produced any great literature, wouldn't we be reading it already?").

I/S: Malfunction

Once we abandon the idea that the imaginary (construed non-psychoanalytically as the "person") corresponds to a monadic subject who might subsequently encounter the symbolic (construed as "external" social conditions), once we grasp their peculiar "equiprimordiality," we are in a position to elaborate more accurately the peculiar conjunction between the imaginary and the symbolic. As Lacan suggests in *Seminar I*, it is only with this dimension of symbolic inscription that we have any insight into that feature of "history" that Freud elaborated under the term *death instinct*, namely, that unnatural dimension within which the ("technical") human relation to the image acquires its maladaptive normalization: "Libidinal captation [by the image] has an irremediably fatal significance for the individual . . . This image is what disrupts the maturity of the libido, the smooth fitting together of reality and the imaginary which should in principle exist, according to our hypothesis—since after all, what do we know about it?—in animals. In animals, the securing of the guide rails is so much more in evidence that it is precisely what has given rise to the great fantasy of *natura mater*... That is how this special fault is introduced, perpetuated in man in the relation to the other who is infinitely more fatal for him than for any animal. This image of the master, which is what he sees in the form of the specular image, becomes confused in him with the image of death. Man can be in the presence of the absolute master. He is in his presence from the beginning."[60] The element of disruption that is introduced by the specifically human relation to the image, then, "subjects" the human to a narcissism that makes the relation to the other, and even the relation to oneself "infinitely more fatal" than for the animal. And this same relation to the image, a relation of rupture ("alienation"), opens onto the domain of the symbolic, which *organizes subjects in groups that do not follow the adaptational lines of nature* that characterize animal societies but rather follow the lines of symbolic exchange, through which desire is obliged to pass.[61] As Lacan puts it in the essay on psychosis: "it is by means of the gap opened up by this prematuration in the imaginary . . . that the human animal is capable of imagining himself as mortal, which does not mean that he would be able to do so without his symbiosis with the symbolic, but that without this gap that alienates him from his own image, this symbiosis with the symbolic, in which he constitutes himself as subject to death, could not have occurred."[62] Here one has not only a glimpse into what distinguishes the symbolic from the concept of 'particular historical conditions,' but also an indication of why we cannot think the relation between the imaginary and the symbolic along the lines of transcendental philosophy (or linguistic and anthropological science), according to which it would be a matter of grounding the contingent (the imaginary) in its conditions of possibility (the symbolic), since it is unmistakably a question here of a different relation between these categories S/I.[63] Let us turn again to the relation between these terms.

This relation, which is one of overlapping (conjunction and disjunction, in *Seminar XI*, under the title "Alienation and Separation"), rather than grounding or constitution, is already evident in the "Mirror Stage" (though little noticed in the secondary literature). In Lacan's account, this maladaptive creature, exposed to the "technique" of the image, is subjected to a "development" that, far from being similar to the "evolutionary" time of natural emergence, on the contrary, turns the "I" of the subject into a "projection," an "apparatus" (elsewhere Lacan calls it a "statue"), that is fundamentally in conflict with the possibility of natural "development" or "adaptation."[64] Narcissism, given with the human relation to the image, thus: "turns the I into that apparatus for which every instinctual thrust constitutes a danger, even though it should correspond to a natural maturation—the very normalization of this maturation being henceforth dependent, in man, on cultural mediation as exemplified, in the case of the sexual object, by the Oedipus complex."[65] Mention of the Oedipal complex here, and of the "sexual object," already in the "Mirror Stage," indicates that the imaginary introduces a non-natural "danger" for the subject that compels a faulty resolution in the symbolic (Freud sees this in the fort-da game, which is nothing but the constitution of the object-relation in accordance with the ordering of symbols, which is quite a different thing from a "psychological" understanding of the object-relation), thereby making "maturation . . . dependent, in man, on cultural mediation," that is to say, on the exchange of symbols.[66] This unexpected and unnatural contrast, indeed conflict, between "instinctual thrust" and "maturation" is what Freud addresses by the distinction between ego libido and object libido, two forms of libidinal energy that would fit together perfectly well, since after all what conflict should there be between "my pleasure" and "my pleasure in the object," were it not that "my pleasure," which is to say the ego's narcissistic pleasure, comes to be fundamentally at odds with my capacity to relate to objects in the world, such that I am threatened with obliteration (death) in the very effort to encounter (love) the other? In short, the ego's relation to itself is not well disposed to "adapt" to what is called the object-relation—not least because its first "object" is itself.[67]

This gives us a glimpse of Lacan's later thesis that "there is no sexual relation" for the human being—a proposition that again underscores the dislocation of human sexuality from its supposed counterpart in natural sexuality.[68] This discussion of the relation between the imaginary and the symbolic should make it clear that, for Lacan, it is a matter, not of the "individual" and the "particular social milieu," but rather of the formation of the *subject* in accordance with the simultaneous facts of imaginary dislocation and inscription within the law of symbolic ordering, which is not *given in history* (as though the symbolic were situated at the same level as a social arrangement produced by human beings—again, according to "contract law," which presupposes a non-psychoanalytic conception of the subject), but is the primordial law *which gives history,* dividing nature and culture at the start. "It can be seen," Lacan writes, "that I do not shrink from seeking the origins of symbolic behavior outside the human sphere."[69]

It should therefore also be clear that Lacan is not interested in establishing, in the fashion of Lévi-Strauss, the "elementary structures of culture," or in providing a science of the symbolic in its autonomy (for that is our question: what is *the object* of this science, if it is a science?); his aim is rather to conceptualize *the subject of the unconscious,* which is not at all Lévi-Strauss's concern. Lacan is quite clear on this point: "Freud's discovery," he says, "was that of the field of the effects in man of his relations to the symbolic order."[70] It is an interest not so much in finding the ethnologist's "laws of culture" or the "elementary structures" that motivates the analyst, then, as it is in finding what the cost in the subject has been of accomodation, not to the social context, but to the law (of which the former is merely the representative). This cost is registered, not by uncovering, like the scientist of culture, the laws of the symbol in its autonomy, but by elaborating the specific relation between the imaginary and the symbolic within the subject.[71] This gives us quite a different orientation towards the relation S/I than is found in Lévi-Strauss (for whom it would be a matter of bracketing the particularity of the individual), and it will bring us toward the category of the real—a category that emerges as central in the final section of the "Rome Discourse," the section that is centered on time and that brings the problem of time together with the question of science, thereby taking Lacan beyond the domain of cultural anthropology altogether: "What is at stake in analysis is the advent in the subject of that little reality that desire sustains in him with respect to the symbolic conflicts and imaginary fixations as the means of their agreement, and our path is the intersubjective experience where this desire makes itself recognized."[72] This focus on the "effects in man of his relation to the symbolic" should now cast light on the earlier temptation to see Lacan's discussion as oriented by Saussure's distinction between speech and language, a distinction that establishes linguistics as a science precisely by bracketing the subject. Such a bracketing of the subject, in the interest of a science of the linguistic or ethnological object, is not at all Lacan's concern: "From this point on," he writes in the second section of the text, "it will be seen that the problem is that of the relation between speech and language *in the subject.*"[73] This will lead Lacan to articulate the relation between the imaginary and the symbolic in the manner that is proper to psychoanalysis: "This is the problem of the grounding that must assure our discipline its place among the sciences: a problem of formalization, which, it must be admitted [*à la vérité*], has not got off to a very good start."[74] At the end of the second section of the essay, he returns to precisely this issue, in the final sentence: Psychoanalysis will provide scientific bases for its theory or for its technique only by formalizing in an adequate fashion the essential dimensions of its experience, which, together with the historical theory of the symbol, are: intersubjective logic and the temporality of the subject.[75]

"IN THE BEGINNING WAS . . ."

Once this distinction is established between the inevitable (not historically contingent) destination of the symbolic and the particular, changing, historical milieu, we are in a position to see why, when Lacan comes to speak of the subject's relation to the symbolic order in *The Four Fundamental Concepts of Psychoanalysis,* he will be able to write: "Before any experience, before any individual deduction . . . something organizes this field, inscribes its initial lines of force."[76] This is what also would make the "priority" of the symbolic apparently incontestable and would motivate a transcendental reading of Lacan, according to which his analysis would center upon the "fundamental order of culture," as that which is constitutive of the subject. In this way, the hierarchy that would appear to have been established between speech and language, in the first section, could be said to overlap with the hierarchy one might pretend to find in the relation between the subject and the symbolic: "Man speaks, then, but it is because the Symbol has made him man."[77] This would be the second version of our temptation, written S/I, by which the "individual," and even the historical community, would be constituted by the symbolic *at the start.* This fact, that "before any experience something organizes this field," would seem to provide the basis not only for an analogy with Lévi-Strauss, but also for what Lacan speaks of as the "scientific" character of psychoanalysis, the topic addressed in the third section of the essay.

Genesis and Structure: A Question of Time

Let us make clear what is at stake in this temptation, which governs so much of the literature on Lacan. One might claim to find here all the attributes of a so-called ahistorical and structuralist formalism, whose links with transcendental philosophy have been amply demonstrated. The mechanisms of the unconscious, far from being personal and unique to the subject (as they are often and more palatably, if mistakenly, taken to be in Freud), turn out in Lacan's reformulation (so the story goes) to entail a generalized determination by a symbolic order (i. e., "social institutions") the anonymity of which is familiar from Lévi-Strauss's work—work that proceeds by bracketing the subjective experience (the register of affect) of the speakers whose community is under investigation (just as Saussure suspends the signified, the subjective meaning of the linguistic sign) in order to reveal the autonomous laws of matrimony, filiation and naming (or, in the case of Saussure, the laws of the signifier itself, prior to the subjective act of signification). In this way, all individual intention, all political acts, all efforts at producing historical change (so the story goes) are said to be imaginary, with no essential bearing on the symbolic order, which would thereby remain—this is the transcendental claim—their condition of possibility. What is at stake in this discussion is therefore nothing less than the notion of grounding that is at work in attempts by transcendental philosophy to provide an a priori foundation for particular and contingent events, the very notion of grounding that is mistakenly used here to characterize the relation between the individual and society, or speech and language, as if these were equivalents for the imaginary and the symbolic.[78]

Contemporary discussions of Lacan are fundamentally impeded at precisely this point. It is often suggested, on the basis of this reading, that the Lacanian notion of the law and the symbolic order commit him to a structuralist point of view in which the possibility of historical change is effectively denied or relegated to a secondary status such that history and, more fundamentally, time would have no decisive bearing on the essentially ahistorical, a priori, and determining character of the law. Lacan's relation to Saussure and Lévi-Strauss, in short, is thought to entail a privileging of the synchronic, which thereby situates his work within the metaphysical tradition of Platonism, insofar as he apparently claims to have discovered the essence of the unconscious, of which there is only one, always.[79]

From Lévi-Strauss to Hegel?

Some advocates of Lacan, on the other hand, playing into this same interpretation from the other side, have pointed out that as a psychoanalyst Lacan can only have been interested in change, insofar as the aim of analysis is in some sense a transformation of the subject's relation to his or her own history. And certainly it is clear that in his discussion of how to handle the transference, or what is to be understood by a properly analytic interpretation, to take only two examples, Lacan was concerned above all with making a cut in the patient's history, so that this history would not be burdened by the symptomatic repetition that brings the neurotic into analysis as one who is destined to have no future, but only a repetition of the past (as Freud put it, hysterics suffer mainly from reminiscences).[80]

It would be possible therefore to believe that, in spite of the apparently ahistorical standpoint that might seem to characterize Lacan's position regarding the symbolic order, he nevertheless entertains the idea that something like "subjective freedom," something like an altered relation to the past and, therefore, a different future is possible. This is the goal of many forms of therapy, and it is not an impossible one. But for Lacan, while the idea that the past and future are altered during the course of analysis is not mistaken, there is nevertheless a fundamental difference between psychoanalysis and psychology with regard to how one conceives of history and the subject's relation to it (for psychotherapy, one learns to change, to adapt differently, or to accept one's past and the limitations that attend it—all of which, for Lacan, is conceived of without the unconscious and on a model of knowing). The conception of history characteristic of most therapy, in Lacan's view, thus amounts to a view of the cure that means nothing less than taking sides with the ego, a cure of the imaginary by the imaginary.[81] Thus, the usual view of how the subject's history is changed and how the future can be liberated from the past is marred, according to Lacan, by an unacknowledged commitment to the ego that it is precisely the aim of analysis to question. This leads to the perhaps unexpected conclusion that we are obliged to consider the distinctive contribution of psychoanalysis and its difference from ego psychology and other non-psychoanalytic therapies in connection with what one might take to be the irrelevant and excessively philosophical issue of how one conceives of history and time. Fundamentally, this issue also entails a certain reevaluation of knowing: in the course of treatment, it is often argued, one comes to know what one wants. As Aristotle says in the *Metaphysics*, "All men by nature *desire to know*." No doubt—but, for Lacan, to suggest that they therefore come to know what they desire would mean the eclipse of Freud's discovery. The conjunction of these two problems—history and knowing—suggest why Lacan will take up together, in the final section of the essay, the joint problem of science and time.

The philosophical stakes of Lacan's argument are perhaps clearer at this point. As long as the discussion of his work remains satisfied with some version of these two alternatives—either structure (determinism) or the subject (freedom), either synchronic law or cultural change, either essentialism or historicism—Lacan's thought will remain a closed book.[82] For the issue in his work is not whether subjectivity or structure has the final word, and it is therefore not a question of choosing one as foundational for the other, according to the dualistic formula S/I; rather, it is a question of how we are to understand the original relation between these terms.[83] In short, we are concerned not with a structural determinism that could be written S/I, or its opposite, individual freedom, but rather with the question of the original temporalization by which the symbolic and the imaginary come into relation—a relation that is one that we can designate, not by "determination" or "freedom," or by the concepts of prior and posterior, but rather along the lines of fate: we might call it a relation to the real that could be characterized as one of "mal-function." Let us not be tempted to believe that the origin, the question of the first things, lies simply in a delineation of the symbolic law, understood as a ground, as a condition of possibility determining the particular individual or group.[84]

Psychoanalysis and Science

What then does it mean to speak of a "science" of psychoanalysis, and what exactly is the link between the symbolic order and what Lacan speaks of as the "formalization" of the analytic enterprise, a formalization he develops through appeal to a certain sort of mathematization? What in fact is the relation between the concept of the 'subject' and the concept of 'structure,' if it is not one of transcendental grounding (S/I) but rather entails a relation to the "real"? This is "the problem of formalization" that "has not got off to a very good start," the issue of the final section of the text and, indeed, of much of Lacan's later work.

The question will already be evident to readers of "The Mirror Stage," in Lacan's remark that the understanding of narcissism that is afforded by an analysis of the image will not be sufficient to develop a genuinely rigorous conception of what Freud's work entails: "If we were to build on these subjective givens alone," Lacan writes there (speaking of the imaginary): "our theoretical attempts would remain exposed to the charge of projecting themselves into the unthinkable of an absolute subject. That is why I have sought in the present hypothesis, grounded in a conjunction of objective data, the guiding grid for a *method of symbolic reduction*."[85] What distinguishes psychoanalysis, properly understood, from those more popular varieties of Freudianism that focus on the "personality" of the client, that act through the "interpersonal relation" of client and therapist and thereby abandon the foundation of speech and the relation of the subject to the symbol to which Lacan urges a return, is that psychoanalysis, precisely by virtue of its discovery of the symbolic order, has a means of understanding subjectivity that goes beyond the *psychological* orientation of many forms of therapy—an orientation that maintains a faith in the ultimate autonomy of the "person" that it was Freud's misfortune and genius to have disrupted. For the symbolic order does show an organization, a machinery that has effects on the subject but that is not at the disposal of the subject who is often taken to be the maker of the symbolic order (as in the historicist thesis, still popular today in theories of social change, according to which the subject is a "social construction," which is to say, a human construction, in keeping with a familiar notion of the social contract, as well as the optimistic but demonic nineteenth century dictum, "Man makes himself").

There is, in other words, a complicity between *psychologistic interpretations* of Freud and the *historicist thesis* that, in spite of historical determination or, indeed, precisely by virtue of historical determination, the subject is able to labor so as to reshape history in his own image (I use the masculine pronoun advisedly here, since it is precisely this humanist understanding of history that makes it impossible to think sexual difference adequately). This thesis regarding history (as constitutive of the subject yet susceptible of re-shaping by the subject) is one whose development Foucault has brilliantly linked to a mode of thought that is particular to the nineteenth century, that promises a transcendental function for "Man" in the very act of demonstrating his finite, empirical situatedness, a mode of "humanism" that is still very popular, but the obsolescence of which is unmistakeable in Foucault's analysis, as it is in Lacan's remark in the course of a devastating appraisal of Jules Masserman: "Let it be known, therefore, since he also prides himself on braving the reproach of anthropomorphism, that it is this last term I would employ in saying that he makes his own being the measure of all things."[86]

It is therefore the concept of the 'symbolic order' that gives psychoanalysis an orientation beyond the usual orientation, which promises an imaginary ideal of human freedom (the "subject," conceived as autonomous and self-determining), over against a "scientific"—which is to say naturalistic—conception of determining "laws" (the "natural," conceived precisely as the machine, as what is not free). It is this alternative that Lacan's work puts in question, and yet it is this alternative that is still used to guide the reading of Lacan, according to which one opposes an "imaginary" freedom against the "determining" power of what one hastily calls "the symbolic law." One can see here that the question of science, just as with Heidegger, will require at one and the same time a rethinking of the "laws" that are taken for granted as the ideal of a scientific form of knowledge and a rethinking of the only popular alternative to this notion of science, namely, the humanistic account of the autonomous human being. Just as Heidegger's question of being overturns philosophy as rigorous science (not to celebrate the freely existing human being, but precisely to put this subject in question), so also Lacan will challenge all the "scientific" models of psychoanalysis: not in order to liberate the authentic desire of the unique individual, but precisely to disclose the illusory and punishing character of this ideal of freedom, an ideal that, as he says in "Aggressivity," has its philosophical culmination in suicide. For both Heidegger and Lacan, the focal point turns out to be this unexpected and symptomatic complicity between these opposites—(1) the notion of rigorous science and its correlate, the idea of nature as governed by predictable, determining laws (the *Gestell*), and (2) the humanistic conception of the autonomous individual as a self-knowing, "self-determining" subject. One could say that the problem of language is nothing other than the locus of this symptom, this paradoxical complicity between freedom and the machine.[87] As other writers have put it, in a manner not entirely removed from our question of fate: does God play dice?[88]

Thus, the symbolic order introduces into the psychoanalytic conception of the subject a dimension that separates psychoanalytic thought both from psychotherapeutic, imaginary and historicist "subjectivism" and also from the "objectivism" or naturalism of medicine, including those forms of psychology that seek to quantify, to provide statistics or criteria of diagnosis, or in some way to "introduce an objective measure" into the field. Unlike psychology, in its effort to be scientific, and unlike medicine, in its treatment of the living organism, psychoanalysis has no way around the particularity of the subject; this would be what allows for a certain mistaken identification between psychoanalysis and various forms of therapy that deal with the "individual" on a case-by-case basis, without avoiding the particularity of the "person." Psychoanalysis, one commonly recognizes, has no other access to its actual field than the particular history and sedimented vocabulary of each individual.[89] It cannot be "applied objectively," like a surgical procedure, to each individual as a "member of a class," without regard for their "individuality"; psychoanalysis, rather, must submit itself to the particularity of the subject; its very "knowledge" must submit to the history and discursive peculiarity of each subject, taking them "one by one."

Such particularity is indeed what distinguishes psychoanalysis from "objective" sciences—those disciplines, "based on principles of the experimental method," which Lacan calls "prejudices that must be swept from our field." But this does not mean that psychoanalysis deals with the "person" or "individual," since such a view would amount to taking over unproblematically the very concept of the 'person' that Freud's work most repudiated. This is why the concept of the 'particular' must be understood in connection with Lacan's elaboration of the real. This is what is at stake in the question of formalization: it is a matter not of discovering the "laws of the symbol" but of developing a theory of the real. This is also what leads Lacan to speak of the *object* of psychoanalysis, namely, the *objet petit a*, the lost object. Such an orientation toward radical particularity would also explain why psychoanalysis is not, strictly speaking, a theory to be applied but always and only a praxis; it would account, moreover, for why analytic training cannot take place in the classroom, why the "tradition" of analysis, so to speak, does not happen as the neutral "handing-down" of a theory or a body of knowledge. And yet if, as we have seen, the point is not to take the symbolic order itself as the *object* of psychoanalytic investigation, what will this formalization entail?

A clue is already evident in the title of the second section, "Structure and Limit of the Field"—particularly in the word limit. For the "structure of the field," as we have seen, turns out to be not merely the structure of the laws governing the symbol in its autonomy but a different structure between the imaginary and the symbolic in which the real is involved. In short, the field has a "structure" that is not determined by the signifier in its autonomy (since, one might say, this Saussurean conception of structure would refer us infinitely from one signifier to the next) but rather by the structuring effect of lack, which introduces a "limit" in a field that would otherwise be lacking all limitation. Put differently, the problem of the relation between the subject and the signifier is the problem of mortality. Freud elaborated this problem through the death drive, which was not a "biological" impulse toward entropy but a peculiar facet of human sexuality in its unnatural relation to representation. We should therefore take note when the word *limit* returns at the end of the text: "so does the death instinct essentially express the limit of the historical function of the subject. This limit is death—not as an eventual coming-to-term of the life of the individual [that is to say, as a point in time], nor as the empirical certainty of the subject [that is to say, a future point in time], but, as Heidegger's formula puts it, as that 'possibility which is one's ownmost, unconditional, unsupercedable, certain and as such indeterminable' [*unüberholbare*], for the subject—'subject' understood as meaning the subject defined by his historicity."[90] All the philosophers have cited this passage, and none has been able to clarify it. Perhaps Lacan's remarks on a certain mathematization will prove helpful. If it is a question, not of a generalized science of the symbol in its autonomy, but of the subject of the unconscious, and, if, moreover, it is a question, not of a science of the synchronic, but of a formalization that will entail a consideration of time ("intersubjective logic and the temporality of the subject"[91]), then how are we to understand this "prior organization of this field" (see "Speech in the Subject," above), which will make it possible to attempt, at a third level, a rigorous formalization, an effort at mathematization? "Speak of chance," Lacan says (he is quoting Freud's *Interpretation of Dreams*, chapter 7), "if you like. In my experience I have observed that there is nothing arbitrary in this field, for it is cross-checked in such a way that *it escapes chance*."[92] As Freud says, the subject suffers not because of a mistake, an accident that has occured (by chance), but because of a more profound "necessity" that keeps coming back, as though it were a matter of some "fate" taking the subject's history into its own hands.

We will therefore have to come back to these words "in the beginning" and "before time." For if we are tempted to believe that the origin, the question of the first things, lies simply in the symbolic law, understood as a "prior" ground, a condition of possibility "determining" the particular subject or group, we will be unable to understand why Lacan claims that the gods, who are at the beginning of things, are real[93] and that their time is, not that of a temporal origin, but rather the time of fate, that rending open of a gap that makes time possible in the first place and that leads Lacan to write again of that particular human fatality, in the essay on psychosis: "it is by means of the gap opened up by this prematuration in the imaginary . . . that the human animal is *capable* of imagining himself as mortal."[94]

Thus, in the third section of the "Rome Discourse," Lacan suggests that the question of "the beginning of things" is not to be located either in the individual who acts or in the structural conditions that might be thought to situate all actions in advance but rather is to be located in *a place exterior to both*: "So when we wish to attain *in the subject* what was *before* the serial articulations of speech, and what is *primordial* to the birth of symbols, we find it in death, from which his existence takes on all the meaning it has."[95] What is this thing "in the subject" ("more in you than you," The Four Fundamental Concepts of Psychoanalysis), this object that never was, lost from the beginning and, precisely by virtue of this fact, giving a *limit*—an originary limit that is marked by that strange temporality of the "first cause" that places it, like the gods, before the very birth of speech or action and primordial even to the symbol, unspeakable, unsymbolizable, but nevertheless that beginning from which "existence takes on all the meaning it has"? It is not an origin that we can place in time, at the beginning, but rather that which makes time possible in the first place, "the limit of the historical function of the subject."[96] Here Lacan adds a sentence: "This mortal meaning reveals *a center exterior to language*" (emphasis added), not symbolic, not imaginary, but that which, he suggests, at the traumatic origin, "is more than a metaphor," though it has everything to do with the primary metaphorization by which the human animal is *capable* of death and *obliged* to speak, without knowing the hour of mortal time or what to say in the face of it.

Science and the Real

By pursuing the question of the relation between the imaginary and the symbolic, then, Lacan finds not only that the notion of determinism will not characterize this relation, but also that the familiar notion of the subject (namely, the conscious one) and the familiar notion of structure (the atemporal one—"conditions of possibility" exterior to the subject) will both prove inadequate. Lacan's later use of topology is intended precisely to address the strange folding over upon one another of these two elements, in accordance with a causality that belongs to neither but, rather, to the real—a real that, as the topological schemas suggest, gives rise to a "structure" that is conceived, not as a priori or synchronic, but rather as a schematization of the original relation between space and time. This is precisely the question of the body: how is the body constituted as a relatively integrated one, capable of detaching itself from the mother and the rest of the world? How is the "body," strictly speaking, established for the subject, since it is not given at birth? How does the difference between what is "inside" and "outside" come into being for a child, a child who will at times clearly refuse this difference, denying the existence of the outside in an effort to prove that the entire world can be taken in through the mouth, thereby repeating the gesture of divine vengeance with which Chronos ate his children, stopping time?[97] This (relative) unity that we call the body (in contrast with the organism) is not given at birth, nor is it accomplished by the assumption of an image (as is often thought). Rather, it is produced by an original loss, the structuring relation to absence that is equiprimordial with the intrusion of the signifier upon the living being.[98]

Let me not enter here into details but simply note the following. We know that Leibniz initially developed topology as a means of questioning the mathematics that favored Euclidean geometry and, in particular, its understanding of the structure of space. Accordingly, topology was first called "analysis situs," the analysis of place. Thus, it was not a question of an account that would entail locating "an object" in space by giving, as one does in school, its coordinates in three dimensions; rather, it was a question of describing the structure of space itself. We know this work was later developed in connection with a non-Euclidean mathematics, namely, one that essentially entails a reference to time and in which space is not uniform or homogeneous. There is, in short, a difference between, on the one hand, the (artificial) "space" that is given geometrical coordinates (this is the "space" of "objective science," upon which Newton insisted when he spoke of that infinite background "in" which all motion occurs) and, on the other hand, that being-in-space that includes the phenomena of "depth"—the "behind" and "in front," the "here" and "there."[99] "Only for a being immersed in space can there be, according to movements that unfold temporally, a before and after, and, consequently, an in front and behind."[100] Such immersion in an organized space is not given at the outset (otherwise there would not be such difficulty in conceptualizing the object-relation and its peculiar genesis), nor is it rendered possible by simple perception, by the simple fact of being "impressed" by an image in the style of Lockean or Hartleian psychology; rather, space is given by the constitution of a peculiar limit in the human animal. This limit is the intrusion of lack upon the organism, that "center exterior to language" and "prior"—"before" the subject's particular speech and "primordial" to the birth of symbols. This "center exterior to language," Lacan says, "is different from the spacialization of a circumference or a sphere, by which we happily schematize the boundary [*les limites*] between the organism and its environment."[101] Space, in particular as it is given in relation to the human body, and the space of the body—the delineation of its inside and outside, the constitution of its limits, all of which entails a consideration of autoeroticism, the relation to the mother and to the first "objects," the very enclosure of the body within its skin, and the first exclusion (lack) that makes exteriority possible—this space is not established by perception, by vision, by the organic fact of seeing and embodied movement (as it presumably is for the animal); and here one can see why the torus and the Möbius strip are not in fact "shapes" or geometrical objects in Euclidean space that one is invited to image; rather, they are to be understood *at the level of the symbol,* as expressing a numerical relation. Space itself, then, is constructed by virtue of a certain relation between the imaginary and the symbol in which the real appears as missing: this is why the human animal, according to Lacan, is a creature not of the imaginary but of the conjunction and disjunction by which the imaginary and the symbolic encounter one another, in such a way that some "thing" comes to be lacking.[102] This is the principal issue of the first two years of Lacan's Seminar.

What is this thing, "in the subject," but not belonging to the subject, this primordial lack that is in some way both "before" the "articulations of speech" and "primordial" to the "birth of symbols," such that it escapes our formula S/I? This is the "first cause" of the subject. The cause, therefore, is not what the symbolic does to us or what the subject might do in spite of external determination; the cause—and this is nothing less than *la chose freudienne,* the "object" of psychoanalysis, the "*objet petit a,* cause of desire"—must be thought by way of the real. It is this rethinking of the cause that will lead us in the direction of what it would mean to call psychoanalysis a "science." "I am well aware," Lacan writes, "that I am entering here on a terrain which, from the point of view of philosophical criticism, suggests a whole world of references."[103] Psychoanalysts cannot, he says, simply abdicate these dilemmas of the philosophical tradition by falling back upon the solution of Newtonian science, which identified causality with the lawful functioning of determining causes and their effects in a linear temporal sequence. "Cause," Lacan insists: is to be distinguished from that which is determinate in a chain, in other words, law. By way of example, think of what is pictured [already we warned that with this picture we are in the imaginary] in the law of action and reaction . . . There is no gap here . . . Whenever we speak of cause, on the other hand, there is always something anti-conceptual, something indefinite . . . there is a hole, and something that oscillates in the interval. In short, there is cause only in something that doesn't work.[104] Our purpose here has been, not to explore in any detail the 1964 seminar, where the real has a complex and fundamental place, but simply to indicate the role of this issue in the more elementary and familiar text of the "Rome Discourse." But it should be clear that Lacan's particular engagement with the strange complicity of subjectivity and structure is unmistakable and distinctive. Even in the first seminar, of 1953, Lacan says: "I must emphasise the fact that Freud progressed on a course of research which is not characterized by the same style as other scientific research. Its domain is that of the truth of the subject. The quest for truth is not entirely reducible to the objective, and objectifying, quest of ordinary scientific method. What is at stake is the realization of the truth of the subject, like a dimension peculiar to it.[105] And perhaps we should hear the reference to speech in the French "dit-mention," the dimension that will turn space inside out, for an entire series of distinctively human acts, from the most excessive, energy-squandering, and life-perverting conquest to the most crippling, incarcerating effects of agorophobia.

Let me conclude here with the remark at the end of the "Rome Discourse" that follows immediately upon the claim that analysis encounters a "mortal meaning that reveals a center exterior to language," something lost, something *excluded* or "impossible," as Lacan says of the real, yet *from which* existence aquires its *limit* and takes on the possibility of meaning. Lacan adds: it corresponds to the relational group that symbolic logic designates topologically as an annulus. If I wished to give an intuitive representation of it, I should call on the three-dimensional form of the torus."[106] Neither the notion of the "individual" nor the notion of "historical conditions," then, can be said to be the cause of the *subject*; rather, it is the original relation between the imaginary and the symbolic, a relation that Lacan conceives as one of malfunction, in which something appears as missing, that Lacan rethinks the cause, as a "first cause" or "origin," that is always already a lost cause, an absolute past that is not, strictly speaking, a moment in time. This is the problem posed by what he calls the "real," and one can see its connection with the (nonnatural) structure of the body in the remark Lacan adds to his reference to the torus: "its peripheral exteriority and its central interiority constitute one single region."[107] This is the function of the symbolic in the constitution of the body, then, which is neither a body organized along the lines of nature nor an "imaginary" body (in which one would have the illusion of a *totality without remainder,* as well as an overwhelming confusion between the subject and the image). This is not to say that the body is simply a "symbolic construction" in the popular sense, but, as Lacan has said, that the lack which is necessary to the constitution of the body could not come to be without the articulation of the symbolic upon the imaginary. Thus, it is a body *given* with the intrusion of a lack, "organ"-ized by a detachment from that which never was, a constitutive separation, one that installs the *subject* as related to lack, which is to say *temporal,* in accordance with the time of a past that was never present, the time of *das Ding,* which makes the human animal *capable* of death, and dependent upon the other and the exchange of symbols for what would otherwise by its "natural" maturation.[108] The radicality of Freud's claim that human sexuality is not a matter of genital maturation could hardly be taken farther. And in a footnote added to this passage in 1966, Lacan indicates that this is the direction his work has gone on to develop.

Notes

INTRODUCTION

1. Cited in Simone De Beauvoir, *The Prime of Life,* trans. Peter Green (New York: Lancer Books, 1966), p. 162.

2. "Rationality," in *Rationality and Relativism,* ed. Martin Hollis and Steven Lukes (New York: Blackwell, 1982), p. 88; cited by Rodolphe Gasché in "Postmodernism and Rationality," *The Journal of Philosophy* 85 (October 1988), p. 533.

3. See, for example, Roderick Chisholm, *The Problem of the Criterion* (Milwaukee: Marquette University Press, 1973).

4. One should add that a similar critique has been leveled against the "spectator" theory of knowledge and its accompanying Platonic view of philosophy by pragmatists such as John Dewey. However, their criticism lacks the ethical bite carried by existential "bad faith."

5. Paul Veyne, *Writing History,* trans. Mina Moore-Rinvolucri (Middletown, Conn.: Wesleyan University Press, 1984), pp. 32ff. and 93.

6. Alphonse de Waelhens pointed this out in his early, classic study, *Une Philosophie de l'ambiguité: L'Existentialisme de Maurice Merleau-Ponty* (Louvian: Nauelerts, 1951).

7. Walter Benjamin, "The Storyteller: Reflections on the Works of Nicolai Leskov," in *Illuminations,* ed. Hannah Arendt, trans. Harry Zohn (New York: Schocken Books, 1969), p. 87.

8. Benjamin, "Storyteller" p. 84.

9. Mikhail Bakhtin, "From the Prehistory of Novelistic Discourse," in *The Dialogic Imagination,* ed. M. Holquist and trans. C. Emerson and M. Holquist (Austin: University of Texas Press, 1981), pp. 41–83.

10. The first official "anti-novel," Charles Sorel's *Le Berger extravagant* (1627), precedes the emergence of the novel as a genre, Mme de Lafayette's *La Princesse de Clèves* (1678).

11. Frederic Jameson, "Postmodernism and Consumer Society," in *The Anti-Aesthetic: Essays on Postmodern Studies,* ed. H. Foster (Washington: Bay Press, 1983), pp. 113–14.

CHAPTER 1

1. Aristotle, *Metaphysics* 1074 b 1–14. Apostle, Hippocrates G., ed. and trans., *Aristotle's Metaphysics,* (Bloomington: Indiana University Press, 1966), 1074b1–14.

2. Parenthetically, the Scriptures describe the devil as the father of lies. The serpent insinuates into the innocent mind of Eve the suspicion that the word of God is not to be taken at face value and without question. So doing, he opens the breach between true and false and in that way begets mendacity. What this does to the self-conception of the philosopher I shall not try to imagine. Suffice it to say that it is consistent with other New Testament references to philosophy.

3. I know: *de me fabula narratur.* But I shall deal with self-reference later on. I can do only one thing at a time. I have to cook my crow before I can eat it.

CHAPTER 2

I am grateful to the National Endowment for the Humanities for its generous support during 1989, which made possible the initial research and writing that went into this paper. Thanks also go to Tom Rosenmeyer and Eric Downing for their encouragement.

1. Friedrich Nietzsche, *The Birth of Tragedy,* trans. Walter Kaufmann (New York: Vintage Books, 1967), pp. 90–91.

2. Nietzsche, *Birth of Tragedy,* p. 91. The conceit originates with the German Romantics (in particular, Friedrich Schlegel). Its most recent exponent is Mikhail Bakhtin; see Bakhtin's *The Dialogic Imagination,* trans. Caryl Emerson and Michael Holquist (Austin: The University of Texas Press, 1981), esp. pp. 22–24.

3. For the extant fragments of Gorgias, see Hermann Diels, *Die Fragmente der Vorsokratiker,* 6th ed., rev. W. Kranz (Berlin: Weidmann, 1952), vol. 2,

pp. 288–294. Other editions to be referred to below are: Francesco Donadi, *Gorgia: "Encomio di Elena" in Bolletino dell' istituto di filologia greca* (Padua: Università di Padova, 1982), suppl. 7; and Otto Immisch, *Gorgiae Helena* (Berlin and Leipzig: W. de Gruyter, 1927). A useful translation, by George Kennedy, of the fragments and testimonia printed in the Diels-Kranz edition is to be found in *The Older Sophists,* ed. Rosamund Sprague (Columbia, S.C.: University of South Carolina Press, 1972), pp. 30–67. References to the *Encomium of Helen* will be given according to the Diels-Kranz (DK) divisions: *Hel.* followed by paragraph number. I have modified the translation in places.

On Not-Being; or, On Nature (here pseudo-Aristotle, *De Melisso, Xenophane, Gorgia,* in *Philosophische und historische Abhandlungen der königlichen Akademie der Wissenschaften zu Berlin* [1900], pp. 1–40) was handed down on two separate reports (the second is given by Sextus Empiricus). Reference will henceforth be *MXG. MXG* (*On Not-Being*) is translated in Mario Untersteiner, *The Sophists,* trans. Kathleen Freeman (Oxford: Blackwell, 1954). Sextus's account (DK 82B3) will be found in Sprague (pp. 42–46) and will also be cited according to the DK divisions (all translations from *On Not-Being* given below are my own).

4. In this view, philosophy is superfetation, resulting from just this kind of hidden causation; cf. Nietzsche, *Birth of Tragedy,* pp. 86–89. Nietzsche asks us to "feel how the enormous driving-wheel of logical Socratism is in motion, as it were, *behind* Socrates," an impetus that "must be viewed through Socrates as through a shadow" (pp. 88–89).

5. G. B. Kerfield, *The Sophistic Movement* (Cambridge: Cambridge University Press, 1981), p. 78: "In its extreme modern form this leads to the doctrine that there are no facts or truth, only ideologies and conceptual models. What happened in the fifth century B.C. hardly went as far as this." But for this thesis to carry conviction, one would need to show that there is for Gorgias knowledge of facts or truth independently of their allegation, or supposition; and this has never been shown (their chief stumbling block, in Kerford's own paraphase, is Gorgias's unbudging claim that "if anything is, it will not be thinkable [or knowable]" [Kerferd, *Sophistic Movement,* p. 97]).

6. Kerferd, *Sophistic Movement,* pp. 78–82. The hypothetical and wistful allusions to "truth" that dot Gorgias's corpus are inconclusive. For a more favorable view promoting "ideology" over "myth" as the object of Pre-Socratic speculation generally, see S. C. Humphreys, in *Anthropology and the Greeks* (London: Routledge and Kegan Paul, 1978), p. 223 with n. 26.

7. Kerferd, *Sophistic Movement,* p. 61.

8. To give further Aristotelian definitions (which obviously could be permutated and combined), dialectic can take the form of "(i) reasoning to opposite conclusions, and (ii) arguing from commonly accepted premises"; G. E. R. Lloyd, *Magic, Reason and Experience: Studies in the Origins and Developments of Greek Science* (Cambridge: Cambridge University Press, 1979), p. 79. These are taken from *Posterior Analytics* 24b10–13; see further G. E. L.

Owen, "Dialectic and Eristic in the Treatment of Forms," in *Logic, Science and Dialectic,* ed. M. Nussbaum (Ithaca, N.Y.: Cornell University Press, 1986), pp. 221–38; 223.

9. Lévi-Strauss has described narrative as "an imaginary resolution of real contradictions," cit. Fredric Jameson, in his foreward to Jean-François Lyotard, *The Postmodern Condition: Report on Knowledge,* trans. Geoff Bennington and Brian Massumi (Minneapolis: University of Minnesota Press, 1984), p. xix; cf. also pp. 28–29.

10. "Dialektik, dem Wortsinn nach Sprache als Organon des Denkens, wäre der Versuch, das rhetorische Moment kritisch zu erretten: Sache und Ausdruck bis zur Indifferenz einander zu nähern" (Theodor Adorno, *Negativ Dialektik* [Frankfurt am Main: Suhrkamp, 1966], p. 66. The translation is adapted from *Negative Dialectics,* trans. E. B. Ashton [New York: Seabury Press, 1973], p. 56. Henceforth, page references to the German text will be given in brackets.

11. Adorno, *Negative Dialectics,* p. 407 [p. 399]. For Gorgias's remarks, see *MXG* 979a12. For details, see the convenient summary in G. E. R. Lloyd, *Polarity and Analogy: Two Types of Argumentation in Early Greek Thought* (Cambridge: Cambridge University Press, 1966), p. 115. On the logic of "presque" ("la limite insaisissable du *presque*"), compare the remarks by Jacques Derrida in *De la grammatologie* (Paris: Minuit, 1967), p. 358.

12. Adorno, *Negative Dialectics,* p. 56 [p. 66].

13. On nervousness in general, see Mick Taussig, *Nervous System* (New York: Routledge, 1992).

14. Cf. Adorno, *Negative Dialectics,* p. 203 [p. 203].

15. Cf. Lloyd, *Polarity and Analogy,* pp. 59–79.

16. Compare *Hel.* 13: "One must study first, the words of *astronomers* who, substituting opinion for opinion, taking away one but creating another, make what is incredible and unclear seem true [or just "appear"] to the eyes of opinion; then, second, logically necessary *debates* in which a single speech, written with art but spoken with truth, bends a great crowd and persuades; [and] third, the verbal disputes of *philosophers* in which swiftness of thought is also shown making the belief in an opinion subject to easy change."

17. See generally, e.g., Christian Meier, *Die Entstehung des Politischen bei den Griechen* (Frankfurt am Main: Suhrkamp, 1980); and W. K. C. Guthrie, *The Sophists* (Cambridge: Cambridge University Press, 1971), pp. 14–26.

18. Joseph Vogt, "Dämonie der Macht und Weisheit der Antike," in *Thukydides,* ed. Hans Herter, *Wege der Forschung,* vol. 98 (Darmstadt: Wissenschaftliche Buchgesellschaft, 1968), p. 290. On "consciousness of power," cf. Guthrie, p. 18

19. On rational exuberance, see Theodor Gomperz, *Greek Thinkers: A History of Ancient Philosophy* (London: John Murray, 1901–12), vol. 1, p. 480,

cited in Guthrie, *Sophists,* p. 49. On the "negative possibilities" of this expansiveness, into which Gorgias also had an insight, see Charles P. Segal, "Gorgias and the Psychology of the Logos," *Harvard Studies in Classical Psychology* 6 (1962), p. 116; see also the surprising parallel with Adorno's "negative dialectic" (Segal, *Gorgias* p. 100). The middle ground is occupied by Thomas G. Rosenmeyer, who emphasizes the literary (and emancipatory) deceptiveness of language in Gorgias; see "Aeschylus, Gorgias and *Apate,*" *American Journal of Philology* 76 (1955), p. 234. Gorgias appears also to be able to accommodate all of the degrees along this spectrum.

20. Cf. Plato, *Gorgias* 456a, and the extant fragments of Gorgias.

21. Cf. however Parmenides's "deceiving *kosmos* of words" (DK 28B8[52]).

22. Isocrates, a student of Gorgias's, balked at the generic confusion exhibited by Gorgias's speech (Isocrates, *Helen* 14). This view of the "eradication" of evil is implied in 14, where Gorgias mentions "a kind of evil persuasion" (to which his own is assumedly opposed), and it is central to readings like those of Segal (*Gorgias,* p. 108) and Kerferd (*Sophistic Movement,* p. 80), which foreground the role of persuasion in Gorgias.

23. On nihilism, see E. R. Dodds, *Plato. Gorgias* (Oxford: Clarendon Press, 1959), p. 8 (debunking the label conferred on Gorgias by Gomperz, *Sophistik und Rhetorik* [Leipzig: Teubner, 1912], p. 35). On nominalism, see Rosenmeyer, "Aeschylus, Gorgias and *Apate,*" pp. 231–32 ("logos creates its own reality"). A definition of nominalism is reproduced in Guthrie, *Sophists,* p. 215.

24. "Kratistos," "most powerful [or best] of men" (Tyndareus); "turannos," "the lord of all" (Zeus); cf. Euripides, Hecuba 816: "Peithō de tēn turannon anthrōpos monēn," etc., "Persuasion (Peithō), the solitary tyrant of men."

25. *Hel.* 3. The Greek is bafflingly compressed and antithetical, to the point of near conflation (as emerges from the final clause even in translation): "patros de tou men genomenou theou, legomenou de thnētou, Tundareō kai Dios, hōn ho men dia to einai edoxen, ho de dia to phanai ēlegchthē, kai ēn ho men andrōn kratistos ho de pantōn turannos." "Physis" by itself contains some of these potential contradictions in Greek (it is not strictly opposed to *genesis,* except on a monastic view). The reading *ēlegchthē,* "was refuted to be," accepted by virtually every editor, has been disputed in MacDowell, "Gorgias, Alkidamas, and the Cripps and Palatine Manuscripts," *Classical Quarterly* 11 (1961), p. 121. Gorgias, however, is entitled to his paradox. (Hence "refuted," not "proved," which is also possible; the indeterminacy between these may just be symptomatic of Gorgias's sophistry.) But my larger point stands, even on the alternative reading.

26. MXG 980b14–15. The thought is paralleled in another fragment: "Gorgias claimed that being is invisible, unless coupled with appearance; and that appearance is strengthless, unless coupled with being" (DK 82B26). Gorgias's ironic "clarity" recalls the philosophers's assurances of self-evidence;

cf. James I. Porter, "Aristotle on Specular Regimes: The Theater of Philosophical Discourse," *Pacific Coast Philology* 21 (1986), pp. 20–24.

27. In *Hel.* 15 the accent falls once again on the defective interchange between saying and being, on the alleged nature of Helen's crime: "tēn tēs legomenēs gegonenai hamartias aitian" (the charge [cause] of the offense that was *said to have taken place* [*to be*]).

28. The neuter plural predicated of singular subjects (any gender) is not uncommon, though it is affected, poetic, or abstract (Raphael Kühner and Bernhard Gerth, *Ausführliche Grammatik der griechischen Sprache* [Hannover and Leipzig: Hahnsche Buchhandlung, 1898], vol. 2, pt. 1, pp. 63–64). The affectation of abstraction is what seems to matter here—especially in a context in which, as the sequel reinforces, "first" things and "beginnings" are suspect (see VI. below).

29. Guthrie (*Sophists,* p. 254) is right to read a (somewhat concealed) "relativism of values "*Hel.* (1)" in this statement.

30. MXG 980b9–14. See [*De Melisso, Xenophane, Georgia*] *Si Parménide,* ed. Barbara Cassin (Lille: Presses Universitaires de Lille, 1980), p. 80, for a suggestive analysis of a single sentence from *On Not-Being* as a three-dimensional object/illusion, whose perspectives are ultimately reducible only to their coincidence in the "material identity" (*l'identité sonore*) of the sentence (p. 79). Strictly, Gorgias would question even this grounding of material identity; any presumed "atomization" of sense and the senses such as Cassin holds will *a fortiori* penetrate here as well (Cassin's "phonic matter," or its "literal transcription"). But there are other considerations besides. See note 53.

31. MXG 980b14–15. Cf. Guido Calogero, *Studi sull' eleatismo* (Rome: Tipografita del Senato, 1932), p. 211; Cassin, *Si Parménide,* p. 557; Alexander P. Mourelatos, "Gorgias on the Function of Language," *Philosophical Topics* 15 (1987), pp. 135–71, 148 (comparing Plato, *Theaetetus* 154a).

32. Correctly, Lloyd remarks: "In neither speech [the *Helen* or the *Palamedes*] are the alternatives such as to be formally mutually exclusive and exhaustive" (*Magic, Reason and Experience,* p. 83).

33. *Hel* 8. On the possible Democritean connection, cf. Giuseppe Mazzara, "Démocrite et Gorgias," *Proceedings of the First International Congress on Democritus* (Xanthe: Diethnes Demokriteio Hidryma, 1984), pp. 125–37. See further Cassin, *Si Parménide,* pp. 95–101; and *MXG* 980a3–8. Guthrie speculates a reverse influence (of Gorgias on Democritus), which is also possible, but not in the present instance (Guthrie, *Sophists,* p. 14). The reference to "invisible body" is at best suggestive. But Gorgias may be thinking of atomistic logic in other ways; see also further below, section VII, on body and void. More generally, concerning these two pre-Socratics and the nascent philology of the time, see the account attempted by Fritz Wehrli, "Der schlichte und erhabene Stil in der poetische-rhetorischen Theorie der Antike," in *Phyllobia für Peter von der Mühll zum 60. Geburtstag,* ed. Olof Gigon et. al. (Basel: B. Schwabe, 1946), pp. 9–34.

34. Kennedy's translation (which follows Diels's proposal) should be corrected to "persuasion does not have the [outward] form of necessity, but it does have the same power." The analogy is clear however the wording is construed (Donadi's recent text provides no solutions).

35. *Hel.* 12. This is most certainly the force of the comparison, whatever the text (Donadi's is adopted here). Cf. the alternative translation of the foregoing sentence: "the persuaded one [Helen], *like* [or *since she is*] one compelled by speech, is wrongly charged." On *hymnos* meaning "speech," cf. Guido Calogero, "Gorgias and the Socratic Principle," in *Sophistik,* ed. Carl Joachim Classen, *Wege der Forschung,* vol. 187 (Darmstadt: Wissenschaftliche Buchgesellschaft, 1976), pp. 416–17.

36. Cf. Aeschylus, *Agamemnon* 385–86, where persuasion, violence, eros, and divine compulsion are already conjoined, and associated with the illusory image of Helen.

37. Rosenmeyer: "Logos is a creator of its own reality" ("Aeschylus, Gorgias and *Apate,*" p. 232). E. R. Dodds, *The Ancient Concept of Progress and Other Essays on Greek Literature and Belief* (Oxford: Clarendon Press, 1973): "Surely what [Gorgias] is trying to prove . . . [is] that an expert propagandist can make a case for any paradox, however fantastic, can in fact 'make it manifest to the eye of faith' " (p. 95).

38. "For that by which we reveal [our thoughts] is *logos,* but *logos* isn't [equivalent to] the underlying realities and beings; therefore, we don't reveal to our fellow creatures what is, but [only] *logos,* which is [irreducibly] other than the underlying realities" (DK 82B3[84]).

39. " 'Reality' for him lies in the human psyche and its malleability and susceptibility to the effects of linguistic coruscation" (Segal, *Gorgias,* p. 110).

40. Guthrie, *Sophists,* p. 211.

41. Cf. Nietzsche, "On Truth and Lie in an Extra-moral Sense," in *Friedrich Nietzsche on Language and Rhetoric,* ed. Sander Gilman, trans. C. Blair (New York: Oxford University Press, 1989). Other modern analogues are equally apt. Compare the following comment by Malcolm Bowie, provoked by Lacan: "Why set in motion such an elaborate machinery of persuasion when there is strictly no one to persuade?" (*Freud, Proust and Lacan: Theory as Fiction* [Cambridge: Cambridge University Press, 1987], p. 130). Helen might be conceived as an imaginary, nodal *point de capiton,* preparing symbolic (re)constructions, while at the same time and from another perspective acting as their common precipitate.

42. Cf. pseudo-Longinus, *On the Sublime* (1.4), which in many ways reads like a commentary on Gorgias's accession to a realm beyond persuasion.

43. Contrast Segal: "These two, psyche and logos, lie both within the realm of tangible experience and become for Gorgias the new reality" (*Gorgias,* p. 110). Here we find smuggled back into the picture of an autonomos logos

the very condition (sensible experience) whose radical otherness is required to argue that autonomy in the first place (cf.: "The *logos* is thus . . . free from exigencies of mimetic adherence to physical reality"; Segal, *Gorgias,* p. 110). Simply to reverse those exigencies is not to dispel them, however, as is evident in the analysis of *Hel.* 14 in terms of unmediated physical adherence and mimetic correspondences (and "equations"; Segal, *Gorgias,* p. 104; cf. as well Segal, *Gorgias,* p. 133), the basis for which is elsewhere recognized for what it is, a "vague analogy" (Segal, *Gorgias,* p. 121).

44. "Egō de boulomai logismon tina tōi logōi dous," *Hel.* 2; "hê piethō prosiousa tōi logōi," *Hel.* 3.

45. Hence, at *Hel.* 9–11, all of the claims made for the effectiveness of logos stand under the aegis of some rhythmical or material attribute. The point is just that logos without this material attribute can make no difference to a hearer—which opens up all over again the question of what logos by itself is. On the indirectness of the effects of logos, see W. J. Verdenius, "Gorgias' Doctrine of Deception," in *Hermes Einzelschriften,* vol. 44, ed. G. B. Kerferd (1981), p. 121 n. 30.

46. No differentiations are made for instance by Kerferd, who speaks in nearly the same breath of "all logos" and "the logos in question" (Kerford, *Sophistic Movement,* p. 81). Immisch takes the dative as instrumental ("minutum corpusculum, de quo loquitur, lingua humana est, un patet vel ex altero epitheto aphanestatōi"; Immisch, p. 23), but even so, it isn't clear that we are entitled to identify *logos* with its instrument. On the locative reading, *logos* is no less easily to be linked to the *"taxis"* that defines its effects (see n. 56 below). Here, Gorgias simply fails (no doubt, deliberately fails) to give us enough information to reconstruct his theoretical intentions in a coherent way.

47. This is the Eleatic argument that was adduced by Melissus, and that was basic even to Aristotle; cf. Harold Cherniss, *Aristotle's Criticism of Presocratic Philosophy* (Baltimore: Johns Hopkins University Press, 1935; reprint New York: Octagon Books, 1964), p. 68 with n. 281.

48. Gorgias did not invent this kind of practical argument. Parmenides's model-Being, conveniently powerful, had already been given new (strictly unwarranted) applications by some of Gorgias's non-Eleatic predecessors. Cf. Cherniss, "The Characteristics and effects of Presocratic Philosophy," where Empedocles's elements are said to be "four physical copies of Parmenidean Being" (in *Studies in Presocratic Philosophy,* vol. 1, ed. R. E. Allen and David J. Furley [London: Routeledge and Kegan Paul, 1975], p. 22).

49. A notable exception is Cassin, who views Gorgias' logos as an inevitable and critical reflex of Parmenidean Being, and thus subordinates logos to the destruction of Eleatic metaphysics (Cassin, *Si Parménide,* pp. 67–68, 98). (However, she too maintains the problematic autonomy thesis). Gorgias can, in other words, and perhaps should be, associated with an "ultra-Parmenideanism" gone askew (Guthrie, *Sophists,* p. 196).

50. *Passim,* and e.g., *Hel.* 8–14, 21, and the statement that Tyndareus's existence, being vouched for by the order of discourse ("because he was said to be") entailed its negation: "he was refuted to be" (*Hel.* 4). This, too, is a play on and against Parmenides's dialectic, which posited, along the way, a straight conformity (identity) between what is, on the one hand, and whatever can be said and thought, on the other (DK 28B2–3).

51. See G. E. L. Owen, "Eleatic Questions," in Allen and Furley, *Studies in Presocratic Philosophy,* vol. 2, pp. 48–81; esp. p. 67; Cassin, *Si Parménide,* e.g., p. 60 (Parmenides's "true" road is contingent upon the negation of the false road; cf. Owen's "by elimination," pp. 57 and esp. 67). Also, Bernard Williams, in *The Legacy of Greece: A New Appraisal,* ed. M. I. Finley (Oxford: Clarendon Press, 1981), who is harsher on Parmenides's fallacy than Owen (who also compares Descartes): "Parmenides has a more primitive conception than this version captures, a notion of language and thought having a content only because they touch or are in contact with what is—the touching and seeing models of thought and meaning operate more directly on Parmenides's ideas than is brought out by the excursion through what *could* be" (220).

52. This alternative follows from a reading that makes Parmenides's dialect self-consciously aporetic. See the brisk arguments advanced by Mary Margaret Mackenzie in favor of Parmenides as a self-deconstructive tactician ("Parmenides' Dilemma," *Phronesis* 27 [1982], pp. 1–12). The destructiveness of Eleatic logic to *all* discursive reasoning was realized by Parmenides's successors, Zeno and Melissus; see Cherniss, *Aristotle's Criticism,* p. 27. One thus did not have to wait for Gorgias to come along and invent an "anti-philosophy" (*Gegenphilosophie,* C. Sicking "Gorgias und die Philosophen" in *Sophistik* ed. Carl Joachim Classen, p. 405); wittingly or not, Parmenides had done the job beautifully himself.

53. Sextus; DK 82B3(86). Cassin views "sonorous identity," the sensuous difference that the physical identity of the word (the "signifier") constitutes, as a subversion of the Parmenidean One. But as we saw, such features are on Gorgias's scheme (in *Helen*) a surplus phenomenom (superadded); which is to say, they are posed in a dialectical relation to logos.

54. MXG 980b6–8; cf. DK 82B3(84). The former follows Cook Wilson's text, on which see Hans-Joachim Newiger, *Untersuchungen zu Gorgias' Schrift Über das Nichtseiende* (Berlin and New York: W. de Gruyter, 1973) p. 152, p. 153 n. 13. Cf. *Palamedes* DK 82B11a(6–7). For the Diels-Kranz passage, see Calogero, where the logical divorce of logos and its material conditions is consequentially carried out (albeit under the assumption that Gorgias's logos reflects Protagorean relativism, an unnecessary and unconvincing attribution; Calogero, p. 209 and esp. 215). Mourelatos takes a slightly different tack and reaches a different result, viz., a Gorgianic critique of private language. But Gorgias's arguments against identity seem to me to be aimed at something other than the private language thesis (see note 67).

55. See Segal, p. 104, n. 37.

56. Segal's suggestion to construe *taxis* as "power" (Segal, *Gorgias,* p. 104) only deepens the surplus/crisis of meanings (giving us three occurrences of "power").

57. This is more emphatic in the Greek, where Gorgias can baffle (but scarcely seduce) the ear with the sonorous jingle of a near tautology: "ton auton de logon echie hê te tou logou dynamics," etc.

58. Cf. Euripides, *Troiades* 892f., where Helen's beauty is said to blind men's eyes with burning desire.

59. A fact rarely acknowledged. But see Franceso Donadi, "Considerazioni in margine all' *Encomio di Elena,*" in *Gorgia e la sofistica: Atti del convegno internazionale,* ed. L. Montoneri and F. Romano (Lentini-Catania, 1983) (*Siculorum Gymnasium,* n.s. 38, n. 1–2 [1985]) pp. 479–85, 482–44.

60. This is one of the pitfalls of a declarative approach like that taken by George Walsh (*The Varieties of Enchantment* [Chapel Hill and London: University of North Carolina Press, 1984], pp. 80–85), who seems to know more of what Gorgias professes himself to (be able to) know. Walsh's position, which rests on a theory of stable after-impressions, is based on a mistranslation (Walsh, *Varieties,* p. 82) of *Hel.* 17. That theory is explicitly denounced in MXG 980b14–17, if we are looking for correspondences between the two treatises. Sensory impressions are susceptible to change over time, "kai nun te kai palai diaphorōs," i.e., nothing guarantees their constancy or their continuity (the more so, if we wish to argue that impressions are in turn "viewed," or "remembered," e.g., "with the eyes of opinion"); moreover, impressions are irretrievably complex, like their perceiving subjects: they are not even self-identical at any given time ("different to the ear and to the eye"). Hence, any principle concerning the "immediacy" of sensory impact will necessarily be complicated by the distribution of differences across a heterogeneous sensorium (this is not quite an "atomization" of sensation, in Cassin's terms, ad. loc.). For a correct understanding of *Hel.* 17, see the editions and translations of Immisch, Donadi, and MacDowell.

61. Hence, the improbability that the tantalizing bits that come down to us through various sources point, ultimately, to any positive theory of the physical world. At best they attest to Gorgias's intense "interest" in such speculation (this is the most Kerferd's lucid arguments for a theory of "pores" can show; Kerferd, "Gorgias and Empedocles," in *Siculorum Gymnasium* n.s. 38 n. 1–2 [1985], pp. 595–605); as does, in its way, *On Not-Being* demonstrate an intense interest, but no positive one, in metaphysical speculation.

62. Ferdinand de Saussure, *Cours de linguistique générale* (Paris: Payot, 1984), p. 163; trans. by Roy Harris under the title *Course in General Linguistics* (La Salle, Ill.: Open Court, 1986) p. 116. Hence a certain materiality is guaranteed even at the center of the semiological system. There are no material identities on the Saussurian model, only material differences between elements of the system, between those elements and what falls outside the system, etc.

63. In "Gorgia: Origine e Struttura materiale della Parola" (*L'Antiquité classique* 52 [1983], pp. 130–40), Giuseppe Mazzura is right to point out that any claim to "autonomy" must be weighed against dependencies upon "corporeal substructures" (p. 134). But as we shall see, in Gorgias these stand in a *dialectical* (and aporetic) relationship to one another; neither term of the polarity is simply "given."

64. Judging from Sextus's report, Gorgias is making some capital of the ambiguity of "logos": as the sum total of words (language) resident within the mind (and hence, as a mental object); and as a given, outward expression (spoken or written). *Both* of these are, in different senses, conceivable as "compounded" of sensations (though to spell out their differences much further than this would take us into speculations not clearly indicated by Gorgias's arguments). See also Kerferd, *Sophistic Movement,* pp. 98, 100.

65. Interestingly, *mēnutikon* + genitive is attested in the sense of "incriminating" (Liddell, Scott and Jones, *Greek-English Lexicon,* 9th ed. [Oxford: Oxford University Press, 1940], s.v. I). In classical Greek, a *mēnutēs* is a legal informant (one who informs *against* another); the verb, *mēnuein,* can likewise mean "to betray." These complications of meaning would potentially hold for Gorgias, whether Sextus is quoting, paraphrasing, or freely elaborating on Gorgias's language. On another option, reality is reduced to signhood (cf. Sextus Empiricus, *Adversus Mathematicos,* 8.202, where the two terms, *mēnutikon* and *parastatikon,* appear together again).

66. Quoted in note 26.

67. Alexander Mourelatos likewise embraces the radical non-transmissibility of "reality" through logos, not simply to others, but with one's self (Mourelatos, "Gorgias on the Function of Language," pp. 138, 150), but then concludes from this (and from *MXG* 980b19) that "linguistic communication is impossible" (Mourelatos, pp. 150, 158). This gives warrant for an alternative, namely a stimulus-response (viz., cause-effect) theory of language. But Gorgias does not disavow the possibility of communicating, only of communicating reality (communication of logos is *per definitionem* imperfect, not impossible; and the incoherence of Gorgias's thesis, if shown, will prove the former, not the latter). This is a physicalist version of the autonomy thesis. But as I have sought to show, logos is not absolutely autonomous, but relatively autonomous—vis-à-vis the world, its effects, and itself. Additional considerations against a stimulus-response thesis will be given in the next note.

68. Even on Gorgias's own logic, the behaviorist thesis, if there is any empirical basis for it, would never be verifiable, e.g., by tracking down causalities to their (putative) external source; nor would it be communicable (as knowledge of an external fact); cf., e.g., the clear implication of MXG 980b12, in Mourelatos's own words: "there is no guarantee, no assurance, no certitude, that [*anything*] will appear alike" (Mourelatos, "Gorgias on the Function of Language," pp. 149–50); or cf. DK 82B3 [77]. So once we accept the categorical argument of *On Not-Being,* the reasons for opting for behaviorism are no

more compelling than those offered by any alternative theory (the categorical argument can in fact just as easily be construed as a critique of stimulus-response theories, *pace;* Mourelatos, p. 163). The same would hold for "firmly established regularities" (Mourelatos, p. 161), a weaker version of causality, but susceptible of the same refutation: there is no linguistic criterion available that could give us their measure (DK 82B3 [84f.]); language cannot exhibit what lies outside language. The affective or "behavioral" thesis is supported by an all too cursory and positive evaluation of the argument from the *Helen* (Mourelatos, pp. 135–36, 156, 164), and more seriously by an impossible rendering of DK 82B3[86], vol. 2, pp. 282, 27–29 (Mourelatos, pp. 158, 163). Its corollary is a narrative of persuasion. But as stated earlier, Gorgias's is an aporetic critique of the pretensions of any discourse (including scientism, or rhetoric for that matter).

69. See note 47 (Melissus).

70. Void is a "physical non-being"; see Cherniss "The Character and Effects of Presocratic Philosophy," in *Studies in Presocratic Philosophy,* p. 25. Cf. also David Sedley, "Two Conceptions of Vacuum," *Phronesis* 27 (1982), pp. 175–93. This consequence is less absurd (or rather, less inconceivable) than first appears; cf. Ptolemy, *Harmonics* 20, reporting (or inferring) the view of certain *harmonikoi,* which reverses the unexpected body-void relation: for them it was "as if the [musical] notes themselves were bodiless and what lay between them were bodies" (*Greek Musical Writings,* ed. Andrew Barker, vol. 2 [Cambridge: Cambridge University Press, 1989], p. 293). The correspondence between these diverse theories may not be due to mere happenstance; I hope to discuss this matter on another occasion.

71. For a recent summary of the background to this much-debated late sixth-century B.C. poem about Helen, see David Sider, "The Blinding Stesichorus," *Hermes* 117 (1989), pp. 423–31; esp. pp. 423–26.

72. Albin Lesky, *A History of Greek Literature,* trans. James Willis and Cornelis de Heer (New York: Corowell, 1976). This is not reduced Gorgias's defense of Helen to a mere "palinode," though it is hard to believe that this connotation would have escaped him either. Relatively closer to the date of our text, on the most common dating of it (to around 415 B.C.) may be reflecting Gorgias's treatment of the myth in more than the obvious ways, on one chronology (for starters, cf. verse 606, and the critical notice by Richard Kannicht, *Euripides, Helena,* vol. 1 [Heidelberg: C. Winter, 1969], p. 58). Ivo Bruns may have been the target of Lesky's reproach (*Vorträge und Aufsätze* [Munich: Beck, 1905], p. 88); but Bruns reads Gorgias's version as a corrective to Stesichorus's (and Euripides's, by his dating) version, not as an *incorporation of a* (Stesichorean) *phantom.*

73. Compare Donadi's rendering, "i motivi per cui si davano le condizioni perché Elena potesse salpare per Troia"). Cf. Immisch, *Gorgiae Helena,* pp. 15 and 53, on this issue (posed without recourse to a Stesichorean phantom) and on the probable date of Gorgias's speech.

74. All such "autonomy" is ultimately a self-refuting notion (revealing hidden contingencies). See further Fredric Jameson, "Periodizing the 60's," in *The Ideologies of Theory: Essays 1971–1986,* vol. 2 (Minneapolis: University of Minnesota Press, 1988), pp. 200–1.

75. Louis Althusser, *Pour Marx* (Paris: Editions la Découverte, 1986), p. 241. Segal captures some of Gorgias's insight into the ideological character of language: "Communication itself, therefore, is a special area of human activity, an invention of society based upon prearranged conventions, and must inevitably involve distortions and rearrangements of the message. There is no such thing as a purely objective transmission of reality" (Segal, *Gorgias,* p. 109). Of course, any conception of "the message," of some unproblematically isolable component of discourse, is an assumption that Gorgias dubiously shares. Moreover, "reality" is not a thing for transmission on Gorgias's philosophy: rather, it just *is* distortion. Differently, Rosenmeyer, "Aeschylus, Gorgias and *Apate,*" p. 231; but see the following remark, which likewise brings us closer to a reading of Gorgias's play of positionalities: "I think it is fair to say, in the light of *On Not-Being,* that in Gorgias's usage the *logos* is *apatelos* [deceptive] primarily in its relation to a *supposed* subject matter, and only secondarily in is effects upon the audience" (Rosenmeyer, p. 233; emphasis added).

CHAPTER 3

1. Victor Farias, *Heidegger et le Nazisme* (Paris: Verdier, 1987).

2. "Letter on Humanism" in Martin Heidegger, *Basic Writings from Being and Time (1927) to The task of thinking (1964),* ed. David F. Krell (New York: Harper and Row, 1977), p. 195. Translated by Frank A. Capuzzi in collaboration with J. Glenn Gray. Translation modified by the author.

CHAPTER 4

1. William J. Richardson, *Heidegger: Through Phenomenology to Thought* (The Hague: M. Nijhoff, 1963); Martin Heidegger, *Being and Time,* trans. John Macquarrie and Edward Robinson (New York: Harper and Row, 1962); cf. also William Barrett, *What is Existentialism?* (New York: Grove Press, 1964).

2. Paul de Man, "Heidegger Reconsidered," in *Critical Writings, 1953–1978,* ed. Lindsay Waters (Minneapolis: University of Minnesota Press, 1989); cf. p. 104.

3. J. Hillis Miller, *Poets of Reality; Six Twentieth-Century Writers* (Cambridge, Mass.: Harvard University Press, Belknap Press, 1965).

4. De Man, "Heidegger Reconsidered," p. 104.

5. De Man, "Heidegger Reconsidered" p. 104.

6. Jean-Paul Sartre, "A More Precise Characterization of Existentialism," in *Selected Prose: The Writings of Jean-Paul Sartre,* ed. Michel Contat and Michel Rybalka, trans. Richard McCleary (Evanston: Northwestern University Press, 1974), vol. 2, pp. 157–58. The article was originally published under the title, "A propos de l'existentialisme: Mise au point," and appeared in *Action,* December 29, 1944.

7. De Man, "Heidegger Reconsidered," pp. 104–5.

8. Heidegger, *Being and Time,* p. 307.

9. Heidegger, *Being and Time,* p. 308.

10. Graeme Nicholson, "The Two Faces of Heidegger," see this volume, chapter 3.

11. De Man, "Heidegger Reconsidered," pp. 105.

12. De Man, "Heidegger Reconsidered," pp. 105.

13. De Man, "Heidegger Reconsidered," pp. 106.

14. De Man, "Heidegger Reconsidered," pp. 104–6.

15. De Man, "Heidegger Reconsidered," pp. 103.

16. We recall that this face of Heideggerian inauthenticity has been developed at length by Günter Grass in a novel about Nazi Germany. See, for example, Störtebeker's Heideggerian description of a pile of corpses—"We must conceive of piledupedness in the openness of Being, the divulgation of care, and endurance to death as the consummate essence of existence." And again, "The most we can say is that here Being has come into unconcealment." Grass, of course, is mocking not only the sincerity of Heidegger's philosophy but the National Socialist practice of using euphemisms to refer to the most ghastly atrocities (*Dog Years,* trans. Ralph Manheim [New York: Fawcett Crest, 1965], p. 314).

CHAPTER 5

1. Wallace Stevens, "A Collect of Philosophy," in *Opus Posthumous,* ed. Samuel French Morse (New York: Vintage Books, 1982), p. 199.

2. Paul de Man, "Intentional Structure of the Romantic Image," in *Romanticism and Consciousness,* ed. Harold Bloom (New York: Norton, 1971), p. 67; hereafter cited as IS.

3. IS, p. 69.

4. In spite of Heidegger's problematic political involvements, one cannot forego a study of his influential thought. Philippe Lacoue-Labarthe rightly claims that to call oneself "Heideggerian" or "anti-Heideggerian" has no meaning or rather "both mean the same thing, namely that one has missed the essential point in Heidegger's thinking, and one is condemned to remain deaf

to the question which the age poses through Heidegger" (*Heidegger, Art and Politics,* trans. Chris Turner [Oxford: Blackwell, 1990], p. 11). Lacoue-Labarthe's concentration on the question that the age poses through Heidegger thus redirects us from a polemical and short-lived confrontation with Heidegger to a more consistent assessment of his work's horizon, which is ultimately determined and clarified by its interpreters. This type of assessment can be done in a critical mode as Habermas does so as to correct its implicit ideological assumptions or in the manner of a hermeneutic reconstruction as practiced by Ricoeur and Gadamer. Both approaches rely directly or indirectly on Schleiermacher's hermeneutic principle, which is trying to understand the author better than he was capable himself. Ricoeur speaks in this context of the world of the work which assumes its independence from its author and remains open to a refiguration of its horizon in the process of reading. In this essay, I will therefore undertake the type of insistent questioning or *Auseinandersetzung* that Lacoue-Labarthe advocates not so much by confronting the concerns of ideology and poetry with one another as by setting them strictly apart. For only in this strict separation is it possible to have a constructive dialogue between poetry and philosophy, one in which neither subordinates the other. This self-limitation should not be misunderstood as a strategy to avoid the political question of Heidegger's work. Rather, we begin to confront it directly by not committing an act of hubris similar to Heidegger's own by staying exclusively within the competence of literature and art. For literature, as the case of Heidegger shows, offers no answers to politics but only to the literary questions it raises for its own survival as a limited and yet special practice of human discourse.

5. For an extensive study on Heidegger's late essays see Gerald Bruns's *Heidegger's Estrangement* (New Haven: Yale University Press, 1989) where he reevaluates the significance of Heidegger's late work as one often underrated by his philosophical followers. My discussion of the late Heidegger differs from Bruns in that I place less emphasis on the hermetic and opaque nature of poetic language. While estranging us from our conventional world, poetic language is not solely a discourse of alienation, as Bruns's discussion would implicitly suggest, but equally one of building and dwelling in constructive insights. A more faithful commentary on the late Heidegger is given in David Halliburton's *Poetic Thinking* (Chicago: University of Chicago Press, 1981). Here more due emphasis is placed on the nearness and proximity of Being warranted even in its apparent strangeness.

6. In using and elaborating on the terms *abstraction* and *empathy,* I am indebted to Wilhel Worringer's *Abstraction and Empathy.* Worringer speaks of abstraction and empathy as two poles that "are only gradations of a common need . . . revealed to us as the deepest and ultimate essence of all aesthetic experience: . . . the need for self-alienation" (*Abstraction and Empathy: A Contribution to the Psychology of Style,* trans. Michael Bullock [New York: World Publishing Company, 1967], p. 23). Whereas abstraction fulfills this need by removing one from "the seeming arbitrariness of organic existence in general, in the contemplation of something necessary and irrefragable," of a

recognizable design or structure of Being, empathy delivers the individual equally beyond his own confines into an absorption with the objective world where he comes to "rest with [his] inner urge to activity within the limits of this objectification" (Worringer, *Abstraction and Empathy,* p. 24).

7. Martin Heidegger, "Poetically Man Dwells," in *Poetry, Language, Thought,* trans. Albert Hofstadter (New York: Harper and Row, 1971), p. 228; hereafter cited as PMD.

8. Martin Heidegger, "The Origin of the Work of Art," in *Poetry, Language, Thought,* p. 29; hereafter cited as OWA.

9. PMD, p. 216.

10. OWA, p. 32.

11. OWA, p. 38.

12. Wallace Stevens, "The Figure of the Youth as Virile Poet," in *The Necessary Angel* (New York: Vintage Books, 1951), p. 65; hereafter cited as *NA.*

13. Paul A. Bové, *Destructive Poetics* (New York: Columbia University Press, 1980), p. 189. Bové's essay is exemplary in dealing with Stevens's and Heidegger's contemporaneity in thought, which both share across their particular cultural horizon and beyond their personality or temperament. Frank Kermode's "Dwelling Poetically in Connecticut," (in *Wallace Stevens: A Celebration,* ed. Frank Doggett and Robert Buttel [Princeton: Princeton University Press, 1980], while likewise establishing such a contemporaneity, does so with perhaps less confidence. It is irrelevant to conjecture, as Kermode does, how Stevens fashions its own poetic persona on Heidegger, whom he had never met nor probably read at any length. Kermode is more convincing when he brings Stevens's poetry and Heidegger's thought actively into a dialogue. Here the affinities between the two thinkers become apparent as the compatibility of a common poetics.

14. Wallace Stevens, "An Ordinary Evening in New Haven," in *The Collected Poems of Wallace Stevens* (New York: Alfred A. Knopf, 1981), p. 486; hereafter cited as *CP.*

15. Wallace Stevens, "Of Modern Poetry," in *CP,* p. 239.

16. Stevens, "Notes" in *CP,* p. 380; "Ordinary Evening" in *CP,* p. 473.

17. Rosalind Krauss, *Passages in Modern Sculpture* (New York: Viking Press, 1977), p. 30.

18. *CP,* pp. 385, 398–99.

19. "Notes," in *CP,* p. 382.

20. "Notes," in *CP,* p. 383.

21. PMD, p. 226.

22. George Santayana, *The Sense of Beauty* (New York: Dover Publications, 1955), p. 25.

23. *CP,* p. 395.

24. "Notes," in *CP,* p. 381.

25. Plato, *The Republic,* in *Plato,* trans. B. Jowett, ed. Louise Ropes Loomis (Roslyn, N.Y.: Walter J. Black, 1942), p. 400.

26. "Notes," in *CP,* p. 380.

27. "Notes," in *CP,* p. 380.

28. "Notes," in *CP,* p. 382.

29. "Description Without Place," in *CP,* p. 345.

30. Stevens, "Of Modern Poetry," pp. 239–40.

31. "Notes," in *CP,* p. 380.

32. *CP,* p. 512.

33. *CP,* p. 512.

34. *CP,* p. 512.

35. PMD, pp. 221–22.

36. Martin Heidegger, "Words," in *On the Way to Language,* trans. Peter D. Hertz (New York Harper and Row, 1971), p. 149.

37. Quoted in Maurice Merleau-Ponty, "Cézanne's Doubt," in *Sense and Non-Sense,* trans. Herbert L. Dreyfus and Patricia Allen Dreyfus (Evanston: Northwestern University Press, 1964), p. 17; hereafter cited as CD.

38. CD, p. 17.

39. OWA, p. 39.

40. CD, p. 17.

41. *CP,* p. 526.

42. *CP,* p. 527.

43. PDM, p. 222.

44. PDM, p. 222.

45. "Notes," in *CP,* p. 406.

CHAPTER 6

1. Martin Heidegger, *Der Satz vom Grund* (Pfullingen: Neske Verlag, 1978), pp. 146–47 (henceforth *SG*).

2. *SG,* p. 150.

3. *SG,* p. 151.

4. *SG,* p. 151.

5. G. W. F. Hegel, *Phänomenologie des Geistes* (Hamburg: Meiner, 1952), p. 163.

6. *SG,* p. 151.

7. Michel Foucault, *The Thought from the Outside,* trans. B. Massumi (Cambridge, Mass.: MIT Press, 1987), p. 13.

8. Foucault, *Thought from the Outside,* p. 25.

9. Hans-Georg Gadamer, *Wahrheit und Methode* (Tübingen: J. C. B. Mohr, 1965), p. 450.

10. Besides a few passing references to Beethoven's late quartets and a special remark dedicated to Mozart (that makes no reference to any musical work in particular) on the two hundredth anniversary of his birth (*SG,* pp. 117–18), one finds, so far as I know, only a very short letter in which Heidegger refers to Stravinsky's "Symphonie of Psalms" and "Persephone" (*Denkerfahrung* [Frankfurt: Klosterman, 1983], p. 113; henceforth *D*).

11. Heidegger, *Unterwegs zur Sprache* (Pfullingen: Neske Verlag, 1975), p. 9 (henceforth *US*).

12. Friedrich Nietzsche, "Götzen-Dämmerung," in *Werke,* vol. 3, ed. Karl Schlechta (Frankfurt: Ullstein Verlag, 1976), p. 451 (henceforth *GD*).

13. Friedrich Nietzsche, "Geburt der Tragödie," in *Werke,* vol. 1, p. 44 (henceforth *GT*).

14. George Steiner, *Real Presences: Is there anything 'in' what we say?* (London: Faber and Faber, 1989), p. 19.

15. Philippe Lacoue-Labarthe, "The Echo of the Subject," in *Typography,* ed. C. Fynsk, trans. B. Harlow (Cambridge, Mass.: Harvard University Press, 1989), p. 145. On the relation of sight and speculation in the formation of the metaphysical tradition see Hans-Georg Gadamer, *Wahrheit und Methode* 4th ed. (Tübingen: J. C. B. Mohr, 1975), pp. 432–49. For a clear statements of the Greek privileging of sight see Aristotle, *De sensu* 473a3, and *Metaphysics* 980b23–25; on music see Aristotle, *Politics* 1339a14ff.

16. Gerald Bruns, *Heidegger's Estrangements* (New Haven: Yale University Press, 1989), p. xv.

17. *US,* p. 182.

18. This is the case in two very different, yet equally influential recent readings of Nietzsche: Maurice Blanchot's "L'expérience-limite" in *L'entretien infini* (Paris: Gallimard, 1969) and Alexander Nehamas' *Nietzsche: Life as Literature* (Princeton: Princeton University Press, 1987). There are, of course, exceptions: besides the Lacoue-Labarthe piece already cited, see, for instance, M. A. Gillespie, "Nietzsche's Musical Politics" in *Nietzsche's New Seas: Ex-*

plorations in Philosophy, Aesthetics, and Politics, ed. Gillespie and Strong, (Chicago: University of Chicago Press, 1988), pp. 117–49.

19. On the figure of "woman" in Nietzsche's work, see David Krell, *Postponements* (Indianapolis: Indiana University Press, 1986); and Drucilla Cornell, "Disastrologies," in *Praxis International* 9, nos. 1–2 (April and July 1989), pp. 183–191. On the relation of women and music, see Eva Rieger, " 'Dolce semplice'?" in *Feminist Aesthetics,* ed. G. Ecker (Boston: Beacon Press, 1985), pp. 135–49.

20. *GD,* p. 393; See also the same remark in the letter to Köselitz dated March 21, 1888.

21. *GD,* pp. 477f.

22. Friedrich Hölderlin, "Brot und Wein" in *Sämtliche Werke,* vol. 6, ed. D. E. Satler (Darmstadt: Luchterhand, 1979), p. 102.

23. Friedrich Nietzsche, "Also Sprach Zarathustra," in *Werke,* vol. 2, pt. 4, no. 3 (henceforth *Z*).

24. E. Bloch, *Prinzip Hoffnung,* vol. 3 (Frankfurt: Suhrkamp, 1973), p. 1243.

25. GT, p. 22.

26. GD, p. 477; for more extended discussions of the philosophical significance of pain, see my "Pain and Fragment" in *Beyond Translation,* ed. David Wood (London: Routledge, 1993); and my "Black Milk and Blue Bodies," in *Word Traces,* ed. A. Fioretos (Baltimore: John Hopkins University Press, 1993)—both forthcoming.

27. Friedrich Nietzsche, "Die Fröliche Wissenschaft," in *Werke,* vol. 2, p. 13 (henceforth FW).

28. GT, p. 91.

29. Nietzsche, "Wille zur Macht," in *Werke,* vol. 4, no. 822 (henceforth WM).

30. Z, p. 544.

31. GT, p. 114.

32. See Theodor Adorno, "Über den Fetischcharakter in der Musik und die Regression des Hörens," in *Dissonanzen: Musik in der verwalteten Welt* (Göttingen: Vandenhoeck & Ruprecht, 1972), pp. 9–45. Also interesting in this context is Adorno's "Musik, Sprache und ihr Verhältnis im gegenwärtigen Komponieren," in *Schriften,* vol. 16 (Frankfurt: Suhrkamp Verlag, 1978), pp. 649–64.

33. Jacques Attali, *Noise: The Political Economy of Music,* trans. Brian Massumi (Minneapolis: University of Minnesota Press, 1985), p. 51.

34. See especially *Republic* 398ff. Full discussion of the political place of music for Plato would need to address the relation that he, like Nietzsche, claims that music bears to both mourning and woman.

35. See, for instance, Aristotle's *Politics* 1340a18–19.

36. Adorno, "Fetischcharakter," p. 31.

37. Edison patented his phonograph in December 1877, the year after Nietzsche published his *Richard Wagner in Bayreuth.*

38. Walter Benjamin, "Das Kunstwerk im Zeitalter seiner technischen Reproduzierbarkeit," *Gesammelte Schriften,* vols. 1, 2, (Frankfurt: Suhrkamp, 1974), p. 474.

39. Benjamin, *Kunstwerk in Zeitalter,* p. 477.

40. Bloch, *Prinzip,* p. 1246.

41. See Igor Stravinsky's criticisms of "mechanically reproduced music" in his *Poetics of Music,* trans. A. Knodel and I. Dahl (Cambridge, Mass.: Harvard University Press, 1942), esp. pp. 134–35.

42. See Theodor Reik, *The Haunting Melody* (New York: Farrar, Straus and Young, 1953), p. 250.

43. Nietzsche, GT, p. 89; "Words and Music," in *The Complete Works of Friedrich Nietzsche,* vol. 2, ed. Oscar Levy, trans. M. Mügge (New York: Macmillan and Co., 1924), pp. 29–47, and 382 (henceforth W); "Sprache und Musik," in *Nietzsche Werke: Fragmente aus 1869–1871* (henceforth abbreviated as SM).

44. GD, p. 112.

45. GD, p. 111.

46. W, p. 29; SM, p. 377.

47. Martin Heidegger, *Nietzsche,* vol. 1 (Pfullingen: Neske Verlag, 1961), p. 119. The passage, full of echoes and puns, resists translation, but means "we live insofar as we [are a] body."

48. Attali, *Noise,* p. 143.

49. Lacoue-Labarthe, "Echo," p. 193.

50. *US,* p. 235.

51. For a more extended treatment of these issues in Heidegger, see my "Changing the Subject: Heidegger, 'the' Epochal, and National," in *Heidegger and the Political,* ed. Marcus Brainard, a special issue of the *Graduate Faculty Journal of the New School,* vol. 14, no. 2–vol. 15, no. 1 (1991), pp. 441–64; as well as "History and Catastrophe," in *Heidegger: Toward the Turn,* ed. J. Risser (Albany: SUNY Press); and "Ruins and Roses: Hegel and Heidegger

on Sacrifice, Memory and Mourning," in *Endings,* ed. R. Comay and J. McCumber (Evanston: Northwestern University Press)—both forthcoming.

52. Friedrich Hölderlin, *Sämtliche Werke,* vol. 4, ed. F. Beissner (Stuttgart: Kohlhammer, 1943), p. 282; cf. also *US,* pp. 65ff.

53. W, p. 382; SM, p. 35.

54. GT, p. 131.

55. W, p. 42.

56. GD, p. 406.

57. Martin Heidegger, *Was Heisst Denken* (Tübingen: Niemeyer, 1954), p. 20.

CHAPTER 7

1. See W. B. Gallie, "Essentially Contested Concepts," in *The Importance of Language,* ed. Max Black (Englewood Cliffs, N.J.: Prentice-Hall, 1962), pp. 121–46; Alasdair MacIntyre, "Social Science Methodology as the Ideology of Bureaucratic Authority," in *Through the Looking-Glass: Epistemology and the Conduct of Inquiry,* ed. Maria J. Falco (Washington, D. C.: University Press of America, 1979), pp. 42–58; William E. Connolly, *The Terms of Political Discourse* 2d ed. (Princeton: Princeton University Press, 1983), pp. 9–44.

2. Max Horkheimer and Theodor W. Adorno, *Dialectic of Enlightenment,* trans. John Cumming (New York: Seabury Press, 1972). Regarding *fin-de-siècle* and ante-bellum Europe, compare Allan Janik and Stephen Toulmin, *Wittgenstein's Vienna* (New York: Simon and Schuster, 1973); also David Frisby, *Fragments of Modernity* (Cambridge: Polity Press, 1985).

3. Hans Blumenberg, *The Legitimacy of the Modern Age,* trans. Robert M. Wallace (Cambridge, Mass.: MIT Press, 1983).

4. Leo Strauss, "The Crisis of Our Time," in *The Predicament of Modern Politics,* ed. Harold J. Spaeth (Detroit: University of Detroit Press, 1964), p. 41.

5. Strauss, "Crisis of Our Time," p. 44.

6. Strauss, "Crisis of Our Time," p. 54. In fairness one should also cite these lines: "The relative success of modern political philosophy has brought into being a kind of society wholly unknown to the classics, a kind of society in which the classical principles as stated and elaborated by the classics are not immediately applicable. Only we living today can possibly find a solution to the problems of today" (p. 54). See also Strauss, *The Political Philosophy of Hobbes: Its Basis and Its Genesis* (Oxford: Clarendon Press, 1936) and *Thoughts on Machiavelli* (Glencoe, Ill.: Free Press, 1958); compare in addition *Ancients and Moderns,* ed. Joseph Cropsey, New York: Basic Books, 1964).

7. Stanley Rosen, *Hermeneutics as Politics* (New York: Oxford University Press, 1987), p. 3.

8. Rosen, *Hermeneutics,* p. 4.

9. Rosen, *Hermeneutics,* p. 5.

10. Rosen, *Hermeneutics,* p. 5.

11. Rosen, *Hermeneutics,* p. 6.

12. Rosen, *Hermeneutics,* p. 7.

13. Rosen, *Hermeneutics,* p. 15.

14. Jürgen Habermas, "Die Moderne—ein unvollendetes Projekt," in *Kleine Politische Schriften I–IV* (Frankfurt am Main: Suhrkamp, 1981), pp. 445, 452–53 (my translations).

15. Jürgen Habermas, *The Philosophical Discourse of Modernity: Twelve Lectures,* trans. Frederick Lawrence (Cambridge, Mass.: MIT Press, 1987), pp. 112–13.

16. Jürgen Habermas, *The Theory of Communicative Action,* trans. Thomas McCarthy (Boston: Beacon Press, 1984 and 1987), vol. 1, *Reason and the Rationalization of Society,* ch. 2; and vol. 2, *Lifeworld and System: A Critique of Functionalist Reason,* ch. 6.

17. William E. Connolly, *Political Theory and Modernity* (Oxford: Blackwell, 1988), p. 2, henceforth, *PT.*

18. *PT,* p. 2.

19. *PT,* p. 4.

20. *PT,* p. 4.

21. *PT,* p. 4.

22. *PT,* p. 4.

23. Rosen, *Hermeneutics,* p. 15.

24. Rosen, *Hermeneutics,* p. 17.

25. Jürgen Habermas, "Modernity versus Postmodernity," *New German Critique* 22 (1981), pp. 3–22; and "Die Utopie des guten Herrschers," in *Kleine Politische Schrifte I–IV,* pp. 318–27.

26. *PT,* pp. 2–3.

27. Rosen, *Hermeneutics,* p. 6.

28. Habermas, *Philosophical Discourse of Modernity,* pp. 83, 106.

29. *PT,* p. 6.

30. *PT,* p. 15.

31. Rosen, *Hermeneutics,* p. 5.

32. Habermas, *Philosophical Discourse of Modernity,* pp. 16–44, 51–69.

33. Michel Foucault, "What is Enlightenment?" in *The Foucault Reader,* ed. Paul Rabinow (New York: Pantheon Books, 1984), p. 34.

34. Foucault, "What is Enlightenment?" p. 38.

35. Foucault, "What is Enlightenment?" p. 42.

36. Foucault, "What is Enlightenment?" p. 43.

37. Foucault, "What is Enlightenment?" p. 45.

38. Foucault, "What is Enlightenment?" p. 45.

39. Foucault, "What is Enlightenment?" p. 45.

40. Foucault, "What is Enlightenment?" p. 45–46.

41. Foucault, "What is Enlightenment?" p. 46. Elaborating on this passage, the essay continues that the criticism is "archaeological—and not transcendental—in the sense that it will not seek to identify the universal structures of all knowledge or of all possible moral action, but will seek to treat the instances of discourse that articulate what we think, say, and do as so many historical events. And this critique will be genealogical in the sense that it will not deduce from the form of what we are what it is impossible for us to do and to know; but it will separate out, from the contingency that has made us what we are, the possibility of no longer being, doing, or thinking what we are, do, or think" (p. 46). Stressing the practical-experimental aspect of critique, Foucault added in a Nietzschean vein: "I shall thus characterize the philosophical ethos appropriate to the critical ontology of ourselves as a historico-practical test of the limits that we may go beyond, and thus as work carried out by ourselves upon ourselves as free beings" (p. 47).

42. Jürgen Habermas, "Taking Aim at the Heart of the Present," in *Foucault: A Critical Reader,* ed. David C. Hoy (Oxford: Blackwell, 1986), p. 107.

43. Habermas, "Taking Aim," p. 108.

44. Hubert Dreyfus and Paul Rabinow, "What Is Maturity? Habermas and Foucault on 'What is Enlightenment?' " in Hoy, *Foucault: A Critical Reader,* pp. 110.

45. Dreyfus and Rabinow, "What Is Maturity?" p. 111.

46. Dreyfus and Rabinow, "What Is Maturity?" p. 118.

47. Dreyfus and Rabinow, "What Is Maturity?" pp. 118–21. (In the above I move somewhat beyond the Dreyfus-Rainbow essay.)

48. Fred Dallmayr, *Twilight of Subjectivity* (Amherst: University of Massachusetts Press, 1981); *Polis and Praxis: Exercises in Contemporary Political Theory*

(Cambridge, Mass.: MIT Press, 1984); *Language and Politics: Why Does Language Matter to Political Philosophy?* (Notre Dame, Ind.: University of Notre Dame Press, 1984); *Margins of Political Discourse* (Albany: State University of New York Press, 1989); compare also *Critical Encounters: Between Philosophy and Politics* (Notre Dame, Ind.: University of Notre Dame Press, 1987).

49. Jean-François Lyotard, *The Postmodern Condition: Report on Knowledge,* trans. Geoff Bennington and Brian Massumi (Minneapolis: University of Minnesota Press, 1984), p. xxiii.

50. Lyotard, *Postmodern Condition,* p. xxiv.

51. Lyotard, *Postmodern Condition,* p. xxv.

52. Lyotard, *Postmodern Condition,* p. 10.

53. Lyotard, *Postmodern Condition,* p. 12.

54. Lyotard, *Postmodern Condition,* pp. 17, 15.

55. Lyotard, *Postmodern Condition,* p. 16.

56. Jean-François Lyotard, *Le Différend* (Paris: Minuit, 1983), pp. 10–11.

57. Arguments akin to those above have been expressed by Albrecht Wellmer in "Zur Dialektik von Moderne und Postmoderne: Vernunftkritik nach Adorno" in *Adorno-Konverenz 1983* (Frankfurt am Main: Suhrkamp, 1985), pp. 48–114—a study that by no means counsels a simple acceptance of modernity.

58. Compare along these lines Ernesto Laclau and Chantal Mouffe, *Hegemony and Socialist Strategy: Towards a Radical Democratic Politics* (London: Verso, 1985); also Dallmayr "Rethinking the Hegelian State," in Dallmayr, *Margins of Political Discourse.*

CHAPTER 8

1. Martin Heidegger, "The Age of the World Picture (henceforth AWP), in *The Question Concerning Technology and Other Essays,* trans. William Lovitt (New York: Harper and Row, 1977).

2. AWP, pp. 130, 132. See also Heidegger's *Nietzsche,* vol. 4, *Nihilism* trans. Frank A. Capuzzi (San Francisco: Harper and Row, 1986), p. 28: "Western history has now begun to enter into the completion of that period we call the *modern,* and which is defined by the fact that man becomes the measure and the center of beings. Man is what lies . . . at the bottom of all objectification and representability." Heidegger's perspectives on the relationship between subjectivity and modernity are given ample critical treatment by David Kolb in *The Critique of Pure Modernity* (Chicago: University of Chicago Press, 1986), pp. 121–27, 137–50; the role of Descartes is the subject of Dalia Judovitz's recent *Subjectivity and Representation in Descartes: The Origins of Modernity* (Cambridge: Cambridge University Press, 1988).

3. Cf. Alexandre Koyré, *From the Closed World to the Infinite Universe* (Baltimore: Johns Hopkins University Press, 1957). See also Hans Blumenberg's discussion of Pascal's sensibility to the new infinity in *The Legitimacy of the Modern Age* (henceforth *LMA*), trans. Robert M. Wallace (Cambridge, Mass.: MIT Press, 1983), pp. 83–85.

4. Descartes, "Mediations II"; in *The Philosophical Works of Descartes,* trans. John Cottingham, Robert Stoothoff, and Dugald Murdoch (Cambridge: Cambridge University Press, 1984), p. 16.

5. AWP, p. 115.

6. In Roberto Mangabreira Unger's view, this is one of the sources of modern "idolatry." See his *Knowledge and Politics* (New York: Free Press, 1975).

7. Jürgen Habermas, *The Philosophical Discourse of Modernity* (henceforth *POM*), trans. Frederick Lawrence (Cambridge, Mass.: MIT Press, 1987), p. 132.

8. This is Unger's formulation for the enigmatic relations between necessity, contextuality, and idolatry in the modern age. See Unger, *Knowledge and Politics* and also *The Critical Legal Studies Movement* (Cambridge, Mass.: Harvard University Press, 1986), esp. p. 119.

9. AWP, pp. 116–17.

10. *POM,* p. 139.

11. *POM,* p. 296.

12. In Rosen's wry view, "we do not need theories telling us how to cross the street or that the best way to communicate with people is by speaking to them" (Stanley Rosen, *Hermeneutics as Politics* [New York: Oxford University Press, 1987], p. 12). The introduction of the concept of 'disenchantment' in this connection is mine; Rosen speaks instead of the "purely procedural, nonreligious, and nonmetaphysical nature of communicative reasoning." For Rosen's critique of "theory," see "Theory and Interpretation" in that same volume, pp. 141–74. There, he characterizes the exuberance of interpretation as "an exacerbation of the nervous sensibility" (p. 143).

13. See, for example, Leo Strauss, "The Crisis of Our Time," in *The Predicament of Modern Politics,* ed. Harold J. Spaeth (Detroit: University of Detroit Press, 1964), pp. 41–54. I owe this reference to Fred Dallmayr's paper "Modernity and Postmodernity" originally presented at the IAPL conference at Emory University, 1989 (included as chapter 7 of this volume).

14. John Milton, *Areopagitica,* in *The Complete Prose Works,* ed. Ernest Sirluck (New Haven: Yale University Press, 1959), vol. 2, p. 549.

15. Stanley Fish, "Critical Legal Studies (I)" (henceforth CLS), *Raritan* 7 (1987), pp. 4–6.

16. Milton, *Areopagitica,* p. 565.

17. CLS, p. 5.

18. CLS, p. 5.

19. *LMA*, p. 9.

20. *LMA*, p. 10; emphasis added.

21. See *POM*, p. 231.

22. Max Weber, "The Sociology of Charismatic Authority," in *From Max Weber: Essays in Sociology*, ed. H. H. Gerth and C. Wright Mills (New York: Oxford University Press, 1946), pp. 248–49.

23. Weber, *General Economic History* (New York: Collier Books, 1961), p. 267.

24. Milton, as cited by Fish, in CLS, p. 3. As Fish explains, "they will be willing followers not at this moment or at that moment but at every moment, since there will be no distance or tension between their own inclinations and the bidding of an *internalized* law" (CLS, p. 3).

25. Georg Lukács, *Theory of the Novel*, trans. Anna Bostock (Cambridge, Mass.: MIT Press, 1971), p. 91. Lukács explains that this freedom is possible "because the lofty norms of his actions and of his substantial ethic are rooted in the existence of the all-perfecting God, are rooted in the idea of redemption, because they remain untouched in their innermost essence by whoever dominates the present, be he God or demon."

26. See Wolfgang Schluchter, "The Paradox of Western Rationalism" in Wolfgang Schluchter and Guenther Roth, *Max Weber's Vision of History* (Berkeley and Los Angeles: University of California Press, 1979), pp. 55–56.

27. Schluchter, "Paradox of Western Rationalism," p. 58.

CHAPTER 9

1. Martin Heidegger, "The End of Philosophy and the Task of Thinking,"in Martin Heidegger *Basic Writings, from Being and Time* trans. Joan Stambaugh, ed. David F. Krell (New York: Harper and Row, 1977), p. 374.

2. Heidegger, "End of Philosophy," p. 374.

3. Heidegger, "End of Philosophy," p. 390.

4. Michel Foucault, *The Order of Things* (henceforth *OT*) (New York: Random House, 1970), p. 67.

5. *OT*, p. 352.

6. *OT*, p. 353.

7. *OT*, p. 386.

8. *OT*, p. 44.

9. Plato, *Republic* 607b. trans. Paul Shorey. *From the Collected Dialogues of Plato,* ed, Edith Hamilton and Huntington Cairns (Princeton: Princeton University Press, 1961), p. 832.

10. Plato, *Republic* 607d.

11. It gives me pleasure to be able to point to Gary Shapiro's reading of Hobbes in "Reading and Writing in the Text of Hobbes's *Leviathan," Journal of the History of Philosophy* (April 1980). Though addressing very different themes in Hobbes, Shapiro emphasizes the extraordinary ways in which Hobbes thinks of writing and representation. And he does note some of the themes I am addressing here. "In his introduction Hobbes gives a piece of advice about how to read the first part of the book, 'Of Man.' Faced with the question whether wisdom comes from reading of books or men, Hobbes quotes the classical maxim *nosce teipsum* but gives it the amazing translation 'read thyself' (rather than 'know thyself'). Nor is this a casual use, for the remainder of the introduction plays elaborately upon the idea that by reading one's self one comes to read other men' (p. 149). I am more interested here in Hobbes's concern with *representing* oneself and others: im-personation.

12. Thomas Hobbes, *Leviathan* (Indianapolis: Liberal Arts Press, 1958), p. 132.

13. Hobbes, *Leviathan,* p. 132.

14. Hobbes, *Leviathan,* p. 132.

15. Little needs to be said of how this view of representation departs from Hobbes's views of representation through words. In relation to words, fiction—untruth—is a constant threat and must be ruthlessly weeded out. He speaks of "compound imagination" as "but a fiction of the mind" (Hobbes, *Leviathan,* p. 29). Far more important, he speaks of four "special uses of speech" with "four correspondent abuses": "First, when men register their thoughts wrong, by the inconstancy of the signification of their words . . . and so deceive themselves. Secondly, when they use words metaphorically . . . and thereby deceive others [etc.]" (p. 38).

16. Niccolo Machiavelli, *The Prince,* trans L. Ricci, rev. E. R. P. Vincent (New York: Random House, 1950), p. 82.

17. Hannah Arendt, *The Human Condition,* (Garden City, N.J.: Doubleday, 1959), p. 45.

18. Arendt, *Human Condition,* p. 48.

19. Arendt, *Human Condition,* p. 53.

20. Arendt, *Human Condition,* pp. 53–54.

21. *OT,* p. xx.

22. *OT,* p. xxi.

23. The notion of "transgression" and its relation to the limit is found in Michel Foucault, "A Preface to Transgression," *Language, Countermemory, Practice* (henceforth *LCP*), trans. Donald F. Bouchard and Sherry Simon ed. D. F. Bouchard (Ithaca, N.Y.: Cornell Uniersity Press, 1977), pp. 29–52.

24. *OT,* p. 16.

25. Marx maintains the distinction between *vertreten* and *darstellen* in *Eighteenth Brumaire of Louis Bonaparte.* Spivak quotes the following: "The small peasant proprietors "cannot represent [*vertreten*] themselves; they must be represented. Their representative must appear simultaneously as their master, as an authority over them, as unrestricted governmental power that protects them from the other classes and sends them rain and sunshine from above" " (Gayatri Spivak, "Can the Subaltern Speak?" *Marxism and the Interpretation of Culture,* ed. Cary Nelson [Urbana: University of Illinois Press, 1988], pp. 276–77).

26. Spivak, "Can the Subaltern Speak? pp. 276–77.

27. Spivak, "Can the Subaltern Speak? p. 275.

28. Spivak, "Can the Subaltern Speak? p. 277.

29. Arendt, *Human Condition,* p. 50.

30. *OT,* p. 306.

31. *OT,* p. 307.

32. Arendt, *Human Condition,* p. 50.

33. *OT,* p. 307–8.

34. *OT,* p. 308.

35. Foucault, "Nietzsche, Genealogy, History," in *LCP,* p. 151.

36. *OT,* p. 312.

CHAPTER 10

1. Jameson's review of *Metahistory,* entitled "Figural Relativism; or, The Poetics of Historiography," first appeared in *Diacritics* 6 (Spring 1976) and has been reprinted in *The Ideologies of Theory: Essays 1971–1986,* vol. 2 (Minneapolis: University of Minnesota Press, 1988), pp. 153–65. Page references to this article given in my text are to *Ideologies of Theory.*

2. Hayden White, *Metahistory: The Historical Imagination in Nineteenth-Century Europe* (Baltimore: Johns Hopkins University Press, 1973), p. 434.

3. Hayden White's "Getting out of History: Jameson's Redemption of Narrative" first appeared in *Diacritics* 12 (Fall 1982) and has been reprinted in

The Content of the Form (Baltimore: Johns Hopkins University Press, 1987), pp. 142–68. All page references to this article given in the text are to the latter; henceforth *CF.*

4. *CF,* p. 167.

5. *CF,* p. 168.

6. In *Metahistory,* White makes a distinction that Jameson picks up on in his preface to Griemas's *On Meaning* (Minneapolis: University of Minnesota Press, 1987), between "the 'bad' Irony of Burckhardt, serene and aestheticizing . . . and the 'good' or strong Irony of Nietzsche from within which Hayden White clearly speaks" (p. xviii). Jameson remarks quite rightly that the significant "slippage" in the concept of irony is essential to its function as the "great magical term on which the text turns" (p. xx), though I would not necessarily draw the Greimassian conclusions that he does. White's problem, to my mind, is simply that he needs another term, and another concept, not a trope, to enable him to get beyond his tropological system and his conception of the ironic stance. While he is quite aware that his Nietzschean irony is not at all the same as the Burckhardtian kind, the shared signifier presents an obstacle to his efforts to define a fundamentally different stance.

7. Jean François Lyotard and Jean-Loup Thébaud, *Au juste* (Paris: Christian Bourgeois Éditeur, 1979); trans. Wlad Godzich, under the title *Just Gaming,* (Minneapolis: University of Minnesota Press, 1984). Page references given in the text are to the English version; henceforth *JG.*

8. Lyotard calls it "modern" here, but in a footnote on p. 16 of the English edition he suggests that the term *postmodern,* which he defined after the publication of the French edition, would be appropriate in this context.

9. *JG, p. 23.*

10. *JG, p.* 17.

11. *JG, p.* 36.

12. *JG, p.* 17.

13. *JG, p.* 27.

14. *JG, pp.* 73–74.

15. *JG, p.* 75.

16. *JG, p.* 80.

17. *JG, p.* 75.

18. Fredric Jameson, *The Political Unconscious: Narrative as a Socially Symbolic Act* (Ithaca, N.Y.: Cornell University Press, 1981), p. 102; henceforth *PU.*

19. *PU,* p. 101

20. *PU,* p. 101.

21. Fredric Jameson, "Modernism and Its Repressed; or, Robbe-Grillet as Anti-Colonialist," in Jameson, *Ideologies of Theory,* vol. 1, p. 179.

22. *CF,* p. 149.

23. *CF,* pp. 150–51.

24. Fredric Jameson, "Marxism and Historicism," in Jameson, *Ideologies of Theory,* vol. 2, p. 169.

25. *CF,* p. 165.

26. On the condition that "modernism" in this sense not be considered as a matter of mere chronology. The article is incorporated in Gérard Genette, *Figures II* (Paris: Seuil, 1969); the typology appears on pp. 98–99.

27. Thus Genette cites Scudéry's observation that "it is true . . . that Chimène married le Cid, but it is not at all plausible for an honorary daughter to marry her father's killer"; and Bussy-Rabutin's remark that "Mme de Clève's confession to her husband is extravagant and could only be told in a true story; but when one freely invents one, it is ridiculous to give one's heroine such an extraordinary sentiment" (*Figures II,* pp. 71–72).

28. Hence the principle of what Genette calls "backward or reverse [*rétrograde*] determination," which means that in the fictional narrative, the means are determined by the end, or the causes by the effects. Thus, in the phrase, "The marquise, in despair, took a pistol and shot her brains out," it is the pistol that determines "in despair," and not the reverse (*Figures II,* pp. 91–92).

29. *PU,* p. 19.

30. *PU,* p. 102.

31. I am referring to a passage in Jean-François Lyotard, *Rudiments païens* (Paris: Union Générale d'Editions, Collection "10/18," 1977) on the strategy of "pagan" practitioners of "theory-fiction," who confront the proponents of "theory-truth" by debating them in a perfect imitation of the latter's own language (p. 30).

32. This is the wording of the *Diacritics* version (p. 4); in *The Ideologies of Theory* it is softened to "the annoyance we feel when heavy artillery is rolled out to dispatch a few (admittedly choice) specimens of game" (vol. 1, p. 156).

33. *CF,* pp. 164–65.

34. Note that "humorous" does not mean "comical." For Jameson's reaction to White's classification of Marx's historiography under a "comic" or "romance" paradigm, see *PU,* pp. 101–3, and chap. 2 in general. It should also be remarked that Jameson is well aware of the difference between the situa-

tion of the French Left and that of its American counterpart, and understands the political motivations behind the former's rejection of the concept of totality and the philosophies of totalization. He explains this in a footnote in which he argues that the American Left must at this stage pursue an "alliance politics." Thus his adoption of totality as finality is not necessarily less strategic than Lyotard's use of the Idea of plurality.

CHAPTER 11

1. See H. Blumenberg, *The Legitimacy of the Modern Age,* trans. Robert Wallace (Cambridge, Mass.: MIT Press, 1983) (henceforth *LM*).

2. By *realism* I simply mean the doctrine that there exists some mind-independent reality to which true beliefs must refer.

3. Despite their reliance on methods of scientific verification, developmental theories of the sort set forth by Piaget, Kohlberg, and Habermas represent, on Blumenberg's account, an illegitimate "reoccupation" of a premodern, metaphysical position.

4. See M. Heidegger, *Being and Time,* trans. John Macquarrie and Edward Robinson (New York: Harper and Row, 1962), pp. 86–134, 414; T. W. Adorno and Max Morkheimer, *Dialectic of Enlightenment* (New York: Herder and Herder, 1972); Michel Foucault, *The Order of Things: An Archaeology of the Human Sciences* (New York: Random House, 1973); *The Birth of the Clinic: An Archaeology of Medical Perception* (New York: Pantheon Books, 1973); and my essay "Foucault and the Frankfurt School: A Discourse on Nietzsche, Power, and Knowledge," *Praxis International* 6, no. 3 (October 1986): pp. 311–27.

5. H. Blumenberg, "An Anthropological Approach to Rhetoric," in *After Philosophy: End or Transformation?,* eds. Kenneth Baynes, James Bohman, and Thomas McCarthy (Cambridge, Mass.: MIT Press, 1987), p. 451.

6. See *The Genesis of the Copernican World,* trans. Robert Wallace (Cambridge, Mass.: MIT Press, 1987), pp. 169–208 (henceforth *GCW*); and Karsten Harries's excellent review, "Copernican Reflections," *Inquiry* 23: no. 2 (June 1980) pp. 253–69.

7. Blumenberg's remarks are directed against those who have sought to ground the theoretical attitude in the nonobjectified experience of a *Lebenswelt.* Blumenberg is sympathetic to Husserl's attempt (in the *Crisis of European Sciences and Transcendental Phenomenology*) to show that the idealization of space, time, subjectivity, and truth begun by the Greeks and completed by modern thinkers is an authentic manifestation of self-transcendence rather than a deficient mode of being, as Heidegger (on Blumenberg's somewhat questionable reading of him) would have it. At the same time, he denies that the *lifeworld* construction can be anything more than a limiting concept, the idea of a *'subjective life'*—richer in meaning, more secure and less alienated than the already objectified *world* we do live in. In this respect, at least, it

functions to legitimate (in a mythic way so to speak) the achievements of rational self-assertion while counteracting its nihilistic side-effects. See H. Blumenberg, *Lebenszeit und Weltzeit* (Frankfurt: Suhrkamp, 1986) and part 3 below.

8. Blumenberg discusses these epochal transitions in the Book of Nature metaphor in *Die Lesbarkeit der Welt* (Suhrkamp: Frankfurt am Main, 1981), pp. 101–7, 171–75 (henceforth *LW*).

9. The claim that Bacon articulated the methodological underpinnings of modern science is only partially true, since his conception of nature was still burdened with theological connotations. Bacon rejected mathematics as the most suitable language for natural science and likened his experimental discovery of laws to a divination of God's commands. His emphasis on prediction and control belies his conceptualization of nature as a quasi-magical text containing the original names of things. For a further discussion of the Book of Nature metaphor in general and its use Bacon's philosophy in particular, see *LW*, especially chap. 8.

10. See R. Pippin, "Blumenberg and the Modernity Problem," *Review of Metaphysics* 40 (1987): pp. 535–57; B. Yack, "Myth and Modernity," *Political Theory* 15 (1987): pp. 244–61; and M. Jay's review of *The Legitimacy of the Modern Age* in *History and Theory* 24 (1985): pp. 183–97. I discuss these critics in my "Blumenberg and the Philosophical Grounds of Historiography," *History and Theory* 29 (1990): pp. 1–15.

11. For a discussion of the differences between Kuhn and Blumenberg on this point, see my essay "The Copernican Revolution Revisited. Paradigm, Metaphor, and Incommensurability in the History of Science: Blumenberg's Response to Kuhn and Davidson," *History of the Human Sciences* (forthcoming).

12. There are interesting similarities between Gadamerian and Davidsonian views regarding the presumption of prior agreement between speaker and interpreter of alien languages (what Davidson calls the "principle of charity"). In this respect, even Gadamer's emphasis on interpreting the *Sache selbst* (the objective truth content of speech or writing) rather than the intentions of the speaker or writer manifests an extensionalist predelection. The Gadamerian assumption of meaning continuity and cross-cultural truth, which even Blumenberg sometimes contests (without ever fully renouncing) is designed to combat relativism, but it cannot establish directional progress in the manner required by Blumenberg. See my discussion of the Blumenberg-Gadamer debate in "Blumenberg and the Philosophical Grounds of Historiography," pp. 9–11. For a comparison of Gadamer and Davidson, see B. Ramberg, *Donald Davidson's Philosophy of Language: An Introduction* (Oxford: Basil Blackwell, 1989).

13. The example of radical translation fits in well with the postulate of referential inscrutability defended by Quine and Davidson. If there is a flaw with this model, it is that the appeal to holistic translation manuals overlooks

the holistic background practices that undergird propositional beliefs. Since Blumenberg and Kuhn do not neglect this background, they can account for the partial (local) incommensurability, or untranslatability, of successive paradigms (or epochs). See H. Blumenberg, *Wirklichkeiten in denen Wir leben* (Stuttgart: Reklam, 1981), pp. 157–58 and my forthcoming essay "The Copernican Revolution Revisited."

14. H. Blumenberg, *Work on Myth,* trans. Robert Wallace (Cambridge, Mass.: MIT Press, 1983), p. 166 (henceforth *WM*).

15. Blumenberg, "An Anthropological Approach," p. 439.

16. G. Vico, *The New Science of Giambattista Vico,* trans. T. G. Bergen and M. H. Fisch (Ithaca: Cornell University Press, 1970), p. 36.; and M. Merleau-Ponty, *The Phenomenology of Perception,* trans. C. Smith (London: Routledge, 1962).

17. See R. C. Tucker, *Philosophy and Myth in Karl Marx* (New York: Cambridge University Press, 1961); J. O'Neill, "Marxism and Mythology" in *Sociology as a Skin Trade* (London: Heinemann, 1972), pp. 137–154.

18. Blumenberg's notion of final myths has much in common with Jean-Luc Nancy's analysis of the relationship between myth and community in the modern age. Both agree that myth functions—often ideologically—to sustain a false sense of community. Thus, one of the final myths of modernity, of the "suppression and inauguration of myth," is articulated in metaphysical foundationalism—what Derrida calls "white mythology." Against this false myth (or illegitimate reoccupation) we have to conceive of myth qua natural and (self)-originating as having been already "interrupted," "unravelled," and "put out of order" in the course of its reception. Myth is beyond justification and hence is "illegitimate." But myth, like literature in general, nonetheless occupies a legitimate place in modern society, namely, the place where we individually and collectively (re)trace the differences and similarities constitutive of who we are. Consequently, as a poetic power of expressivity, myth, too, culminates in a self-overcoming that affirms responsibility. See J.-L. Nancy, *La Communauté désoeuvrée* (Paris: Christian Bourgeois, 1986), and my study "The Retreat of the Political in the Modern Age: Jean-Luc Nancy on Totalitarianism and Community," *Research in Phenomenology* 18 (Fall 1988), esp. pp. 109–115.

19. See J. Habermas, *The Theory of Cummunicative Action,* vol. 1, *Reason and the Rationalization of Society,* trans. T. McCarthy (Boston: Beacon Press, 1984), pp. 73–74. I discuss Habermas's evolutionary scheme in my book *Habermas and the Dialectic of Reason* (New Haven: Yale University Press, 1987), pp. 132ff.

20. This conclusion would be contested by those who, like Robert Wallace, claim that the "'time-testedness' (of cultural artifacts) simply creates a (refutable) general presumption that they should be respected as meeting some kind of human need." This presumption is simply inadequate to establish the

kind of relative progress requisite to legitimate modernity as Blumenberg understands it. Although Wallace presents the "Darwinism of culture" as a middle alternative to the rationalism of Habermas and the traditionalism of Gadamer, it seems that the "time-tested" validity of culture is precisely what Gadamer has in mind when he appeals to the authoritative power of tradition. Conversely, when Blumenberg stresses optimality he voices a position that is not obviously different from the teleological evolutionism defended by Habermas. See R. Wallace, "Blumenberg's Third Way, between Habermas and Gadamer," Chapter 12 in this volume, p. 211.

21. See Stephen Jay Gould, *Hen's Teeth and Horse's Toes* (1983) and *The Flamingo's Smile,* published by Norton and Company (New York).

22. See J.-F. Lyotard, *The Postmodern Condition: A Report On Knowledge,* trans. B. Massumi and G. Bennington (Minneapolis: University of Minnesota Press, 1984) and my discussion of Lyotard's political thought in "Legitimacy of the Postmodern Condition: The Political Thought of Jean-Francois Lyotard," *Praxis International* 7, nos. 3–4 (Winter 1987–78): pp. 285–303.

CHAPTER 12

I would like to thank Anthony Appiah, Tom Benningson, Bruce Krajewski, Tom McCarthy and Carol Roberts for helpful questions, comments, and objections.

1. See Jürgen Habermas, "A Review of Gadamer's *Truth and Method,*" in *Understanding and Social Inquiry,* ed. Fred R. Dallamyr and Thomas A. McCarthy (Notre Dame, Ind.: University of Notre Dame Press, 1977), and "On Hermeneutics' Claim to Universality," in *The Hermeneutics Reader: Texts of the German Tradition from the Enlightenment to the Present,* ed. Kurt Mueller-Vollmer (New York: Continuum, 1985); and Hans-Georg Gadamer, "On the Scope and Function of Hermeneutical Reflection," in his *Philosophical Hermeneutics,* ed. G. B. Hess and R. E. Palmer (Berkeley and Los Angeles: University of California Press, 1976), and "Rhetoric, Hermeneutics and the Critique of Ideology: Metacritical Comments on *Truth and Method,*" in Mueller-Vollmer, *Hermeneutics Reader.*

2. As Thomas McCarthy calls it in his "Rationality and Relativism: Habermas' 'Overcoming' of Hermeneutics," in *Habermas, Critical Debates,* ed. David Held and John B. Thompson (Cambridge, Mass.: MIT Press, 1982), p. 60.

3. See Seyla Benhabib, *Critique, Norm and Utopia: A Study of the Foundation of Critical Theory* (New York: Columbia University Press, 1986), pp. 276–67.

4. Hans Blumenberg, *The Genesis of the Copernican World,* trans. Robert M. Wallace (Cambridge, Mass.: MIT Press, 1987), p. 170.

5. Hans Blumenberg, "Ernst Cassirers gedenkend," in his *Wirklichkeiten in denen wir leben* (Stuttgart: P. Reclam, 1981), p. 169; alluding to Lessing's

"The Education of the Human Race" (1977). In his "Idea for a Universal History with a Cosmopolitan Purpose" (1784), under the "Third Proposition," Kant remarks on the "disconcerting" fact that the earlier generations in the development of human reason "seem to perform their laborious tasks only for the sake of the later ones." I should add, though, that it is not altogether clear that Kant himself (whose philosophy of history has *mainly* to do with the development of political institutions) is committed to the view that members of earlier generations were incapable, as individuals, of full *Mündigkeit*—as Habermas's parallelism of species and individual "competence," and their development, seems clearly to imply.

6. Note that I have taken care not to commit *myself* to describing Gadamer's position as "relativist." Like others to whom rationalists apply the label, Gadamer rejects it. But whether one uses that label or some other (e.g., simply "anti-rationalist"), everyone is familiar with the dispute that I'm referring to. And, as I make clear in the course of this paper, I think each side has good (not merely polemical) grounds for criticizing the other.

7. Jürgen Habermas, *Communication and the Evolution of Society* (Boston: Beacon Press, 1979), pp. 140, 154, 171.

8. It is striking that in none of Habermas's discussions of the origin and nature of modernity (including those in *The Theory of Communicative Action,* in which he alludes to the works of Blumenberg) does he come to grips with Blumenberg's account of the genesis of modernity in *The Legitimacy of the Modern Age.* I imagine that this omission has something to do with the dissatisfaction that I impute to "the rationalist," here; together, perhaps, with a reluctance to make fully explicit the teleological assumptions (about the genesis and status of modern rationality) on which his thinking, in contrast to Blumenberg's, is based.

9. Hans-Georg Gadamer, *Truth and Method* (New York: Crossroad, 1982), p. 432; 2d rev. ed. (New York: Crossroad, 1989), p. 474. Combined citations to these two editions will be given below as (for example) "p. 432/474."

10. Hans Blumenberg, *Die Lesbarkeit der Welt* (Frankfurt am Main: Suhrkamp, 1981), pp. 20, 21. A complete account even of the surface features of the complex Gadamer/Blumenberg relationship—an account that I can hardly provide here—would have to examine, also, their debate about the concept of secularization (which Gadamer defended in his review of Blumenberg's *Legitimacy of the Modern Age,* in *Philosophische Rundschau 15* [1968]: 201–9; see Blumenberg's response in his revised edition [p. 17 in the English translation]) and Blumenberg's appropriation and major novel application of Gadamer's and Collingwood's notion of interpretation as involving understanding the question to which the text is an answer (see *Legitimacy of the Modern Age,* p. 483 [cf. p. 48] and *Truth and Method,* pp. 333ff./369ff.).

11. Hans Blumenberg, *Work on Myth* (Cambridge, Mass.: MIT Press 1985), pp. 163–64.

12. Blumenberg, *Work on Myth,* p. 164.

13. I do not mean to suggest that Gadamer thinks that prejudices should not be subject to criticism (which is a charge that he has convincingly denied), but only that he has not made clear when and how it is appropriate to criticize them, and what kind of defense can appropriately be expected. (In fact, as will become evident, Blumenberg is able to concede less to Habermas, on this score, than Gadamer seems to, because Blumenberg has a clear conception of what criticism of tradition is rationally appropriate and what is not.) For the confusion in which, as it seems to me, Gadamer leaves us, see the passages cited in notes 21 and 22, below.

14. Blumenberg, *Work on Myth,* p. 166.

15. This solution by Blumenberg, of the problem of unmanageable demands on our capacity for establishing rational foundations, seems to me to be identical, in principle, to what Christopher Cherniak (drawing on the common law tradition of the "reasonable man," and on Pierce, Neurath, and J. L. Austin, and addressing the same problem of human finitude that Blumenberg is addressing) describes and advocates as the "special reasons requirement" in pragmatic nondeductive reasoning: see pt. 2, chap. 5 of his *Minimal Rationality* (Cambridge, Mass.: MIT Press, 1986). For references to similar arguments by other recent German writers see Odo Marquard, *Farewell to Matters of Principle: Philosophical Studies* (New York and Oxford: Oxford University Press, 1989), p. 20 n. 25.

16. Blumenberg, *Work on Myth,* p. 152.

17. "When we speak of evolution," Habermas writes, "we do in fact mean cumulative processes that exhibit a direction" (*Communication and the Evolution of Society,* p. 141). And he argues that that direction, in the case of social evolution, is toward increased "development of productive forces and maturity of forms of social intercourse" (p. 142). Perhaps, then, we need to distinguish between theories of "evolution," in this sense, and theories of survival due to environmental selection—survival that may or may not be associated with increased productive forces or "maturity." To the extent that Habermas thematizes *survival* at all, the primary unit that he thinks of as surviving is a society (pp. 172–73), so that the *environment* in question is still, primarily, nature; whereas for Blumenberg what survives is a cultural "artefact" or Institution, and its environment is, primarily, its human users. (Thus Blumenberg's "Darwinism of culture" is clearly in no sense an "extension" of natural selection—as it may still be, in one way or another, in other social-theoretical appropriations of the idea of evolution.) Blumenberg's conception makes it much easier for him to find a variety-generating mechanism comparable to mutation and an exclusion-principle comparable to natural selection. This is more difficult for Habermas, who observes, in discussing the problem of finding a social analogue to mutation, that "whereas the mutation process produces chance variations, the ontogenesis of structures of consciousness is a highly selective and directional process" (p. 172). Clearly Habermas is not distinguishing between the production and the reception/rejection processes

within society, for if he had his eye on the latter, the occurrence of bright ideas to individuals would be sufficiently random, in comparison to the massive statistical objectivity of the acceptance and survival of such ideas across generations, to be regarded as analogous to random mutation. See p. xxxix n. 1 to my introduction to Blumenberg, *Work on Myth.*

18. For a recent proposal that parallels Blumenberg's quite closely, see Phillipe Van Parijs, *Evolutionary Explanation in the Social Sciences: An Emerging Paradigm* (Totowa, N.J.: Rowan and Littlefield, 1981).

19. Hans Blumenberg, "An Anthropological Approach to the Contemporary Significance of Rhetoric," trans. Robert M. Wallace, in *After Philosophy: End or Transformation?* ed. Kenneth Baynes, James Bohman, and Thomas A. McCarthy (Cambridge, Mass.: MIT Press, 1987), p. 439.

20. Blumenberg himself speaks of a "Darwinism in the realm of words" (Blumenberg, *Work on Myth,* p. 159) in connection with his account of myth, but perhaps the phrase I suggest will be a useful way of referring to his theory in its full generality.

21. See, for example, Gadamer, *Truth and Method,* p. 249/280: "That which has been sanctioned by tradition and custom has an authority that is nameless, and our finite historical being is marked by the fact that the authority of what has been handed down to us—and not just what is clearly grounded—always has power over our attitudes and behavior." (But do we have *reason* to grant it such power?) Gadamer asserts that "authority has nothing to do with obedience, but rather with knowledge" (p. 248/279), but he does not explain the relationship between this "knowledge" and what has been transmitted but is not "clearly grounded." So his "tradition" remains wide open to rationalist objections, like the one I have just made.

22. Gadamer comes closest to producing it, perhaps, in "On the Scope and Function of Hermeneutic Refection" (1967), in his *Philosophical Hermeneutics,* p. 34, where he writes: "Tradition is no proof and validation of something, in any case not where validation is demanded by reflection. But the point is this: where does reflection demand it? Everywhere? I would object to such an answer on the grounds of the finitude of human existence and essential particularity of reflection." But of course he still grants too much "reflection" when he grants it the right to "demand proof and validation" at all. Tradition does not have to justify itself explicitly; instead criticism/"reflection" has to justify *rejecting* tradition, in particular cases. Neither Heidegger nor Gadamer is enough of a rationalist to get into focus the real problems that human finitude creates for rationality, or (consequently) the need for, and the specific rationality of, tradition.

CHAPTER 13

1. The most important article is Albrecht Wellmer, "Truth, Semblance, Reconciliation: Adorno's Aesthetic Redemption of Modernity," trans. Maeve

Cook *Telos* 62 (Winter 1984–85): 89–115. This is a translation of "Wahrheit, Schein, Versöhnung: Adornos ästhetische Rettung der Modernität," first published in *Adorno-Konferenz 1983* (Frankfurt am Main: Suhrkamp, 1983), pp. 138–76, and republished in Wellmer's *Zur Dialektik von Moderne und Postmoderne: Vernunftkritik nach Adorno* (Frankfurt am Main: Suhrkamp, 1985), pp. 9–47 (henceforth WSV). Other articles in this last volume, and their translations, include the following: "Zur Dialektik von Moderne und Postmoderne: Vernunftkritik nach Adorno," pp. 48–114; translated as "On the Dialectic of Modernism and Postmodernism," trans. David Roberts *Praxis International* 4 (January 1985): 337–62. "Kunst und industrielle Produktion: Zur Dialektik von Moderne und Postmoderne," pp. 115–34; translated as "Art and Industrial Production," trans. Karen G. Jefchak *Telos* 57 (Fall 1983): 53–62. "Adorno, Anwalt des Nicht-Identischen: Eine Einführung," pp. 135–66. Citations from these articles will give the pagination in the German, followed by the pagination of the translation, if any. The first three articles listed here have subsequently appeared in Albrecht Wellmer, *The Persistence of Modernity: Essays on Aesthetics, Ethics and Postmodernism,* trans. David Midgley (Cambridge: Mass.: MIT Press, 1991).

2. For a particularly instructive account, see Wellmer, "Communications and Emancipation: Reflections on the Linguistic Turn in Critical Theory," in *On Critical Theory,* ed. John O'Neill (New York: Seabury Press, 1976), pp. 231–63. See also the chapter "The Latent Positivism of Marx's Philosophy of History," in Wellmer's *Critical Theory of Society* [1969], trans. John Cumming (New York: Herder and Herder, 1971), pp. 67–119. A more recent attempt is titled "Reason, Utopia, and the Dialectic of Enlightenment," *Praxis International* 3 (July 1983): 83–107. This article has been republished in *Habermas and Modernity,* ed. Richard J. Bernstein (Cambridge, Mass.: MIT Press, 1985), pp. 35–66. For extended interpretations and criticisms of Habermas's universal-pragmatic theory of language and communicative action, see Wellmer's *Praktische Philosophie und Theorie der Gesellschaft: Zum Problem der normativen Grundlagen einer kritischen Sozialwissenschaft* (Konstanz: Universitätsverlag Konstanz, 1979), and *Ethik und Dialog: Elemente des moralischen Urteils bei Kant und in der Diskursethik* (Frankfurt am Main: Suhrkamp, 1986).

3. Jürgen Habermas, "The Entwinement of Myth and Enlightenment: Max Horkheimer and Theodor Adorno," in *The Philosophical Discourse of Modernity: Twelve Lectures* [1985], trans. Frederick Lawrence (Cambridge, Mass.: MIT Press, 1987), p. 119. For an earlier version of this article, see "The Entwinement of Myth and Enlightenment: Re-Reading *Dialectic of Enlightenment,*" *New German Critique* 26 (Spring-Summer 1982), 13–30.

4. I have discussed Wellmer's criticisms at greater length in the final chapter of *Adorno's Aesthetic Theory: The Redemption of Illusion* (Cambridge, Mass.: MIT Press, 1991), pp. 275–307. Titled "History, Art, and Truth," the chapter is a revision and expansion of this essay. I am grateful to MIT Press for permission to publish this earlier and shorter version.

5. "Zur Dialektik," pp. 49–50; "On the Dialectic," p. 338.

6. The path-breaking statement of this theory is Jürgen Habermas, "Wahrheitstheorien," in *Wirklichkeit und Reflexion: Walter Schulz zum 60 Geburtstag,* ed. Helmut Fahrenbach (Pfullingen: Neske, 1973), pp. 211–65.

7. WSV, p. 32; "Truth, Semblance, Reconciliation," p. 106.

8. WSV, p. 32; "Truth, Semblance, Reconciliation," p. 106.

9. WSV, p. 16; "Truth, Semblance, Reconciliation," p. 95. The translation renders "gegenständliche Warheit" as "representational truth" or "cognitive truth."

10. WSV, pp. 16–18; "Truth, Semblance, Reconciliation," pp. 95–96.

11. WSV, p. 30; "Truth, Semblance, Reconciliation," p. 105.

12. WSV, pp. 30–37; "Truth, Semblance, Reconciliation," pp. 105–9.

13. WSV, pp. 36–37; "Truth, Semblance, Reconciliation," p. 109.

14. Theodor W. Adorno, *Ästhetische Theorie* [1970], 2d ed., in *Gesammelte Schriften* (Frankfurt am Main: Suhrkamp, 1972), vol. 7, p. 530; *Aesthetic Theory,* trans. C. Lenhardt (London: Routledge and Kegan Paul, 1984), p. 489.

15. See in this connection the excellent issue on "Analytic Aesthetics" guest-edited by Richard Shusterman in *The Journal of Aesthetics and Art Criticism* 46 (Special Issue 1987).

16. I am indebted to Albrecht Wellmer for making this point clear in his comments on an earlier draft of this paper.

17. *Perchronic* is a term suggested by Calvin Seerveld to describe traditions that "recur" in various historical periods. He distinguishes these enduring traditions from the synchronic patterns that make up an historical period and the diachronic patterns that differentiate various styles. My own suggestions are partially indebted to his approach, as presented in Calvin Seerveld, "Towards a Cartographic Methodology for Art Historiography," *Journal of Aesthetics and Art Criticism* 39 (Winter 1980–81): pp. 143–54; reprinted in *Opuscula Aesthetica Nostra,* ed. Cécile Cloutier and Calvin Seerveld (Edmonton: Academic Printing & Publishing, 1984), pp. 51–62.

18. Adorno, "Wozu noch Philosophie" [1962–63], in *Eingriffe: Neun kritische Modelle* [1963], *Gesammelte Schriften* vol. 10, pt. 2 (Frankfurt am Main: Suhrkamp, 1977), p. 465.

CHAPTER 14

1. Gerald Prince, for example, defines narrative in the following terms: "The representation of at least two real or fictive events or situations in a time

sequence neither of which presupposes or entails the other" (*Narratology* [Berlin: Mouton, 1982]). For Mieke Bal, "une histoire est une série d'événements logiquement reliés entre eux, et causés ou subis par des acteurs" (Mieke Bal, *Narratologie: Les Instances du récit* [Paris: Klincksieck, 1977], p. 4). Gérard Genette provides us with the following definition of narrative: "la représentation d'un événement ou d'une suite d'événements, réels ou fictifs, par le moyen du langage, et plus particulièrement, du langage écrit" ("Frontières du récit," in *Figures II* [Paris: Seuil, 1969], p. 49. Finally, Peter Brooks, in *Reading for the Plot* (New York: Alfred A. Knopf, 1984), adopts Todorov's definition of narrative in as far as it "brings into relation different actions, combines them through perceived similarities . . . , appropriates them to a common plot, which implies the rejection of merely contingent (or unassimilable) incident or action [Aristotle's *alogon*]. Plot is the structure of action in closed and legible wholes." In each case the Aristotelian definition of *mythos* as representation of a complete action is preserved; indeed, Aristotle states: "our thesis is that tragedy consists in the representation of a completed action which constitutes a whole and is of certain magnitude" (Aristotle, *Poetics,* ed. R. Kassel [Oxford: University Press, 1965] ch. 7, 50b21).

2. M. de M'Uzan, "Le même et l'identique," *Revue française de psychanalyse* 3 (May 1970), p. 444; quoted by Kristeva in *Revolution du langage poétique* (Paris: Seuil, 1974), pp. 86–87; unless otherwise stated, all quotations in the essay are given in my own translation.

3. Julia Kristeva, *Polylogue* (Paris: Seuil, 1977), p. 121.

4. Jacques Lacan, "Fonction et champ de la parole et du langage," in *Ecrits I* (Paris: Seuil, 1971), pp. 157–58.

5. Jean-Pierre Vernant and Pierre Vidal-Nacquet, *Mythe et tragédie en Grèce Ancienne* (Paris: François Maspero, 1981), vol. 1 p. 15.

6. Vernant and Vidal-Nacquet, p. 15.

7. Lacan, "Le stade du miroir comme formateur de la fonction du Je," in *Ecrits I,* pp. 90–91.

8. Lacan, *Ecrits I,* p. 94.

9. I am referring to recent research conducted in the Laboratory of Child Biopsychology in the CNRS and to the presentation entitled "Evolution des compétences à communiquer chez l'enfant," given by P. M. Beaudonnieres, the director of research in this laboratory, on April 21, 1989, at the Hôpital de la Salpêtrière.

10. Kristeva quotes Freud, *Totem et Tabou* (Paris: Payot, 1965), p. 104, in *Pouvoirs de l'horreur* (Paris: Seuil, 1980), p. 77.

11. Sarah Kofman, *L'enfance de l'art* (Paris: Payot, 1972), p. 163.

12. I borrow this term from Guattari and Deleuze in order to distance this moment from any formation of identity.

13. Cf. Aristotle, *Poetics,* chaps. 24, 11.

14. Jacques Derrida, *Psyché* (Paris: Galilée, 1987), pp. 22–23.

15. See Bakhtin's analysis of polylogical novel or Nietzsche's assertion on origins of the novel in the Platonic dialogues.

16. Already in the Aristotelian definition of tragedy and the epic arises a paradox: while *alogon,* the irrational, has to be maintained outside the tragic story (the model of which serves also the purpose of defining the epic and the narrative), it is nevertheless recognized as properly narrative when Aristotle recognizes the capacity of the epic to represent *polla merè* (see *Poetics* chaps. 24, 11).

17. An example of such an effort of analysis may be found in Gerald Prince's recent formulation of the "dénarré."

18. Kristeva, *Pouvoirs de l'horreur,* p. 76.

19. Freud, Sigmund, *Studies on Hysteria* (London: The Hogarth Press and the Institute of Psychoanalysis, 1955).

20. Kristeva, *La Révolution du language poétique,* p. 96.

21. Ann Banfield, "Describing the Unobserved: Events Grouped around an Empty Centre," in *The Linguistics of Writing,* ed. Nigel Fabb (Manchester: Manchester University Press; New York: Metheun, 1987), pp. 265–85.

22. Kristeva, *La Révolution du langage poétique,* p. 121.

CHAPTER 15

1. Paul de Man, "The Rhetoric of Temporality," in *Blindness and Insight* (Minneapolis: University of Minnesota Press, 1983), p. 206.

2. Walter Benjamin, "The Storyteller: *Reflections on the Works of Nicolai Leskov,*" in *Illuminations,* ed. Hannah Arendt, trans. Harry Zohn (New York: Schocken Books, 1979), pp. 83–109.

3. Oscar Wilde, *The Picture of Dorian Gray* (Baltimore: Penguin Books, 1976), p. 5.

4. See George Meredith, *The Egoist* (London: Oxford University Press, 1974), p. 288.

5. See Martha Craven Nussbaum, " 'Finely Aware and Richly Responsible': Literature and the Moral Imagination," in *Literature and the Question of Philosophy,* ed. Anthony J. Cascardi (Baltimore: Johns Hopkins University Press, 1987), pp. 169–91.

6. Percy Bysshe Shelley, "A Defence of Poetry," in *Shelley's Poetry and Prose,* ed. Donald H. Reiman and Sharon B. Powers (New York: Norton, 1971), p. 505.

7. Jacques Derrida, "White Mythology," in *Margins of Philosophy,* trans. Alan Bass (Chicago: University of Chicago Press, 1982), p. 241.

8. Sigmund Freud, *Beyond the Pleasure Principle,* in *The Standard Edition of the Complete Psychological Works of Sigmund Freud,* trans. and ed. James Strachey (London: Hogarth Press, 1953–74), vol. 18, p. 22.

9. George Eliot, *Daniel Deronda* (Baltimore: Penguin Books, 1967).

10. Eliot, *Daniel Deronda,* p. 761.

11. Jacques Derrida, "Like the Sound of the Sea Deep within a Shell: Paul de Man's War," *Critical Inquiry* 14 (Spring 1988), p. 594.

12. Derrida, "White Mythology," p. 241.

13. Derrida, "White Mythology," p. 246.

14. Sigmund Freud, "The Uncanny," in *The Standard Edition of the Complete Psychological Works of Sigmund Freud,* vol. 17, p. 219.

15. Benjamin, "The Storyteller," p. 91.

16. Harold Bloom, *Poetry and Repression* (New Haven: Yale University Press, 1976), p. 140.

17. Derrida, "Paul de Man's War," p. 595.

18. Derrida, "Paul de Man's War," p. 639.

19. Derrida, "Paul de Man's War," p. 636.

20. Eliot, *Daniel Deronda,* p. 746.

21. Eliot, *Daniel Deronda,* p. 831.

CHAPTER 16

1. *Brecht on Theatre; The Development of an Aesthetic,* ed. and trans. John Willett (New York: Hill & Wang, 1964), pp. 281–82; henceforth *B.*

2. *B,* p. 203.

3. *B,* p. 55.

4. *B,* p. 201.

5. Kenneth Burke, *Language as Symbolic Language: Essays on Life, Literature, and Method* (Berkeley and Los Angeles: University of California Press, 1968), p. 36.

6. *B,* p. 125.

7. *B,* p. 194.

8. *B,* p. 89.

9. *B,* p. 122.

10. *B,* p. 126.

11. *B,* p. 126.

12. *B,* p. 165.

13. Cf. *B,* pp. 163–68.

14. *B,* p. 126.

15. David Halliburton, "Endowment, Enablement, Entitlement: Toward a Theory of Constitution," in *New Directions in Philosophy and Literature,* ed. Anthony J. Cascardi (Baltimore: Johns Hopkins University Press, 1987), pp. 242–64.

16. *B,* p. 200.

17. John Dewey, *Later Works, 1927–1953,* ed. Jo Ann Boylston (Carbondale: Southern Illinois University Press, 1988), vol. 1, *Experience and Nature,* p. 232.

18. Dewey, p. 232.

19. Alphonso Lingis, "The Elemental Background," in *New Essays in Phenomenology: Studies in the Philosophy of Experience,* ed. James M. Edie (Chicago: Quadrangle, 1969), p. 36.

20. Dewey, *Experience and Nature,* p. 232.

21. Dewey, *Experience and Nature,* p. 233.

22. *B,* p. 90.

23. Georg Lukàcs, *History and Class-Consciousness: Studies in Marxist Dialectics,* trans. Rodney Livingstone (Cambridge: Mass.: MIT Press, 1971), p. 299.

24. Lukàcs, p. 299.

25. Hannah Arendt, *On Revolution* (1963; reprint 1981), Harmondsworth: Penguin), pp. 262ff.

26. Ronald Hayman, *Artaud and After* (Oxford: Oxford University Press, 1977), p. 105.

27. *The Oxford English Dictionary* (Oxford: Oxford University Press, 1971) 1868.

28. *OED* 1.1535.

29. *OED* b.1639.

30. Martin Heidegger, *Hegel's Concept of Experience* (New York: Harper and Row, 1970), pp. 46–47.

31. *The Political Thought of Mao Tse Tung,* ed. Stuart R. Schram (New York: Praeger, 1969), p. 423.

32. Bertolt Brecht, *The Modern Theatre,* ed. Eric Bentley (New York: Doubleday, 1960), vol. 6, *The Measures Taken,* p. 277; henceforth *MT.*

33. *MT,* p. 279.

34. *MT,* p. 259.

35. *MT,* p. 263.

36. *MT,* p.270.

37. *MT,* p. 270.

38. Sheila Delany, "The Politics of the Signified in Bertolt Brecht's 'The Measures Taken,'" *Clio: A Journal of Literature, History and the Philosophy of History* 16 (1981), p. 70.

39. *MT,* p. 272.

40. Delany, "Politics of the Signified," p. 70.

41. *MT,* p. 283.

42. Jean-Paul Sartre, *The Critique of Dialectical Reason: Theory of Practical Ensembles,* ed. Jonathan Rée, trans. Alan Sheridan-Smith (London: New Left Books, 1976), p. 523.

43. *B,* p. 193.

44. *B,* p. 46.

45. *B,* p. 186.

46. *MT,* p. 281.

47. *MT,* p. 281.

48. Hannah Arendt, *The Life of the Mind,* vol. 2 (New York: Harcourt Brace & Jovanovich, 1978), p. 50.

49. "Wo aber Gefahr is, wächst / Das Rettende auch"; cf. Martin Heidegger, *The Question Concerning Technology and Other Essays,* trans. William Lovitt (New York: Harper and Row, 1977), pp. 28ff.

CHAPTER 17

Our thanks to Fedrico Borges, Welch Everman, Ellen Fine, Portia Goltz, and Lauren Marsh. Michael Deneen and Steven Youra participated in the formulation of many of the ideas in this paper. We are especially grateful to Sandor Goodhart and Dalia Judovitz who have helped us rework this paper at various stages in the writing.

1. Ludwig Wittgenstein, *Lectures on the Foundations of Mathematics,* ed. Cora Diamond (Ithaca, N.Y.: Cornell University Press, 1976), p. 206.

2. Ludwig Wittgenstein, *Remarks on the Foundation of Mathematics,* ed. G. H. von Wright, R. Rhees, G. E. M. Anscombe, trans. G. E. M. Anscombe (Cambridge, Mass.: MIT Press, 1967), p. 51.

3. Wittgenstein, *Lectures on the Foundations of Mathematics,* pp. 206–7.

4. Wittgenstein, *Remarks on the Foundations of Mathematics,* p. 186.

5. Ludwig Wittgenstein, "On Heidegger on Being and Dread," in *Heidegger and Modern Philosophy,* ed. Michael Murray (New Haven: Yale University Press, 1978), pp. 80–81.

6. Wittgenstein, *Lectures on the Foundations of Mathematics,* p. 207.

7. Charles Sanders Peirce, *Collected Papers of Charles Sanders Peirce,* ed. Charles Hartshorne and Paul Weiss (Cambridge, Mass.: Harvard University Press, 1933), vol. 3, p. 211.

8. A revisionist argument, as summarized by Jean-François Lyotard, *The Differend, Phrases in Dispute,* trans. George Van Den Abbeele (Minneapolis: University of Minnesota Press, 1988), pp. 3–4.

9. Lyotard, *Differend,* p. xi.

10. Lyotard, *Differend,* p. xii.

11. Lyotard, *Differend,* p. 3.

12. Lyotard, *Differend,* p. 4.

13. Lyotard, *Differend,* p. 9.

14. Wittgenstein, *Remarks on the Foundations of Mathematics,* p. 130.

15. Wittgenstein, *Remarks on the Foundations of Mathematics,* p. 130.

16. Wittgenstein, *Remarks on the Foundations of Mathematics,* p. 207.

17. Ludwig Wittgenstein, *On Certainty,* ed. G. E. M. Anscombe and G. H. von Wright (New York: Harper and Row, 1972), p. 6.

18. Ludwig Wittgenstein, *Philosophical Grammar,* ed. R. Rhees, tr. Anthony Kenny (Berkeley and Los Angeles: University of California Press, 1978), p. 205.

19. Wittgenstein, *Philosophical Grammar,* p. 205.

20. Wittgenstein, *Philosophical Grammar,* p. 205.

21. Plato, *The Republic,* trans. Paul Shorey, in *Collected Dialogues,* ed. Edith Hamilton and Huntington Cairns (New York: Pantheon Books, 1963), p. 747.

22. Wittgenstein, *Philosophical Grammar,* p. 205.

23. Lyotard, *Differend,* p. 94. For contextual consistency, we have modified Lyotard's notation, using the symbols *x, not-x,* and *y,* in place of *p, not-p,* and *q*.

24. Lyotard, *Differend,* p. 6.

25. Ludwig Wittgenstein, *Remarks on the Foundations of Mathematics,* p. 52; for further discussion, see also Wittgenstein, *Philosophical Investigations,* trans. G. E. M. Anscombe (New York: Macmillan, 1958), and Wittgenstein, *Philosophical Remarks,* ed. R. Rhees, trans. Raymond Hargreaves and Roger White (Chicago: University of Chicago Press, 1975).

26. Lyotard, *Differend,* p. 6. Self-reference involves what the protocols of the formalization permit to stand as a referent; it produces an effect in which *x* is also *not-x*: "something is said about *all* cases of some kind, and from what is said a new case seems to be generated, which both is and is not the same kind" (Alfred North Whitehead and Bertrand Russell, *Principia Mathematica to *56* [Cambridge: Cambridge University Press, 1962), p. 62.

27. Kurt Gödel, "On Undecidable Propositions of Formal Mathematical Systems," in *Collected Works,* ed. Solomon Feferman, John W. Dawson, Jr., Stephen C. Kleene, Gregory H. Moore, Robert M. Solovay, Jean von Heijanoort. (Oxford: Clarendon Press, 1986.), vol. 1, p. 362–63.

28. Gödel, "On Undecidable Propositions," p. 363.

29. Michael Dummet, *The Interpretation of Frege's Philosophy* (Cambridge, Mass.: Harvard University Press, 1981), p. 83.

30. Gödel regarded the Liar as "a heuristic argument for the existence [in a formal system] of an undecidable proposition" ("On Undecidable Propositions," p. 363). Formal proof of undecidability might in turn be taken as an argument for the value of an indexical semantics—even in an idiom (the formalization of mathematics) where the attempt to exclude indexical imperfections has been rigorous.

A proposition is undecidable with relation to a formal system when it can be *expressed* in that system but neither the proposition nor its negation is *provable.* Gödel constructed an undecidable proposition in a modified version of *Principia Mathematica.* The result might be summarized as follows: the undecidable proposition takes the form of a generalization whose proof implies a negative instance; at the same time, proof of the negation of the generalization coexists with proof of every instance of the generalization.

"The formulas of a formal system . . . in outward appearance are finite sequences of primitive signs" to which particular meanings have been assigned (Gödel, "On Formally Undecidable Propositions of *Principia Mathematica* and Related Systems I," in *Collected Works,* vol. 1, p. 147). Thus, for example, *V* can be taken as the primitive sign which represents *for all.* "For metamathematical considerations it does not matter what objects are chosen as primitive signs," and "[Gödel] assign[s] natural numbers to this use" (Gödel, "On Formally Undecidable Propositions," p. 147). Thus, for example, *9* instead of *V* becomes the sign which represents *for all* (Gödel, "On Formally Undecidable Propositions," p. 157). Gödel demonstrates that if natural numbers are assigned this use, then—for specific formulas and sequences of formulas in *Principia Mathematica*—there will be corresponding arithmetic relations for the numbers assigned to the formulas. These arithmetizations, which are not *in Principia Mathematica* can be *represented in Principia Mathematica* as instances of a specific generalization, and both the generalization and its instances can then be arithmeticized.

Like any formalization, *Principia Mathematica* operates in terms of *implication,* and the representation in *Principia Mathematica* for the arithmeticization of *Principia Mathematica* and the formalization of this arithmetization must operate in terms of application as well. This allows for the following: if the formula in *Principia Mathematica* for which *x* is the number is *not* a proof of the formula in *Principia Mathematica* for which *y* is the number, an arithmetic relation (*rel*) will exist between the numbers *x* and *y,* and this arithmetic relation can in turn be formalized as an instance of a generalization for which *g* will be the number. The generalization has the form: for all *x* in relation to *y* (where *x* is any number and *y* is the number of some specified formula). When we substitute *g* for *y,* the result (*G*) turns out to be undecidable. It can be shown that proof of *G* will imply a negative instance of *G* (i.e., proof of *G* will be arithmetized as a relation between numbers which implies the existence in *Principia Mathematica* of a negative instance of *G*). On the other hand, inasmuch as we cannot prove *G* without contradiction (that is, there is no formula that can be a proof of *G*), any formula will lead to the proof of an instance of *G.* This leads to the conclusion that the *negation* of *G* should also be unprovable since it would coexist with the provability of *every* instance of *G,* a result which is formally unsatisfactory but indexically illuminating (see Gödel, "On Formally Undecidable Propositions," pp. 173–77). In retrospect, Gödel regarded his results as evidence that intuitive mathematics is not the equivalent of its formalization: "I never held the view that mathematics is syntax of language. Rather this view, understood in any reasonable sense, can be *disproved* by my results" (quoted in Hao Wang, *Reflections on Kurt Gödel* [Cambridge, Mass.: MIT Press, 1982], p. 20). Frege may have predicted this result when he wrote that "formal arithmetic can remain alive only by being untrue to itself . . . To take formal arithmetic seriously is to overthrow formal arithmetic" (Gottlob Frege, "Frege Against the Formalists," in *Philosophical Writings of Gottlob Frege,* ed. and trans. Peter Geach and Max Black [Oxford: Blackwell, 1977], p. 233).

If it is "asked what importance Gödel's proof has for our work," the "answer is that the situation, into which such a proof brings us, is of interest to us" (Wittgenstein, *Remarks on the Foundations of Mathematics,* p. 177). The situation results from a particular "projection": proof of *G* could not be said to imply a counterexample of *G* if the arithmetization of the proof (i.e., of the numbers that express the proof) as *rel* were not subsumed by *Principia Mathematica* as a formal implication. Gödelian undecidability occurs after we "project" expressibility in terms of implication through the numeric representation of *Principia Mathematica statements,* but the mere fact that *G* can be expressed by some natural number does not require that proof of *G* "imply" the formal equivalent of *rel.* The conventions through which the proof implies this formal equivalent (and thus, a negative instance of *G*) lead to a contradiction. The contradiction produces evidence through the undecidable, by *pointing* to a conclusion that might have been expressed otherwise but for the restricted nature of the formal idiom. Thus the undecidable signifies indexically, apart from any intention to signal, any convention within the formalization. The inevitability of this evidence might be called "the inevitability of the indexical."

31. Peirce, *Collected Papers,* (Cambridge, Mass.: Harvard University Press, 1931), vol. 2, p. 135.

32. Peirce, *Collected Papers,* vol. 2, p. 170.

33. Raul Hilberg, *The Destruction of the European Jews,* vol. 1 (New York: Holmes and Meier, 1985), p. x.

34. Adolph Eichmann, *Eichmann Interrogated: Transcripts from the Archives of the Israel Police,* ed. Jochen von Lang, trans. Ralph Manheim (New York: Vintage Books, 1984), p. 108.

35. Emmanuel Levinas, "The Trace of the Other," trans. A. Lingis, in *Deconstruction in Context: Literature and Philosophy,* ed. Mark C. Taylor (Chicago: University of Chicago Press, 1986), p. 356.

36. Levinas, "Trace of the Other," p. 357.

37. Claude Lanzmann, *Shoah* (New York: Pantheon Books, 1985), p. 13.

38. Levinas, "Trace of the Other," p. 357.

39. Levinas, "Trace of the Other," p. 357.

40. Walter Benjamin, *Charles Baudelaire: A Lyric Poet in the Era of High Capitalism,* trans. Harry Zohn (London: New Left Books, 1973), p. 169; cf. also Benjamin's "Thesis on the Philosophy of History," in *Illuminations,* ed. Hannah Arendt, trans. Harry Zohn (New York: Schocken Books, 1978), pp. 253–64, for further remarks.

41. Friedrich Nietzsche, *The Will to Power,* ed. Walter Kaufmann, trans. Walter Kaufmann and R. J. Hollingdale (New York: Vintage Books, 1968), p. 267.

42. Uwe Dietrich Adam, "The Gas Chamber," in *Unanswered Questions,* ed. François Furet (New York: Schocken Books, 1989), p. 154.

43. Christopher R. Browning, "The Decision Concerning the Final Solution," in *Unanswered Questions,* p. 99.

44. Pierre Vidal-Nacquet, "Theses on Revisionism," in Furet, *Unanswered Questions,* p. 308.

45. Adam, "Gas Chamber," p. 154.

46. Adam, "Gas Chamber," p. 154.

47. Saul Friedländer, "From Anti-Semite to Extermination," in Furet, *Unanswered Questions,* p. 30.

48. Nadine Fresco, "The Denial of the Dead: On the Faurisson Affair," *Dissent* (Fall 1981), p. 474.

49. Adam, "Gas Chamber," p. 154.

50. Robert Faurisson, *The "Problem of the Gas Chambers"* (Institute for Historical Review, Undated brochure), pp. 6–7.

51. Faurisson, *"Problem of the Gas Chambers,"* p. 8.

52. From Benjamin's Arcades Project (*Gesammelte Schriften,* vol. 5, p. 1058), cited in Alexander Gelley, "History and Actualization in Walter Benjamin's *Arcades Project*" (Paper delivered at the 1988 meeting of the International Association of Philosophy and Literature, Notre Dame University). The awakening involves a particular mode of citation ("to write history . . . means to *quote* history" (Benjamin, "N [Theoretics of Knowledge, Theory of Progress]," trans. Leigh Hafrey and Richard Seiburth, *The Philosophical Forum* 15 [Fall-Winter, 1983–84], p. 24) where quotation is a response to the "legibility" of the "historical datum" (*Gesammelte Schriften,* vol. 5, p. 577; quoted in Gelley): "the possibility of moving the present back into the past and bringing the past forward into the present" (Gelley). Just as the possibility of quotation is indicative of this movement of legibility, so the past is given to legibility, to the transformation of events into their afterlife, the evidence of their occurrence. Afterlife, traces, images are characterized by their "historical index," which "doesn't simply say that they belong to a specific time" but that "they only come to legibility at a specific time," when "the past and present moment flash into a constellation" (Benjamin, "N," p. 8).

53. Lyotard, *Differend,* p. 123.

54. Wittgenstein, cited in Friedrich Waismann, *Ludwig Wittgenstein and the Vienna Circle,* ed. Brian McGuiness (Oxford: Blackwell, 1979), p. 115.

55. Waismann, *Ludwig Wittgenstein,* p. 97.

56. Waismann, *Ludwig Wittgenstein,* p. 93.

57. Emmanuel Levinas, "Beyond Intentionality," trans. Kathleen McLaughlin, in *Philosophy in France Today,* ed. Alan Montefiore (Cambridge: Cambridge University Press, 1983), p. 111.

58. Emmanuel Levinas, *Quatre Lectures talmudiques* (Paris: Minuit, 1968), p. 105.

59. Cited in Lanzmann, *Shoah,* p. 164.

60. Filip Müller, *Eyewitness Aushwitz: Three Years in the Gas Chamber,* ed. and trans. Susanne Flateuer (New York: Stein and Day, 1979), p. 113.

61. Lyotard, *Differend,* p. 13.

62. Herman Rapaport, "Review: *Le Différend,*" *Substance* 49 (1986), p. 85. "For me," Rapaport writes, "Lyotard's discussion of the Holocaust "marks a limit where certain modes of poststructuralist interpretation reveal major inadequacies as methods of philosophical reflection" (Rapaport, p. 86).

63. Primo Levi, *The Drowned and the Saved,* trans. Raymond Rosenthal (New York: Collier Books, 1988), p. 12.

64. Lyotard, *Differend,* p. 13.

65. Lyotard, *Differend,* p. 65.

66. G. W. F. Hegel, *The Phenomenology of Mind* (New York: Harper and Row, 1967), pp. 151–53.

67. Sigmund Freud, "Negation," *Collected Papers,* vol. 5, pp. 151–53.

68. Lyotard, *Differend,* p. 33.

69. Lyotard, *Differend,* p. 57.

70. Lyotard, *Differend,* p. 57.

71. Geoffrey Hartman, *Bitburg in Moral and Political Perspective,* ed. Hartman (Bloomington: Indiana University Press, 1986), p. 8. Hartman describes his response to the woman as follows: "I felt unnecessary, and yet I had to be 'there' myself as a belated witness to that act" (Hartman, p. 8).

72. Yaffa Eliach, from a conversation.

73. Mark Weber, *The Holocaust: Let's Hear Both Sides* (Institute for Historical Review, Undated brochure).

74. Friedländer, "From Anti-Semite to Extermination," p. 29. Consider this case: in denying the existence of gas chambers, Faurisson argues that what have been "present[ed] . . . as homicidal 'gas chambers'" were actually "sterilizers . . . intended to disinfect clothing with gas" (quoted in Nadine Fresco, "The Denial of the Dead," p. 475). In this he repeats Louis Darquier de Pellepoix, the General Commissioner of Jewish Affairs in the Vichy government (May 1942 to February 1944), who recently insisted that "the only thing gassed in Auschwitz was the lice" (Fresco's paraphrase; Nadine Fresco, "The Denial of the Dead," p. 468). In 1943, Himmler had remarked that "it is the same with anti-Semitism as with delousing. To remove lice has nothing to do with a world view. It is a question of cleanliness" (quoted in Nadine Fresco, "The Denial of the Dead," p. 475).

75. Robert Jay Lifton, *The Nazi Doctors: Medical Killing and the Psychology of Genocide* (New York: Basic Books, 1986), p. 3.

76. Lifton, *Nazi Doctors,* p. 3.

77. Carolyn Forsche, *The Country Between Us* (New York: Harper and Row, 1981), p. 11.

78. Primo Levi, *The Reawakening,* trans. Stuart Woolf (New York: Collier Books, 1986), p. 193.

79. Primo Levi, *Survived in Auschwitz,* trans. Stuart Woolf (New York: Collier Books, 1961), p. 23.

80. Levi, *The Drowned and the Saved,* pp. 119–20.

CHAPTER 18

1. To take only two examples, Lacan writes in *Seminar,* bk. 2 of Freud's early *Project,* a text in which Freud seeks to establish the scientific status of psychology by constructing a model of the energy-flow within the mental apparatus: this is the system of relations between the unconscious, preconscious and conscious systems, a model Freud uses to explain the relations between perception, thought, memory, and other functions that must be located at different levels. One of the shocking conclusions he draws is that "consciousness" has to be located at a radically different level than "perception"—despite the usual equivalence that is maintained between these two concepts. And the principle reason for their dissociation has to do with the fact that consciousness, far from being "immediate awareness," involves something like what Husserl would have called "protentions and retentions," a series of repetitions and a degree of memory whereby the so-called immediate experience of a thing can come to be experienced as "one and the same thing," as precisely "an object," identical to itself over time. Thus *consciousness,* understood as this complex phenomenon by which time is folded over upon itself, cannot really be derived from our usual conception of "perception," according to which the mental apparatus would simply receive one thing after another. Thus, Lacan writes: Freud "conceives the function of perception in the psychic economy as something primary, not composite, but elementary. For him, the organism is essentially impressionable. . . . That is where the whole problem lies—can what happens at the level of the phenomena of consciousness be in any way purely and simply assimiliated to the elementary phenomena of perception?" We see, then, that with this first distinction of levels, already in the *Project,* Freud has discovered that the *being of consciousness* cannot be understood on the basis of matter, impressionable matter—in which case one has a rather difficult problem knowing what consciousness is: "What may be said in Freud's favor, is that at this naive level, he doesn't evade the difficulty of the existence as such of consciousness . . . He succeeds in dealing with it *without turning it into a thing.*" See *The Seminar of Jacques Lacan,* bk. 2, *The Ego in Freud's Theory and in the Technique of Psychoanalysis, 1954–55,* ed. Jacques-Alain Miller, trans. Sylvana Tomaselli, with notes by John Forrester (New York: Norton, 1988), p. 143. All references to *Seminar,* bk. 2 will be to this edition. Consider, as a second example, Lacan's

parodic but quite serious claim in "The Freudian Thing" (see note 2) that efforts at "introducing psychoanalysis into the laws of general psychology" reduce the subject to a thing no different than his desk: "How does this [conception]," he asks, "distinguish rationally what one makes of the notion of the ego in analysis from the current usage of any other thing, of this desk to take the first *thing to hand?*" (emphasis added). Jacques Lacan, *Ecrits* (Paris: Seuil, 1966), p. 421; *Ecrits: A Selection,* trans. Alan Sheridan (New York: Norton, 1977), p. 132. The untranslated portion of the French volume is in preparation in English. References will henceforth appear in the text, preceded by E (for *Ecrits*), French pagination first, English second. Translations are occasionally modified.

2. *E,* p. 242/34.

3. *E,* p. 527/175.

4. *E,* p. 527/174. See, in addition to "The Freudian Thing," the remarks in *Seminar,* bk. 2 on the thing, the entity, and "entification" (Lacan's word, p. 143, is *chosifier*).

5. Martin Heidegger, *Metaphysische Anfangsgrunde der Logik im Ausgang von Leibniz* (Vittorio Klostermann, 1978), pp. 199–200; trans. Michael Heim, under the title *The Metaphysical Foundations of Logic* (Bloomington: Indiana University Press, 1984); henceforth *MFL,* followed by page number following the German edition.

6. Heidegger, *MFL,* pp. 199–200. One also finds in this section of *The Metaphysical Foundations of Logic* a remark worthy of consideration in connection with the question of repeating and remembering in psychoanalysis: "Fundamental ontology is always only a repetition of [what is] ancient . . . But what is ancient gets transmitted to us by repetition, only if we grant it the possibility of transformation [overturning]." Heidegger adds: "characteristically, the tradition, i.e. externalized transmission, deprives the problem of this very transformation in a repetition." This "externalized transmission" corresponds exactly to the view of history as a "present that has been," which one might also, in somewhat more psychoanalytic terms, call the past conceived of as "passed," that is to say as incapable of being rewritten, a *fait accompli*—which is to say cut off from its relation to the future—the past as *factum,* as *dead,* or, in Ranke's famous phrase, the past as *an object of knowledge,* the past *wie es eigentlich gewesen ist.* The philosophical problem of what tradition is, and how a "community of speakers" retains its identity through a tradition which is in fact *not identical to itself* is thus close to the analytic problem of how personal history and the temporality of the subject is to be understood; it is in neither case a matter of historical "facts," but of how they are "historized" (cf. *E,* pp. 259–62, 285–86/50–53, 74).

7. Jacques Lacan, *Le Seminaire,* book 11 *Les Quatres concepts fondamentaux de la psychanalyse,* ed. Jacques-Alain Miller (Paris: Seuil, 1973); trans. Alan Sheridan under the title *The Four Fundamental Concepts of Psychoanalysis* (New York: Norton, 1978); *FFC,* followed by French pagina-

tion first, English second, in this case, p. 34/33. Translations are occasionally modified.

8. The obvious text is "The Freudian Thing," but see also the opening pages of "The Subversion of the Subject and the Dialectic of Desire" in *Ecrits*. Juliet Flower MacCannell is one of the few commentators to acknowledge the problem of truth. See *Figuring Lacan: Criticism and the Cultural Unconscious* (Lincoln: University of Nebraska Press, 1986), esp. pp. xvii–xviii and 20–21.

9. See also *FFC*, pp. 246–48/265.

10. *FFC*, p. 12/7.

11. This is clear in the C manuscripts and in the Crisis, in particular "The Origin of Geometry." See *The Crisis of European Sciences and Transcendental Phenomenology: An Introduction to Phenomenological Philosophy*, trans. David Carr (Evanston: Northwestern University Press, 1970). For the role of history in Husserl's career, see also Paul Ricoeur, "Husserl and the Sense of History" in *Husserl: An Analysis of his Philosophy*, trans. Edward G. Ballard and Lester E. Embree (Evanston: Northwestern University Press, 1967), pp. 143–74; Ludwig Landgrebe, "The Problem of a Transcendental Science of the A Priori of the Life-World" in *The Phenomenology of Edmund Husserl: Six Essays*, ed. Donn Welton (Ithaca, N.Y.: Cornell University Press, 1981), pp. 176–200; and Jacques Derrida, *Edmund Husserl's "Origin of Geometry": An Introduction*, trans. John P. Leavey, ed. David B. Allison (Stony Brook: Nicolas Hays, 1978). David Carr's *Phenomenology and the Problem of History* (Evanston: Northwestern University Press, 1974) is an excellent introduction. This rethinking of the link between history and logic is clearly central to *The Metaphysical Foundations of Logic* as well; here, our purpose is to explore Lacan's initial formulation of the problem.

12. *FFC*, p. 13/8.

13. *FFC*, p. 14/9.

14. Heidegger, *Being and Time*, p. 435.

15. In *Beyond the Pleasure Principle* Freud speaks of "a repetition of the same fatality [*Schicksals*]" and of "being pursued by a malignant fate, possessed by a demonic power [*verfolgenden Schicksals, eines dämonischen Zuges eines dämonischen Zuges*]" Sigmund Freud, *The Standard Edition of the Complete Psychological Works of Sigmund Freud*, ed. and trans. James Strachey in collaboration with Anna Freud et. al. (London: The Hogarth Press and the Institute of Psychoanalysis, 1955), vol. 18, p. 12. References will henceforth appear in the text, preceded by SE (for Standard Edition). In a letter of October 1, 1911 to Else Voigtlander he writes of the peculiar relation between these "accidental" events and "fate," saying we must recognize that "*daimon kai tuche* [fate and chance] and not one *or* the other are decisive." This indicates again that "fate" is not to be equated with determinism. To be precise, the "fate" of which Freud speaks here—being pursued by a malignant destiny—is precisely an "avoidance of one's fate," as the obsessional for example engages

in rituals that keep at a distance something that is nevertheless still determining for him ("him," since the obsessional is typically male). Thus, analysis would be concerned with an "encounter" with this fate, rather than an avoidance. As tragedy makes clear, however, fate is that which comes whether one flees from it (the "inauthenticity" of Oedipus who looks elsewhere for the criminal) or embraces it (Antigone, whose "desire for death" one might call more "authentic")—which is not to say there is no difference whatsoever between these two modes of fate's coming. Some of this material has been usefully discussed by John Forrester in *The Seductions of Psychoanalysis: Freud, Lacan and Derrida* (Cambridge: Cambridge University Press, 1990), esp. chap. 8.

16. Heidegger, *Being and Time,* p. 438.

17. *E,* pp. 416/127, 284/72.

18. *E,* p. 274/63, my emphasis.

19. A word on the "act" of speech. The temptation to read Lacan in this way would lead to the idea that one can understand speech as an "act" that is governed in advance by its conditions of possibility, those of the signifier in its internal legality. Following these lines, John Forrester has recently written on the similarity between Derrida's remarks on Austin's theory of speech acts, and Lacan's treatment of the relation between speech and action. Although it is true that, for Lacan, speech is to be understood, not simply as the communication of a message (in accordance with certain aspects of information theory), but rather as an effort to produce effects, to "change the world," in particular (following Kojève) to attain recognition, it is nevertheless also true that, for both Kojève and Austin, the conception of *the act* of speech, its "performative" character, can be elaborated *without any reference whatsoever to the unconscious.* And obviously Lacan's conception of what he calls, in this first section of the "Rome Discourse," "speech *in the subject,*" entails an understanding of the *subject as unconscious.* The difference between Lacan and this Kojève-Austin has not been sufficiently marked in the secondary literature. In addition to the problem of performatives, it is not clear that the construal of speech as an act, as one finds it in Austin, would allow one to address what Lacan means when he speaks of "the act," a term that, among other things, has primarily to do with time. Lacan's development of the term *act* has also received little attention, but it is in fact a central topic in the "Rome Discourse," one that we touch on only briefly. See John Forrester, *The Seductions of Psychoanalysis.* Jonathan Scott Lee has also followed this line of argument concerning performatives, in *Jacques Lacan,* Twayne's World Author Series, vol. 817 (Boston: Twayne, 1990).

20. E, p. 495/148, my emphasis.

21. See Eugenio Donato, "Of Structuralism and Literature" in *Velocities of Change: Selected Essays from MLN,* ed. Richard Macksey (Baltimore: Johns Hopkins University Press, 1974).

22. *FFC,* p. 14/9.

23. *E,* p. 284/72, italics mine.

24. *E,* pp. 272–75/62–64.

25. *E,* p. 252/44, italics mine.

26. *E,* p. 258/49.

27. *E,* p. 256/48.

28. This becomes especially important in 1964. See *FFC,* pp. 49–50/50: "Repetition is not reproduction . . . To reproduce is what one thought one could do in the optimistic days of catharsis. One had the primal scene . . . But what Freud showed when he made his next steps—and it did not take him long—is that nothing can be grasped, destroyed, or burnt, except in a symbolic way."

29. *E,* p. 253/44–45.

30. *E,* p. 258/49.

31. *E,* p. 255/46.

32. *E,* pp. 255–56/47, my emphasis.

33. *E,* p. 260/51, my emphasis.

34. *E,* pp. 256/48, 260/51.

35. *E,* p. 318/403.

36. *E,* p. 274/66.

37. Two writers who have recently criticised this parallel in a particularly clear way are Joan Copjec, in "Cutting Up," in *Between Feminism and Psychoanalysis,* ed. Theresa Brennan (New York: Routledge, 1989), pp. 227–46, and Jacqueline Rose, in *Sexuality in the Field of Vision* (London: Verso, 1986); see "Feminism and the Psychic," esp. pp. 7–9, and "Femininity and its Discontents," esp. pp. 83–93. Both point out that if the notion of "determination" by the symbolic (understood as a "context" *exterior to the subject*) were intended seriously, one could not speak of suffering, which implies a dis-ease, a maladjustment, which is to say a *failure* of complete determination by the law. Obviously, then, the idea that the symbolic, equated with external social conditions, "determines" or "constitutes" the subject, cannot be maintained, nor does such a view coincide with a conception of the subject of unconscious. It is therefore clear that Lacan must mean something else by the symbolic order.

38. Lacan denies, of course, that the symbolic can be equated with a particular social order, but the reasons for his assertion are not clear in the secondary literature; instead, this denial is taken as a refusal to acknowledge the "implicit patriarchal values" of his theory. This challenge should by no

means be dismissed, but neither should it be taken for granted that it accurately construes Lacan's position. In particular, for our purposes here, what must not be taken for granted is the equation of the concept "symbolic order" with the notion of "socio-historical conditions."

39. This currently popular opposition between the "historical" and the "ahistorical" (according to which one is either "in" history or "out of it," just as one is either in time or not in time—it being taken for granted what history is), however, is not a self-evident opposition, but particular to the nineteenth century and should not itself be established as the absolute criterion by which the validity of a discourse is to be measured—though it is clearly used in many cases today, for example, in the reception of some French feminism, which, if it speaks of "the feminine," is immediately and absurdly taken to be promoting an "ahistorical essence," and thereby violating the one unquestionable demand to "historicize everything" (our one universal), as though this demand did not itself have a specific, indeed a questionable and perhaps even obsolete lineage. I would add that the logic we are following here, by which arguments such as "historicize everything" *must include themselves,* lest they function as absolutes, is precisely the argument one can find in Lacan's account of sexual difference in *Encore,* according to which the rule produces its own exception—so that the "masculine" side of Lacan's diagram, for instance, reads "All X is subject to the phallic function," which might be given the analogy "All statements are political," a statement that means "This one too," so that the "universal" character of the proposition does not make it itself immune to the fact that it announces. This leaves us with a strange phenomenon which one might call "the contingency of the law" or, perhaps better, the *incompleteness* of the law (Lacan therefore writes *A,* the Other, with a slash mark through it); thus, the "All" of the statement, its "universal" element, is subject to exception by its own truth: "All statements are political (rather than universal)" means "This one too." In the terms of set theory, the set of "all objects" is closed by the exclusion of something that does not participate in the set, but stands in an essential relation to it. Where then are we to locate the "universality" that the "All" implies, if even this statement is subject to the qualification "is political"? Similarly, in the proposition "All men are castrated," the status of the universal, the closure of the set, that is, the possibility of this proposition containing all possible objects, is put into question by the logic of the schema itself, so that the rule generates its own exception, which is precisely the proposition "There is one that is not castrated," a proposition that, of course, names the mythical father, the figure examined in Freud's text on the primal horde, the father who does not exist (all are castrated) and who is nevertheless always said to exist (there is one that). As there is not space to elaborate this here, I would only indicate that the graph of sexual difference in *Encore* examines this peculiar logic of the relation between the universal ("All are . . . ") and the particular ("There is one that . . . ").

40. For other instances of this claim regarding the inadequacy of historicism, see *Post-Structuralism and the Question of History,* ed. Derek Attridge and Geoff Bennington (Cambridge: Cambridge University Press, 1987).

41. This point in regard to Lacan would obviously bear comparison with Derrida's remarks on the incest taboo in his discussion of Levi-Strauss, who claims that this singular "institution," which as an instituted phenomenon would be understood to be historical, nevertheless has the character of being *also* natural," since it can be attributed to *all cultures* (this fact qualifying it as "natural" according to Levi-Strauss's definition). See Jacques Derrida, *Of Grammatology,* trans. Gayatri Spivak (Baltimore: Johns Hopkins Univeristy Press, 1974).

42. The "Rome Discourse" is in fact decisively oriented in certain respects by the terms *freedom* and *determinism;* even the well-known essay on the mirror stage has the following sentence, in which these terms are unmistakable and prominent: "I have shown," Lacan writes, "why human knowledge has greater autonomy than animal knowledge in relation to the field of force of desire, but also why human knowledge is determined in that 'little reality' which the Surrealists, in their restless way, saw as its limitation" (*E* 96/4). The difference between the human and the animal is thus at once greater freedom and greater determinism, as Lacan shows in considerable detail in *Seminar,* bk. 1, *Freud's Papers on Technique: 1953–54,* ed. Jacques-Alain Miller, trans. with notes by John Forrester (New York: Norton, 1988). At the very least, this suggests we are dealing, not simply with the usual notions of freedom and determinism, but with a reformulation of these concepts, above all a reformulation that detaches them from the orientation that they normally take from the understanding in which what is free is the *will,* whereas the "determined" is that which is subject to *natural laws.* The concept of the imaginary is precisely the arena in which these notions of natural law and free will receive their first reformulation. In the "Rome Discourse," one sees the same vocabulary, this time in connection with our theme of history, in the claim (to give only one example), that "in psychoanalytic anamnesis, it is not a question of reality but of truth, because the effect of full speech is to reorder past contingencies by conferring on them the sense of necessities to come, such as they are constituted by the little freedom through which the subject makes them present" (*E,* p. 256/48). See also pp. 43, 52, 58–9, 66, 68, not to mention the discussion of "freedom for death" and the master-slave relation (Hegel-Heidegger) at the conclusion to the essay. This issue is clearly linked to the question of ethics, as we suggested at the start: "an individual who . . . would aim to transform the subject in his present by learned explanations of his past, betrays well enough by his very intonation the anxiety he wishes to spare himself—namely the anxiety of having to think that his parent's freedom may depend upon freedom from his own intervention" (*E,* p. 251/42–3).

43. We could push this thesis about history and suggest that history itself cannot be said to happen simply as the work (labor) of conscious subjects, but is also the unfolding of an "inhuman" discourse that can never be reduced to the intentions of its purported authors. One might put it in psychoanalytic language as follows: do not mistake the superego for a power invented *by someone;* you will find yourself fighting human enemies (representatives of the law, in Derrida's phrase), when the problem is more unspeakable, more

inhuman, than you believe, more mechanistic and demonic than the weapons of humanism are fitted for. Freud says: the father only came back stronger than ever, when he was killed, as the ghosts return in our horror movies, more powerful once they are dead. *This* is the machinery of the law. This does not mean that "instituted" laws should go unquestioned, but that change in what is wrongly called "the symbolic order" (that is, historical conditions) cannot afford to neglect the force and logic of the law that lies beyond human "contractual law."

44. Even the reception of Saussure that takes the *parole/langue* distinction to be parallel to the distinction a posteriori/a priori is questionable. See Derek Attridge, "Language as history/history as language: Saussure and the romance of etymology," *Post-Structuralism and the Question of History,* pp. 183–211.

45. *E,* p. 271/60, emphasis added.

46. *E,* p. 242/34.

47. See Jacques Derrida, *Dissemination,* trans. Barbara Johnson (Chicago: University of Chicago Press, 1981), where there is not only a similar distinction between the "law" and the "patriarch," but also the claim that this distinction is necessary in order to understand or "investigate something like paternity": "The father is not the generator or procreator in any 'real' sense *prior to* or outside all relation to language emphasis added . . . it is precisely *logos* that enables us to perceive and investigate something like paternity" (p. 80). See also pp. 108–111, and 292: "no one is allowed on these premises who is afraid of machines . . . technicity as a metaphor that transports life into death—is not added as an excess, a simple surplus, to the living."

48. See Jacques Derrida, "Before the Law," in *Kafka and the Contemporary Critical Performance,* ed. Alan Udoff (Bloomington: Indiana University Press, 1987): "The present interdiction of the law is not an interdiction in the sense of an imperative constraint." This interdiction, in other words, is not an "imperative" or "constraint" in the usual sense of a moral or legal convention, what I have called here an "instituted law," a law given in history. Derrida adds: "the law is the forbidden . . . this does not mean that it forbids, but that it is itself forbidden, a forbidden place . . . one cannot reach the law and in order to have a rapport of respect [he is thinking of Kant] with it, *one must not—one must not* have a rapport with it" (p. 140–41, emphasis added). This is why Lacan writes *A*—the "Great Other"—with a slash mark through it, designating a relation of nonrelation. It is not possible to fulfill the law, to occupy this place of the "good citizen." This idea, this fantasy of the good, Lacan says, wishes you ill.

49. *E,* p. 274/66.

50. *E,* p. 496/148.

51. We are thus given three terms: "nature" names the biological order of instinct, while "society" refers to *animal* groups, which clearly exists and even

use communication, but which are in turn distinguished from "culture," which refers to *groups formed in accordance with language.* Only the third group has "history," properly speaking, the animal society having what we call "evolution." See also, for example, the remark: "it is this [the distinction between society and culture] that distinguishes a society founded in language from an animal society." And he adds that such a "society [i.e., that which is formed by language] may no longer be defined as a collection of individuals, when the inmixture of subjects makes it a group with quite a different structure" ("The Freudian Thing," *E,* p. 415/127). One can see here, in the terms "structure" and "group," the initial bearings that orient Lacan's work in topology.

52. *E,* pp. 495–96/148, emphasis added. The place of history in Structuralism, as in transcendental philosophy, is far more complicated, and is addressed with far more sophistication, than is usually thought. This is not to say that it is addressed adequately. The point here is that, as I hope to make clear, it is not a matter of naming names (structuralist, poststructuralist), as if that could by some wish substitute for thinking. See the essays on history in Lévi-Strauss, *Anthropologie structurale* (Paris: Plon, 1958, 1973); vols. 1 and 2 trans. by Claire Jacobson and Brooke Grundfest Schoef as *Structural Anthropology* (New York: Basic Books, 1963, 1976) vols. 1 and 2. See also Jean Piaget, *Le Structuralisme* (Paris: PUF, 1968); trans. by Chaninah Maschier as *Structuralism* (New York: Basic Books, 1970).

53. *E,* p. 272/61.

54. Cf. Lacan, *Ecrits,* pp. 22–3, 61, 89, 122, 142, 144. See also Moustafa Safouan on "gift" and "debt" in *Le Structuralism en psychanalyse* (Paris: Seuil, 1968), in particular pp. 58–64. For a discussion of "gift" and "debt" in another context, see Samuel Weber, "The Debts of Deconstruction and Other, Related Assumptions" in Jacques Derrida, William Kerrigan and Joseph H. Smith, *Taking Chances* (Baltimore: Johns Hopkins University Press, 1984) pp. 33–65.

55. See Jacques Derrida *Of Grammatology,* p. 67. The link with Freud is also clear: Derrida adds that this obliges us to think the time by which "an experience [can] be determined, in its very present, by a present which would not have preceded it immediately [as our usual conception of the past suggests] but would be considerably 'anterior' to it. It is the problem of the deferred effect (*Nachtraglichkeit*) of which Freud speaks."

56. Jean Laplanche, *Life and Death in Psychoanalysis,* trans. Jeffrey Mehlman (Baltimore: Johns Hopkins University Press, 1976), p. 66. "Narcissism," he adds, "however 'primary' its designation, can no more be there at the beginning than the ego. What remains to be grasped, of course, is by what necessity both narcissism and the ego pass themselves off to us, mythically, as 'primal'" (p. 72).

57. Laplanche, in chap. 3 of *Life and Death,* distinguishes two separate models of the ego, the metaphoric and the metonymic. The latter he regards as a relation of contiguity between the ego and the organism; his discussion regards the metaphoric model as more fruitful. *Synecdoche* would be the term

closest to my account at the moment, but the main point is that his account of the (less fruitful) "metonymic" model of the ego is, it should be recognized, actually a means of characterizing ego-psychology and adaptational accounts of psychic development. The ego, he argues, cannot be regarded as the "delegate" of the whole, the "higher, synthesizing function" that would provide a welcome balance between the Id and the Superego—because we must recognize that this ego misrepresents the whole. This is simply to acknowledge its imaginary character.

58. This is closer than one might think to what Derrida has called "the law of the law": "That is the law of the law, the process of a law of whose subject we can never say, 'there it is,' it is here or there. It is neither natural nor institutional." "Before the Law," pp. 141, emphasis added.

59. *E,* p. 262/53.

60. *Seminar,* bk. 1 pp. 148–49, emphasis added.

61. Again, one might stress the difference between the usual argument separating nature and culture, an argument that suggests that nature repeats while humanity has freedom and history, which this position, according to which the separation between nature and culture gives us, not natural law set against social change, but rather biological organization as contrasted with linguistic organization. One might well wonder whether this position corresponds with recent research in biocultural evolution. It has been suggested that the only adequate way of arguing for a properly "evolutionary" theory of culture—according to which culture is conceived as adaptationally advantageous—is to abandon the strict argument for "genetic" inheritance at the level of the organism or population and to speak, instead, of an inheritance of the signifier, by which the biological organization of the species is displaced. See Robert Boyd and Peter J. Richardson, *Culture and the Evolutionary Process* (Chicago: University of Chicago Press, 1985).

62. *E,* p. 552/196.

63. See *Seminar,* bk. 2 chaps. 9–15, pp. 116–99.

64. Lacan speaks here of a "genetic order," "archaic stages," "primary" and "secondary" narcissism—the temporality of which is enormously complex, and little noticed by his readers (*E,* p. 98/5–6).

65. *E,* p. 98/5–6.

66. In the "Rome Discourse," Lacan directs our attention to this by remarking, in the introduction, on one of the central problems in the analytic literature, especially in object-relations theory and its understanding of libido: this is "the concept of the libidinal object relations" in which one finds in the literature "a clear-cut reaction taking place in favor of a return to the technical pivot of symbolization"—a topic he identifies as his starting point in the second section of the text.

67. This difficulty in the constitution of the ego is elaborated in detail by Jean Laplanche in *Life and Death in Psychoanalysis.*

68. Miller, *Seminar,* book 1, p. 141; on the thesis "there is no sexual relation," see "Aristote et Freud: l'autre satisfaction" in *Le Seminaire,* book 20, *Encore,* ed. Jacques-Alain Miller (Paris: Seuil, 1975), pp. 49–59.

69. *E,* p. 272/62. Lacan explicitly remarks on the term *contract* at this point.

70. *E,* p. 275/64.

71. See Marie-Hélène Brousse, "La Formule du fantasme? $\$ \diamond a$," in *Lacan,* ed. Gérard Miller (Paris: Bordas, 1987), pp. 107–22, esp. 112–16, and 120–22.

72. *E,* p. 279/68, emphasis added.

73. *E,* p. 279/68, emphasis added.

74. *E,* p. 284/72.

75. *E,* p. 289/77. See *FFC,* p. 47/45.

76. *FFC,* p. 23/20.

77. *E,* p. 276/65.

78. And Lacan does speak of a certain "grounding" in connection with the formalization of psychoanalysis: "This is the problem of the grounding that must assure our discipline its place among the sciences: a problem of formalization" (*E,* p. 284/72). But it is perfectly clear that the notion of "grounding" that is usually taken to mean the securing of a science by isolating the object of inquiry from all accidental, subjective, inessential, or otherwise extraneous considerations by a rigorous method, is in question in the case of psychoanalysis, the method of which is not the same as one finds in "objective" sciences, the so-called sciences of nature.

79. This would be the "essentialist" reading that has come to terms neither with the sense in which psychoanalysis encounters the notion of "particularity" nor with the question of history that is central to analytic theory, the same problem that has emerged in the "essentialist" reading—a misreading and non-reading—of Irigaray.

80. *Seminar,* bk. 1, p. 14.

81. The analyst's task, on this psychological view, will be to help the analysand not to construct himself or herself in the alienated form of an ego; the analyst will keep the client from such self-objectification. One recent author writes: "How the analyst replies to the analysand will determine whether the analysand is caught as an object in the symbolic, or emerges as a fully fledged human subject, assuming his status as *the hero of a narration*" (p. 79). And later: "*The truth* of the human subject . . . *is eventually captured* in the *discourse as narrated*" (p. 90). Consequently, "the analysand is now in a position *to exploit* the special *resources* of this language *in the telling of his history*" (p. 75). In fact, however, it is not a matter of taking history in hand, in order to "exploit its resources," and when Lacan speaks of the "hero of the

narration," it is only to expose the illusory character of this heroism, and to stress in its place that never-to-be-outstripped (*unüberholbare*) discontinuity between this person who constructs a narrative (a principal model for current theories of history), and that *in the discourse,* that irrevocable and nonappropriable alterity, which is the truth of the subject, unassimilable, unspeakable, and real. As Lacan says, the unconscious is disturbing for all psychology, precisely "insofar as this domain reveals the *reality* of *the discourse in its autonomy*" (*E,* p. 50). See Jonathan Scott Lee, *Jacques Lacan.*

82. This is a point that has been made recently, in another context, by Rodolph Gasché, who remarks, in regard to the recent and enormously popular "return to history," that "under the banner of diachrony and the factual, empiricism, now disguised as post-structuralism, pretends to have come to grips with nothing less than the ideology of Platonism." The problem is, he suggests, that in this purported dismissal of essences, the new (old) historicism *only repeats* more insidiously than ever the *complicity between* Platonism and historicism. The "relation of structure and genesis, system and history," he suggests, was in fact more deeply interrogated and "opened up by structuralism" than by those who claim to have transcended its ahistorical bias. The interrogation of this complicity, moreover, is to be found not only in structuralism, but in phenomenology as well: "No one was more aware of this complicity between structure and genesis, between platonism and empiricism, than Husserl. It was precisely this" he says, "which led to Husserl's development of phenomenology." See Gasché, "Of Aesthetic and Historical Determination," in Attridge and Bennington, *Post-Structuralism and the Question of History,* pp. 139–61.

83. Derrida has of course made a number of points on the basis of this temporal dimension of structuralist thought, notably in Saussure and Lévi-Strauss, though also in Husserl and elsewhere. Other writers have cast light on this as well. See, for example, Françcois Wahl's statement in the introduction to *Le Structuralism en psychanalyse,* by Moustafa Safouan (Paris: Seuil, 1968): "In the sign, the latest thing is not the signified but its relation to the signifier, and one might be tempted—I personally would be tempted—to think that it is by the latter that structuralism is to be defined . . . But this definition would doubtless be too restrictive. For in putting back into question the parallel between the two parts of the sign, one would be quickly led—by that epochal step to which I just alluded, which owes somehing to philosophy, which is thus no longer simply science, and which even risks rebounding upon our very conception of science—to overturn a whole series of 'self-evident propositions': the anteriority of what one means to say over what one says, in place of which we encounter the 'unthinkable' in an upsurge of the letter that eclipses meaning; the position, in the present and at the center, of a support for discourse, in place of which we must learn to think as intrinsic to the signifier the overwhelming of the center, and the eternal recoil of the origin; the final autonomy of the speaking subject in relation to the languages he uses, in place of which we will discover the constitutive effects of the signifier and the fact that it is perhaps in it that what is most irreducible about each 'subject' resides."

84. *FFC,* p. 44/41.

85. *E,* p. 98/5, Lacan's emphasis.

86. *E,* p. 275/64. The fact that psychoanalysis occupies a place in Foucault's book that is that of a "counter-science," rather than a "science of man," has not been given much attention. Here I would only point out that the figure of "man" which Foucault has done so much to unravel is still maintained by those who follow the pattern of post-enlightenment thought, and the invention of the figure of "man" as the "empirico-transcendental doublet," a figure overrun by history and external conditions but, nevertheless, on the very basis of this situatedness, able to control the forces to which he is subjected—and the masculine is intended, for it is the "man" of humanism, who, in spite of all external determination, can nevertheless come to *know* and *take in hand* that which determines him, thereby putting himself once more at the center of history. Foucault shows quite clearly the extent to which this model loses its efficacity, already by the time of Husserl's late work—which does not keep us today from repeating its obsolete gestures. Even our understanding of therapeutic techniques today is still caught in this impoverished theoretical model of history and its relation to the subject. Foucault (this so-called early Foucault), like Lacan, is nevertheless still read as a "structuralist" thinker, as though history were not one of the central problems in his work. See Michel Foucault, *Les Mots et les choses* (Paris: Gallimard, 1966), chaps. 9–10.

87. Lacan suggests that Lévi-Strauss, far from maintaining the opposition between freedom and the laws of nature, in fact develops a conception of the symbolic that "destroys" this opposition: Mannoni comments, "After Lévi-Strauss one has the impression that we can no longer use the notions of culture and nature." *Seminar,* bk. 2, p. 39.

88. See *Seminar,* bk. 2, pp. 294–308.

89. For *Sein und Zeit,* too, the question of access is a significant one precisely for determining the "primordiality" of Heidegger's investigation, the status of fundamental ontology as a "rigorous science," in Husserl's phrase.

90. *E,* p. 318/103, emphasis added.

91. *E,* p. 289/77.

92. *FFC,* pp. 45–46/45, emphasis added. The term *cross-checking* is Lacan's term for what Freud calls "the work of gathering associations": this work shows that even—to use the example Freud gives in the *Traumdeutung*—a "randomly" chosen number can be shown to *have its cause.* See also *Seminar,* bk.2, p. 56. At the same time, one must not therefore be immediately led into the usual notion of causality that is said to characterize the natural sciences: "one has only to go back to the works of Freud to realize to what a secondary and hypothetical place he relegates the theory of instincts. The theory cannot in his eyes stand for a single instant against the least important particular fact of a history" (*E,* p. 264/54). See also Jacques Derrida, "Mes Chances/My Chances: A Rendezvous with some Epicurean Stereophonies."

93. *FFC,* p. 45/45.

94 *E,* pp. 552/196, Lacan's emphasis. The structure of "condition and conditioned" that we have been examining here—that which determines and that which is determined—could be followed specifically through Kant's discussion of transcendental ideas. We might refer the reader to Kant, for whom it is a question of totality, a question of whether one can speak of "being as a whole"; the same question concerns both Lacan and Kant. See John Sallis, *The Gathering of Reason* (Athens, Ohio: Ohio University Press), esp. chap. 4, pp. 116–22.

95. *E,* p. 320/105, emphasis added.

96. For one of many moments in which Lacan refuses not only psychology, but also its complicity with the Hegelianism of particular and universal, see *FFC,* p. 201/221: "It is with the *Vorstellung* that we are dealing in psychology, when the objects of the world are taken in charge . . . Here is situated the subjectivity on which the theory of knowledge is suspended. Of course, every representation requires a subject, but this subject is never a pure subject . . . Things might be thus, were there in the world subjects, entrusted with the task of representing certain conceptions of the world. Indeed, this is the central flaw in philosophical idealism. There is no subject without, somewhere, aphanisis." The reference to Hegel follows.

97. Wilfred ver Eecke tells the story of his children asking "where were we, Mommy and Daddy, before you met us?" The limit of life, not only at the end but also at the beginning, is not the most natural thought in the world, and it is some time before it takes up its residence in us. See the introduction to Alphonse de Waelhens's *Schizophrenia: A Philosophical Reflection on Lacan's Structuralist Interpretation,* trans. with introduction and notes by Wilfred ver Eecke (Pittsburgh: Dusquesne University Press, 1978).

98. *Seminar,* bk. 2, pp. 137, 163. I discuss some of this in "Biology and History: some Psychoanalytic Aspects of the Writing of Luce Irigaray," *Textual Practice,* 6, 1 (1992), pp. 47–86.

99. Clearly, a development of Heidegger's analysis of "Being-in" would be possible here.

100. Jeanne Granon-Lafont, *La Topologie ordinaire de Jacques Lacan* (Paris: Point Hors Ligne, 1985), p. 14.

101. *E,* p. 320/105.

102. On the first "object" as lack, see Michele Montrelay, "The Story of Louise," exerpted from *L'Ombre et le nom* (Paris: Edition de Minuit, 1977) in *Returning to Freud: Clinical Psychoanalysis in the School of Lacan,* ed. and trans. Stuart Schneiderman (New Haven: Yale University Press, 1980), pp. 75–93, esp. pp. 83–85.

103. *FFC,* p. 24/21.

104. *FFC,* p. 25/22.

105. *Seminar,* bk. 1, pp. 20–21.

106. *E,* p. 320/105.

107. *E,* p. 321/105.

108. On the difference between imaginary as opposed to symbolic "identification," and between that "unity" that is given with the installation of lack and that "totality" that is imaginary, see Jacqueline Rose, "The Imaginary," in *Sexuality in the Field of Vision,* esp. pp. 183–84.

Notes on Contributors

CAROL L. BERNSTEIN is Fairbank Professor in the Humanities at Bryn Mawr College. Her recent book is *The Celebration of Scandal: Toward the Sublime in Victorian Urban Fiction,* and she is currently working on the trajectory of the sublime toward the spectacle from Burke through Benjamin.

TONY BRINKLEY is Associate Professor of English at the University of Maine at Orono where Joseph Arsenault studies mathematics and music. They are completing a book on the theory and practice of an indexical criticism. Brinkley is co-editor with Keith Hanley of *Romantic Revisions* (Cambridge Univeristy Press, 1992), a collection of essays on the production of the texts of British Romanticism.

ANTHONY J. CASCARDI is Professor of Comparative Literature, Rhetoric, and Spanish at the University of California, Berkeley, and General Editor of the Penn State series in Literature and Philosophy. He has published *The Limits of Illusion, The Bounds of Reason,* and most recently, *The Subject of Modernity,* and he is editor of the volume *Literature and The Question of Philosophy.*

FRED DALLMAYR is Packey Dee Professor of Political Theory at the University of Notre Dame. A native of Germany, he holds a Doctor of Law degree from the University of Munich and a Ph.D. degree in political science from Duke University. Before joining the University of Notre Dame in 1978, he taught at the University of Wisconsin-Milwaukee, at the University of Georgia, and at Purdue University where he also served as department chair for five years. He has also been a visiting professor at Hamburg University in Germany and at the New School for Social Research in New York; in addition, he has been a research fellow at Nuffield College in Oxford and a senior

Fulbright scholar in India. Among his publications are: *Beyond Dogma and Despair* (1981); *Twilight of Subjectivity* (1981); *Polis and Praxis* (1984); *Language and Politics* (1984); *Critical Encounters: Between Philosophy and Politics* (1987); *Margins of Political Discourse* (1989); and *Life-World, Modernity, and Critique* (1991).

DAVID HALLIBURTON is Professor of English, Comparative Literature, and Modern Thought & Literature at Stanford University. His most recent publications are *The Color of the Sky: A Study of Stephen Crane* (Cambridge UP) and "Reconstructing Theory" in *Comparative Criticism*, Annual of the British Comparative Literature Association (Cambridge UP). He has recently completed *The Fateful Discourse of Worldly Things*, an interdisciplinary study of literary, philosophical, and political discourses. His main work in progress is a study of cultural memory.

DAVID INGRAM is an Associate Professor of Philosophy at Loyola University in Chicago. Major publications include *Habermas and the Dialectic of Reason* (Yale, 1987); *Critical Theory and Philosophy* (Paragon, 1990); *Critical Theory: The Essential Readings*, co-edited with Julia Simon-Ingram (Paragon, 1991). He is currently working on a book on legitimation problems in the Modern age.

MATTHIAS KONZETT received his Ph.D. in English from Emory University (1991) and is presently teaching in the graduate program of German literature at the University of Chicago. A native of Austria, his current areas of research include Austrian literature and the relation between philosophy and theory.

CANDACE D. LANG is Associate Professor of French at Emory University. She is the author of *Irony/Humor: Critical Paradigms* (The Johns Hopkins University Press, 1988) and has published articles on nineteenth and twentieth century French literature and critical theory. She is currently writing a book on questions of autobiography.

LOUIS MACKEY is Professor of Philosophy and a member of the faculty in Comparative Literature at The University of Texas at Austin. He is the author of *Kierkegaard: a Kind of Poet* (1971) and *Points of View; Readings of Kierkegaard* (1986), as well as articles on medieval philosophy and literary topics. Among the latter are essays on Thomas Pynchon, Gilbert Sorrentino, Robert Coover, Umberto Eco, and Northrop Frye.

GRAEME NICHOLSON is Professor of Philosophy at Trinity College in the University of Toronto. He is author of *Seeing and Reading* (1984) and *Illustrations of Being—Drawing Upon Heidegger and Upon Metaphysics* (1992) both of which appeared in the series *Contemporary Studies in Philosophy and the Human Sciences* with Humanities Press International. He is also co-editor, with Dieter Misgeld, of *Hans-Georg Gadamer on Education, Poetry and His-*

tory (SUNY Press, 1992) and, with Louis Greenspan, of *Fackenheim: German Philosophy and Jewish Thought* (University of Toronto Press, 1992).

JAMES I. PORTER is Associate Professor of Classics and Comparative Literature at the University of Michigan–Ann Arbor. He is the author of articles on classical literature and literary aesthetics, Aristotle, Aeschyllus, Philodemus, Crates of Mallos, Philo of Alexandria, and a forthcoming book *Nietzsche's Poetry of Atoms* (Stanford University Press).

HERMAN RAPAPORT is Professor of English and Comparative Literature at the University of Iowa. His most recent book is *Heidegger and Derrida: Reflections on Time and Language.* Another book, *Between the Sign and the Gaze,* will go into publication soon and focuses on the French psychoanalytical concept of the *fantasme.*

STEPHEN DAVID ROSS is Professor of Philosophy and Comparative Literature at the State University of New York at Binghamton. He is the author of *Transition to an Ordinal Metaphysics; Philosophical Mysteries; Perspective in Whitehead's Metaphysics; A Theory of Art: Inexhaustibility by Contrast;* and more recently, *Metaphysical Aporia and Philosophical Heresy* and *The Ring of Representation,* all published by SUNY Press. He is also the author of *Inexhaustibility and Human Being: An Essay on Locality,* with Fordham University Press, as well as several other books and many articles.

DANA RUDELIC is currently teaching and practicing psychoanalysis in Paris. She has a doctorate in French literature from Duke University and a doctorate in psychoanalysis and literature from University of Paris-Jussieu. She has published extensively on French literature, Vian, St. Réal, Maupassant, and is currently completing a book on the works of Julia Kristeva.

DENNIS J. SCHMIDT is Professor of Philosophy and Comparative Literature and Director of Graduate Studies at SUNY–Binghamton. He is the author of *The Ubiquity of the Finite,* editor of the SUNY Press series in Continental Philosophy and translator of *Natural Law and Human Dignity* as well as works by Gadamer. He is presently finishing a book on the idea of tragedy in German Idealism.

CHARLES SHEPHERDSON has contributed to *The Princeton Encyclopedia of Poetry and Poetics,* and is the author of articles on Kant, Foucault, Irigaray, and Derrida as well as Lacan. Recently a visiting fellow at the University of Virginia's Commonwealth Center for Literary and Cultural Change, he currently teaches in the Department of English at the University of Missouri–Columbia.

ROBERT M. WALLACE translated and wrote introductions to Hans Blumenberg's *The Legitimacy of the Modern Age, Work on Myth,* and *The Genesis of the Copernician World.* He is a graduate student in the philosophy department at Cornell University, and is completing a dissertation on Hegel's argument for the rationality of ethics, and the affinity between that argument and classical eudaemonism (Plato, Aristotle, and the Stoics).

LAMBERT ZUIDERVAART is Professor of Philosophy and Chair of the Philosophy Department at Calvin College. He is author of *Adorno's Aesthetic Theory: The Redemption of Illusion* (MIT Press, 1991) and a co-author of *Dancing in the Dark: Youth, Popular Culture, and the Electronic Media* (Eerdmans, 1991). He is currently writing a book on *Cultural Politics and Artistic Truth: Aesthetics after Heidegger.*

Notes on Editors

THOMAS R. FLYNN is Samuel Candler Dobbs Professor of Philosophy at Emory University. Author of *Sartre and Marxist Existentialism. The Test Case of Collective Responsibility* (Chicago, 1984), he is currently writing a two-volume study of Sartre, Foucault and reason in history, an essay in comparative rationalities. His most recent publications include "Sartre and the Poetics of History" and "Foucault's Mapping of History" in the respective *Sartre*- and *Foucault*-volumes of the Cambridge "Companion to the Philosopher" series, as well as "Foucault and the Spaces of History" in *The Monist,* Vol. 74, 2 (April, 1991).

DALIA JUDOVITZ is Associate Professor of French and Director of the Comparative Literature Program at Emory University. She is the author of *Subjectivity and Representation in Descartes: The Origins of Modernity* (Cambridge University Press, 1988). She has published extensively on French Baroque and Classical Aesthetics, philosophy and literature and critical theory and has recently completed a book *Unpacking Duchamp: Art in Transit* (forthcoming). She is co-editor with James Porter of a new series *The Body, In Theory* (at The University of Michigan Press).

Index